Table of Contents

Part 2: Expanding Basic Skills   59

Part 3: Interacting with People   129

Part 4: Daily Life   213

Part 5: Getting Around   301

Part 6: Hobbies and Vacations   393

Preface

This book will introduce you to the Italian language in a simple yet comprehensive way. It is made up of brief units (instead of long and complicated chapters), with digestible information in them. This will allow you to gain skills gradually and effortlessly.

This book can be used profitably by:

- all those who want to learn Italian from scratch on their own;
- students enrolled in a primary level Italian language course, whether it be in a middle or high school, a college, a university, or a continuing studies program;
- those who know some Italian already and wish to improve upon their knowledge of the language;
- anyone preparing to take elementary proficiency tests in the language (since it can also be used as a reference and study manual).

Here are some study hints to take into consideration as you work your way through the book:

- Always refer to the pronunciation guides provided when attempting to pronounce new words.
- Read the dialogues out loud.
- Dramatize the dialogues with friends or other students.
- Listen to spoken Italian at every opportunity—on radio, on television, in the movies, and so on.
- Speak Italian to anyone who will listen to you!
- Consult Barron's various Italian language CDs (available at most bookstores), for these will expose you to the spoken language in complementary ways.

About This Book

This book starts off with a preliminary unit that will introduce you to the fundamentals of Italian pronunciation. Do not skip it! It will help you get your feet wet in the language, so to speak.

There are thirty units in this text, subdivided into six 5-unit sequences, each completed by a review unit. The thematic content of each sequence is based on a specific discourse area. The first five units introduce you to the fundamentals of communication (greeting people, talking about yourself, etc.). These skills are extended in units 6–10. Units 11–15 are designed to illustrate how Italian is used typically to interact with people, 16–20 to negotiate situations in daily life, 21–25 to get around, and 26–30 to talk about hobbies and vacations.

An important feature of this thematic approach is that the grammar is introduced in a gradual "bit-by-bit" manner. The separate forms of a grammatical category are given to you a little at a time and then summarized later on. In this way, you will get the whole "grammatical picture" in small digestible chunks. By the end of the book, you will still know all the grammar that you will need to go on to higher levels of study.

Each of the 30 units consists of five sections.

CONVERSAZIONE

Each unit starts with a brief conversation that will show you how Italian is used typically for social interaction—to introduce people, say hello and good-bye, talk about the weather, and so on. English translations of each conversation are provided for your convenience. The 30 conversations are designed as a continuing narrative about Dina Siracusa and her friends studying Italian in the Umbrian city of Perugia. This adds a connective story element to the book that cuts across units. Read each dialogue out loud several times. If you have forgotten what a word from a previous unit means, consult the glossaries at the back of the book.

COMPRENSIONE

This section tests your comprehension of the dialogue contents. Five types of exercises are used throughout for this purpose:

- *True and false:* You must indicate if the given statement is true or false based on the contents of the conversation.
- *Multiple choice:* You must choose response **a** or **b** as the correct or appropriate one on the basis of the contents.
- *Completions:* You must complete each partial statement according to the contents of the dialogue.
- *Questions:* You must answer each question on the basis of what you have read.
- *Matches:* You must match the items in the left and right columns in an appropriate fashion, again on the basis of the contents of the conversation.

VOCABOLARIO

This section lists the new words, phrases, verb forms, structures, and expressions found in the dialogue. Pronunciation guides are provided to help you pronounce difficult new items. Go over this list several times until you have familiarized yourself with it. The list is followed by activities that will allow you to use the new vocabulary right away, both in a controlled fashion and in creative ways.

If this book is used in a classroom situation with a teacher, the latter is encouraged to provide additional activities and fill in gaps of vocabulary that may arise in classroom interaction.

LINGUA

This section explains, illustrates, and expands upon new items of grammar and usage found in the dialogue. Read it over carefully several times until you have mastered its contents.

The technique used in presenting grammar is a "piecemeal" one and thus very easy to follow. For example, you are introduced to the forms of the definite article in different stages in the early units. Then in Unit 10 all the forms are summarized for you in a chart. This method allows you to learn the more difficult components of a grammatical *system*, such as the definite article forms, in "bits and pieces" and then to see the system in its entirety in a later unit.

The explanations are followed by exercises and activities that will allow you to put your new knowledge to work immediately.

If this book is used in a classroom situation with a teacher, the latter is again encouraged to provide additional activities to reinforce or expand upon what has been covered in the unit.

In a textbook designed for a primary level of study, obviously not all the details and complexities of Italian grammar can be covered. The treatment of grammar is therefore limited to those areas that are absolutely crucial for developing basic conversational skills. The subjunctive tenses, for example, will not be covered in this text, since these involve advanced notions of grammar and because they are less frequently used in common conversations. Nevertheless, you will find in this textbook many (if not all) of the topics covered in more elaborate and complicated treatments.

NOTA CULTURALE

In this final section, you will find out something about Italian culture that is related to the unit theme. These are brief modules that, over 30 units, can provide an in-depth picture of Italy and the Italians.

REVIEW UNITS

At the end of every five units, you will find a review unit containing activities designed to help you reinforce what you have learned.

Pronunciation and Spelling

When new words and expressions are introduced in units, a pronunciation guide will be provided to make it easy for you to pronounce them correctly. This preliminary unit will introduce you to a few general principles and features of Italian pronunciation and spelling.

VOWELS

The Italian vowels are a, e, i, o, u. They are pronounced as follows:

Letters	Pronunciation	As in...	Examples	Meanings
a	ah	*bah*	cane	*dog*
e	eh	*bet*	bene	*well*
i	eeh	*beet*	vino	*wine*
o	oh	*bought*	oro	*gold*
u	ooh	*boot*	uso	*use*

In words where the i and u come before or after another vowel (in the same syllable), they are pronounced instead as follows:

Letters	Pronunciation	As in...	Examples	Meanings
i	y	*yes*	ieri	*yesterday*
i	y	*say*	mai	*never*
u	w	*way*	uomo	*man*
u	w	*cow*	causa	*cause*

SINGLE CONSONANTS

Italian has both single and double consonants. The pronunciation of single consonants is summarized in the chart below:

Letters	Pronunciation	As in...	Examples	Meanings
b	b	*bat*	bene	*well*
c (before a, o, u)	k	*cat*	cane	*dog*
ch (before e, i)			chi	*who*
c (before e, i)	ch	*chin*	cena	*dinner*
ci (before a, o, u)			ciao	*hi/bye*
d	d	*dip*	dopo	*after*
f	f	*fair*	fare	*to do*
g (before a, o, u)	g	*gas*	gatto	*cat*
gh (before e, i)			ghetto	*ghetto*
g (before e, i)	j	*gym*	gente	*people*
gi (before a, o, u)			giacca	*jacket*
gli	ly	*million*	figlio	*son*
gn	ny	*canyon*	bagno	*bathroom*
l	l	*love*	latte	*milk*

Letters	Pronunciation	As in...	Examples	Meanings
m	m	*man*	mano	*hand*
n	n	*name*	nome	*name*
p	p	*pen*	pane	*bread*
q	k(w)	*quick*	qui	*here*
r	r	*brrrrr...*	rosso	*red*
s (voiceless)	s	*sip*	sale	*salt*
		spin	specchio	*mirror*
s (voiced)	z	*zip*	casa	*house*
			sbaglio	*mistake*
sc (before a, o, u)	sk	*skill*	scuola	*school*
sch (before e, i)			schema	*scheme*
sc (before e, i)	sh	*shave*	scena	*scene*
sci (before a, o, u)			sciarpa	*scarf*
t	t	*tent*	tanto	*a lot*
v	v	*vine*	vino	*wine*
z	ts or ds	*cats or lads*	zio	*uncle*

DOUBLE CONSONANTS

Double consonants are not sounded in English, even though double letters are often used (but they represent single consonant sounds). The Italian double consonants last approximately twice as long as corresponding single ones and are pronounced with more intensity. They occur between vowels or between a vowel and l or r.

Examples	Meanings
arrivederci	*good-bye*
basso	*short*
bello	*beautiful*
caffè	*coffee*
camminare	*to walk*
faccia	*face*
formaggio	*cheese*
mamma	*mom*
nonno	*grandfather*
occhio	*eye*
pizza	*pizza*

SPELLING PECULIARITIES

In general, there is a one-to-one correspondence between a sound and the letter (or letters) used to represent it. The main exceptions are as follows.

Words with a stressed final vowel are written with an accent mark on the vowel. The mark is usually grave. But in some words, especially those ending in -ché, the acute accent mark may be used.

Examples	Meanings
caffè	*coffee*
città	*city*
perché	*why, because*
poiché	*since*

Words spelled with j, k, w, x, and y are words that Italians have adopted from other languages, especially English.

Examples	Meanings
il jazz	*jazz*
il karatè	*karate*
il weekend	*weekend*

The letter h is used only in several present indicative tense forms of the verb avere *to have*. It is always silent.

Examples	Meanings
io ho	*I have*
tu hai	*you have (familiar)*
Lei ha	*you have (polite)*
lui / lei ha	*he / she has*
loro hanno	*they have*

As in English, capital letters are used at the beginning of sentences and to write proper nouns (names of people, countries, etc.). However, there are a few different conventions worth noting: the pronoun io, *I*, titles, months of the year, days of the week, and adjectives and nouns referring to languages and nationalities are not capitalized.

Examples	Meanings
dottore	*Dr.*
professore	*Professor*
signora	*Ms., Mrs.*
cinese	*Chinese*
inglese	*English*
italiano	*Italian*
gennaio	*January*
settembre	*September*
ottobre	*October*
lunedì	*Monday*
martedì	*Tuesday*

On the other hand, the polite pronoun Lei, *you,* and other corresponding polite forms are capitalized (although this is optional).

Part 1: Basic Skills

Part I consists of 5-unit groups dealing with the basics of the Italian language. You will also learn how to communicate and interact with native speakers of Italian. At the end of the 5-unit sequence you will find a review unit.

E Lei, come si chiama?

Unit 1

Come si chiama?

CONVERSAZIONE

[Dina Siracusa and Paul Giannetti have decided to go to the beautiful Umbrian city of Perugia on a "study in Italy" program. Both have studied a little Italian back home in the U.S., and they have come to Italy in order to learn more about the language, the Italian people, and their culture. This is their first day of class at the *Università per Stranieri* (University for Foreigners). The *Università* has special types of courses for foreign students at all levels, from high school to university. Their instructor is la professoressa Maria Giusti (Professor Maria Giusti). Another American student, Mark Cardelli, is also enrolled in the class. Mark met Professor Giusti yesterday.]

Giusti	Signorina, come si chiama?	*Young lady, what's your name?*
Dina	Mi chiamo Dina Siracusa.	*My name is Dina Siracusa.*
Giusti	Lei è americana, no?	*You're American, aren't you?*
Dina	Sì. Sono di Chicago.	*Yes. I'm from Chicago.*
Giusti	E Lei, signore?	*And you, sir?*
Paul	Mi chiamo Paul Giannetti.	*My name is Paul Giannetti.*
Giusti	Anche Lei è americano, vero?	*You're American too, right?*
Paul	Sì, ma sono italiano d'origine.	*Yes, but I'm of Italian origin.*
Dina	Anch'io sono italiana d'origine.	*I'm also of Italian origin.*
Giusti	Vi presento Mark Cardelli, un altro americano d'origine italiana.	*Let me introduce (the two of) you to Mark Cardelli, another American of Italian origin.*
Paul	Molto lieto!	*Delighted!*
Dina	Piacere!	*A pleasure!*
Mark	Il piacere è mio!	*The pleasure's mine!*

COMPRENSIONE

A. Vero o falso? *(True or False?)*

_____V_____ 1. Dina è americana.

_____V_____ 2. Paul è d'origine italiana.

_____F_____ 3. La professoressa si chiama Maria Cardelli.

_____F_____ 4. Dina è la professoressa.

_____V_____ 5. Anche Mark è americano, ma è d'origine italiana.

_____F_____ 6. Paul è di Chicago.

VOCABOLARIO

[In each vocabulary section a capital letter will be used to indicate the accented syllable in the pronunciation guides in parentheses. These guides are provided only for new items whose pronunciation might be difficult to figure out.]

PAROLE NUOVE (NEW WORDS)

Americano

Italiana

altro	*other*
americano / americana	*American (male / female)*
anche (Ahn-keh)	*also, too*
come	*how (what)*
di	*of, from*
e	*and*
io (Eeh-oh)	*I*
italiano / italiana (eeh-tah-lyAh-noh)	*Italian (male / female)*
Lei (lEh-eeh)	*you (polite)*
lieto / lieta	*delighted (masculine / feminine)*
ma	*but*
molto	*very*
no	*no*
origine (oh-rEEh-jeeh-neh)	*origin*
sì	*yes*
signore	*Mr., gentleman, sir*
signorina	*Ms., Miss, young lady*
vero	*true*

ESPRESSIONI E MODI DI DIRE (EXPRESSIONS AND WAYS OF SPEAKING)

anch'io	*I too*
d'origine (oh-rEEh-jeeh-neh)	*of origin, originally*
no? / vero?	*no?/right?/aren't you?...*
un altro / un'altra	*another (male / female)*

Mi chiamo Marco Antonio Mazzini
Della Rovere. Piacere.

Mi chiamo Bob. Hi!

PRESENTAZIONI **(INTRODUCTIONS)**

Come si chiama? (kyAh-mah)	*What is your name? (polite)*
Il piacere è mio!	*The pleasure's mine!*
Mi chiamo… (kyAh-moh)	*My name is…*
Molto lieto / lieta (lyEh-toh)	*Delighted (to meet you)! (male / female)*
Piacere! (pyah-chEh-reh)	*A pleasure!*
Vi presento… / Le presento…	*Let me introduce you to… (plural) / (polite, singular)*

STRUTTURE VERBALI **(VERB STRUCTURES)**

(io) sono (sOh-noh)	*I am*
(Lei) è	*you are (polite)*

ATTIVITÀ

B. Come si dice in italiano? *(How do you say this in Italian?)*

Note
To form questions
(1) Just add intonation:
Mark è americano?   *Is Mark American?*
(2) Add intonation and put the subject at the end:
È americano, Mark?   *Is Mark American?*

1. Delighted to meet you (spoken by a male).

_____

2. Delighted to meet you (spoken by a female).

_____

3. The pleasure's mine!

_____

4. Is Paul another Italian?

_____

5. Is Dina another American?

_____

6. Let me introduce you to Dina Siracusa (*plural*).

_____

7. Let me introduce you to Mark Cardelli (*polite, singular*).

_____

8. Young lady, you are American, right?

_____

9. Sir, you are also American, aren't you?

_____

C. Domande personali. (*Personal questions.*)

1. Come si chiama Lei?

_____

2. Lei è americano / americana?

_____

3. Di che origine è (*of what origin are you*)?

_____

D. Gioco! (*Game!*)

Find the Italian equivalents of the given words in the search puzzle.

1. young lady
2. Mr.
3. American (female)
4. Italian (male)
5. I am
6. also
7. origin
8. other (masculine)

A	M	E	R	I	C	A	N	A	I
S	A	S	I	G	N	O	R	E	T
C	D	A	S	C	D	R	S	A	A
S	I	G	N	O	R	I	N	A	L
O	D	C	B	B	N	G	S	N	I
N	A	C	A	D	B	I	A	C	A
O	S	M	L	L	D	N	A	H	N
M	A	L	T	O	D	E	M	E	O
C	L	E	R	C	C	D	A	S	L
L	C	E	O	D	A	M	M	A	S

E. Composition!

Write a summary of the encounter between Professor Giusti and the three American students in your own words. Here are a few expressions you might need:

Useful Vocabulary		
si chiama	*is called*	(La professoressa si chiama Maria Giusti.)
lei	*she*	
lui	*he*	
lui/lei presenta	*he / she introduces…*	

chiama Maria Giusti. Lei

Mark

and Tijuana

LINGUA

Polite Address

The pronoun form Lei, *you*, is part of a system of polite speech. You must use polite forms to address people with whom you are not on a first-name basis, such as strangers and those who have social authority. These forms convey respect, courtesy, and formality, and you must use them to avoid being considered rude.

Lei

Masculine vs. Feminine Forms

Noun and adjective forms ending in -o, such as those used by the male speakers in the dialogue, are to be distinguished from those ending in -a, such as those used by the female speakers. They indicate the gender of the speaker.

Male Speaker	Female Speaker
Molto lieto! / *Delighted!*	Molto lieta! / *Delighted!*
(Io) sono italiano. / *I am Italian.*	(Io) sono italiana. / *I am Italian.*
(Io) sono americano. / *I am American.*	(Io) sono americana. / *I am American.*

The Forms è and e

The accent mark on the verb è distinguishes it from e, which is the conjunction *and*.

Mark è d'origine italiana.	*Mark is of Italian origin.*
E Lei?	*And you?*

Introductions

In the dialogue you came across two examples of how to introduce people. One involved introducing someone to another person using polite (formal) speech; the other involved introducing someone to more than one person at the same time.

Le presento ....

Introducing Someone to Another Person Formally

Le presento...	*Let me introduce you to...*
Le presento Dina Siracusa	*Let me introduce you to Dina Siracusa*

Vi presento ....

Introducing Someone to More than One Person at the Same Time

Vi presento…	*Let me introduce you to…*
Vi presento Dina Siracusa	*Let me introduce you to Dina Siracusa*

ATTIVITÀ

F. Supply the missing ending.

1. *Mark*:   Molto liet___!

2. *Dina:*   Molto liet___!

3. *Mark:*   Io sono american___

4. *Giusti:*   Io sono italian___

5. *Paul:*   Io sono un altr___ american___

6. *Dina:*   Anch'io sono un'altr___ american___

G. Supply the missing word.

1. Mark _____ d'origine italiana.

2. Dina _____ americana.

3. _____ Lei, come si chiama?

4. Mi _____ Maria Giusti.

5. _____ Paul è americano.

H. First, introduce the following people to Professor Giusti, following the model.

> *Model:* Mark Cardelli
> *Professoressa Giusti, Le presento Mark Cardelli.*

1. Dina Siracusa

_____

2. Paul Giannetti

_____

3. Jim Carducci

_____

4. Debbie Di Nardo

_____

Now introduce them to two other people, following the model.

> *Model:* Mark Cardelli
> *Vi presento Mark Cardelli.*

5. Dina Siracusa

_____

6. Paul Giannetti

_____

7. Jim Carducci

_____

8. Debbie Di Nardo

_____

Finally, indicate what each person might say, following the model.

> *Model:* Mark Cardelli
> *Mi chiamo Mark Cardelli. Sono americano, ma sono d'origine italiana.*

9. Dina Siracusa

_____

10. Paul Giannetti

_____

11. Jim Carducci

_____

12. Debbie Di Nardo

_____

I. Cruciverba! *(Crossword!)*

Horizontal

1 Mark Cardelli è un … italiano d'origine.
4 Anche Paul Giannetti è …. d'origine.
5 Come si …?
6 Io sono italiano. … Lei?
9 Anch'… sono italiana d'origine.
10 Molto …!
11 Il piacere è …
12 Le … Mark Cardelli.

Vertical

2 Io sono italiano d'origine. E …?
3 Sì, … la professoressa è italiana.
7 Piacere! … lieto!
8 Il … è mio!
11 Come si chiama? … chiamo Dina Siracusa.
13 Lei è italiano? …, sono italiano d'origine.

NOTA CULTURALE

Greeting Someone in Italy

When greeting strangers in Italy, shaking hands is all that is really required. However, when greeting a friend that you haven't seen for a while, it is normal to give a kiss on both cheeks, barely making contact, while patting him or her on a shoulder.

J. How would you greet the following people in Italy?

1. a complete stranger

_____

2. a friend whom you see often

_____

3. a friend whom you haven't seen in a while

_____

Buongiorno!

Unit 2

Buongiorno!

CONVERSAZIONE

[Mark Cardelli, whom you met in the previous unit, runs into la signora Martini (Mrs. Martini), an assistant to la professoressa Giusti, on a main street of Perugia. They exchange greetings.]

Martini	Buongiorno signor Cardelli, come va?	Good day Mr. Cardelli, how's it going?
Cardelli	Buongiorno signora Martini. Io sto bene, e Lei come sta?	Hello, Mrs. Martini. I'm well, and how are you?
Martini	Non c'è male, grazie! ArrivederLa!	Not bad, thank you! Good-bye!
Cardelli	A presto!	See you soon!

[Dina, Paul, and Mirella, Dina's new Italian friend, run into each other near the *Università per Stranieri*.]

Dina	Ah, ecco Paul! Ciao Paul! Come stai?	Ah, here's Paul! Hi, Paul! How are you?
Paul	Molto bene, Dina, e tu?	Very well, Dina, and you?
Dina	Io, invece, sto così, così. Ti presento Mirella.	I, instead, feel so-so. Let me introduce you to Mirella.
Paul	Ciao, Mirella! Di dove sei?	Hi, Mirella! Where are you from?
Mirella	Sono di qui.	I'm from here.
Dina	Dove vai, Paul?	Where are you going, Paul?
Paul	In centro!	Downtown!
Dina	Arrivederci!	Good-bye!
Mirella	Ciao!	Bye!
Paul	Ci vediamo!	See you!

COMPRENSIONE

A. Which response, a or b, is the correct or appropriate one?

_____1. Buongiono, signor Cardelli, …
        a. come va?
        b. a presto

_____2. Buongiorno, signora Martini. Come sta?
        a. Non c'è male, grazie!
        b. A presto!

_____3. Come va?
        a. Buongiorno.
        b. (Io sto) bene.

_____ 4. ArrivederLa!
        a. Come va?
        b. A presto!

_____ 5. Ah, … Paul!
        a. ecco
        b. dove

_____ 6. Ciao, Paul, …
        a. Come stai?
        b. Come sta?

_____ 7. Sto molto bene, Dina, e tu?
        a. Sono di qui!
        b. Io, invece, sto così, così!

_____ 8. Ti presento Mirella.
        a. Ciao!
        b. Ci vediamo!

_____ 9. Di dove sei?
        a. Sono di qui.
        b. In centro.

_____10. Dove vai?
        a. Ci vediamo!
        b. In centro!

VOCABOLARIO

Ecco!   Grazie!

PAROLE NUOVE

bene (bEh-neh)	*well*
il centro (chEhn-troh)	*downtown*
come	*how*
così	*so, thus, like this*
dove	*where*
ecco	*here is / here are*
grazie (grAh-tsyeh)	*thank you*

in	in
invece (eehn-vEh-cheh)	instead
qui	here
tu	you (familiar)

ESPRESSIONI E MODI DI DIRE

Come sta / Come stai? (stAh-eeh)	How are you? (polite / familiar)
Come si chiama? / Come ti chiami?	What's your name? (polite / familiar)
Come va?	How's it going?
Di dove è? / Di dove sei?	Where are you from? (polite / familiar)
Dove va? / Dove vai?	Where are you going? (polite / familiar)
molto bene	very well
Non c'è male (cheh mAh-leh)	(I'm) not bad
(Io) sono di …	I'm from…
(Io) sono di qui (kwEEh)	I'm from here
(Io) sto bene	I'm well
(Io) sto così, così (koh-zEEh)	I'm so-so
Ti presento…	Let me introduce you to… (familiar, singular)

SALUTI (GREETINGS)

A presto!	See you soon!
Arrivederci! (ah-reeh-veh-dEhr-cheeh)	Good-bye! (familiar)
ArrivederLa!	Good-bye! (polite)
Buongiorno! (bwohn-jOhr-noh)	Hello! / Good day! / Good morning!
Ci vediamo! (cheeh veh-dyAh-moh)	See you!
Ciao! (chAh-oh)	Hi! / Bye!

Signora   Signore   Signorina

TITOLI (TITLES)

dottore	Dr. (male)
dottoressa	Dr. (female)
professore	Professor (male) / high school teacher
professoressa	Professor (female) / high school teacher
signora	Mrs. / Ms. / madam
signore (seeh-nyOh-reh)	Mr. / sir
signorina	Miss

ATTIVITÀ

B. Say the following things, following the model.

Model: Point out that Paul is arriving
Ecco Paul!

1. Ask Dina how she is _____
2. Ask Mrs. Martini how she is _____
3. Say that you are well _____
4. Say that you are not bad _____
5. Say good-bye to Mrs. Martini _____
6. Say hello to Mrs. Martini _____
7. Introduce Dina to Mark _____
8. Ask Dina where she is going _____
9. Greet Paul _____
10. Say bye to Paul _____

C. Comunicazione!

1. Say hello to someone in your class or in your family.

_____

2. Introduce someone in your class / family to someone else. Use polite form.

_____

3. Now introduce the same person to someone else, using familiar form.

_____

4. Ask someone what his / her name is. Use polite form.

_____

5. Ask someone what his / her name is. This time use familiar form.

_____

6. Give your name.

_____

7. Say good-bye to everyone.

_____

8. Ask someone how he / she is. Use polite form.

_____

9. Ask someone how he / she is. This time use familiar form.

_____

10. Ask someone where he / she is from. Use polite form.

_____

11. Ask someone where he / she is from. This time use familiar form.

_____

12. Ask someone where he / she is going. Use polite form.

_____

13. Ask someone where he / she is going. This time use familiar form.

_____

14. Say that you are from Chicago.

_____

15. Say that you are from here.

_____

D. Fill-in the blanks with appropriate words in their correct forms.

Franca	(1) _____, Dino!
Dino	Ciao, come (2) _____?
Franca	Non c'è (3) _____. E tu?
Dino	Così (4) _____. Dove vai?
Franca	In (5) _____. Ciao!
Dino	Ci (6) _____!

LINGUA

Come stai?

Come sta?

Polite vs. Familiar Speech

The pronoun form tu / _you_ is part of a system of familiar speech. Familiar forms are used to address family members, friends, children, and anyone with whom you are on a first-name basis. The corresponding polite form is Lei, as you learned in the previous unit.

Differences between polite and familiar speech characterize everyday communication and must be maintained so as to avoid being considered impolite or unsociable.

Polite		Familiar
Lei		tu
Come si chiama?	*What's your name?*	Come ti chiami?
Come sta?	*How are you?*	Come stai?
Le presento…	*Let me introduce you to…*	Ti presento…

Greetings

Polite and familiar speech distinctions also apply to greetings, as you may have noticed

Polite		Familiar
Lei		tu
Buongiorno!	*Hello! / Good-bye!*	Ciao!
ArrivederLa!	*Good-bye!*	Arrivederci!/Ciao!

Titles: Part 1

Titles are used commonly in Italy, much more than they are in North America. The ones for *Mr./Mrs./Ms., Dr.,* and *Prof.*, however, are used equally in both. By convention, the final -e of masculine titles is dropped before a name:

Masculine	Feminine
Mr./Mrs./Ms./Miss	
signore	signora
signor Cardelli	signora Martini
signor Smith	signora Smith
	signorina Siracusa
Dr.	
dottore	dottore / dottoressa
dottor Cardelli	dottoressa Martini
dottor Giannetti	dottoressa Siracusa
dottor Smith	dottoressa Smith
Prof.	
professore	professoressa
professor Cardelli	professoressa Martini
professor Giannetti	professoressa Siracusa
professor Smith	professoressa Smith

Notice that titles are not capitalized in Italian unless, of course, they are the first words in sentences.

Also, note that the title of professore / professoressa is used not only with university professors but also with middle and high school teachers.

ATTIVITÀ

E. Ask each of the following people how he or she is.

> *Model:* Mr. Martini
> *Signor Martini, come sta?*

1. Mr. Cardelli

_____

2. Mrs. Martini

_____

3. Miss Siracusa

_____

4. Dr. Franchi (a female)

_____

5. Dr. Bruni (a male)

_____

6. Prof. Gianmarchi (a female)

_____

7. Prof. Santucci (a male)

_____

8. Dina

_____

9. Mark

_____

10. your instructor

_____

F. Fill in each blank with the appropriate familiar or polite expression.

> *Model:* Ask Angela how she is
> *Angela, come stai?*

Say hello to …

1. Dr. Giusti (a male) _____

2. Dina _____

Say good-bye to …

3. Prof. Martini (a female) _____

4. Mark _____

Ask … how he is

5. Mr. Santucci _____

6. Paul _____

Ask … what his or her name is

7. a little girl _____

8. a stranger _____

Introduce…

9. Mrs. Martini to Mr. Giusti _____

10. Gino to Mirella _____

G. Write a brief composition or dialogue on the following theme.

Debbie è d'origine italiana!

_____

_____

_____

_____

_____

_____

_____

_____

_____

_____

_____

_____

H. Cruciverba!

Horizontal

1 the familiar form for *good-bye*
5 the familiar counterpart of *Lei*
6 the polite counterpart of *Arrivederci*
10 Ciao, Mirella, come …?
11 Molto …!
12 Come ti …?
13 … presento Mirella *(familiar)*
14 Io … di qui.
16 Mrs.
17 Di … sei?
19 E Lei, come si …?
20 Ti … Mark.
22 Anch'io sono di ….
23 Ci …!
26 … ti chiami?
28 Thank you!

Vertical

2 Io, …, sto così, così.
3 It means both *Hi!* and *Bye!*
4 Good day!
7 Come … chiama, Lei?
8 A …!
9 Di dove …?
10 the form of *signore* in front of Carducci.
15 the polite counterpart of *tu*
16 Buongiorno, signora Martini, come …?
18 Mark, dove …?
19 Io, invece, sto …, così.
21 Ah, … Paul!
24 Non c'è …!
25 downtown
27 Come …?

NOTA CULTURALE

The Use of Titles in Italy

Titles referring to professions are used more commonly in Italy than they are in North America. Here are some titles that are used in Italy but not in North America:

Avvocato	Lawyer
Geometra	Draftsman / Draftswoman
Ingegnere	Engineer
Ragioniere	Accountant

Note also that the title dottore *(masculine)* / dottoressa *(feminine)* is used not only to address medical doctors but anyone with a university degree. Finally, the title professore *(masculine)* / professoressa *(feminine)* is used not only to address university professors but also middle and high school teachers.

When used with a name, the final -e of masculine titles is dropped:

Buongiorno, ingegnere.	Good morning, Engineer.
Buongiorno, ingegner Marchi.	Good morning, Engineer Marchi.

Finally, titles may or may not be capitalized, as a matter of style. The choice is yours (unless, of course, it is the first word in a sentence).

I. Greet the following people using their titles. Follow the model.

> *Model:* Engineer Marchi *(masculine)*
> *Buongiorno, Ingegner Marchi.*

1. Lawyer Martini

_____

2. Accountant Nardini *(a male)*

_____

3. Mr. Di Nardo

_____

4. Mrs. Rossini

_____

5. Draftswoman Martelli

_____

6. Professor Giusti *(a female)*

_____

7. Professor Verdi *(a male)*

_____

8. Dr. Brunetti *(a male)*

_____

9. Dr. Carducci *(a female)*

_____

Buonasera, professor Binni!

Unit 3

Che cosa è?

CONVERSAZIONE

[Dina has decided to take a quick trip to Pisa to see the leaning tower. It is early evening. At the train station in Perugia she runs into one of her instructors, il professor Binni. She takes advantage of the situation by asking Professor Binni what a *schedule* is called in Italian.]

Dina	Buonasera professore, come sta?	Good evening, Professor, how are you?
Binni	Abbastanza bene. E Lei?	Quite well. And you?
Dina	Molto bene. Che cosa è quello?	Very well. What's that?
Binni	In italiano si chiama «orario».	In Italian it's called «schedule».
Dina	Grazie. Quando arriva il treno?	Thank you. When is the train arriving?
Binni	Fra qualche minuto.	In a few minutes.
Dina	Grazie!	Thank you!
Binni	Prego! Dove va? A Firenze?	You're welcome! Where are you going? To Florence?
Dina	No, a Pisa. È bella?	No, to Pisa. Is it nice/beautiful?
Binni	Sì, molto. Ecco il mio treno! ArrivederLa!	Yes, very. Here's my train! Good-bye!
Dina	ArrivederLa!	Good-bye!

COMPRENSIONE

A. Complete each statement or question in an appropriate fashion.

1. _____ professore, come sta?

2. _____ bene. E Lei?

3. E Lei? _____ bene.

4. _____ cosa è quello?

5. In italiano si chiama _____.

6. _____ arriva il treno?

7. Fra _____ minuto.

8. _____ va? A Pisa?

9. _____ il mio treno!

25

VOCABOLARIO

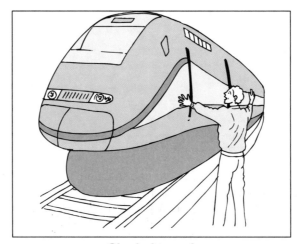

Che bel treno!

PAROLE NUOVE

a	*to, at*
abbastanza (ah-bbah-stAhn-tsah)	*quite, enough*
arrivare	*to arrive*
bello	*nice, beautiful*
che	*what*
fra	*in, between, among*
l'italiano	*Italian (the language)*
il minuto	*minute*
molto	*a lot, very much*
l'orario (oh-rAh-ryoh)	*schedule, timetable*
qualche	*some*
quando (kwAhn-doh)	*when*
quello	*that*
tra	*in, between, among*
il treno	*train*

ESPRESSIONI E MODI DI DIRE

Abbastanza bene!	*Quite well!*
Buon pomeriggio (poh-meh-rEEh-jjoh)	*Good afternoon!*
Buonasera! (bwoh-nah-sEh-rah)	*Good afternoon! / Good evening!*
che cosa (keh kOh-zah)	*what*
Che cosa è quello? (kwEh-lloh)	*What is that?*
Dove va?	*Where are you going (polite)?*
fra qualche minuto (kwAhl-keh)	*in a few minutes*
il mio	*my (masculine, singular)*
Prego!	*You're welcome!*
Quando arriva il treno?	*When is the train arriving?*

STRUTTURE VERBALI

arriva	*it is arriving*
è	*it is*
si chiama	*it is called*

ATTIVITÀ

B. Come si dice in italiano?

> *Model:* Good morning!
> *Buongiorno!*

1. Good evening!

Buona sera

2. Quite well, thank you!

Molto bene, grazie

3. The train is arriving in a few minutes.

Il treno arriva in qualche minuto

4. What is that?

Che cosa è quello

5. You're welcome!

Prego

6. It's a schedule in Italian.

In italiano si chiama horario

7. When is the train arriving?

8. Where are you going, Ms. Siracusa?

9. To Florence. Is it nice?

10. Yes, very!

11. Good afternoon!

C. Fill in the blanks with the appropriate words in their correct forms.

Nora: Claudio, (1) _____ è quello?

Claudio: È il (2) _____ che va a Pisa.

Nora: Quando (3) _____?

Claudio: Fra qualche (4) _____.

Nora: Grazie, e arrivederci!

Claudio: (5) _____!

D. Do the following things.

> *Model:* Greet someone in the afternoon.
> *Buon pomeriggio!*

1. Indicate that you are feeling quite well.

_____

2. Ask what something is.

_____

3. Ask where the schedule is.

_____

4. Ask when the train is coming.

_____

5. Greet someone in the evening.

_____

E. Give the Italian equivalent for each of the following.

> *Model:* Hi!
> *Ciao!*
> *Ciao, Debbie, come va?*

1. Good-bye (*formal*)

_____

2. Good-bye (*informal*)

_____

3. Bye!

_____

4. Hello in the morning / Good morning!

_____

5. Hello in the afternoon! / Good afternoon!

_____

6. Hello in the late afternoon (early evening) / Good evening!

_____

7. What's your name? (*formal*)

_____

8. What's your name? (*informal*)

_____

9. How are you? (*formal*)

_____

10. How are you? (*informal*)

_____

11. Where are you from? (*formal*)

_____

12. Where are you from? *(informal)*

_____

13. Delighted to meet you! *(spoken by a male)*

_____

14. Delighted to meet you! *(spoken by a female)*

_____

15. Let me introduce you to ... *(familiar, singular)*

_____

16. Let me introduce you to ... *(polite, singular)*

_____

17. Let me introduce you to ... *(familiar, plural)*

_____

F. Now greet various people in the class or in your family.

LINGUA

The Forms che, fra, and tra

The interrogative forms **Che? Cosa?** or **Che cosa?** can be used alternatively. Each one means *What?* The prepositions **fra** and **tra**, meaning *among*, *between*, or *in* (a certain amount of time), are also interchangeable:

Che cosa è quello?	*What is that?*	**Che è quello? / Cosa è quello?**
fra qualche minuto	*in a few minutes*	**tra qualche minuto**

Che cosa è quello?

Masculine and Feminine Nouns

In Italian, nouns are either masculine or feminine. Singular masculine nouns generally end in -o and singular feminine nouns end in -a:

Masculine	Feminine
treno / *train*	signora / *lady*
orario / *schedule*	dottoressa / *doctor*
minuto / *minute*	signorina / *young lady*

The Article: Part 1

Un corresponds to the English indefinite article form *a / an*. It is used before singular masculine nouns beginning with any vowel or consonant except *z* or *s + consonant:*

un orario	*a timetable*
un treno	*a train*
un italiano	*an Italian*
un americano	*an American*

Il corresponds to the English definite article form *the*. It is used before masculine singular nouns beginning with any consonant except *z* or *s + consonant* (as you will see in subsequent units).

il treno	*the train*
il minuto	*the minute*

Hellos and Good-byes

Here is a summary of greeting protocols in Italian.

Buonasera, signorina!

Hellos:
- **Buongiorno** is used to greet someone formally or simply to say *Good morning* to anyone in general. It is also used to say *good day* during the morning hours.
- **Buon pomeriggio** is used to greet anyone in general in the early afternoon. It means *Good afternoon.*

- **Buonasera** is used to greet someone formally in the late afternoon and in the evening. It means *Good evening.*
- **Ciao** is used to greet someone informally at any time of the day.

Good-byes:
- The same expressions are used to say *good-bye* at the same times of the day: **Buongiorno** in the morning, **Buon pomeriggio** in the afternoon, **Buonasera** in the evening, and **Ciao** at any time of the day (in informal speech situations).
- **ArrivederLa** is a formal equivalent for *Good-bye*; it can be used at any time of the day.
- **Arrivederci** is an informal equivalent for *Good-bye*; it too can be used at any time of the day.

Note that **buongiorno** and **buonasera** can also be written as two separate words: **buon giorno** and **buona sera**.

ATTIVITÀ

G. Choose the appropriate response, **a**, **b**, or **c**.

1. … è quello?
   a. Che
   b. Quando
   c. Come

2. … arriva il treno?
   a. Che
   b. Quando
   c. Come

3. … vai, Dina?
   a. Dove
   b. Che cosa
   c. Sì

4. Il treno arriva …
   a. tra qualche minuto.
   b. Buon pomeriggio!
   c. Buonasera!

5. … signora Marchi!
   a. Buongiorno
   b. Ciao
   c. Di dove sei

6. … professor Giusti!
   a. Buon pomeriggio
   b. Ciao
   c. Come stai

7. … Dina!
   a. ArrivederLa
   b. Come
   c. Arrivederci

H. Put the correct ending on each noun.

> *Model:* tren__
> *treno*

1. minut___

2. tren____

3. orari___

4. signorin___

5. dottoress___

I. Put the definite and indefinite articles in front of the given nouns:

> *Model:* ____ treno / _____ treno
> *il treno / un treno*

NOTE
As you will soon learn, some nouns end in -e. Note also that the titles for *professor* and *doctor* can also be used as nouns referring to the two professions: professore / *professor*　　　dottore / *doctor*

1. ____ centro / ____ centro

2. ____ minuto / ____ minuto

3. ____ dottore / _____ dottore

4. ____ professore / _____ professore

J. Cruciverba!

Horizontal

2 Il treno arriva tra qualche …
7 fra … minuto
9 the form of the article in front of *orario*
10 the form of the article in front of *minuto*
11 È un …
13 Quando … il treno?
14 Ma … cosa è quello?
16 to arrive
17 Ma … arriva il treno?

Vertical

1 Ah, … bene. E Lei?
3 the form of the article in front of *treno*
4 Quando arriva il …?
5 an alternative form for *fra*
6 good evening
8 an alternative form for *Che*?
12 Buonasera …, come sta?
15 You're welcome!

NOTA CULTURALE

Transportation in Italy

As elsewhere, cars are the main means of transportation in Italy. Buses and subway systems in large cities such as Rome and Milan are also used commonly to get around within cities and from town to town. Trains and airplanes are used to travel longer distances. Train travel is still very popular.

l'aereo	*airplane*
l'autobus	*bus*
l'automobile	*automobile*
la metropolitana	*subway*
il treno	*train*

K. Here's an exercise that will test your knowledge of Italian geography. You may have to look up these places in an encyclopedia or on the Internet. If you are using this book in a classroom situation, do this activity with a partner.

You are given two places (cities, regions, etc.). Give the most likely mode or modes of transportation used to get from one to the other.

Model: dalla Sicilia alla Lombardia *(from Sicily to Lombardy)*
    con l'aereo / con il treno (da = *from;* con = *with*)

1. da Roma a Milano

_____

2. da Roma centro *(downtown Rome)* all'EUR *(a part of Rome)*

_____

3. da Firenze a Siena

_____

4. dal Piemonte alla Sicilia

_____

Dove vai?

Unit 4

Dove vai?

CONVERSAZIONE

[Dina and Mark are chatting on a street bench in downtown Perugia, discussing the class they attended in the morning. It has been a long day for Dina and it is late at night. So, she suddenly gets up to leave.]

Mark	Dina, dove vai?	*Dina, where are you going?*
Dina	Vado a dormire.	*I'm going to bed / sleep.*
Mark	Perché?	*Why?*
Dina	Perché ho sonno.	*Because I'm sleepy.*
Mark	Sei stanca?	*Are you tired?*
Dina	Sì, sono molto stanca. E domani ho un appuntamento.	*Yes, I'm very tired. And tomorrow I have an appointment.*
Mark	Con chi?	*With whom?*
Dina	Con un'amica. Buonanotte!	*With a friend. Good night!*
Mark	Buonanotte!	*Good night!*

COMPRENSIONE

A. Rispondi alle seguenti domande con frasi intere. (*Answer the following questions with complete sentences.*)

1. Dove va Dina? (*Where is Dina going?*)

_____

2. Perché?

_____

3. È stanca Dina?

_____

4. Che cosa ha domani Dina?

_____

5. Con chi?

_____

VOCABOLARIO

Ho sonno!

PAROLE NUOVE

l'amico / l'amica (ah-mEEh-koh)	*friend (male / female)*
l'appuntamento	*appointment, date*
avere	*to have*
chi (kEEh)	*who / whom*
con	*with*
domani	*tomorrow*
dormire	*to sleep*
essere (Eh-sseh-reh)	*to be*
molto	*very*
perché (pehr-kEh)	*because, why*
il sonno	*sleep*
stanco (stAhn-koh) / stanca	*tired (masculine / feminine)*

ESPRESSIONI E MODI DI DIRE

avere sonno	*to be sleepy*
(Io) ho sonno	*I'm sleepy*
Buonanotte! (bwoh-nah-nOh-tteh)	*Good night!*

STRUTTURE VERBALI

(io) ho	*I have*
(io) sono	*I am*
(io) vado	*I'm going*
(tu) sei	*you are (familiar)*

ATTIVITÀ

B. Each statement is false. Correct it in an appropriate manner, according to the content of the dialogue on page 35.

> *Model:* Dina va a Pisa.
> *No, Dina va a dormire.*

1. Mark ha sonno.

_____

2. Mark è stanco.

_____

3. Dina ha un appuntamento con la professoressa Giusti.

_____

4. Mark ha un appuntamento domani.

_____

C. Change each statement to the opposite form: if it is masculine change it to feminine; if it is feminine change it to masculine.

> *Model:* Lui è americano.
> *Lei è americana.*

NOTE	
Masculine / Male	Feminine / Female
il professore / *the professor*	la professoressa / *the professor*
il dottore / *the doctor*	la dottoressa / *the doctor*
un amico / *a friend*	un'amica / *a friend*
l'amico / *a friend*	l'amica / *a friend*
il signore / *the gentleman*	la signora / *the lady*

1. Lui è italiano.

_____

2. Il signore è stanco.

_____

3. Lui ha un appuntamento con un amico.

_____

4. Il dottore è italiano.

_____

5. Lui è stanco.

_____

6. L'amico di Mark è americano.

_____

7. Il professore ha sonno.

_____

D. Answer the questions as indicated.

> *Model:* Chi è Dina? (*an American*)
> *Dina è un'americana.*

1. Che cosa è? (*a schedule*)

_____

2. Dove vai? (*to Florence*)

_____

3. Perché vai a dormire? (*because I'm tired and I'm sleepy*)

_____

4. Con chi hai un appuntamento domani? (*with a friend*)

_____

5. Buonanotte! (*Good night!*)

_____

E. Reconstruct the question that produced each answer.

> *Model:* Marco ha sonno.
> *Chi ha sonno? / Che cosa ha Marco?*

1. Marco è stanco.

_____

2. Dina ha sonno.

_____

3. Ho un appuntamento domani con un amico.

_____

4. Sto molto bene, grazie.

_____

5. Mi chiamo Dina Siracusa.

_____

6. Sono di Palermo.

_____

7. Vado a dormire perché ho sonno.

_____

LINGUA

Gender

As you already know from the previous unit, singular masculine nouns generally end in -o and feminine ones in -a. These endings indicate *grammatical gender*. As you have also discovered, these endings often allow you to identify the gender of an individual:

Masculine	Feminine
amico / *friend*	amica / *friend*
italiano / *Italian*	italiana / *Italian*
americano / *American*	americana / *American*

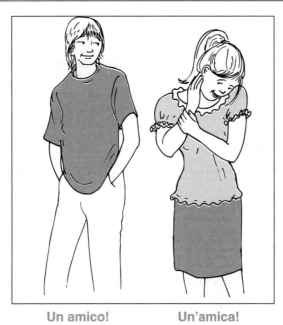

Un amico!   Un'amica!

The Article: Part 2

In the previous unit you learned that the indefinite article form un is used in front of masculine nouns that begin with any vowel and any consonant (except *z* and *s* + *consonant*): un treno, un orario. Note that the form un', introduced above, is used instead before feminine nouns beginning with any vowel:

Masculine	Feminine
un amico / *a friend*	un'amica / *a friend*
un americano / *an American*	un'americana / *an American*

The Adjective stanco

The adjective form stanco is masculine singular. The corresponding feminine form is stanca, as you may have figured out. Adjectives agree in gender and number with the nouns they modify:

With Masculine Singular Noun	With Feminine Singular Noun
Paul è stanco / *Paul is tired* Il signore è stanco / *The man is tired*	Dina è stanca / *Dina is tired* La signora è stanca / *The lady is tired*

The Verb essere: Part 1

The present indicative forms of the verb essere / *to be* that you have encountered so far are summarized below. The present indicative allows you, as its name implies, to indicate present or ongoing action or states:

(io) sono	*I am*
(tu) sei	*you are (familiar, singular)*
(lui / lei) è	*he / she is*
(Lei) è	*you are (polite, singular)*

Subject Pronouns: Part 1

Note that the subject pronouns are optional in simple sentences. The pronouns you have encountered so far are given below:

io (not capitalized)	*I*
tu	*you (familiar, singular)*
lui	*he*
lei	*she*
Lei (usually capitalized)	*you (polite, singular)*

ATTIVITÀ

F. Put the appropriate ending on each noun and then put the correct form of the indefinite article before the noun.

> *Model:* _____ american__ *(female)*
> *un'americana*

1. _____ tren__

2. _____ amic__ *(female)*

3. _____ italian__ *(female)*

4. _____ italian__ *(male)*

5. _____ amic__ *(male)*

6. _____ orari__

7. _____ minut__

G. Say or ask the following things in Italian. Use subject pronouns whenever needed.

> *Model:* Say that you (yourself) are tired
> *Io sono stanco / stanca.*

Say that…

1. you (yourself) are sleepy

_____

2. Dina is sleepy

_____

3. Dina is Italian

_____

4. he too is Italian

_____

5. you (yourself) are American

_____

6. she is tired

_____

7. he is tired

_____

Ask Dina…

8. where she is from

_____

9. if she is sleepy

_____

10. if she is tired

_____

11. if she is from here

_____

Ask Professor Giusti…

12. where she is from

_____

13. if she is sleepy

_____

14. if she is tired

_____

15. if she is from here

_____

H. Cruciverba!

<table>
<tr><td>

Horizontal

1 Dina è …
4 *because* and *why*
7 *an* appuntamento
8 I am
9 the feminine counterpart of *italiano*
10 Sono … stanco.
12 What one does when one goes to bed.
14 Dina ha …
16 Good night!
17 Con … ?
18 to have

</td><td>

Vertical

1 Anche Mark è …
2 Ho un appuntamento con un'…
3 Domani ho un …
5 Vado a dormire perché … sonno.
6 Sì, … a dormire.
8 you are *(familiar)*
11 Ho un appuntamento … un'amica.
12 tomorrow
13 to be
15 Dove …?

</td></tr>
</table>

NOTA CULTURALE

Schooling in Italy

The schooling system in Italy can be gleaned from the terms used to describe the various levels and schools. Here are the main ones in chronological order:

la scuola materna	*nursery school*
l'asilo infantile	*kindergarten*
la scuola elementare	*elementary school*
la scuola media	*junior high school*
il liceo	*secondary school, high school*
l'università	*university*

Sono stanco!

There are various kinds of secondary schools from which students can choose. For example, there are the liceo classico / *arts and letters secondary school* and the liceo scientifico / *science secondary school*. These allow students to specialize in areas which interest them.

I. Here is a research project for you. Look up each of the following in an encyclopedia or on the Internet. Identify the normal age (or age range) at which one starts and the age (or age range) at which one ends going to the school. If you are using this book in a classroom situation, do this activity with a partner.

1. la scuola materna

_____

2. l'asilo infantile

_____

3. la scuola elementare

_____

4. la scuola media

_____

5. il liceo

_____

6. l'università

_____

Basta, basta!

Unit 5

Uno, due, tre, . . .

CONVERSAZIONE

[In class one day, Dina asks her instructor to teach her how to count in Italian.]

Dina	Voglio imparare a contare.	*I want to learn how to count.*
Insegnante	Va bene! Uno, due, tre, quattro, cinque, sei, sette, otto, nove, dieci.	*OK! 1, 2, 3, 4, 5, 6, 7, 8, 9, 10.*
Dina	E poi?	*And then?*
Insegnante	Undici, dodici, tredici, quattordici, quindici, sedici, diciassette, diciotto, diciannove, venti.	*11, 12, 13, 14, 15, 16, 17, 18, 19, 20.*
Dina	E da venti in poi?	*And from twenty on?*
Insegnante	Venti, trenta, quaranta, cinquanta, sessanta, settanta, ottanta, novanta, cento.	*20, 30, 40, 50, 60, 70, 80, 90, 100.*
Dina	Mi può insegnare altri numeri?	*Can you teach me other numbers?*
Insegnante	Sì. Duecento, trecentodue, novecento novantadue.	*Yes. 200, 302, 992.*
Dina	Mamma mia! Come sono lunghi!	*My heavens! How long they are!*
Insegnante	Mille, duemila, centomila, un milione, tre milioni, un miliardo...	*1,000, 2,000, 100,000, 1,000,000, 3,000,000, a billion...*
Dina	Basta così, grazie!	*That's enough, thank you!*

COMPRENSIONE

A. Match the items in the two columns in an appropriate fashion.

1. Voglio imparare ...   a. dieci

2. Uno, due, tre, quattro, cinque, sei, sette, otto, nove, ...   b. quindici

3. Undici, dodici, tredici, quattordici, ...   c. in poi

4. Sedici, diciassette, diciotto, diciannove, ...   d. a contare

5. E da venti ...?   e. numeri

6. Venti, trenta, quaranta, ...   f. venti

7. Sessanta, settanta, ottanta, novanta, ...   g. cinquanta

8. Mi può insegnare altri ...?   h. centomila

9. Duecento, trecentodue, novecento ...   i. cento

10. Mille, duemila, ...   j. miliardo

11. un milione, tre milioni, un ...   k. Basta

12. ... così, grazie!   l. novantadue

VOCABOLARIO

PAROLE NUOVE

contare	*to count*
da	*from*
imparare (eehm-pah-rAh-reh)	*to learn*
l'insegnante (eehn-seh-nyAhn-teh)	*teacher (masculine and feminine)*
insegnare	*to teach*
lungo	*long*
il miliardo	*billion*
il milione	*million*
il numero (nOOh-meh-roh)	*number*
poi (pOh-eeh)	*then*

ESPRESSIONI E MODI DI DIRE

Basta così!	*That's enough!*
in poi	*(from) then on*
Mamma mia!	*My heavens! (literally: My mother!)*
Mi può insegnare?	*Can you teach me? (polite)*
Va bene!	*OK!*

Uno, due, tre, ...

I NUMERI CARDINALI

0 zero	18 diciotto (deeh-chOh-ttoh)
1 uno	19 diciannove (deeh-chah-nnOh-veh)
2 due	20 venti
3 tre	30 trenta
4 quattro	40 quaranta (kwah-rAhn-tah)
5 cinque (chEEhn-kweh)	50 cinquanta (cheehn-kwAhn-tah)
6 sei	60 sessanta
7 sette	70 settanta
8 otto	80 ottanta
9 nove	90 novanta
10 dieci (dyEh-cheeh)	100 cento (chEhn-toh)
11 undici (Oohn-deeh-cheeh)	200 duecento
12 dodici (dOh-deeh-cheeh)	300 trecento
13 tredici (trEh-deeh-cheeh)	1000 mille
14 quattordici (kwah-ttOhr-deeh-cheeh)	2000 duemila
15 quindici (kwEEhn-deeh-cheeh)	3000 tremila
16 sedici (sEh-deeh-cheeh)	...
17 diciassette (deeh-chah-ssEh-tteh)	

STRUTTURE VERBALI

sono   *they are*
(io) voglio (vOh-lyoh)   *I want*

ATTIVITÀ

B. Do the following things in Italian.

1. Count from 0 to 10 (writing out the numbers in letters).

_____

2. Count from 11 to 19 (writing out the numbers in letters).

_____

_____

3. Count from 20 to 100 in tens (writing out the numbers in letters).

_____

_____

C. *Quiz numerico!* Write out each response in letters.

> *Model:* the number of days in a week
> *sette*

1. the number of pennies in a dollar

_____

2. the number of months in a year

_____

3. the product of 10×3

_____

4. the product of 10×30

_____

5. the number of U.S. states

_____

6. half of eighty

_____

7. the result of adding 40 to itself

_____

8. ten less than a hundred

_____

9. twice thirty-five

_____

10. twice thirty

_____

Cinquanta euro

Note
The Italian currency is the **euro** (Euro). It is an invariable masculine noun (that is, it never changes its form): **un euro** / *one euro*   **due euro** / *two euros*

D. Say the following things in Italian.

1. My heavens!

_____

2. Can you teach me to count?

_____

3. Who is the instructor?

_____

4. I want to learn the numbers from one to ten.

_____

5. How long they are!

_____

6. He has one million euros.

_____

7. No, he has one billion euros!

_____

8. That's enough!

_____

9. OK!

_____

10. Here are other numbers.

_____

LINGUA

Cento, duecento ... mille!

Cardinal Numbers

Above you learned all the cardinal numbers from 0–20. The numbers from 20 on are easy to construct. Use the pattern of "adding on" the number as shown in the chart below:

22	=	20 + 2	ventidue
39	=	30 + 9	trentanove
112	=	100 + 12	centododici
279	=	200 + 79	duecento settantanove
915	=	900 + 15	novecento quindici
1505	=	1000 + 500 + 5	mille cinquecento cinque

If the resulting word is rather long, such as duecentosettantanove, then break it up in a numerically logical way, as shown in the chart above.

When uno / *one* or otto / *eight* is added to a number, the final vowel of the number is dropped:

21	=	20 + 1	venti + uno	=	ventuno
38	=	30 + 8	trenta + otto	=	trentotto
91	=	90 + 1	novanta + uno	=	novantuno
78	=	70 + 8	settanta + otto	=	settantotto

An accent mark is added to numbers ending in tre:

23	=	20 + 3	ventitré
73	=	70 + 3	settantatré
93	=	90 + 3	novantatré

Plural Forms

The plural forms of mille, un milione, and un miliardo are respectively mila, milioni, and miliardi. Please note that the rules for thousands and decimals are reversed in Italian: commas are used for decimals and periods for thousands.

2000	duemila
2005	duemila cinque
3900	tremila novecento
5000	cinquemila
5972	cinquemila novecento settantadue
100.000	centomila
120.000	cento ventimila
500.505	cinquecento mila cinquecento cinque
992.000	novecento novantadue mila
1.000.000	un milione
30.000.000	trenta milioni
1.000.000.000	un miliardo
5.000.000.000	cinque miliardi

The Article: Part 3

So far you have encountered the form il of the definite article, which is used before a masculine singular noun beginning with any consonant except *z* or *s + consonant*: il treno / *the train*.

In this unit, the form l' has been introduced. This is the form used in front of any singular noun, masculine or feminine, beginning with a vowel:

l'amica	*friend (feminine)*
l'amico	*friend (masculine)*
l'insegnante	*instructor (masculine or feminine)*
l'orario	*schedule*

ATTIVITÀ

E. Write out the following numbers in letters.

Model: 234
duecento trentaquattro

1. 86, 95, 63, 22, 88, 94, 98, 71, 72

_____

_____

2. 123, 245, 378, 421, 553, 621, 798, 888, 999

_____

_____

3. 2343, 5678, 9871, 7549

_____

_____

4. 12,458, 25,789

_____

_____

5. 345,798, 989,421

_____

_____

6. 1,654,893, 2,343,789

_____

_____

7. 1,456,798,345, 5,555,555,555

_____

_____

F. Put the appropriate definite article form in front of the following nouns.

> _Model:_ _____ treno
> _il treno_

1. _____ amico
2. _____ amica
3. _____ americano
4. _____ americana
5. _____ appuntamento
6. _____ centro
7. _____ insegnante
8. _____ italiano
9. _____ italiana
10. _____ milione
11. _____ miliardo
12. _____ minuto
13. _____ numero
14. _____ orario
15. _____ euro

G. Choose the correct or appropriate response.

1. 348 euros
    a. trecento quarantaotto euro
    b. trecento quarantotto euro

2. 563 euros
    a. cinquecento sessantatre euro
    b. cinquecento sessantatré euro

3. 3451
    a. tremila quattrocento cinquantuno
    b. tremila quattrocento cinquantauno

4. Mi può insegnare a contare … cento in poi?
    a. da
    b. di

5. Mamma …!
    a. mia
    b. così

6. Mi può insegnare … numeri?
    a. altri
    b. altro

7. Come sono …!
    a. lungo
    b. lunghi

H. Cruciverba!

Horizontal

1   the plural of *milione*
6   uno, …, tre
8   otto, …, dieci
9   100.000
11 number
13 E … venti in poi?
16 ventisette, …, ventinove
17 109
18 trentadue, …, trentaquattro
21 one
22 teacher
23 ventinove, …, trentuno
24 to learn
25 undici, …, tredici

Vertical

1   one billion
2   93
3   long
4   nove, …, undici
5   sette, …, nove
7   E da venti in …?
10 trenta, …, trentadue
12 Voglio imparare a …
14 Mi può … altri numeri?
15 Va …!
19 tre, …, cinque
20 sei, …, otto

NOTA CULTURALE

Mille lire

Dieci euro

Un dollaro

Italian Currency

As you may know, the **euro** is used in Italy as the basic currency, as it is in many other European countries. It has replaced the **lira,** which was the previous unit of currency. One **euro** is designed to provide the same "buying power" as one dollar, although the exchange rates will vary. Do you know what the rate is right now?

The noun **euro** is invariable:

un euro	*one euro*
venti euro	*twenty euro*

I. First, indicate how to say the following figures in Italian. Then, give the exchange value by looking it up on the Internet. If you are using this book in a classroom situation, do this activity with a partner.

1. 25 euro

_____

2. 150 euro

_____

3. 1,500 euro

_____

4. 21,000 euro

_____

Review Part 1

[This very brief unit allows you to go over the basic notions in units 1–5 with practical exercises.]

A. Come si dice in italiano?

1. Delighted to meet you (spoken by a male).

_____

2. Delighted to meet you (spoken by a female).

_____

3. Let me introduce you to Mark Cardelli *(plural)*.

_____

4. Let me introduce you to Dina Siracusa *(polite, singular)*.

_____

5. Good evening!

_____

6. You're welcome!

_____

7. Good afternoon!

_____

8. My heavens!

_____

9. I want to learn how to count from one to ten.

_____

10. OK!

_____

B. Comunicazione! Carry out the following commands in Italian.

> *Model:* Introduce Dina Siracusa to Professor Giusti *(a female)*.
> *Professoressa Giusti, Le presento Dina Siracusa.*

1. Introduce Paul Giannetti to both Dina and Mark.

_____

2. Introduce Debbie Di Nardo to Jim Carducci.

_____

3. Ask Dina how she is.

_____

4. Ask Dr. Martini *(a female)* how she is.

_____

5. Say good-bye to Dr. Martini.

_____

6. Ask Dina where she is from.

_____

7. Ask Dr. Martini where she is from.

_____

8. Ask Paul how he is.

_____

9. Ask Mr. Franchi how he is.

_____

10. Ask Mark if he is sleepy.

_____

11. Ask Professor Giusti if she is Italian.

_____

12. Ask Professor Giusti if she is tired.

_____

C. Domande personali. *(Personal questions.)*

1. Come ti chiami?

_____

2. Sei americano / americana?

_____

3. Di che origine sei?

_____

4. Come stai?

_____

D. Write a brief dialogue in which various people meet each other for the first time in an Italian classroom.

La classe d'italiano!

_____

_____

_____

_____

_____

_____

_____

_____

_____

E. Word Search Puzzle!

There are 20 words hidden in the word search puzzle below: 10 can be read from left to right (horizontally) and 10 in a top-down direction (vertically). Can you find them? The clues given below will help you look for them. The numbers of the clues do not reflect any particular order or arrangement to the hidden words.

M	I	N	U	T	O	E	R	T	C	B	S	Q	W	E	R	T	Y	U	I
A	S	D	F	G	H	J	K	L	H	Z	O	X	C	V	B	N	M	G	Q
W	E	R	T	Y	I	T	A	L	I	A	N	O	T	Y	U	I	O	R	P
A	S	D	F	G	H	J	K	L	A	Z	O	X	C	V	B	S	T	A	I
N	M	Q	W	E	R	T	Y	U	M	I	O	P	P	O	U	I	Y	Z	T
C	H	I	A	M	A	G	F	D	O	V	E	D	S	A	Q	W	E	I	R
E	Q	S	T	T	T	N	Q	Q	Z	Z	X	C	C	B	N	M	E	J	
N	Z	Z	X	X	C	C	V	B	U	O	N	A	S	E	R	A	W	W	B
T	C	V	V	W	W	R	R	T	Y	U	U	Y	T	N	R	E	W	W	U
R	A	N	O	V	A	N	T	O	T	T	O	R	Q	T	Q	Q	N	N	O
O	W	W	E	R	T	Y	T	W	N	W	W	D	W	O	W	W	O	M	N
X	Z	P	E	R	C	H	É	Z	M	Z	Z	O	Z	M	Z	Z	V	K	G
Q	X	R	X	X	X	Q	G	X	B	X	X	M	X	I	X	X	E	L	I
A	C	E	C	C	C	W	X	C	B	C	C	A	C	L	C	C	M	O	O
Z	V	G	V	V	V	E	X	V	E	V	V	N	V	A	V	V	I	K	R
X	B	O	B	B	B	R	X	B	S	B	B	I	B	A	B	B	L	M	N
C	N	G	N	N	N	T	G	N	S	N	N	N	E	N	N	A	N	O	
V	M	G	M	M	M	Y	G	M	E	M	M	M	A	M	M	K	Q	E	
G	B	G	B	B	B	N	G	B	R	B	B	B	C	E	N	T	O	Q	R
B	U	O	N	A	N	O	T	T	E	B	B	A	G	G	G	G	G	Q	Q

Horizontal
1 the masculine counterpart of *italiana*
2 Come si …?
3 Ciao, Mark, come …?
4 Di … sei?
5 Good evening.
6 Il treno arriva tra qualche …
7 It means both *because* and *why.*
8 Good night!
9 ninety-eight
10 one hundred

Vertical
11 Io … italiano.
12 Mi … Alessandro.
13 downtown
14 Thank you!
15 You're welcome!
16 Good morning!
17 tomorrow
18 to be
19 nine thousand
20 one hundred thousand

Part 2: Expanding Basic Skills

A che ora parte?

Unit 6

Che ora è?

CONVERSAZIONE

[Dina has made a new Italian friend, Alessandro. They are at the bus station in Perugia. The new bus schedule is confusing because of recent route changes that have not as yet been completely implemented.]

Dina	Che ora è?	*What time is it?*
Alessandro	Sono le dieci precise.	*It's exactly ten.*
Dina	Veramente? Proprio in punto?	*Really? Right on the dot?*
Alessandro	Sì.	*Yes.*
Dina	A che ora parte l'autobus ogni giorno?	*At what time does the bus leave every day?*
Alessandro	Forse alle dieci e venti.	*Maybe at 10:20.*
Dina	Non alle dieci e mezzo?	*Not at half past ten?*
Alessandro	Non sono sicuro. Di solito parte alle undici meno un quarto.	*I'm not sure. Usually it leaves at a quarter to eleven.*
Dina	Non capisco.	*I don't understand.*
Alessandro	C'è un orario differente. Forse l'informazione non è precisa.	*There's a different schedule. Maybe the information is not precise.*

COMPRENSIONE

A. Vero o falso?

_____ 1. Che ora è? Sono le dieci e cinque minuti.

_____ 2. Sono le dieci in punto.

_____ 3. Forse l'autobus parte alle dieci e venti.

_____ 4. Forse parte alle undici meno un quarto.

_____ 5. C'è un orario differente.

_____ 6. L'informazione è precisa.

VOCABOLARIO

PAROLE NUOVE

l'autobus	bus
capire	to understand
differente	different
forse	maybe
il giorno (jOhr-noh)	day
l'informazione (eehn-fohr-mah-tsyOh-neh)	information
meno	less, minus
mezzo	half
ogni (Oh-nyeeh)	every
l'ora	hour
partire	to leave
preciso	precise
proprio (prOh-preeh-oh)	really
il punto	dot, point
quarto	quarter
sicuro	sure
veramente	actually, truly

ESPRESSIONI E MODI DI DIRE

c'è	there is
di solito	usually
non	not

Che ora è?   È l'una.

L'ORA (TIME)

A che ora?	At what time?
a un'ora differente	at a different time
all'una	at one o'clock

alle dieci e mezzo (mEh-dsdsoh)	*at half past ten*
alle dieci e venti	*at 10:20*
alle nove meno un quarto	*at a quarter to nine*
Che ora è?	*What time is it?*
È l'una.	*It's one o'clock.*
Sono le due, le tre, ...	*It's two, three, ... o'clock.*
Sono le dieci e cinque.	*It's 10:05.*
Sono le dieci precise (preh-chEEh-zeh).	*It's exactly ten o'clock.*
Sono le dieci in punto.	*It's ten on the dot.*

STRUTTURE VERBALI

(io) capisco (kah-pEEhs-koh)	*I understand*
(io) non capisco	*I don't understand*
parte	*it leaves, it is leaving*

ATTIVITÀ

B. Say the following things in Italian.

1. What time is it?

_____

2. It's eleven right on the dot.

_____

3. Really?

_____

4. When is the bus leaving?

_____

5. I'm not sure.

_____

6. Usually it leaves at a quarter past nine every day.

_____

7. I don't understand.

_____

8. There's a different schedule tomorrow.

_____

9. The information is not precise.

_____

C. Indicate what time it is.

> *Model:* 5:10
> *Sono le cinque e dieci.*

Che ora è?

1. 1:12

_____

2. 2:20

_____

3. 3:15

_____

4. 4:30

_____

5. 5:45

_____

6. 6:05

_____

7. 7:59

_____

8. 8:00

_____

9. 1:00

_____

10. 9:30

_____

11. 10:20

_____

12. 11:15

_____

13. 12:40

_____

D. Now say that the bus usually leaves at the indicated hours.

> *Model:* 3:45
> *Di solito l'autobus parte alle tre e quarantacinque.*

A che ora parte l'autobus di solito?

1. 9:50

_____

2. 1:30

_____

3. 12:15

_____

4. 5:00

_____

5. 6:45

_____

E. Domande personali. Indicate at what time you do the following things every day.

> *Model:* Get up.
> *Alle sette e mezzo. / Alle otto precise. / ...*

Ogni giorno…

1. Get up

_____

2. Go to school / work

_____

3. Eat lunch

_____

4. Eat dinner

_____

5. Go to bed

_____

LINGUA

Telling Time

What time is it?
Che ora è?   or   Che ore sono?

As you have probably figured out by now, in telling time you use the cardinal numbers to refer to the hour preceded by the feminine plural form of the definite article. That form is le for all hours except *one o'clock*, which is the only "singular hour":

l'una	*one o'clock*
le due	*two o'clock*
le tre	*three o'clock*
le quattro	*four o'clock*
le cinque	*five o'clock*

The reason why the feminine form is used is because the complete expression for telling time includes le ore / *the hours*: le ore due / *two hours = two o'clock*. In general, however, the complete expression is not used (unless it is needed):

The minutes are indicated simply by adding them on to the hours with the conjunction e / *and*. Again, the complete expression includes the word for minutes: le ore due e venti minuti / *two o'clock and twenty minutes*. In general, however, the complete expression is not used (unless it is needed):

l'una e dieci	*one ten*
le due e ventitré	*two twenty-three*
le tre e cinquantadue	*three fifty-two*
le quattro e venti	*four twenty*

There are some points on the clock that can be rendered alternatively as follows:

:30	=	mezzo / *half past*		
:15	=	un quarto / *a quarter*		
12:00 A.M.	=	la mezzanotte / *midnight*	= È mezzanotte. / *It's midnight.*
12:00 P.M.	=	il mezzogiorno / *noon*	= È mezzogiorno. / *It's noon.*

Within 15 minutes to the next hour, you can use meno / *minus* as shown in the chart below:

4.30	le quattro e trenta	= le quattro e mezzo	*half past four*
10.30	le dieci e trenta	= le dieci e mezzo	*half past ten*
1.15	l'una e quindici	= l'una e un quarto	*a quarter past one*
5.15	le cinque e quindici	= le cinque e un quarto	*a quarter past five*
3.55	le tre e cinquanta-cinque	= le quattro meno cinque	*five minutes to four* (literally: four minus five)
9.57	le nove e cinquanta-sette	= le dieci meno tre	*three minutes to ten* (literally: ten minus three)

Che ore sono?   È mezzanotte!

Official time in Italy is based on the twenty-four-hour clock:

le otto e dieci	8:10 A.M.
le venti e dieci	8:10 P.M.
le dieci e venti	10:20 A.M.
le ventidue e venti	10:20 P.M.

The words il mattino / *morning*, la sera / *evening*, and il pomeriggio / *afternoon* are used alternatively in everyday speech:

le otto e dieci del mattino	8:10 A.M. *(of the morning)*
le otto e dieci della sera	8:10 P.M. *(of the evening)*
le due e un quarto del mattino	2:15 A.M. *(of the morning)*
le due e un quarto del pomeriggio	2:15 P.M. *(of the afternoon)*

The Article: Part 4

As we saw in the previous unit, l' is the form of the definite article used before any singular noun (masculine or feminine) beginning with any vowel:

l'ora	*the hour*
l'amico	*the friend (male)*

Le is the form used before any feminine plural noun (beginning with any vowel or consonant):

l'ora	*the hour*	le ore	*the hours*
l'amica	*the friend*	le amiche	*the friends*

Contractions: Part 1

Contractions are forms that result when two words are united and shortened. For example, in English the form *won't* is a contraction of *will not*; the form *it's* is a contraction of *it is,* and so on. In Italian, common prepositions such as a / *to* and di / *of* contract with the definite article. Here are some examples of prepositional contractions introduced in this unit:

alle	=	(a + le):	alle due	*at two o'clock*
all'	=	(a + l'):	all'una	*at one o'clock*
del	=	(di + il):	del mattino	*of the morning*
della	=	(di + la):	della sera	*of the evening*

ATTIVITÀ

F. Che ore sono? Give all equivalent ways of telling each time.

> *Model:* 6:30 P.M.
> *Sono le sei e trenta della sera. / Sono le sei e mezzo della sera.*
> *Sono le diciotto e trenta. / Sono le diciotto e mezzo.* (colloquial)

1. 1:00 A.M.

_____

2. 1:15 P.M.

_____

3. 2:45 A.M.

_____

4. 3:45 P.M.

_____

5. 4:10 A.M.

_____

6. 5:55 P.M.

_____

7. 6:30 A.M.

_____

8. 7:30 P.M.

_____

9. 8:00 A.M.

_____

10. 9:00 P.M.

_____

11. 10:12 A.M.

_____

12. 11: 01 P.M.

_____

13. 12:00 A.M.

_____

14. 12:00 P.M.

_____

G. Put the appropriate form of the definite article or of the contraction in front of each word.

> _Model:_ Sono _____ sette _____ sera.
> _Sono le sette della sera._

1. L'autobus parte _____ otto _____ mattino.

2. È _____ una precisa _____ pomeriggio.

3. Sono _____ nove e trenta _____ sera.

4. Il treno parte _____ una e dieci _____ pomeriggio.

5. Sono _____ venti in punto.

H. Cruciverba!

NOTE	
non...mai / *never (not ever)*	Non parte mai all'una / *It never leaves at one.*
per / *for*	Grazie per l'informazione / *Thanks for the info.*

Horizontal

1 Sono le undici ... cinque (= 10:55).
4 Che ... sono?
7 ... non parte all'una.
9 Sono le nove ... sera.
10 Ma ... l'autobus parte alle nove e venti.
11 Sono le ... e venti (= 9:20).
12 Grazie per l'...
17 Parte a un'ora ... ogni giorno.
18 Ma non parte ... *(mai)* all'una precisa.
20 Ogni ... parte a un'ora differente.
22 Sono le cinque ... (= 5:00).
23 to leave
25 Sono le sette in ... (= 7:00).

Vertical

1 È l'una e ... (= 1:30).
2 Sono le ... precise (= 8:00).
3 A che ora parte l'...?
4 Che ... è?
5 to understand
6 L'autobus parte ... nove e mezzo.
8 the masculine counterpart of *amica*
9 Sono le undici ... mattino.
11 L'autobus ... parte all'una.
13 Sì, ... giorno parte a un'ora differente.
14 Alessandro, ... sono le dieci e cinque.
15 Grazie ... l'informazione.
16 *the* ore
19 the opposite of *sì*
21 Veramente? Sono ... le cinque in punto?
24 Sono le ... e un quarto (= 2:15).

NOTA CULTURALE

L'una del pomeriggio   Le tredici precise

Italian Time

The 24-hour clock is used more commonly in Italy than it is in North America. Thus 5 P.M. is usually rendered nowadays as **le diciassette** rather than as **le cinque del pomeriggio**. This is especially true in the case of media and official "time situations" (travel schedules, school timetables, etc.). You will simply have to get used to this method of telling time when you are in Italy!

I. Give the more common version of the indicated times. Also, try to guess what may be happening at those hours in Italy. If you are using this book in a classroom situation, do this activity with a partner.

> *Model:* le quattro del pomeriggio
> *le sedici*

1. l'una del pomeriggio

_____

2. le sette di sera

_____

3. le undici di sera

_____

4. le sei di sera

_____

5. le nove di sera

_____

Fa molto caldo, no?

Unit 7

Che bel tempo!

CONVERSAZIONE

[Dina is chatting with Mirella in a downtown espresso bar. Dina just loves the weather in Perugia, even though it is winter. Mirella, who has a keen sense of humor, is in the mood to pull Dina's leg.]

Dina	Che bel tempo!	*What nice weather!*
Mirella	Sì, oggi è proprio una bella giornata!	*Yes, today is really a beautiful day!*
Dina	Che tempo fa generalmente d'inverno?	*What's the weather like usually in the winter?*
Mirella	Di solito fa brutto tempo! Fa freddo, tira vento e nevica.	*Usually the weather's awful! It's cold, it's windy, and it snows.*
Dina	E d'estate?	*And in the summer?*
Mirella	Fa troppo caldo!	*It's too hot!*
Dina	E di primavera?	*And in the spring?*
Mirella	Di primavera e d'autunno piove sempre e fa fresco!	*In the spring and in the fall it always rains and it is cool!*
Dina	Scherzi, vero?	*You're joking, aren't you?*
Mirella	Certo!	*Of course!*

COMPRENSIONE

A. Which response, a or b, is the correct or appropriate one?

1. Che ... tempo!
   a. bel
   b. bello

2. È proprio una ... giornata!
   a. bel
   b. bella

3. Che tempo fa generalmente d'inverno?
   a. Di solito fa brutto tempo.
   b. È una bella giornata.

4. Fa freddo, tira vento e ...
   a. d'estate
   b. nevica

5. D'estate fa…
      a. troppo caldo
      b. troppo freddo

6. Di primavera e d'autunno…
      a. scherza
      b. piove sempre

VOCABOLARIO

Che bel tempo!   Lei scherza, no?

PAROLE NUOVE

bello	*beautiful, nice*
brutto	*ugly, awful*
il caldo	*heat (hot, warm)*
certo	*certainly*
il freddo	*cold*
fresco	*cool, fresh*
generalmente	*generally*
la giornata (johr-nAh-tah)	*day (in the sense of all day long)*
nevicare	*to snow*
oggi (Oh-jjeeh)	*today*
piovere (pyOh-veh-reh)	*to rain*
scherzare (skehr-tsAh-reh)	*to joke (around)*
sempre	*always*
il tempo	*weather*
troppo	*too (much)*
il vento	*wind*

LE STAGIONI (THE SEASONS)

la primavera / di primavera, in primavera	*spring / in the spring*
l'estate / d'estate, in estate	*summer / in the summer*
l'autunno / d'autunno, in autunno	*fall / in the fall*
l'inverno / d'inverno, in inverno	*winter / in the winter*

IL TEMPO (THE WEATHER)

Che bel tempo!	*What nice weather!*
Che tempo fa?	*How's the weather?*
È proprio una bella giornata!	*It's really a nice day!*
Fa brutto tempo!	*The weather's awful!*
Fa freddo!	*It's cold!*
Fa troppo caldo!	*It's too hot!*
Tira vento!	*It's windy!*

STRUTTURE VERBALI

nevica (nEh-veeh-kah)	*it snows, it is snowing*
piove (pyOh-veh)	*it rains, it is raining*

ATTIVITÀ

B. Say or ask the following things.

> *Model:* Say that it is nice weather.
> *Fa bel tempo.*

Say that…

1. it is really a beautiful day

_____

2. usually the weather is awful

_____

3. it is cold today

_____

4. it is windy

_____

5. it is snowing today

_____

6. in the spring it rains too much and it is cool

_____

7. it is windy in the fall

_____

8. it is cold in the winter

_____

9. it is always hot in the summer

_____

Ask…

10. how the weather is generally in the winter

_____

11. how the weather is usually in the spring

_____

12. how the weather is generally in the summer

_____

13. how the weather is generally in the fall

_____

14. Alessandro if he is joking

_____

C. Che tempo fa? Indicate the weather and/or season that each picture suggests.

1.

_____

2.

_____

3.

_____

4.

_____

5.

_____

6.

_____

D. **Domande personali.** Indicate the following in Italian.

> _Model:_ Your favorite season.
> _La primavera._

1. Your favorite season.

_____

2. How the weather is in your hometown each season.

_____

3. What the weather is like today.

_____

LINGUA

Fa caldo!

Fa freddo!

The Weather

As you have seen, in Italian the verb fare / *to do, to make* is used to refer to the weather as being hot or cold:

Fa caldo	*It is hot*
Fa freddo	*It is cold*
Fa fresco	*It is cool*

Note that the verb essere / *to be* can be used alternatively:

È caldo	*It is hot*
È freddo	*It is cold*
È fresco	*It is cool*

The Adjective bello: Part 1

Descriptive adjectives are words that modify nouns. They describe attributes, features, and other characteristics such as color, shape, size, and so on. They generally follow the noun in Italian. However, some can be used before the noun or after it.

The adjective bello is one of those adjectives that can be used before or after the noun. When used before its forms vary. Following are its singular forms:

Before a masculine singular noun beginning with any consonant except *z* or *s + consonant:* bel

bel tempo   *nice weather*
bel giorno   *nice day*

Before a masculine singular noun beginning with *z* or *s + consonant:* bello

bello studente   *nice student (male)*

Before a feminine singular noun beginning with any consonant: bella

bella giornata   *nice day*
bella signora   *beautiful lady*

Before any singular noun, masculine or feminine, beginning with any vowel: bell'

bell'amico   *handsome friend (male)*
bell'amica   *beautiful friend (female)*

Una bella signora!

The Verbs nevicare and piovere

The verbs nevicare / *to snow* and piovere / *to rain* can be used only in the third person singular, of course, when referring to weather conditions:

nevicare *to snow*	piovere *to rain*
Oggi nevica.	*Today it is snowing.*
Domani piove.	*Tomorrow it's going to rain.*

ATTIVITÀ

E. Say that...

1. today it is snowing, but tomorrow it will be beautiful

_____

2. usually it is windy in the fall

_____

3. in the winter it is always cold but it is not cold today

_____

4. in the summer it is always too hot

_____

5. it is a very beautiful day today, but it is quite (very) windy

_____

6. in the fall it is always very cool

_____

7. in the spring it is also very cool and windy

_____

F. Put the appropriate form of bello in the spaces.

1. Oggi è una _____ giornata.
2. Di solito fa _____ tempo in estate.
3. Chi è quel _(that)_ _____ studente?
4. Dina ha una _____ amica.
5. Ha anche un _____ amico.
6. Perugia ha un _____ centro.
7. Oggi è un _____ giorno.

G. Composition. Write a brief weather forecast.

    Model: Domani piove e tira vento. Di solito fa molto caldo, ma non domani...

Il tempo di domani!

_____

_____

_____

_____

_____

_____

H. Cruciverba!

Horizontal	Vertical
1 No, non fa bel tempo! Fa … tempo!	1 *nice* student
2 nice friend (male)	2 nice friend *(female)*
4 No, non fa brutto tempo! Fa … tempo!	3 No, non fa freddo! Fa …!
6 Che tempo …?	4 È proprio una … giornata.
8 an alternative word for *giornata*	5 an alternative word for *giorno*
10 Che … fa generalmente d'estate?	6 No, non fa caldo! Fa …!
13 Tira vento e …	7 to rain
15 Che tempo fa generalmente d'… ?	9 It is snowing.
16 Sì, …. vento.	11 winter
17 Di … fa bel tempo d'autunno.	12 spring
20 summer	14 Tira …
21 fall	18 D'estate fa … caldo!
22 to snow	19 Sì, … di primavera fa bel tempo.

NOTA CULTURALE

The People and Regions of Italy

Most of Italy's people live in urban areas. Italy's largest cities, in order of population, are Rome (Roma), Milan (Milano), and Naples (Napoli). Each has more than a million people. Many of the country's cities are surrounded by large metropolitan areas.

The most densely populated areas of the country are the industrialized regions of Lombardy (la Lombardia) and Liguria (la Liguria) in the northwest and the region of Campania (la Campania) in the south. The areas with the lowest population density are the mountains of both the north and south.

About 98 percent of Italy's people are ethnic Italians. The only sizable ethnic minorities are Germans who live in the Trentino-Alto Adige (il Trentino Alto Adige) region, which borders Austria, and Slovenes who inhabit the Trieste area, along the border of Italy and Slovenia. A number of ethnic French people live in the Valle d'Aosta (la Valle d'Aosta) region, near Italy's border with France and Switzerland.

I. There are 20 Italian regions. Do you know what they are? If you are using this book in a classroom situation, do this activity with a partner, looking them up on a map.

1. _____

2. _____

3. _____

4. _____

5. _____

6. _____

7. _____

8. _____

9. _____

10. _____

11. _____

12. _____

13. _____

14. _____

15. _____

16. _____

17. _____

18. _____

19. _____

20. _____

Ciao, Dina, sono io!

Unit 8

Pronto?

[Mark calls Mirella on his cellphone (il cellulare). He pretends to have lost his mind. His real aim is to get Mirella's attention, especially since she is hosting a party at her house on Sunday which he badly wants to attend.]

Mark	Pronto? Dina, sono io, Mark.	Hello? Dina, it's me, Mark.
Mirella	Ciao, Mark. Che c'è?	Hi, Mark. What's up?
Mark	Che giorno della settimana è, lunedì, martedì, mercoledì o giovedì?	What day of the week is it, Monday, Tuesday, Wednesday, or Thursday?
Mirella	Ma che dici? Hai perso la testa?	What are you saying? Have you lost your mind?
Mark	Forse.	Maybe.
Mirella	Oggi è venerdì. Domani vado in centro come ogni sabato. Vieni anche tu alla festa domenica?	Today is Friday. Tomorrow I'm going downtown like every Saturday. Are you also coming to the party on Sunday?
Mark	Sì, se vuoi tu.	Yes, if you want me to.
Mirella	Certo.	Of course I do.
Mark	Che mese dell'anno è?	What month of the year is it?
Mirella	Hai veramente perso la testa! È novembre. Fa già molto freddo!	You've really lost your mind! It's November. It's already very cold!
Mark	Fa sempre freddo in questo paese, a dicembre, gennaio, febbraio, marzo e aprile?	Is it always cold in this country, in December, January, February, March, and April?
Mirella	Non sempre. A maggio, giugno, luglio e agosto fa assai caldo.	Not always. In May, June, July, and August it gets quite hot.
Mark	Anche a settembre e ottobre fa bel tempo.	Even in September and October it's nice.
Mirella	Hai ragione.	You're right.
Mark	Che giorno è oggi?	What's today's date?
Mirella	È il cinque novembre. Uffa! Hai veramente perso la testa!	It's the fifth of November. Heck! You've really lost your mind!

COMPRENSIONE

A. Complete each statement or question in an appropriate fashion with the missing word or expression.

1. Mark telefona a *(phones)* _____.

2. Mark chiede a *(asks)* Dina che _____ della settimana è.

3. I giorni della settimana sono: _____.

4. Ma che dici? Hai perso la _____?

5. Domani Dina va in _____ come ogni sabato.

6. Vieni anche tu alla festa _____?

7. Se _____ tu.

8. Che _____ dell'anno è?

9. I mesi dell'anno sono: _____.

10. È novembre e fa già molto _____.

11. Fa sempre freddo in questo _____.

12. Che giorno è oggi? È _____.

VOCABOLARIO

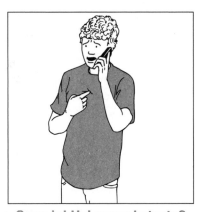

Sono io! Hai perso la testa?

PAROLE NUOVE

andare	*to go*
l'anno	*year*
assai	*quite*
il cellulare	*cellphone*
certo	*of course, certainly*
come	*like*
di	*of*
dire	*to say, to tell*
la festa	*party*
già (jAh)	*already*
il mese	*month*
o	*or*
il paese (pah-Eh-zeh)	*country*
perdere (pEhr-deh-reh)	*to lose*
se	*if*
la settimana	*week*
la testa	*head*
venire	*to come*

ESPRESSIONI E MODI DI DIRE

avere ragione (rah-jOh-neh) / **hai ragione**	*to be right / you're right (familiar)*
Che c'è? (keh chEh)	*What's up?*
Che giorno è oggi?	*What's today's date? / What day is it today?*
Hai perso la testa?	*Have you lost your mind?*
Pronto?	*Hello? (on the phone)*
Sono io!	*It's me! (on the phone)*

FORMA DIMOSTRATIVA

questo paese (kwEhs-toh)	*this country*

I GIORNI DELLA SETTIMANA (DAYS OF THE WEEK)

lunedì (looh-neh-dEEh)	*Monday*
martedì	*Tuesday*
mercoledì	*Wednesday*
giovedì (joh-veh-dEEh)	*Thursday*
venerdì	*Friday*
sabato (sAh-bah-toh)	*Saturday*
domenica (doh-mEh-neeh-kah)	*Sunday*

Il quindici settembre

I MESI DELL'ANNO (MONTHS OF THE YEAR)

gennaio (jeh-nnAh-yoh)	*January*
febbraio (feh-bbrAh-yoh)	*February*
marzo (mAhr-tsoh)	*March*
aprile	*April*
maggio (mAh-jjoh)	*May*
giugno (jOOh-nyoh)	*June*
luglio (lOOh-lyoh)	*July*
agosto	*August*
settembre	*September*
ottobre	*October*
novembre	*November*
dicembre (deeh-chEhm-breh)	*December*

STRUTTURE VERBALI

(io) vado	*I'm going*
(tu) vieni	*you are coming (familiar)*
(tu) dici	*you are saying (familiar)*

ATTIVITÀ

B. Say or ask the following things.

Say …

1. hello on the phone

_____

2. «of course»

_____

3. «if you want to»

_____

4. «not always»

_____

5. «you're right» to Sara

_____

Say that…

6. it is you on the phone

_____

7. today you are going downtown like every Saturday

_____

8. it is always very cold in this country

_____

9. it is already quite cold

_____

10. it's the tenth of October

_____

Ask …

11. what's up

_____

12. what day of the week it is

_____

13. someone if he or she has lost his or her mind

_____

14. someone what he or she is saying

_____

15. Alessandro if he too is coming to the party

_____

16. what month of the year it is

_____

17. what day it is

_____

18. where the cellphone is

_____

19. Sara if she has a cellphone

_____

C. Give the day or month that comes after (dopo).

> _Model:_ lunedì
> _Il giorno dopo è martedì._

1. martedì

_____

2. giovedì

_____

3. sabato

_____

4. gennaio

_____

5. marzo

_____

6. maggio

_____

7. luglio

_____

8. settembre

_____

9. novembre

_____

D. Domande personali. Answer the questions.

1. Hai un cellulare?

_____

2. Vai a una festa sabato o domenica?

_____

3. Com'è il tempo in questo paese?

_____

4. Qual è il tuo giorno della settimana preferito *(What is your favorite day of the week)?*

_____

5. Qual è il tuo mese dell'anno preferito *(What is your favorite month of the year)?*

_____

E. Now, make up a phone conversation between yourself and someone else, similar to the one on page 85.

Pronto?

_____

_____

_____

_____

_____

_____

_____

_____

_____

_____

_____

_____

_____

_____

_____

_____

_____

LINGUA

Ma che data è?

Dates

Dates are expressed with the definite article in the masculine singular form, il, followed by the appropriate cardinal number and the month:

Che data è? / *What's the date?*	
il tre maggio	*May 3*
il quindici settembre	*September 15*
il ventun settembre	*September 21*
il quattro aprile	*April 4*
il quattro dicembre	*December 4*
il ventitré giugno	*June 23*

There is one exception to this rule. The ordinal number primo is used to indicate the first of each month:

il primo gennaio	*January 1*
il primo ottobre	*October 1*

In front of vowels, l' is the required article form, of course:

l'otto gennaio	*January 8*
l'undici ottobre	*October 11*

To indicate the year, just write and read the year as a number:

1994	Mille novecento novantaquattro
1998	Mille novecento novantotto
2001	Duemila e uno
2004	Duemila e quattro
2005	Duemila e cinque

Contractions: Part 2

In this unit you have encountered three other prepositional contractions. They are listed below:

alla	=	(a + la):	alla festa / *to the party*
della	=	(di + la):	della settimana / *of the week*
dell'	=	(di + l'):	dell'anno / *of the year*

Subject Pronouns: Part 2

The complete system of subject personal pronouns is given below.

io	*I*
tu	*you (familiar)*
Lei	*you (polite)*
lui	*he*
lei	*she*
noi	*we*
voi	*you (plural)*
loro	*they*

As mentioned in Unit 4, in general, these pronouns are optional:

Tu che dici? / Che dici?	*What are you saying?*
Io sono italiano / Sono italiano	*I'm Italian*

However, they are used for emphasis or to avoid ambiguity, especially when two or more subjects are involved:

For emphasis

Sono io!	*It is I!*
È proprio lui!	*It is really him!*

To avoid ambiguity or for clarity

Lui è italiano ma lei è americana.	*He is Italian but she is American.*
Io sono stanca, ma non lui.	*I am tired, but not him.*

Present Indicative of dire, andare, and venire

In this unit you have come across three verbs, dire / *to say, tell,* andare / *to go,* and venire / *to come* used in the present indicative tense. This is the tense that allows you to refer to actions in the present or near present time, as well as to continuous or ongoing actions: as in English *I go, I am going, I do go, I have been going.*

These three verbs are all "irregular," that is, they do not follow a regular pattern of conjugation. Their conjugations are given below. You will learn how to conjugate regular verbs in the present indicative in subsequent chapters. Learn these ones now, because they are used often in common speech:

dire *to say,* andare *to go, and* venire *to come*	
(io) dico	*I say, I am saying*
(io) vado	*I go, I am going*
(io) vengo	*I come, I am coming*
(tu) dici	*you say, you are saying (familiar)*
(tu) vai	*you go, you are going (familiar)*
(tu) vieni	*you come, you are coming (familiar)*
(Lei) dice	*you say, you are saying (polite)*
(Lei) va	*you go, you are going (polite)*
(Lei) viene	*you come, you are coming (polite)*
(lui / lei) dice	*he / she says, he / she is saying*
(lui / lei) va	*he / she goes, he / she is going*
(lui / lei) viene	*he / she comes, he / she is coming*
(noi) diciamo	*we say, we are saying*
(noi) andiamo	*we go, we are going*
(noi) veniamo	*we come, we are coming*
(voi) dite	*you say, you are saying (plural)*
(voi) andate	*you go, you are going (plural)*
(voi) venite	*you come, you are coming (plural)*
(loro) dicono	*they say, they are saying*
(loro) vanno	*they go, they are going*
(loro) vengono	*they come, they are coming*

To make any verb negative, just put non in front of it:

Loro vengono alla festa / *They are coming to the party*
Loro non vengono alla festa / *They are not coming to the party*

Noi andiamo domani / *We are going tomorrow*
Noi non andiamo domani / *We are not going tomorrow*

ATTIVITÀ

F. Give the indicated date, following the model.

> *Model:* February 28, 1999
> *È il ventotto febbraio, mille novecento novantanove.*

Che data è?

1. September 21, 1998

_____

2. May 3, 1972

_____

3. December 4, 1971

_____

4. September 15, 1994

_____

5. October 1, 2004

_____

6. January 1, 2006

_____

7. February 19, 2007

_____

G. Answer the question.

1. Che data è oggi?

_____

H. Say the following in Italian.

1. Alessandro is coming to the party Sunday. He is going with Dina. And she says that *(che)* it is true.

_____

2. I say that Sara and Dina are going to the party. What do you say?

_____

3. What are they saying? Are they coming? If not, are you *(plural)* coming?

_____

4. Where are you *(plural)* going? We are going to the party.

_____

5. We are coming too, if you *(plural)* say where it is.

_____

6. I am also going to the party. I am coming with Dina.

_____

I. First, ask Dina…

1. if she is going downtown

_____

2. what she is saying

_____

3. with whom she is coming to the party

_____

Now, ask Professoressa Giusti…

1. if she is going downtown

_____

2. what she is saying

_____

3. with whom she is coming to the party

_____

Finally, ask Dina and Alessandro…

1. if they are going downtown

_____

2. what they are saying

_____

3. with whom they are coming to the party

_____

J. Cruciverba!

Horizontal

1 you come *(polite)*
2 Che giorno … settimana è?
5 to go
7 we go
8 they
10 to come
11 you come *(plural)*
12 Saturday
16 you are going *(plural)*
17 you are coming *(familiar)*
20 Alessandro, … giorno è oggi?
21 we are saying
22 they are coming
25 Sono …!
27 Fa … molto freddo.
28 *I* (dico)
29 È il … dicembre.
31 *you* (vieni)
34 È l'… gennaio.
35 È il … ottobre.
36 Che giorno è …?
39 August
43 Wednesday
44 Che mese dell'… è?
46 Monday
48 Hai veramente … la testa!
49 March
52 Ma che dici? Hai perso la …?
53 June
54 February
56 September

Vertical

1 they are going
2 to say
3 he
4 they say
6 November
8 she
9 we are coming
11 she is going
13 I am coming
14 I am saying
15 he says
17 I am going
18 Che … dell'anno è?
19 you are going *(familiar)*
21 you are saying
22 *you* (dite)
23 January
24 *we* (diciamo)
26 July
29 *this* paese
30 Tuesday
32 May
33 Vieni … festa domenica?
37 Sunday
38 Che giorno della … è?
40 Thursday
41 Friday
42 Hai …, anche a settembre fa bel tempo.
45 certainly
47 Domani vado in centro … ogni sabato.
48 *Hello?* Sono io, Alessandro.
50 Fa caldo … primavera.
51 Che giorno è …?
55 April

NOTA CULTURALE

Italian Holidays

The main Italian holidays are as follows:

il Natale	*Christmas* (25 dicembre)
il Capo d'Anno	*New Year's* (1 gennaio)
la Pasqua	*Easter* (varies)
il Ferragosto	*the Assumption* (15 agosto)

In Italy, most homes and churches have a presepio (Nativity scene). On Christmas Eve, the family prays while the mother places a figure of the Bambino (Christ child) in the manger. Many Italians serve eels for dinner on Christmas Eve. They also bake a Christmas bread called panettone, which contains raisins and candied fruit. Italian children receive gifts from la Befana, a kindly old lady, on the eve of Epiphany, January 6.

Easter is preceded by **Carnevale** throughout Italy. Most carnivals today are small and are held in towns and small cities, setting up their attractions in streets and parking lots. The Mardi Gras in New Orleans is a famous American carnival of this type.

Il Natale **Il Capo d'Anno**

La Pasqua **Il Ferragosto**

J. Give the Italian for each of the following. If you are using this book in a classroom situation, look up each feast with a partner and then describe it.

1. Christmas

_____

2. New Year's

_____

3. Easter

_____

4. the Assumption

_____

5. Nativity scene

_____

6. Christ child

_____

7. Christmas bread

_____

8. Carnival

_____

9. the lady who comes on the eve of the Epiphany

_____

Ecco la mia famiglia!

Unit 9

Ho una famiglia grande!

CONVERSAZIONE

[Dina and Alessandro are at a café. The topic of conversation is their families.]

Dina	Io vorrei conoscere la tua famiglia.	I would like to became acquainted with your family.
Alessandro	Va bene! Mio padre si chiama Paolo. Lui è molto alto.	OK! My dad's name is Paolo. He is very tall.
Dina	E tua madre?	And your mother?
Alessandro	Lei si chiama Maria. Anche lei è molto alta. Ho anche un fratello, Mario, e una sorella, Claudia. Anche tu hai un fratello e una sorella, vero?	Her name is Maria. She too is very tall. I also have a brother, Mario, and a sister, Claudia. You too have a brother and sister, don't you?
Dina	Sì, ho una famiglia grande! Abbiamo anche il nonno, la nonna, lo zio e la zia in casa con noi. La nostra casa è molto grande.	Yes, I have a large family. We also have my grandfather, grandmother, uncle and aunt living with us. Our house is very big.

COMPRENSIONE

A. Rispondi alle seguenti domande con frasi intere.

1. Che cosa vuole conoscere *(want to know)* Dina?

_____

2. Come si chiama il padre di Alessandro?

_____

3. Com'è il padre di Alessandro?

_____

4. Come si chiama la madre di Alessandro?

_____

5. Com'è la madre di Alessandro?

_____

6. Chi altro c'è *(Who else is there)* nella *(in the)* famiglia di Alessandro?

_____

7. Com'è la famiglia di Dina?

_____

8. Com'è la casa di Dina?

_____

9. Chi vive con loro *(Who lives with them?)*

_____

VOCABOLARIO

PAROLE NUOVE

alto	*tall*
la casa (kAh-zah)	*house, home*
conoscere (koh-nOh-sheh-reh)	*to know, to be acquainted with*
la famiglia (fah-mEEh-lyah)	*family*
grande	*big, large*
il parente / la parente	*relative (male / female)*

ESPRESSIONI E MODI DI DIRE

(lui / lei) si chiama... (kyAh-mah)	*his / her name is...*
vero?	*don't you?/ right? / isn't that so?*

Il nonno   La nonna

LA FAMIGLIA E I PARENTI **(THE FAMILY AND RELATIVES)**

il fratello	*brother*
la madre	*mother*
la nonna	*grandmother*
il nonno	*grandfather*
il padre	*father*
la sorella	*sister*
la zia (tsEEh-ah)	*aunt*
lo zio (tsEEh-oh)	*uncle*

FORME POSSESSIVE

mio padre	*my father*
tua madre	*your mother*
la tua famiglia	*your family*
la nostra casa	*our house*

STRUTTURE VERBALI

(io) ho	*I have*
(tu) hai	*you have (familiar)*
(noi) abbiamo	*we have*
(voi) avete	*you have (plural)*
(io) vorrei (voh-rrEh-eeh)	*I would like*

ATTIVITÀ

B. Comunicazione! Say the following things.

Say that …

1. you would like to know Alessandro's family

_____

2. it's OK

_____

3. your father is very tall

_____

4. your mother is also very tall

_____

5. you also have a brother and a sister

_____

6. you have a large family

_____

7. you have your grandfather and grandmother in your house

_____

8. you also have your uncle and aunt in your house

_____

9. your house is very big

_____

C. Complete the chart by providing the corresponding male or female family member or relative, as the case may be: for example, if you are given the word for *brother*, provide the word for *sister*.

La famiglia e i parenti	
padre	1. _____
2. _____	nonna
fratello	3. _____
4. _____	zia

D. Domande personali. Answer each question.

1. Come si chiama tua madre?

_____

2. Come si chiama tuo padre?

_____

3. Hai un fratello? Se sì, come si chiama?

_____

4. Hai una sorella? Se sì, come si chiama?

_____

5. Come si chiama tuo nonno?

_____

6. Come si chiama tua nonna?

_____

7. Hai una zia? Se sì, come si chiama?

_____

8. Hai uno zio? Se sì, come si chiama?

_____

E. Write a brief composition on your family and relatives, simply identifying who they are.

La mia famiglia!

_____

_____

_____

_____

_____

_____

_____

LINGUA

Family and Relatives

Notice that the word for *family* is **la famiglia**. The word for *parent* is **il genitore** (male) and **la genitrice** (female). The word for *relative* is **il parente** (male) and **la parente** (female). Be careful! All this can be a bit confusing. Here is a summary:

Family	=	la famiglia
Parent (male)	=	il genitore
Parent (female)	=	la genitrice
Relative (male)	=	il parente
Relative (female)	=	la parente

Genitori!

Masculine forms are used when referring to a parent or relative in general:

Hai un genitore qui? / *Do you have a parent here?*
Hai un parente qui? / *Do you have a relative here*

In this unit, several possessives have been introduced. As you might suspect, they have both masculine and feminine forms:

Masculine	Feminine
My	*My*
mio zio / *my uncle*	mia zia / *my aunt*
mio fratello / *my brother*	mia sorella / *my sister*
Your (familiar, singular)	*Your (familiar, singular)*
tuo padre / *your father*	tua madre / *your mother*
tuo nonno / *your grandfather*	tua nonna / *your grandmother*

Generally, possessives are preceded by the definite article:

> la mia famiglia / *my family*
> il mio amico / *my friend*
> la nostra casa / *our house*
> il nostro professore / *our professor*

However, if the noun refers to a family member or to a relative, it is dropped (as you have seen).

Nouns Ending in -e

Recall that nouns ending in -o are generally masculine and those ending in -a feminine. There is a third type of noun that ends in -e. In this case the noun can be either masculine (il padre) or feminine (la madre). You will simply have to memorize which is which.

The chart below summarizes the system of regular singular nouns:

Masculine		Feminine	
-o		-a	
amico	*friend (male)*	amica	*friend (female)*
zio	*uncle*	zia	*aunt*
fratello	*brother*	sorella	*sister*
Masculine		**Feminine**	
-e		-e	
padre	*father*	madre	*mother*
paese	*country*	informazione	*information*

The Article: Part 5

In addition to the singular article forms you have encountered so far, there is the indefinite article form uno and the corresponding definite article form lo, both of which are used before any masculine singular noun beginning with *z* or *s + consonant*:

> uno zio / *an uncle*
> lo zio / *the uncle*
>
> uno studente / *a student*
> lo studente / *the student*

Now you know all the singular forms of both the definite and indefinite article. The chart below summarizes them for you:

Before *z* or *s + consonant*			
Masculine		**Feminine**	
uno		una	
lo		la	
uno zio	*an uncle*	una zia	*an aunt*
lo zio	*the uncle*	la zia	*the aunt*
Before any other consonant			
Masculine		**Feminine**	
un		una	
il		la	
un padre	*a father*	una madre	*a mother*
il padre	*the father*	la madre	*the mother*
Before any vowel			
Masculine		**Feminine**	
un		un'	
l'		l'	
un amico	*a friend (male)*	un'amica	*a friend (female)*
l'amico	*the friend (male)*	l'amica	*the friend (female)*

The Present Indicative of avere and essere

The verbs avere / *to have* and essere / *to be*, are irregular in the present indicative. You have already learned some of the forms of both verbs in this and in previous units. The following two charts summarize the present indicative forms of both these verbs:

avere	to have
(io) ho	*I have*
(tu) hai	*you have (familiar)*
(Lei) ha	*you have (polite)*
(lui / lei) ha	*he / she has*
(noi) abbiamo	*we have*
(voi) avete	*you have (plural)*
(loro) hanno	*they have*

essere	to be
(io) sono	*I am*
(tu) sei	*you are (familiar)*
(Lei) è	*you are (polite)*
(lui / lei) è	*he / she is*
(noi) siamo	*we are*
(voi) siete	*you are (plural)*
(loro) sono	*they are*

ATTIVITÀ

F. First ask Alessandro a question as indicated in the model. Then answer it on his behalf, also as in the model. If you are using this book in a classroom, do this activity with a partner.

> *Model:* brother / tall
> —*Alessandro, tuo fratello è alto?*
> —*Sì, mio fratello è alto.*

1. sister / beautiful

_____

2. uncle / tired

_____

3. aunt / tall

_____

4. brother / handsome

_____

5. mother / tired

_____

6. father / precise

_____

7. grandmother / beautiful

_____

8. grandfather / precise

_____

G. Put the appropriate ending on each noun and then give both the definite and indefinite article forms that go before it.

> *Model:* genitor__
> *il genitore / un genitore*

1. genitric__

_____

2. parent__ *(masculine)*

_____

3. parent__ *(feminine)*

_____

4. famigli__

_____

5. zi__ *(masculine)*

_____

6. zi___ *(feminine)*

_____

7. amic___ *(feminine)*

_____

8. orari___

_____

9. cellular___

_____

10. giorn___

_____

11. giornat___

_____

12. mes___

_____

13. origin___

_____

14. amic___ *(masculine)*

_____

15. zer___

_____

H. Come si dice in italiano?

1. I have a large family.

_____

2. I am tired.

_____

3. Dina is tired.

_____

4. Alessandro is not tired.

_____

5. We have a large family.

_____

6. We are not of Italian origin.

_____

7. Alessandro and Dina have a large family.

_____

8. They are downtown today.

_____

I. Comunicazione! Do the following things.

Ask Dina…

1. if she is sleepy

_____

2. if she is tired

_____

Now, ask Professoressa Giusti…

3. if she is sleepy

_____

4. if she is tired

_____

Finally, ask Mark and Paul…

5. if they are sleepy

_____

6. if they are tired *(stanchi)*

_____

J. Cruciverba!

Horizontal	Vertical
1 Tu … una sorella, vero?	2 to have
4 Anch'io … una famiglia grande.	3 (voi) *are*
6 Dina … un fratello.	4 (loro) *have*
8 Io … stanco.	5 Mia sorella si … Francesca.
9 to be	7 the female counterpart of *nonno*
13 *the* fratello	8 you are *(familiar)*
15 Abbiamo anche lo zio e la zia in …	10 we are
16 Sì, mia sorella è alta, e anche mio fratello è …	11 Vorrei conoscere la tua …
17 Noi … una famiglia grande.	12 Ho un fratello e una …
18 Anche mio padre è …	14 *the* sorella
19 Ti presento … fratello.	15 Vorrei … tua madre.
21 Ho … zio molto alto.	17 you have *(plural)*
23 Anche tu hai una famiglia grande, …?	20 brother
24 Ho un fratello e … sorella.	22 grandfather
25 Vorrei conoscere la … famiglia.	28 Mia … è molto alta.
26 Mia … è molto alta.	
27 Anche mio … è molto alto.	
28 Lo … di Dina è alto.	
29 Io ho una famiglia …	

NOTA CULTURALE

La famiglia tradizionale

The Italian Family

The typical Italian family today is very similar to the North American one, consisting of a married couple with children. Italy, incidentally, has one of the lowest birth rates in the world, which means that there tend to be one or two children in a typical family today. The traditional Italian family included grandparents and other close relatives either living in the same house or near each other. This type of family still exists somewhat in rural areas.

Throughout the country there is a strong sense of family.

K. Domande personali. *(Personal Questions.)* Answer the questions in Italian as best you can.

1. Secondo te *(In you opinion)*, qual è il numero ideale *(ideal number)* di bambini in una famiglia?

_____

2. Chi c'è nella tua famiglia? *(Who's in your family?)*

_____

Vuoi vedere le mie foto?

Unit 10

Chi è quell'uomo?

CONVERSAZIONE

[Dina and Mirella are chatting over coffee one afternoon. Mirella has brought some photographs with her.]

Mirella	Dina, vuoi vedere queste fotografie?	Dina, do you want to see these photographs?
Dina	Sì. Chi è quell'uomo?	Yes. Who's that man?
Mirella	È il migliore amico di mio padre.	He's the best friend of my father.
Dina	E quella donna?	And that woman?
Mirella	È un'amica di mia madre. Vedi quei due ragazzi?	She's a friend of my mother's. Do you see those two boys?
Dina	Sì.	Yes.
Mirella	Quel ragazzo piccolo lì è mio nipote, e quell'altro più grande è mio cugino.	That small boy there is my nephew, and that other bigger one is my cousin.
Dina	E quelle due ragazze?	And those two girls?
Mirella	Sono due amiche di mia sorella. Vedi quei due bambini?	They're two of my sister's friends. Do you see those two children?
Dina	Sì. Chi sono?	Yes. Who are they?
Mirella	Sono i bambini di mia cugina.	They are my cousin's children.
Dina	Che belle fotografie!	What beautiful photographs!

COMPRENSIONE

A. Match the items in the two columns in an appropriate fashion.

1. Chi vuole vedere le fotografie?

2. Chi è la donna nella fotografia?

3. Chi è l'uomo nella fotografia?

4. Chi sono i due ragazzi?

5. Chi sono le due ragazze?

6. Chi sono i due bambini?

7. Come sono le fotografie, secondo *(according to)* Dina?

a. Secondo Dina le fotografie sono belle.

b. Sono i bambini della cugina di Mirella.

c. Sono due amiche della sorella di Mirella.

d. Dina vuole vedere le fotografie.

e. È il miglior amico del padre di Mirella.

f. È un'amica della madre di Mirella.

g. Uno è il nipote di Mirella e l'altro è il cugino di Mirella.

VOCABOLARIO

PAROLE NUOVE

il bambino / la bambina	*child (male / female)*
la donna	*woman*
la fotografia (foh-toh-grah-fEEh-ah)	*photograph*
lì	*there*
migliore	*best*
piccolo	*small*
più	*more, plus*
la ragazza (rah-gAh-tsah)	*girl*
il ragazzo	*boy*
l'uomo (wOh-moh)	*man*
vedere (veh-dEh-reh)	*to see*

Una fotografia di mio nipote

LA FAMIGLIA E I PARENTI

il cugino / la cugina (kooh-jEEh-noh)	*cousin (male / female)*
i genitori	*parents*
il nipote / la nipote	*nephew / niece*
i parenti	*relatives*

FORME DIMOSTRATIVE **(DEMONSTRATIVE FORMS)**

questa fotografia (kwEhs-tah)	*this photograph*
queste fotografie	*these photographs*
quel ragazzo (kwEhl)	*that boy*
quei due bambini	*those two children*
quei due ragazzi	*those two boys*
quell'altro	*that other one*
quell'uomo	*that man*
quella donna	*that woman*
quelle due ragazze	*those two girls*

STRUTTURE VERBALI

(tu) vedi	*you see (familiar)*
(tu) vuoi (vwOh-eeh)	*you want (familiar)*

113

ATTIVITÀ

B. Do the following things.

Ask Sara…

1. if she wants to see the photographs you have

_____

2. if she sees those two boys

_____

3. who that woman is

_____

4. who that man is

_____

5. who those two girls are

_____

6. if she sees those two children

_____

7. who are those children

_____

Say that…

8. that man is the best friend of your father

_____

9. that woman is a friend of your mother

_____

10. that small boy is your nephew

_____

11. that other bigger boy is your cousin

_____

12. they are two female friends of your sister

_____

13. they are your female cousin's children

_____

14. what beautiful photos they are

_____

C. Give the "opposite" of each item. For example, if you are given **quel ragazzo** / *that boy*, then the only logical choice is **quella ragazza**.

1. quell'uomo

_____

2. quella bambina

_____

3. grande

_____

4. meno

_____

5. quella cugina

_____

6. quella genitrice

_____

7. quella nipote

_____

D. Write a brief dialogue, similar to the one on page 112, in which you are showing photos to a friend.

Vuoi vedere queste fotografie?

_____

_____

_____

_____

_____

_____

_____

_____

_____

_____

LINGUA

Plural Nouns

As in English, Italian nouns have singular and plural forms. To make a regular Italian noun plural, change the final vowel of the singular noun as follows: -o to -i, -a to -e, and -e to -i. The chart below summarizes how to form plural nouns in Italian

Masculine Singular		Masculine Plural	
-o		-i	
-e		-i	
zio	uncle	zii	uncles
ragazzo	boy	ragazzi	boys
amico	friend (male)	amici	friends
padre	father	padri	fathers
Feminine Singular		**Feminine Plural**	
-a		-e	
-e		-i	
zia	aunt	zie	aunts
ragazza	girl	ragazze	girls
amica	friend (female)	amiche	friends
madre	mother	madri	mothers

Note that amiche is written with an "h" in order to indicate that the "hard c" sound is to be retained in the feminine plural (ah-mEEh-keh). In the case of the masculine plural form amici, the "soft sound" is the required one (ah-mEEh-chee).

The Article: Part 6

The definite article also has plural forms. These are summarized in the chart below:

Masculine Singular Forms		Masculine Plural Forms	
lo (before z or s + consonant)		gli	
il (before any other consonant)		i	
l' (before any vowel)		gli	
lo zio	the uncle	gli zii	the uncles
il ragazzo	the boy	i ragazzi	the boys
l'amico	the friend	gli amici	the friends
il padre	the father	i padri	the fathers
Feminine Singular Forms		**Feminine Plural Forms**	
la (before any consonant)		le	
l' (before any vowel)		le	
la zia	the aunt	le zie	the aunts
la ragazza	the girl	le ragazze	the girls
l'amica	the friend	le amiche	the friends
la madre	the mother	le madri	the mothers

Demonstrative Adjectives

Demonstrative adjectives are words that indicate whether something is relatively near *(this photo)* or far *(that photo)*. You have come across a number of demonstrative adjectives previously. The following charts summarize the complete demonstrative adjective system:

This			
Masculine Singular		**Feminine Singular**	
questo quest' (before a vowel)		questa quest' (before a vowel)	
questo zio	*this uncle*	questa zia	*this aunt*
questo bambino	*this child*	questa bambina	*this child*
quest'amico	*this friend*	quest'amica	*this friend*
These			
Masculine Plural		**Feminine Plural**	
questi		queste	
questi zii	*these uncles*	queste zie	*these aunts*
questi bambini	*these children*	queste bambine	*these children*
questi amici	*these friends*	queste amiche	*these friends*

Questa bambina è mia nipote

117

That		Those	
Masculine Singular Forms		**Masculine Plural Forms**	
quello (before *z* or *s* + *cons.*)		quegli	
quel (before any other consonant)		quei	
quell' (before any vowel)		quegli	
quello zio	*that uncle*	quegli zii	*those uncles*
quel bambino	*that child*	quei bambini	*those children*
quell'amico	*that friend*	quegli amici	*those friends*
Feminine Singular Forms		**Feminine Plural Forms**	
quella (before any consonant)		quelle	
quell' (before any vowel)		quelle	
quella zia	*that aunt*	quelle zie	*those aunts*
quella bambina	*that child*	quelle bambine	*those children*
quell'amica	*that friend*	quelle amiche	*those friends*

Possession

Possession is expressed with the preposition di / *of*, as you may have figured out by now.

> **il bambino di mia cugina:**
> *my cousin's child* = *the child of my cousin*
>
> **l'amico di mio padre:**
> *my father's friend* = *the friend of my father*
>
> **la madre del signor Bruni (del = di + il):**
> *Mr. Bruni's mother* = *the mother of Mr. Bruni*
>
> **l'amica della signora Bruni (della = di + la):**
> *Mrs. Bruni's friend* = *the friend of Mrs. Bruni*
>
> **il fratello dello zio (dello = di + lo):**
> *the uncle's brother* = *the brother of the uncle*
>
> **i genitori dell'uomo (dell' = di + l'):**
> *the man's parents* = *the parents of the man*

The Irregular Noun uomo

The noun uomo / *man* has an irregular plural form:

uomo	*man*	uomini (wOh-mee-neeh)	*men*
l'uomo	*the man*	gli uomini	*the men*
quest'uomo	*this man*	questi uomini	*these men*
quell'uomo	*that man*	quegli uomini	*those men*

ATTIVITÀ

E. Make the following plural.

> *Model:* l'amico
> *gli amici*

1. l'americana

_____

2. l'uomo

_____

3. il bambino

_____

4. la donna

_____

5. lo zero

_____

6. la fotografia

_____

7. il ragazzo

_____

8. la ragazza

_____

9. la nipote

_____

10. il nipote

_____

11. il parente

_____

12. il genitore

_____

13. l'italiano

_____

14. l'anno

_____

15. il cellulare

_____

16. lo zio

_____

17. lo studente

_____

18. l'italiana

_____

F. Below are noun phrases (a phrase made up of a noun plus the article). Replace each article with the corresponding form of the indicated demonstrative adjective *(this)*. Then make the whole phrase plural. Follow the model.

        Model: il ragazzo
                questo ragazzo / questi ragazzi

1. il cugino

_____

2. la ragazza

_____

3. l'amico

_____

4. l'amica

_____

5. lo studente

_____

6. il cellulare

_____

7. lo zio

_____

8. la donna

_____

9. l'uomo

_____

G. Here are the same noun phrases. This time replace each article with the corresponding form of the other demonstrative adjective *(that)*. As before, make the whole phrase plural. Follow the model.

        Model: il ragazzo
                quel ragazzo / quei ragazzi

TIP
The forms of the demonstrative adjective **quello** correspond to the forms of the definite article.

quel	corresponds to **il**	**il ragazzo / quel ragazzo**
quello	corresponds to **lo**	**lo zio / quello zio**
quell'	corresponds to **l'**	**l'amico / quell'amico**
		l'amica / quell'amica
quella	corresponds to **la**	**la ragazza / quella ragazza**
quei	corresponds to **i**	**i ragazzi / quei ragazzi**
quegli	corresponds to **gli**	**gli zii / quegli zii**
		gli amici / quegli amici
quelle	corresponds to **le**	**le ragazze / quelle ragazze**
		le amiche / quelle amiche

1. il cugino

_____

2. la ragazza

_____

3. l'amico

_____

4. l'amica

_____

5. lo studente

_____

6. il cellulare

_____

7. lo zio

_____

8. la donna

_____

9. l'uomo

_____

H. Quiz logico! Can you figure out who each person is?

Vocabulary Note	
il figlio / _son_	**la figlia** / _daughter_

Model: Chi è il figlio di tuo zio.
Il figlio di mio zio è mio cugino.

Chi è...

1. la figlia di tua zia?

_____

2. la sorella di tua madre?

_____

3. il fratello di tuo padre?

_____

4. il padre di tua madre?

_____

5. la madre di tua madre?

_____

6. il figlio di tuo fratello?

_____

7. la figlia di tua sorella?

_____

I. Domande personali. Answer each question.

> *Model:* Come si chiama il bambino di tua cugina?
> *Il bambino di mia cugina si chiama Tom / Mark / ...*

1. Come si chiama la figlia di tua zia?

_____

2. Come si chiama il tuo migliore amico / la tua migliore amica?

_____

3. Come si chiama il tuo professore / la tua professoressa d'italiano?

_____

4. Chi è il più grande *(biggest)* della tua famiglia?

_____

5. Chi è il più piccolo *(smallest)* della tua famiglia?

_____

J. Cruciverba!

Horizontal

6 the plural of *uomo*
10 Chi sono … donne?
11 Vuoi … questa fotografia?
14 Chi è quel …?
17 Lei è mia …
19 Quell'altro è … cugino.
20 Quel ragazzo lì è mio …
21 the form of *the* before *zii*
23 Lui è il mio … amico.
26 Vuoi vedere questa …?
27 Chi sono … ragazzi?
28 boy
30 girl
31 *those* in front of *zii*
34 the plural of *ragazza*
35 *these* in front of *bambine*
36 the form of *the* before *uomini*
38 the plural of *madre*

Vertical

1 *that* in front of *bambino*
2 Lui è l'amico … mio fratello.
3 Dov'è la fotografia … Dina?
4 relatives
5 Chi è … uomo?
7 Chi è … ragazzo?
8 Chi è … donna?
9 the form of *the* before *amiche*
12 Chi è quella …?
13 Lui è mio …
14 the female counterpart of *bambino*
15 Quell'altro è … cugino
16 Dina, … vedere questa fotografia?
18 Mirella, … quei due bambini lì?
22 the form of *the* before *donne*
24 Il padre e la madre sono i …
25 Sì, … ragazza è mia cugina.
29 the plural of *ragazzo*
31 *this* in front of *bambino*
32 *these* in front of *bambini*
33 the plural of *padre*
37 the form of *the* before *ragazze*

NOTA CULTURALE

In luna di miele!

Italian Weddings

The word for wedding in Italian is lo sposalizio, although the word il matrimonio / *matrimony* is commonly used. Unlike what many in North America might think, Italian weddings are small-scale affairs, taking place in a church and followed by a late lunch. The bride (la sposa) and the groom (lo sposo) generally follow up the ceremony by leaving for a honeymoon (la luna di miele).

The bridesmaids at a wedding are called le damigelle and the ushers i cavalieri. The best man is called il compare d'anello and the maid of honor la damigella d'onore.

K. Give the Italian equivalents of each term. Try to describe in your own words what each one is.

1. maid of honor

_____

2. best man

_____

3. bridesmaids

_____

4. ushers

_____

5. wedding

_____

6. matrimony

_____

7. bride

_____

8. groom

_____

9. honeymoon

_____

Review Part 2

A. Come si dice in italiano?

1. What time is it?

_____

2. It's midnight.

_____

3. It's five thirty in the afternoon.

_____

4. It's nine fifty at night.

_____

5. The bus usually leaves at one on the dot.

_____

6. Hello (on the phone).

_____

7. I will come to the party on Saturday if you want.

_____

8. They have a large family.

_____

9. They are of Italian origin.

_____

B. Comunicazione!

Say that…

1. it is an awful day

_____

2. usually the weather is beautiful

_____

3. it is always cold and windy

_____

4. it snows generally in the winter

_____

5. in the summer it rains too much

_____

6. it is you on the phone

_____

7. tomorrow you are going downtown like every Friday

_____

8. it's the fifteenth of September

_____

9. you would like to know Sara's family and relatives

_____

10. you have a large family

_____

11. your house is very big

_____

Ask ...

12. what's up

_____

13. someone what he or she is saying

_____

14. Sara if she too is coming to the party

_____

15. Sara if she is going downtown tomorrow

_____

16. Mrs. Martini what she is saying

_____

17. Mark and Paul with whom they are coming to the party

_____

18. Dina if she wants to see those photographs

_____

19. Dina who these two girls are

_____

20. Dina who those children are

_____

C. Domande personali. Answer the following questions.

1. Che giorno è oggi?

_____

2. Che mese è?

_____

3. Che stagione è?

_____

4. Che tempo fa?

_____

5. Hai un cellulare? Che marca *(brand)* è?

_____

6. Chi c'è nella tua famiglia *(Whose in your family)*?

_____

7. Chi è il tuo migliore amico / la tua migliore amica?

_____

D. Tema da svolgere! *(Composition to write.)* Write a brief composition on the following topic.

Io e la mia famiglia

_____

_____

_____

_____

_____

_____

_____

_____

_____

_____

_____

_____

_____

_____

_____

_____

_____

_____

_____

_____

E. There are 20 words hidden in the word search puzzle below: 10 can be read from left to right (horizontally) and 10 in a top-down direction (vertically). Can you find them? The clues given below will help you look for them. The numbers of the clues do not reflect any particular order or arrangement to the hidden words.

A	Z	Q	E	D	C	V	G	M	T	Y	U	I	O	P	A	S	D	S	D
H	K	J	L	G	I	O	Z	I	X	C	V	T	E	M	P	O	M	A	L
L	G	I	O	R	N	A	T	A	D	J	K	L	K	J	H	G	B	B	M
P	S	D	F	A	B	B	B	A	A	A	Q	R	T	Y	P	S	N	A	M
A	S	A	S	N	D	P	R	O	N	T	O	R	R	R	L	S	M	T	M
D	D	D	D	D	D	D	D	G	G	G	C	C	C	R	B	U	R	O	N
R	C	D	A	E	G	C	D	A	G	C	B	R	U	T	T	O	T	U	N
E	S	Z	C	X	Z	C	X	Z	C	X	Z	D	A	R	B	M	T	R	N
X	T	R	O	P	P	O	S	D	F	G	C	A	A	R	N	O	T	D	S
X	X	X	Q	Q	Q	S	S	S	R	B	X	G	A	F	N	A	F	Q	E
X	X	X	R	Q	Q	Q	P	R	E	C	I	S	E	F	B	C	R	Z	T
C	F	S	A	Q	Z	X	V	X	R	B	Z	C	A	F	E	M	A	X	T
C	A	S	G	D	D	D	X	T	R	C	C	D	A	T	L	M	T	C	E
A	M	M	A	Q	G	I	O	R	N	O	X	A	A	T	L	M	E	V	M
D	I	M	Z	E	Q	Y	X	S	T	S	Z	G	A	T	A	N	L	B	B
A	G	M	Z	D	E	Y	X	Q	T	R	C	C	A	T	Q	Y	L	N	R
A	L	D	I	Y	D	Y	X	I	N	F	O	R	M	A	Z	I	O	N	E
Q	I	D	R	Y	Y	V	Z	Q	T	Q	X	D	A	B	Q	T	T	T	O
Q	A	U	T	O	B	U	S	Z	V	S	E	T	T	I	M	A	N	A	M
D	Z	Z	X	X	X	Q	R	Z	V	Q	V	A	A	B	Q	G	T	B	N

Horizontal

1 Che ora è? Sono le dieci …
2 A che ora parte l'…?
3 Ogni … parte a un'ora differente.
4 Grazie per l'…
5 Sì, è proprio una bella …
6 Che … fa generalmente d'inverno?
7 Di solito fa … tempo!
8 E d'estate? Fa … caldo!
9 Dina, …? Sono io, Alessandro.
10 Che giorno della … è?

Vertical

11 Domani vado in centro come ogni …
12 E anche a … e ottobre fa bel tempo.
13 Io vorrei conoscere la tua …
14 Mio … si chiama Paolo.
15 Anche tu hai un … e una sorella, vero?
16 Sì, noi abbiamo una famiglia …
17 Chi è quell'…?
18 Vedi quei due …?
19 Sono i bambini di … cugina.
20 Che … fotografia!

Part 3: Interacting with People

A destra del semaforo c'è via Garruba!

Unit 11

Scusi?

CONVERSAZIONE

[One day in downtown Perugia, Dina notices two tourists, Bill and Karen, asking a woman to help them find a street. She listens in.]

Bill	Scusi, Lei parla inglese?	Excuse me, do you speak English?
Donna	No, purtroppo non lo parlo.	No, unfortunately, I don't speak it.
Karen	Io e mio marito non parliamo bene. Ci può aiutare a trovare via Garruba?	My husband and I do not speak well. Can you help us find Garruba Street?
Donna	Certo. Ma voi parlate molto bene.	Certainly. But you (both) speak very well.
Bill	Lei è molto gentile. Mia moglie parla bene e anche nostro figlio e nostra figlia parlano bene. Ma io no!	You are very kind. My wife speaks well and our son and daughter also speak well. But I do not!
Donna	Lei è molto umile! Dunque, per via Garruba dovete andare qui a sinistra fino al semaforo.	You are very humble! So, to get to Garruba Street you must go here to the left until you reach the traffic light.
Karen	E poi?	And then?
Donna	Subito a destra c'è la via.	Immediately to the right you'll find the street.
Bill e Karen	Grazie!	Thank you!
Donna	Prego!	You're welcome!

COMPRENSIONE

A. Vero o falso?

_____ 1. La donna non parla inglese.

_____ 2. Karen e Bill non parlano inglese.

_____ 3. Karen vuole trovare via Garruba.

_____ 4. Karen non parla italiano.

_____ 5. Il figlio e la figlia di Karen e Bill parlano italiano bene.

_____ 6. Per via Garruba Bill e Karen devono andare a sinistra fino al semaforo.

_____ 7. Subito a destra c'è via Garruba.

VOCABOLARIO

PAROLE NUOVE

aiutare	*to help*
la destra	*right*
gentile (jehn-tEEh-leh)	*kind*
l'inglese (eehn-glEh-zeh)	*English (language)*
l'italiano	*Italian (language)*
parlare	*to speak*
per	*for, in order to, through*
purtroppo	*unfortunately*
il semaforo (seh-mAh-foh-roh)	*traffic light*
la sinistra	*left*
subito (sOOh-beeh-toh)	*right away (after)*
trovare	*to find*
umile (Ooh-meeh-leh)	*humble*
la via	*street*

A destra o a sinistra?

ESPRESSIONI E MODI DI DIRE

a destra	*to the right*
a sinistra	*to the left*
c'è (chEh)	*there is*
Ci può aiutare?	*Can you help us (polite)?*
Cosa desidera (deh-zEEh-deh-rah)?	*What would you like?*
dunque (dOOhn-kweh)	*so, therefore*
fino a	*up to, until*
scusi (skOOh-zeeh)	*excuse me (polite)*

LA FAMIGLIA

la figlia (fEEh-lyah)	*daughter*
il figlio	*son*
il marito	*husband*
la moglie (mOh-lyeh)	*wife*

FORME POSSESSIVE

nostro figlio	*our son*
nostra figlia	*our daughter*

STRUTTURE VERBALI

(io) parlo	*I speak*
(Lei) parla	*you speak (polite)*
(lei) parla	*she speaks*
(noi) non parliamo	*we don't speak*
(voi) parlate	*you speak (plural)*
(loro) parlano (pAhr-lah-noh)	*they speak*
(voi) dovete andare	*you must go (plural)*

ATTIVITÀ

Ma non parlo italiano!

B. Comunicazione! Say or ask the following things.

Say …

1. that unfortunately you do not speak Italian

_____

2. that you and your husband do not speak Italian well

_____

3. to two people (*use* voi) that they speak Italian very well

_____

4. to two people (*use* voi) that to get to Garibaldi Street they have to go to the left until they reach the traffic light

_____

5. to the right there's the street

_____

Ask …

6. someone (a stranger) if he or she speaks English

_____

7. someone (a stranger) if he or she can help you (and someone else together) find Garibaldi Street

_____

C. Come si dice in italiano?

1. Excuse me *(polite)*!

_____

2. You are very kind *(polite, singular)*.

_____

3. You are very kind *(familiar, singular)*.

_____

4. You are very kind *(plural)*.

_____

5. You speak very well *(polite, singular)*.

_____

6. You speak very well *(familiar, singular)*.

_____

7. You speak very well *(plural)*.

_____

8. My wife speaks very well.

_____

9. Our son and our daughter do not speak Italian.

_____

10. You are very humble *(polite, singular)*.

_____

11. You are very humble *(familiar, singular)*.

_____

12. You are very humble *(plural)*.

_____

13. So!

_____

D. Questions and answers! First ask the indicated question and then provide the indicated answer. If you are using this book in a classroom situation, do this activity with a partner—one asks the question, the other answers it. Follow the model.

> *Model:* Ask ... where the traffic lights are / to the right
> —*Dov'è il semaforo?*
> —*Il semaforo è a destra.*

Ask ...

1. where Boccaccio Street is / to the left

_____

2. someone to help you *(plural)* find the traffic light / to the right

_____

3. someone if he or she speaks English / yes, he or she does speak it

_____

4. someone if you can help him or her / unfortunately he or she does not speak Italian

_____

E. Dov'è la via? Write down a set of instructions on how to get from your house to the nearest traffic light. If you are using this book in a classroom situation, do this activity with a partner. In the latter case, indicate how to get from the classroom to the nearest traffic light.

Dov'è il semaforo?

_____

_____

_____

_____

_____

_____

_____

_____

_____

LINGUA

Possessive Adjectives: Part 1

You have already come across and used several possessive adjectives in this and in previous units. Their forms are summarized in the chart below. Since they are adjectives, they agree in gender and number with the noun they modify. Notice that, unlike English, they are preceded by the definite article:

My
il mio (before a masculine singular noun):   **il mio amico**   *my friend (male)*
la mia (before a feminine singular noun):   **la mia amica**   *my friend (female)*
i miei (before a masculine plural noun):   **i miei amici**   *my friends*
le mie (before a feminine plural noun):   **le mie amiche**   *my friends*

I miei amici!

Your (familiar, singular)

il tuo (before a masculine singular noun):
il tuo amico   *your friend (male)*

la tua (before a feminine singular noun):
la tua amica   *your friend (female)*

i tuoi (before a masculine plural noun):
i tuoi amici   *your friends*

le tue (before a feminine plural noun):
le tue amiche   *your friends*

Our

il nostro (before a masculine singular noun):
il nostro amico   *our friend (male)*

la nostra (before a feminine singular noun):
la nostra amica   *our friend (female)*

i nostri (before a masculine plural noun):
i nostri amici   *our friends*

le nostre (before a feminine plural noun):
le nostre amiche   *our friends*

As you already know, when the possessive adjective is used with singular and unmodified nouns referring to family members and relatives, the article is dropped. It is put back when the noun is plural and/or modified:

Singular		Plural	
mio fratello	*my brother*	i miei fratelli	*our brothers*
tua zia	*your aunt*	le tue zie	*your aunts*
nostro figlio	*our son*	i nostri figli	*our sons*
Unmodified		**Modified**	
mio fratello	*my brother*	il mio fratello alto	*my tall brother*
tua zia	*your aunt*	la tua zia alta	*your tall aunt*
nostro figlio	*our son*	il nostro figlio umile	*our humble son*

I miei amici non ci sono!

The Verb esserci

The verb **esserci** is made up of **essere** plus **ci**. The latter precedes the verb when it is conjugated. It means *to be here / there*. There are only third-person singular and plural forms of this verb.

Singular	Plural
C'è Maria	Ci sono Maria e Dina
Maria is here / there	*Maria and Dina are here / there*
Il mio amico non c'è	I miei amici non ci sono
My friend is not here / there	*My friends are not here / there*

The Present Indicative of Regular First Conjugation Verbs

Verbs whose infinitive ending is -are are known as *first conjugation* verbs. To conjugate them in the present indicative, drop the -are and then add the following endings to the resulting stem:

Singular	
1st person	-o
2nd person	-i
3rd person	-a

Plural	
1st person	-iamo
2nd person	-ate
3rd person	-ano

Below is the verb parlare / *to speak,* fully conjugated for you:

parlare → parl-	*to speak*
(io) parlo	*I speak, I am speaking*
(tu) parli	*you speak, you are speaking (familiar)*
(Lei) parla	*you speak, you are speaking (polite)*
(lui / lei) parla	*he / she speaks, he / she is speaking*
(noi) parliamo	*we speak, we are speaking*
(voi) parlate	*you speak, you are speaking (plural)*
(loro) parlano (pAhr-lah-noh)	*they speak, they are speaking*

The present indicative allows you to refer to actions that are occurring, ongoing, continuous, or connected to the present in some way:

Dina parla italiano molto bene.	*Dina speaks Italian very well.*
Dina trova l'Italia molto bella.	*Dina finds Italy (to be) very beautiful.*

In effect, this Italian verb tense corresponds to the following three English verb tenses:

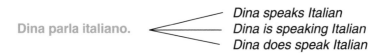

Dina parla italiano.
Dina speaks Italian
Dina is speaking Italian
Dina does speak Italian

Negative Verbs

Negative verbs are formed simply by putting non before the verb:

Affirmative	Negative
Io parlo italiano	Io non parlo italiano
I speak Italian	*I do not speak Italian*

Contractions: Part 3

In this unit you have come across one other prepositional contraction:

al = (a + il): al semaforo	*at / to the traffic lights*

ATTIVITÀ

F. C'è? / Ci sono? Ask if the indicated people are here. Use the indicated possessive pronoun in its appropriate form. Follow the model.

> *Model:* My...friend
> *C'è il mio amico?*

My...

1. friend *(male)*

_____

2. friend *(female)*

_____

3. cousin *(male)*

_____

4. cousin *(female)*

_____

5. beautiful mother

_____

6. parents

_____

7. tall brother

_____

8. grandparents

_____

9. cousins *(female)*

_____

10. friends *(female)*

_____

Your *(familiar, singular)*...

11. friend *(male)*

_____

12. friend *(female)*

_____

13. cousin *(male)*

_____

14. cousin *(female)*

_____

15. beautiful mother

_____

16. parents

_____

17. tall brother

_____

18. grandparents

_____

19. cousins *(female)*

_____

20. friends *(female)*

_____

Our...

21. friend *(male)*

_____

22. friend *(female)*

_____

23. cousin *(male)*

_____

24. cousin *(female)*

_____

25. beautiful mother

_____

26. parents

_____

27. tall brother

_____

28. grandparents

_____

29. cousins *(female)*

_____

30. friends *(female)*

_____

G. Come si dice in italiano?

I...

1. speak Italian

_____

2. always help my friends

_____

3. usually arrive early *(presto)*

_____

4. teach English

_____

5. do not always joke around

_____

You *(familiar, singular)...*

6. speak Italian

_____

7. always help your friends

_____

8. usually arrive early *(presto)*

_____

9. teach English

_____

10. do not always joke around

_____

You *(polite, singular)...*

11. speak Italian

_____

12. always help your friends *(i suoi amici)*

_____

13. usually arrive early *(presto)*

_____

14. teach English

_____

15. do not always joke around

_____

He / She ...

16. speaks Italian

_____

17. always helps his / her friends *(i suoi amici)*

_____

18. usually arrives early *(presto)*

_____

19. teaches English

_____

20. does not always joke around

_____

We ...

21. speak Italian

_____

22. always help our friends

_____

23. usually arrive early *(presto)*

_____

24. teach English

_____

25. do not always joke around

_____

You *(plural)* ...

26. speak Italian

_____

27. always help your friends *(i vostri amici)*

_____

28. usually arrive early *(presto)*

_____

29. teach English

_____

30. do not always joke around

_____

They …

31. speak Italian

_____

32. always help their friends *(i loro amici)*

_____

33. usually arrive early *(presto)*

_____

34. teach English

_____

35. do not always joke around

_____

H. Domande personali. Answer the questions.

1. Come si chiama la tua via?

_____

2. Come si chiamano i tuoi amici migliori?

_____

3. Tu parli italiano bene?

_____

4. Tu scherzi sempre?

_____

5. Tu sei umile?

_____

6. Tu sei gentile?

_____

I. Cruciverba!

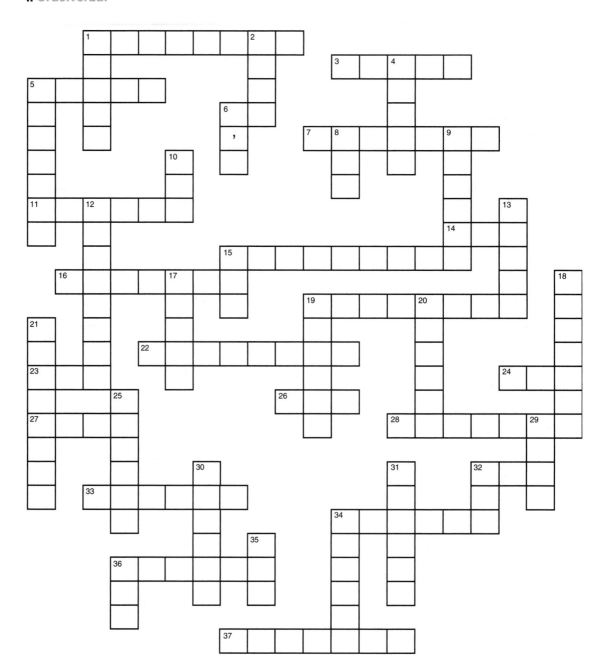

Horizontal

1 Noi … italiano.
3 Signore, …, Lei parla inglese?
5 Tu … inglese, vero?
6 No, i miei genitori non … sono.
7 No, purtroppo non parlo …
11 Anche … figlio parla bene l'italiano.
14 Anche … moglie parla italiano, vero?
15 No, … lei non parla italiano.
16 Scusi, ci può … a trovare via Garruba?
19 Cosa …?
22 Io e mio marito non parliamo bene l'…
23 Ti presento … moglie.
24 Dov'è … Garruba?
26 Scusi, ci … aiutare a trovare via Garruba?
27 Dovete andare qui a sinistra … al semaforo.
28 Voi … italiano molto bene.
32 Chi è … marito?
33 Nostro … parla italiano molto bene.
34 Loro sono le … amiche.
36 Le presento mio …
37 Lei è molto …

Vertical

1 Anch'io … italiano.
2 Dina e Paul sono i … migliori amici.
4 Lei è molto …
5 I tuoi amici … inglese, vero?
6 Subito a destra … la via.
8 No, io … parlo inglese.
9 E poi? … a destra c'è via Garruba.
10 Quel ragazzo è … figlio.
12 Dovete andare qui a … fino al semaforo.
13 Scusi, Lei … italiano?
15 Dunque, … via Garruba dovete andare a destra.
17 he helps
18 to speak
19 So!
20 Subito a … c'è la via.
21 Dovete andare qui a sinistra fino al …
25 Mia … parla italiano molto bene.
29 Chi sono i … amici?
30 Nostra … parla italiano molto bene.
31 Lei è … figlia.
32 Quelle bambine sono le … figlie, vero?
34 Loro sono i … amici.
35 Noi … parliamo inglese molto bene.
36 Quelle due bambine sono le … figlie.

NOTA CULTURALE

L'italiano! Che bella lingua!

The Italian Language

L'italiano is the official language of Italy and one of the official languages of Switzerland. It is also spoken by many people in areas of France and Slovenia that lie near Italy. More than 60 million people speak Italian as their native language. Like French and Spanish, it is a Romance language, one of the modern languages that developed from Latin.

Many words in other languages come from Italian. For example, English has borrowed the words *balcony*, *carnival*, *costume*, *malaria*, *opera*, *piano*, *pilot*, *stucco*, *studio*, *umbrella*, and *volcano*. Many other English words, such as *bankrupt*, *gazette*, and *infantry*, came from French, but their roots were Italian.

J. Using a dictionary, identify the Italian root word for the following English words.

1. balcony

_____

2. carnival

_____

3. costume

_____

4. malaria

_____

5. opera

_____

6. piano

_____

7. pilot

_____

8. stucco

_____

9. studio

_____

10. umbrella

_____

11. volcano

_____

Ecco il vostro indirizzo!

Unit 12

Capisce l'italiano?

CONVERSAZIONE

[Two recently arrived American students, Debbie and Sharon, have also come to Perugia to study Italian. They are at a post office near the *Università per Stranieri*, requesting a temporary mailing address.]

Impiegata	Signorina, Lei capisce l'italiano?	Miss, do you understand Italian?
Debbie	Certo che lo capisco! E lo scrivo bene! Sono due anni che lo studio.	Of course I understand it! And I write it well! I've been studying it for two years.
Impiegata	Lei lo parla anche veramente bene!	You also speak it very well!
Debbie	Grazie. Io e la mia amica capiamo quasi tutto.	Thank you. My friend and I understand almost everything.
Impiegata	Dovete scrivere i vostri nomi qui, altrimenti non vi posso aiutare.	You must write your names here, otherwise I can't help you.
Sharon	Va bene. Altro?	OK. Anything else?
Impiegata	No. Ecco il vostro indirizzo postale qui in Italia.	No. Here's your mailing address here in Italy.
Sharon	Grazie!	Thank you!
Impiegata	Prego!	You're welcome!

COMPRENSIONE

A. Which response, a or b, is the correct or appropriate one?

1. Debbie … l'italiano bene.
   - a. capisce
   - b. non capisce

2. Debbie anche … l'italiano bene.
   - a. scrive
   - b. non scrive

3. Sono … anni che Debbie studia l'italiano.
   - a. due
   - b. quattro

4. Debbie e Sharon … quasi tutto.
   - a. capiscono
   - b. capisce

5. Dovete … i vostri nomi qui.
    a. scrivere
    b. capire

6. … non vi posso aiutare.
    a. Quasi
    b. Altrimenti

7. Ecco il vostro … postale qui in Italia.
    a. indirizzo
    b. nome

VOCABOLARIO

PAROLE NUOVE

altrimenti	*otherwise*
capire	*to understand*
che (kEh)	*that, which*
l'impiegata (eehm-pyeh-gAh-tah)	*employee, clerk (female)*
l'indirizzo (eehn-deeh-rEEh-ttsoh)	*address*
l'Italia	*Italy*
il nome	*name*
postale	*postal, mailing*
quasi	*almost*
scrivere (skrEEh-veh-reh)	*to write*
studiare	*to study*
tutto	*everything*

Altro?

ESPRESSIONI E MODI DI DIRE

Altro?	*Anything else?*
(Io) non vi posso aiutare	*I can't help you (plural)*

FORME POSSESSIVE

il vostro indirizzo	*your (plural) address*
i vostri nomi	*your (plural) names*

STRUTTURE VERBALI

(io) studio	*I study*
(io) scrivo	*I write*
(Lei) capisce (kah-pEEh-sheh)	*you understand (polite)*
(noi) capiamo	*we understand*
(voi) dovete scrivere	*you have to write (plural)*

ATTIVITÀ

B. Comunicazione! Say or ask the following things.

Say that …

1. you understand Italian and that you write it well

_____

2. you have been studying Italian for many years

_____

3. you and your friend understand almost everything

_____

Tell Debbie and Sharon that…

4. they must write out their names, otherwise you cannot help them

_____

Ask …

5. Debbie if she speaks Italian

_____

6. who speaks Italian really well

_____

7. Debbie and Sharon if they have a mailing address here in Italy

_____

C. Come si dice in italiano?

1. I study Italian every evening.

_____

2. I write Italian very well.

_____

3. Anything else?

_____

4. We understand everything.

_____

5. It is almost nine o'clock.

_____

6. The clerk says that she understands English.

_____

7. My friends Debbie and Sharon say that they are coming to the party as well.

_____

D. Domande personali. Answer the questions.

1. Tu capisci l'italiano molto bene?

_____

2. Tu scrivi l'italiano molto bene?

_____

3. Qual è *(What is)* il tuo indirizzo postale?

_____

4. Capisci altre lingue *(languages)*?

_____

E. Tema da svolgere! Write a brief composition on your knowledge of the language you are studying, indicating how you speak it, write it, and so on.

Io e la lingua italiana!

_____

_____

_____

_____

_____

_____

_____

_____

_____

LINGUA

Possessive Adjectives: Part 2

In the previous unit you learned the possessive adjectives corresponding to English *my, your* (singular, familiar), and *our*. Summarized in the charts below are the possessive adjectives corresponding to English *your* (second person plural) and *their* (third person plural).

Recall that possessives are adjectives and, thus, must agree in gender and number with the noun they modify. The exception to this is **loro** / *their*, which is invariable.

Your (plural)
il vostro (before a masculine singular noun):
il vostro amico　　　　　*your friend (male)*
la vostra (before a feminine singular noun):
la vostra amica　　　　　*your friend (female)*
i vostri (before a masculine plural noun):
i vostri amici　　　　　*your friends*
le vostre (before a feminine plural noun):
le vostre amiche　　　　*your friends*

Their (invariable)
il loro (before a masculine singular noun):
il loro amico　　　　　*their friend (male)*
la loro (before a feminine singular noun):
la loro amica　　　　　*their friend (female)*
i loro (before a masculine plural noun):
i loro amici　　　　　*their friends*
le loro (before a feminine plural noun):
le loro amiche　　　　*their friends*

As mentioned in previous units, when possessive adjectives are used with singular and unmodified nouns referring to family members and relatives, the article is dropped:

Singular		**Plural**	
vostro fratello	*your brother*	i vostri fratelli	*your brothers*
vostra zia	*your aunt*	le vostre zie	*your aunts*
Unmodified		**Modified**	
vostro fratello	*your brother*	il vostro fratello alto	*your tall brother*
vostra zia	*your aunt*	la vostra zia gentile	*your kind aunt*

The exception to this rule is, again, loro, which must always be preceded by the article:

il loro fratello	*their brother*	i loro fratelli	*their brothers*
la loro zia	*their aunt*	la loro zia gentile	*their kind aunt*

The Present Indicative of Regular Second Conjugation Verbs

Verbs whose infinitive ending is -ere are known as *second conjugation* verbs. In a similar manner to first conjugation verbs (Unit 11), these verbs are conjugated by dropping the -ere and adding the following endings to the resulting stem:

Singular	
1st person	-o
2nd person	-i
3rd person	-e

Plural	
1st person	-iamo
2nd person	-ete
3rd person	-ono

Below is the verb scrivere / *to write*, fully conjugated for you:

scrivere → scriv- *to write*	
(io) scrivo	*I write, I am writing*
(tu) scrivi	*you write, you are writing (familiar)*
(Lei) scrive	*you write, you are writing (polite)*
(lui / lei) scrive	*he / she writes, he / she is writing*
(noi) scriviamo	*we write, we are writing*
(voi) scrivete	*you write, you are writing (plural)*
(loro) scrivono (skrEEh-voh-noh)	*they write, they are writing*

Io scrivo solo e-mail d'amore!

The Present Indicative of Regular Third Conjugation Verbs: Part 1

Verbs whose infinitive ending is -ire are known as *third conjugation* verbs. There are two conjugation patterns in this case. The one you have encountered in the previous dialogue is formed by dropping the -ire and adding the following endings to the resulting stem (you will learn about the second pattern in the next unit):

Singular	
1st person	-isco
2nd person	-isci
3rd person	-isce

Plural	
1st person	-iamo
2nd person	-ite
3rd person	-iscono

Below is the verb capire / *to understand,* fully conjugated for you:

capire → cap-	*to understand*
(io) capisco (kah-pEEhs-koh)	*I understand*
(tu) capisci (kah-pEEh-sheeh)	*you understand (familiar)*
(Lei) capisce (kah-pEEh-sheh)	*you understand (polite)*
(lui / lei) capisce	*he / she understands*
(noi) capiamo	*we understand*
(voi) capite	*you understand (plural)*
(loro) capiscono (kah-pEEhs-koh-noh)	*they understand*

Non capisco!

As discussed in the previous unit, the present indicative allows you to refer to actions that are occurring, ongoing, continuous, or connected to the present in some way:

Dina capisce l'italiano	*Dina understands Italian*
Carla studia l'inglese da molti anni	*Carla has been studying English for many years*

ATTIVITÀ

F. C'è / Ci sono? Ask if the indicated person or persons are here. Use the suggested possessive pronoun in its appropriate form. Then answer that the person is (in fact) there. Follow the model. If you are using this book in a classroom situation, do this exercise with a partner—one of you will ask the question and the other will answer it as in the model.

> *Model:* Your *(plural)*...instructor *(male)*
> —*C'è il vostro insegnante?*
> —*Sì, ecco il nostro insegnante.*
>
> Their...instructor *(female)*
> —*C'è la loro insegnante?*
> —*Sì, ecco la loro insegnante.*

Your *(plural)...*

1. friend *(male)*

_____

2. friend *(female)*

_____

3. brother

_____

4. sister

_____

5. beautiful mother

_____

6. parents

_____

7. tall cousin *(male)*

_____

8. grandparents

_____

9. cousins *(female)*

_____

10. friends *(female)*

_____

Their...

11. friend *(male)*

_____

12. friend *(female)*

_____

13. brother

_____

14. sister

_____

15. beautiful mother

_____

16. parents

_____

17. cousin *(male)*

_____

18. grandparents

_____

19. cousins *(female)*

_____

20. friends *(female)*

_____

G. Come si dice in italiano?

I...

1. write Italian very well

_____

2. understand Italian and English

_____

3. know their cousins (recall that **conoscere** means *to know*)

_____

You *(familiar, singular)*...

4. write Italian very well

_____

5. understand Italian and English

_____

6. know their cousins

_____

You *(polite, singular)*...

7. write Italian very well

_____

8. understand Italian and English

_____

9. know their cousins

_____

He / she …

10. writes Italian very well

_____

11. understands Italian and English

_____

12. knows their cousins

_____

We...

13. write Italian very well

_____

14. understand Italian and English

_____

15. know their cousins

_____

You *(plural)*...

16. write Italian very well

_____

17. understand Italian and English

_____

18. know their cousins

_____

They...

19. write Italian very well

_____

20. understand Italian and English

_____

21. know our cousins

_____

H. Cruciverba!

Horizontal	**Vertical**
1 Io non … l'italiano.	1 Certo … capisco.
3 otherwise	2 Ecco il vostro indirizzo postale qui in …
8 Altrimenti non vi … aiutare.	3 Anything else?
10 Io e la mia amica capiamo …	4 address
13 Ecco il vostro indirizzo … qui in Italia.	5 name
14 il … *(their)* amico	6 employee *(female)*
15 la … *(their)* amica	7 to study
17 le … *(your) (plural)* sorelle	9 to write
18 *your (plural)* cugina	11 *your (plural)* nome
21 Mia sorella non … l'italiano.	12 *your (plural)* nomi
23 A chi … ?	16 Tu … l'italiano, vero?
26 Debbie e Sharon … l'italiano.	19 Anche voi … l'italiano, vero?
27 Voi non … mai.	20 Io … l'italiano molto bene.
28 Loro non … mai.	22 Voi non … molto bene, vero?
	24 Mio fratello non … mai.
	25 Noi non … mai.

NOTA CULTURALE

Italian Addresses

In writing Italian addresses, the number is put after the street, and the postal code precedes the city. So the address for 38 Papiniano Avenue in Milan is:

> Viale Papiniano, 38
> 20123 Milano

Here's how to read an e-mail address in Italian:

dina@perugia.provider.it		
↓ ↓ ↓ ↓ ↓ ↓↓		
1 2 3 4 5 6 7		
1.	Nome utente	*User name*
2.	Chiocciola	*at*
3./5.	Nome di dominio	*Domain name*
4./6.	Punto	*dot*
7.	Italia	*Italy*

I. Do the following things.

1. Give your address in Italian.

_____

2. What is your **nome utente**?

_____

3. What is your **nome di dominio**?

_____

4. Give your complete e-mail address, naming its various parts in Italian.

_____

Scusi, dov'è la stazione?

Unit 13

Mi sa dire?

CONVERSAZIONE

[One day after class, as she is taking a long stroll by herself, Dina notices a tourist talking to a policewoman. Always curious to find out how things are said in Italian, Dina listens in.]

Turista	**Scusi, mi sa dire dov'è la stazione ferroviaria? Il mio treno parte fra qualche minuto!**	*Excuse me, can you tell me where the train station is? My train is leaving in a few minutes!*
Vigilessa	**Sì, è qui vicino. Vada diritto per due isolati.**	*Yes, it's near here! Go straight ahead for two blocks.*
Turista	**E poi?**	*And then?*
Vigilessa	**Al semaforo giri a destra. A due passi dopo c'è la stazione.**	*At the traffic light, turn right. Two paces after you'll find [there is] the train station.*
Turista	**Grazie.**	*Thank you.*
Vigilessa	**Prego!**	*You're welcome!*

COMPRENSIONE

A. Complete each statement or question in an appropriate fashion with the missing word or expression.

1. Scusi, mi _____ dire dov'è la stazione ferroviaria?

2. Il mio treno _____ fra qualche minuto!

3. Sì, è qui _____.

4. _____ diritto per due isolati.

5. Al semaforo _____ a destra.

6. A due _____ dopo c'è la stazione.

VOCABOLARIO

Mi sa dire
dov'è la
stazione
ferroviaria?

Vada lì!

PAROLE NUOVE

diritto	*straight*
dopo	*after*
ferroviario (feh-rroh-vyAh-reeh-oh)	*railway (of the railway)*
girare	*to turn*
l'isolato (eeh-zoh-lAh-toh)	*street block*
partire	*to leave*
il passo	*pace*
la stazione (stah-tsyOh-neh)	*station*
il treno	*train*
il turista / la turista	*tourist (male / female)*
vicino (veeh-chEEh-noh)	*near*
il vigile (vEEh-jeeh-leh) / **la vigilessa**	*policeman / policewoman (traffic)*

ESPRESSIONI E MODI DI DIRE

a due passi	*two paces (ahead)*
Mi sa dire?	*Can you tell me?*

STRUTTURE VERBALI

Giri! (jEEh-reeh)	*Turn (polite)!*
Vada!	*Go (polite)!*

ATTIVITÀ

B. Comunicazione! Say or ask the following things.

Say that…

1. your train is leaving in a few minutes

_____

2. the train station is near here

_____

3. the station is a few paces after the traffic light

_____

Tell someone to…

4. go straight ahead for two blocks

_____

5. turn left at the traffic light

_____

Ask …

6. someone if he or she can tell you where the train station is

_____

C. Questions and answers. Ask the indicated question and then answer it. Follow the model. If you are using this book in a classroom situation, do this activity with a partner—one of you asks the question and the other answers it.

> _Model:_ train station / near here
> —_Mi sa dire dov'è la stazione ferroviaria?_
> —_La stazione ferroviaria è qui vicino._

1. train station / two paces from here

_____

2. the street block / straight ahead

_____

3. the policeman / near here

_____

4. the policewoman / two blocks straight ahead

_____

5. the tourist / to the right

_____

D. Give instructions (as best you can) to a stranger on how to get to the train station of your city. Use a dictionary if you need to. If you are using this book in a classroom situation, do this activity with a partner together.

Dov'è la stazione ferroviaria?

_____

_____

_____

_____

_____

_____

_____

_____

_____

_____

_____

LINGUA

The Present Indicative of Regular Third Conjugation Verbs: Part 2

As pointed out in the previous unit, there are two conjugation patterns in the case of -ire verbs. As you learned, the verb capire exemplifies the first pattern. The verb partire, used in the dialogue on page 162, exemplifies the second pattern.

Drop the -ire and then add the following endings to the resulting stem:

Singular	
1st person	-o
2nd person	-i
3rd person	-e

Plural	
1st person	-iamo
2nd person	-ite
3rd person	-ono

Here is partire fully conjugated for you:

partire → part- *to leave*	
(io) parto	*I leave, I am leaving*
(tu) parti	*you leave, you are leaving (familiar)*
(Lei) parte	*you leave, you are leaving (polite)*
(lui / lei) parte	*he / she leaves, he / she is leaving*
(noi) partiamo	*we leave, we are leaving*
(voi) partite	*you leave, you are leaving (plural)*
(loro) partono (pAhr-toh-noh)	*they leave, they are leaving*

A che ora parte il treno?

From this point on, third conjugation verbs that are conjugated like capire (first pattern) will be identified with (-isc) in parentheses when they are first introduced.

As discussed in the two previous units, the present indicative allows you to refer to actions that are occurring, ongoing, continuous, or connected to the present in some way:

Dina parte domani	*Dina is leaving tomorrow*
Carla non capisce l'inglese	*Carla doesn't understand English*

The Irregular Verbs dare, fare, and volere

In Unit 8 you memorized the present indicative conjugations of dire, andare, and venire, and in Unit 9 of avere and essere. Review them if you have forgotten them.

Following are the present indicative conjugations of three other commonly used irregular verbs. You will have to memorize these as well.

dare	to give	
(io) do	I give, I am giving	
(tu) dai	you give, you are giving (familiar)	
(Lei) dà	you give, you are giving (polite)	
(lui / lei) dà	he / she gives, he / she is giving	
(noi) diamo	we give, we are giving	
(voi) date	you give, you are giving (plural)	
(loro) danno	they give, they are giving	

fare	to do, to make	
(io) faccio (fAh-choh)	I do, I am doing	
(tu) fai	you do, you are doing (familiar)	
(Lei) fa	you do, you are doing (polite)	
(lui / lei) fa	he / she does, he / she is doing	
(noi) facciamo (fah-chAH-moh)	we do, we are doing	
(voi) fate	you do, you are doing (plural)	
(loro) fanno	they do, they are doing	

volere	to want	
(io) voglio (vOh-lyoh)	I want	
(tu) vuoi	you want (familiar)	
(Lei) vuole	you want (polite)	
(lui / lei) vuole	he / she wants	
(noi) vogliamo (voh-lyAh-moh)	we want	
(voi) volete	you want (plural)	
(loro) vogliono (vOh-lyoh-noh)	they want	

The Imperative of Regular Verbs

The *imperative* is a verb tense that allows you to command, order, or suggest that something be done:

Parla italiano, Dina!	Speak Italian, Dina!
Signorina, parli!	Young lady, speak!

There is no first person singular form of the imperative (you cannot command yourself to do something, linguistically speaking of course). To form the imperative of the other persons, drop the infinitive ending and then add the following endings to the resulting stem.

Note that there is a polite plural form (Loro):

FIRST CONJUGATION VERBS

Singular			Plural		
1st person	—		1st person	-iamo	
2nd person familiar	-a		2nd person familiar	-ate	
3rd person polite	-i		3rd person polite	-ino	

167

Parla italiano, Dina!

Here's **parlare** / *to speak,* fully conjugated for you:

parlare → parl- to speak	
(tu) parla	*speak (familiar, singular)*
(Lei) parli	*speak (polite, singular)*
(noi) parliamo	*let's speak*
(voi) parlate	*speak (familiar, plural)*
(Loro) parlino (pAhr-leeh-noh)	*speak (polite, plural)*

SECOND CONJUGATION VERBS

Singular			Plural		
1st person	—		*1st person*	-iamo	
2nd person familiar	-i		*2nd person familiar*	-ete	
3rd person polite	-a		*3rd person polite*	-ano	

Here's **scrivere** / *to write,* fully conjugated for you:

scrivere → scriv- to write	
(tu) scrivi	*write (familiar, singular)*
(Lei) scriva	*write (polite, singular)*
(noi) scriviamo	*let's write*
(voi) scrivete	*write (familiar, plural)*
(Loro) scrivano (skrEEh-vah-noh)	*write (polite, plural)*

THIRD CONJUGATION VERBS (FIRST PATTERN)

Singular			Plural		
1st person	—		*1st person*	-iamo	
2nd person familiar	-isci		*2nd person familiar*	-ite	
3rd person polite	-isca		*3rd person polite*	-iscano	

Here's the verb finire / *to finish* fully conjugated for you:

finire → fin- *to finish*	
(tu) finisci (feeh-nEEh-sheeh)	*finish (familiar, singular)*
(Lei) finisca (feeh-nEEhs-kah)	*finish (polite, singular)*
(noi) finiamo	*let's finish*
(voi) finite	*finish (familiar, plural)*
(Loro) finiscano (feeh-nEEhs-kah-noh)	*finish (polite, plural)*

THIRD CONJUGATION VERBS (SECOND PATTERN)

Singular			**Plural**	
1st person	—		*1st person*	-iamo
2nd person familiar	-i		*2nd person familiar*	-ite
3rd person polite	-a		*3rd person polite*	-ano

Here's the verb partire / *to leave* fully conjugated for you:

partire → part- *to finish*	
(tu) parti	*leave (familiar, singular)*
(Lei) parta	*leave (polite, singular)*
(noi) partiamo	*let's leave*
(voi) partite	*leave (familiar, plural)*
(Loro) partano (pAhr-tah-noh)	*leave (polite, plural)*

The Loro forms are used in very formal situations:

Familiar / Informal

Singular
Dina, parla italiano!
Dina, speak Italian!

Plural
Studenti, parlate italiano!
Students, speak Italian!

Polite / Formal

Singular
Signora Martini, parli italiano!
Mrs. Martini, speak Italian!

Plural
Signore e signori, parlino italiano!
Ladies and gentlemen, speak Italian!

The Imperative of Irregular Verbs

The imperative forms of the irregular verbs you have encountered so far are summarized below:

andare *to go*	
(tu) va'	*go (familiar, singular)*
(Lei) vada	*go (polite, singular)*
(noi) andiamo	*let's go*
(voi) andate	*go (familiar, plural)*
(Loro) vadano (vAh-dah-noh)	*go (polite, plural)*

avere	to have	
(tu) abbi	have (familiar, singular)
(Lei) abbia	have (polite, singular)
(noi) abbiamo	let's have
(voi) abbiate	have (familiar, plural)
(Loro) abbino (Ah-beeh-noh)	have (polite, plural)

dare	to give	
(tu) da'	give (familiar, singular)
(Lei) dia	give (polite, singular)
(noi) diamo	let's give
(voi) date	give (familiar, plural)
(Loro) diano (dEEh-ah-noh)	give (polite, plural)

dire	to tell, to say	
(tu) di'	tell (familiar, singular)
(Lei) dica	tell (polite, singular)
(noi) diciamo	let's tell
(voi) dite	tell (familiar, plural)
(Loro) dicano (dEEh-kah-noh)	tell (polite, plural)

essere	to be	
(tu) sii	be (familiar, singular)
(Lei) sia	be (polite, singular)
(noi) siamo	let's be
(voi) siate	be (familiar, plural)
(Loro) siano (sEEh-ah-noh)	be (polite, plural)

fare	to do, to make	
(tu) fa'	do (familiar, singular)
(Lei) faccia (fAh-chah)	do (polite, singular)
(noi) facciamo (fah-chAh-moh)	let's do
(voi) fate	do (familiar, plural)
(Loro) facciano (fAh-chah-noh)	do (polite, plural)

venire	to come	
(tu) vieni	come (familiar, singular)
(Lei) venga	come (polite singular)
(noi) veniamo	let's come
(voi) venite	come (familiar, plural)
(Loro) vengano (vEhn-gah-noh)	come (polite, plural)

ATTIVITÀ

E. Come si dice in italiano?

I...

1. am leaving tomorrow for Italy

2. am finishing at 3:30

3. always sleep till late *(tardi)* (recall that dormire means *to sleep*; it is conjugated like partire)

4. give everything to my brother

5. do everything in the house

6. want to go downtown

You *(familiar, singular)*...

7. are leaving tomorrow for Italy

8. are finishing at 3:30

9. always sleep till late

10. give everything to your brother

11. do everything in the house

12. want to go downtown

You *(polite, singular)*...

13. are leaving tomorrow for Italy

14. are finishing at 3:30

_____

15. always sleep till late

_____

16. give everything to your *(Suo)* brother

_____

17. do everything in the house

_____

18. want to go downtown

_____

He / she …

19. is leaving tomorrow for Italy

_____

20. is finishing at 3:30

_____

21. always sleeps till late

_____

22. gives everything to his / her *(suo)* brother

_____

23. does everything in the house

_____

24. wants to go downtown

_____

We …

25. are leaving tomorrow for Italy

_____

26. are finishing at 3:30

_____

27. always sleep till late

_____

28. give everything to our brother

_____

29. do everything in the house

_____

30. want to go downtown

_____

You *(plural)*...

31. are leaving tomorrow for Italy

_____

32. are finishing at 3:30

_____

33. always sleep till late

_____

34. give everything to your brother

_____

35. do everything in the house

_____

36. want to go downtown

_____

They ...

37. are leaving tomorrow for Italy

_____

38. are finishing at 3:30

_____

39. always sleep till late

_____

40. give everything to their brother

_____

41. do everything in the house

_____

42. want to go downtown

_____

F. Comunicazione! Tell the following people to do the indicated things. Use the appropriate form of the imperative in each case.

> *Model:* Tell Dina to speak Italian
> *Dina, parla italiano!*

Tell Dina to ...

1. speak Italian

_____

2. write to *(alla)* Professoressa Giusti

_____

3. sleep until noon

_____

4. finish the coffee *(il caffè)*

_____

5. go downtown

_____

6. have patience *(pazienza)*

_____

7. give everything to her brother

_____

8. always tell the truth *(la verità)*

_____

9. always be kind

_____

10. do everything in the house

_____

11. come to the party

_____

Now, tell Mrs. Martini to …

12. speak Italian

_____

13. write to *(alla)* Professoressa Giusti

_____

14. sleep until noon

_____

15. finish the coffee *(il caffè)*

_____

16. go downtown

_____

17. have patience *(pazienza)*

_____

18. give everything to Mr. Martini

_____

19. always tell the truth *(la verità)*

_____

20. always be kind

_____

21. do everything in the house

_____

22. come to the party

_____

Now, tell Alessandro and Sara to …

23. speak Italian

_____

24. write to *(alla)* Professoressa Giusti

_____

25. sleep until noon

_____

26. finish the coffee *(il caffè)*

_____

27. go downtown

_____

28. have patience *(pazienza)*

_____

29. give everything to their mother

_____

30. always tell the truth *(la verità)*

_____

31. always be kind *(Be careful! The adjective is in the plural!)*

_____

32. do everything in the house

_____

33. come to the party

_____

Now tell Mr. and Mrs. Martini to …

34. speak Italian

_____

35. write to *(alla)* Professoressa Giusti

_____

36. sleep until noon

_____

37. finish the coffee *(il caffè)*

_____

38. go downtown

_____

39. have patience *(pazienza)*

_____

40. give everything to their relatives

_____

41. always tell the truth *(la verità)*

_____

42. always be kind *(Be careful again!)*

_____

43. do everything in the house

_____

44. come to the party

_____

Finally, give the Italian equivalent of …

45. Let's speak Italian!

_____

46. Let's write to *(alla)* Professoressa Giusti!

_____

47. Let's sleep until noon!

_____

48. Let's finish the coffee *(il caffè)*!

_____

49. Let's go downtown!

_____

50. Let's have patience *(pazienza)*!

_____

51. Let's give everything to our friends!

_____

52. Let's always tell the truth *(la verità)*!

_____

53. Let's always be kind!

_____

54. Let's do everything in the house!

_____

55. Let's come to the party!

_____

G. Cruciverba!

Horizontal

1 to leave
4 Carla, ... diritto per due isolati!
5 Scusi, dov'è la ... ferroviaria?
7 Vada diritto per un ...!
9 policewoman (traffic)
10 la stazione ...
13 Domani io ... alle dodici e mezzo.
14 policeman (traffic)
15 Loro ... alle diciassette domani.
16 Signor Martini, ... qui l'indirizzo!
17 Noi ... domani all'una.
21 Io parto fra ... minuto.
22 E voi a che ora ...?
23 Leave! *(familiar)*
25 block
27 Leave! *(plural)*
28 Understand! *(polite)*
29 Understand! *(plural)*

Vertical

1 A due ... c'è la stazione.
2 tourist
3 Signor Rossini, al semaforo ... a destra!
4 Signora Martini, ... diritto per un isolato!
6 Alessandro, al semaforo ... a destra!
8 Il mio ... parte fra qualche minuto.
11 near
12 Carla, a che ora ... domani?
15 Il treno ... tra qualche minuto.
16 Dina e Sara, ... qui il vostro indirizzo.
17 Sara e Carla, ... italiano!
18 Il treno parte tra qualche ...
19 Mark, ... italiano!
20 Carla, ... il tuo indirizzo qui!
22 Signora Martini, ... italiano!
23 Leave! *(polite)*
24 Understand! *(familiar)*
26 Scusi, mi ... dire dov'è la stazione?

NOTA CULTURALE

Rome

Italian Cities

Italian cities started out as city-states, little nations with their own governments, politics, and traditions. City-states were often ruled by a king, by a dictator, or by a small group of powerful citizens. In some cases, political life was controlled by city dwellers, and in other cases by people of both the countryside and the city. During the Middle Ages, some Italian cities became self-governing and almost entirely independent. They included Florence, Genoa, Milan, and Venice.

Florence

Some well-known Italian cities are:

Torino	*Turin*	**L'Aquila**	*Aquila*
Milano	*Milan*	**Ancona**	*Ancona*
Venezia	*Venice*	**Roma**	*Rome*
Trieste	*Trieste*	**Napoli**	*Naples*
Genova	*Genoa*	**Potenza**	*Potenza*
Bologna	*Bologna*	**Bari**	*Bari*
Firenze	*Florence*	**Siracusa**	*Syracuse*
Siena	*Siena*	**Catanzaro**	*Catanzaro*
Perugia	*Perugia*	**Cagliari**	*Cagliari*

Venice

H. Look up each city previously named and give one reason (among many) why it is well-known. If you are using this book in a classroom situation, do this activity with a partner.

_____

_____

_____

_____

_____

_____

_____

_____

_____

_____

_____

_____

_____

_____

_____

_____

_____

Pronto, pronto, chi parla?

Unit 14

Sono io!

CONVERSAZIONE

[Dina is out shopping with Carla. All of a sudden, Carla receives a call on her cellphone from her brother Claudio.]

Carla	**Pronto? Chi parla?**	*Hello? Who is it?*
Claudio	**Carla, sono io, Claudio. Dove sei? Che fai? A che ora torni a casa?**	*Carla, it's me, Claudio. Where are you? What are you doing? At what time are you returning home?*
Carla	**Faccio delle spese in centro. Torno fra un'ora.**	*I'm doing some shopping downtown. I'll be back in an hour.*
Claudio	**Puoi comprare qualcosa per me?**	*Can you buy something for me?*
Carla	**Cosa vuoi?**	*What do you want?*
Claudio	**Ho bisogno del pane, dell'olio, dello zucchero, degli spaghetti e della carne.**	*I need some bread, some oil, some sugar, some spaghetti, and some meat.*
Carla	**Perché?**	*Why?*
Claudio	**Perché stasera faccio io da mangiare! Perché non compri anche qualcosa per la mamma? Fra una settimana è il suo compleanno.**	*Because tonight I'm doing the cooking! Why don't you also buy something for mom? In a week it's her birthday.*
Carla	**Hai ragione. Che cosa devo comprare, dei pantaloni, delle scarpe, degli orecchini,…?**	*You're right. What should I buy, pants, shoes, earrings, …?*
Claudio	**Non importa! Decidi tu! Forse è più facile comprare gli orecchini, no?**	*It doesn't matter! You decide! Maybe it's easier to buy earrings, right?*
Carla	**Va bene! Ciao!**	*OK! Bye!*
Claudio	**Ciao!**	*Bye!*

COMPRENSIONE

A. Rispondi alle seguenti domande con frasi intere.

1. Chi chiama Carla?

_____

2. Dov'è Carla?

_____

3. Cosa fa Carla?

_____

4. Quando torna a casa Carla?

_____

5. Di che cosa ha bisogno Claudio?

_____

6. Perché?

_____

7. Che cosa c'è fra una settimana?

_____

8. Che cosa è più facile comprare, secondo _(according to)_ Claudio?

_____

VOCABOLARIO

PAROLE NUOVE

la carne	_meat_
il compleanno	_birthday_
comprare	_to buy_
decidere (deh-chEEh-deh-reh)	_to decide_
facile	_easy_
la mamma	_mom_
mangiare (mahn-jAh-reh)	_to eat_
l'olio	_oil_
l'orecchino (oh-reh-kkEEh-noh)	_earring_
il pane	_bread_
i pantaloni	_pants_
potere	_to be able to_
qualcosa (kwahl-kOh-zah)	_something_
la scarpa	_shoe_
gli spaghetti	_spaghetti_
la spesa / le spese	_food shopping / shopping in general (plural)_
stasera	_tonight, this evening_
tornare	_to return, to get back_
lo zucchero (dsOOh-keh-roh)	_sugar_

ESPRESSIONI E MODI DI DIRE

avere bisogno (beeh-zOh-nyoh) di	_to need_
fare delle spese	_to shop in general_
fare la spesa	_to shop for food_
fra / tra un'ora / settimana	_in an hour / a week_
Non importa!	_It doesn't matter!_
per me	_for me_

Fare delle spese!

FORME PARTITIVE (PARTITIVE FORMS)

del pane	some bread
dei pantaloni	some pants
dello zucchero	some sugar
dell'olio	some oil
degli spaghetti	some spaghetti
degli orecchini	some earrings
della carne	some meat
delle scarpe	some shoes

ATTIVITÀ

B. Say or ask the following things.

Say that …

1. it is you (on the phone)

_____

2. you are shopping downtown

_____

3. you'll be back in an hour

_____

4. you need some bread

_____

5. Claudio needs some oil

_____

6. Carla and Claudio need some sugar

_____

7. you need some spaghetti

_____

8. your parents need some meat

_____

9. you are doing the cooking this evening

_____

10. in a week it's your birthday

_____

11. you want to buy pants

_____

12. your brother wants to buy shoes

_____

13. your sister wants to buy earrings

_____

14. it does not matter

_____

15. maybe it's easier to buy earrings

_____

Ask …

16. who it is (on the phone)

_____

17. Carla where she is

_____

18. Claudio what he is doing

_____

19. Sara when she is coming back home

_____

20. Carla if she can buy something for you

_____

21. Claudio what he wants

_____

22. Claudio what you should buy

_____

Tell Carla to...

23. buy something for mom

_____

24. do the cooking

_____

C. Che cosa vuoi? Give the indicated answer.

> _Model:_ some meat
> _Voglio della carne._

Che cosa vuoi?

1. some oil

_____

2. some earrings

_____

3. some bread

_____

4. some pants

_____

5. some shoes

_____

6. some spaghetti

_____

7. some sugar

_____

D. Comunicazione.

Say that...

1. your birthday is in a month

_____

2. Italian is easy

_____

3. you always shop for food in _(nella)_ your family

_____

4. you always go shopping downtown

_____

5. you need something tonight

_____

6. you are going back home in a few minutes

_____

E. Domande personali. Answer the questions.

1. Mangi la carne?

_____

2. Quando è il tuo compleanno?

_____

3. Mangi gli spaghetti?

_____

4. Hai bisogno di qualcosa? Se sì, di che?

_____

5. Quando fai la spesa generalmente?

_____

6. Dove fai le spese di solito?

_____

F. Make a list of ten things you would like for your next birthday. Use a dictionary to look up words you do not know. If you are using this book in a classroom situation, do this activity with a partner.

Per il mio compleanno, vorrei...

1. _____

2. _____

3. _____

4. _____

5. _____

6. _____

7. _____

8. _____

9. _____

10. _____

LINGUA

Possessive Adjectives: Part 3

In previous units you have learned all of the Italian possessive adjectives, except those corresponding to *his, her,* and *its* (third person singular):

His / Her / Its	
il suo (before a masculine singular noun):	
il suo amico	*his / her friend (male)*
la sua (before a feminine singular noun):	
la sua amica	*his / her friend (female)*
i suoi (before a masculine plural noun):	
i suoi amici	*his / her friends*
le sue (before a feminine plural noun):	
le sue amiche	*his / her friends*

Signorina, è Suo questo?

Sì, ma non lo voglio!

Note that this possessive adjective, like all adjectives, agrees in gender and number with the noun it modifies. This use of the possessive is clearly different from English usage and, thus, you must be careful!

Lui è l'amico di Paolo	*He is Paul's friend*
Lui è il suo amico	*He is his friend*
Lui è l'amico di Francesca	*He is Francesca's friend*
Lui è il suo amico	*He is her friend*
Lei è l'amica di Paolo	*She is Paul's friend*
Lei è la sua amica	*She is his friend*
Lei è l'amica di Francesca	*She is Francesca's friend*
Lei è la sua amica	*She is her friend*

This form of the possessive is also used for polite address. In writing, it is sometimes capitalized in order to distinguish it from the other meanings it has.

> Signor Santucci, dov'è la Sua amica?
> *Mr. Santucci, where's your friend (female)?*
>
> Signora Dini, dov'è il Suo amico?
> *Mrs. Santucci, where is your friend (male)?*

As indicated in previous units, when the possessive is used with singular and unmodified nouns referring to family members and relatives, the article is dropped:

Singular		Plural	
suo fratello	*his / her brother*	i suoi fratelli	*his / her brothers*
sua zia	*his / her aunt*	le sue zie	*his / her aunts*
Suo figlio	*your son*	i Suoi figli	*your sons*
Unmodified		**Modified**	
suo fratello	*his / her brother*	il suo fratello alto	*his / her tall brother*
sua zia	*his / her aunt*	la sua zia alta	*his / her tall aunt*
Suo figlio	*your son*	il Suo figlio gentile	*your kind son*

The Partitive: Part 1

The *partitive* is a structure that renders the idea of English *some, a bit, a little,* etc. It is constructed with the preposition di plus the definite article:

del = (di + il)		
del pane	*some bread*	(= di + il pane)
dei = (di + i)		
dei pantaloni	*some pants*	(= di + i pantaloni)
dell' = (di + l')		
dell'olio	*some oil*	(= di + l'olio)
dello = (di + lo)		
dello zucchero	*some sugar*	(= di + lo zucchero)
degli = (di + gli)		
degli spaghetti	*some spaghetti*	(= di + gli spaghetti)
degli orecchini	*some earrings*	(= di + gli orecchini)
della = (di + la)		
della carne	*some meat*	(= di + la carne)
delle = (di + le)		
delle scarpe	*some shoes*	(= di + le scarpe)

Notice that the partitive allows you to put "indefinite" noun phrases into the plural:

Singular		*Plural*	
un ragazzo	*a boy*	dei ragazzi	*some boys*
una ragazza	*a girl*	delle ragazze	*some girls*
uno zio	*an uncle*	degli zii	*some uncles*
un'amica	*some friends*	delle amiche	*some friends*

The Present Indicative of potere

In this unit you have come across a very useful verb: potere / *to be able to.* Like volere / *to want* (previous unit) it is called a "modal" verb. This means that it is generally used with an infinitive to convey "mood," "state," and the like:

Voglio venire, ma non posso	*I want to come, but I can't*
Vuole venire anche lui, ma non può	*He also wants to come, but he cannot*

Here are the present indicative forms of potere:

potere	*to be able to*
(io) posso	*I can / am able to*
(tu) puoi	*you can / are able to (familiar)*
(Lei) può	*you can / are able to (polite)*
(lui / lei) può	*he / she can / is able to*
(noi) possiamo	*we can / are able to*
(voi) potete	*you can / are able to (plural)*
(loro) possono (pOh-ssoh-noh)	*they can / are able to*

ATTIVITÀ

G. Ask where each indicated person is, following the model:

Model: his brother
—*Dov'è suo fratello?*

1. his sister

_____

2. her brother

_____

3. her friend *(male)*

_____

4. her friend *(female)*

_____

5. his friend *(male)*

_____

6. his friend *(female)*

_____

7. her tall uncle

_____

8. his tall uncle

_____

9. her shoe

_____

10. his shoe

_____

11. her number

_____

12. his number

_____

13. your *(polite, singular)* friend *(male)*

_____

14. your *(polite, singular)* friend *(female)*

_____

15. your *(polite, singular)* cousin *(male)*

_____

16. his sisters

_____

17. her brothers

_____

18. her friends *(male)*

_____

19. her friends *(female)*

_____

20. his friends *(male)*

_____

21. his friends *(female)*

_____

22. her uncles

_____

23. his uncles

_____

24. her shoes

_____

25. his shoes

_____

26. her numbers

_____

27. his numbers

_____

28. your *(polite)* friends *(male)*

_____

29. your *(polite)* friends *(female)*

_____

30. your *(polite)* cousins *(male)*

_____

H. Ask Dina if she wants the indicated thing.

      Model: some sugar
              Dina, vuoi dello zucchero?

1. some oil

_____

2. some bread

_____

3. some spaghetti

_____

4. some cellphones

_____

5. some shoes

_____

6. some pants

_____

7. some meat

_____

8. some euros

_____

9. some earrings

_____

I. Come si dice in italiano?

1. I want to go to Italy, but I can't this year.

_____

2. You *(familiar, singular)* want to go shopping today, but you can't.

_____

3. He wants to eat meat, but he can't.

_____

4. She wants to eat spaghetti, but she can't.

_____

5. We can eat only meat.

_____

6. You _(plural)_ can eat meat, right?

_____

7. My parents can't eat meat.

_____

J. Cruciverba!

Horizontal

1 you can *(plural)*
4 Ho bisogno della …
5 they can
6 Voglio … qualcosa per la mamma.
9 Anch'io … delle spese in centro oggi.
13 Noi … delle spese ogni sabato in centro.
14 I can
15 I want
16 Voglio … zucchero.
17 they want
18 she wants
19 Voglio … olio.
21 Voglio comprare … scarpe per nostra madre.
23 Ho bisogno … pantaloni.
26 Anche tu vuoi comprare dei …, vero?
28 Anche voi volete comprare dell'…, vero?
29 Loro sono le amiche di Dina. Sono le … amiche.
31 earring
34 Sì, fra una settimana è il compleanno della …
35 shoe
37 to want
38 to decide
39 Alessandro vuole del …
40 Anch'io voglio comprare … pantaloni.
41 sugar

Vertical

1 we can
2 to do
3 Tu sei l'amico di Paul? Sì, sono il … amico.
5 he can
7 Mia sorella ha molti …
8 they make
10 Mia sorella … delle spese in centro oggi.
11 Anche voi … delle spese in centro, vero?
12 we want
13 Quando … delle spese tu, generalmente?
14 you can *(familiar)*
15 you want *(plural)*
16 Ho bisogno … spaghetti.
18 you want *(familiar)*
19 Lei vuole … carne, vero?
20 Anche tuo fratello vuole … spaghetti, vero?
22 Non …! Decidi tu!
24 Mia sorella è l'amica di Paul? Sì, lei è la … amica
25 Loro sono gli amici di Maria? Sì, è vero sono i … amici
26 Perché non compri qualcosa … la mamma?
27 to return
30 Fra una settimana è il … della mamma.
32 Non compro mai la …
33 Domani noi facciamo delle … in centro.
36 Non importa! … tu!

NOTA CULTURALE

La Repubblica Italiana

Italian Government

Italy set up its present form of government in 1946. That was the year when the people voted to change their nation from a monarchy ruled by a king to a republic headed by a president. King Umberto II immediately left the throne. The voters elected a group of 556 members, called a

Constituent Assembly, to write a constitution. The constitution was approved in 1947 and became effective on January 1, 1948. The constitution established a governing system made up of a president, a cabinet called the Council of Ministers headed by a prime minister, and a Parliament made up of a Senate and a Chamber of Deputies.

K. Give the English equivalent of each one, using a dictionary if necessary, and then give the name of the present Italian office holder, if you know it. If you are using this book in a classroom situation, do this activity with a partner.

1. il presidente della repubblica

_____

2. il primo ministro

_____

3. il ministro degli affari esteri

_____

4. il ministro dell pubblica istruzione

_____

Che bel televisore!

Unit 15

Certo che mi piace!

CONVERSAZIONE

[Every afternoon Dina watches the soaps on Italian TV. She does this to improve her command of the language. A furniture commercial comes on at a certain point one afternoon; it revolves around a husband and wife discussing their new home.]

Moglie	Allora, ti piace la nostra casa nuova?	So, do you like our new house?
Marito	Certo che mi piace. Ha un salotto grande e anche una bella cucina, delle belle finestre e delle belle porte.	Of course I like it. It has a large living room, and also a beautiful kitchen, beautiful windows, and beautiful doors.
Moglie	Sì, e delle camere molto spaziose.	Yes, and some very spacious bedrooms.
Marito	Ma abbiamo bisogno di mobilia e di elettrodomestici.	But we need furniture and appliances.
Moglie	Sì, specialmente di un tavolo, una poltrona, un divano, delle sedie,…	Yes, especially a table, an armchair, a sofa, some chairs,…
Marito	E anche di un televisore, un frigorifero…,	And also a TV set, a refrigerator…
Moglie	Basta, per adesso! E sai dove andare, vero, per comprare tutto?	That's enough, for now! And you know where to go, right, to buy everything?
Marito	Certo!	Of course!

COMPRENSIONE

A. Match the items in the two columns in an appropriate fashion.

1. Ti piace la nostra casa nuova?	a. grande
2. Ha un salotto …	b. bella
3. Ha una cucina …	c. mobilia e elettrodomestici
4. Ha anche delle belle …	d. un tavolo, una poltrona, un divano, delle sedie
5. Ha delle … molto spaziose.	e. Certo che mi piace.
6. La moglie e il marito hanno bisogno di …	f. camere
7. Hanno bisogno specialmente di …	g. finestre e porte

VOCABOLARIO

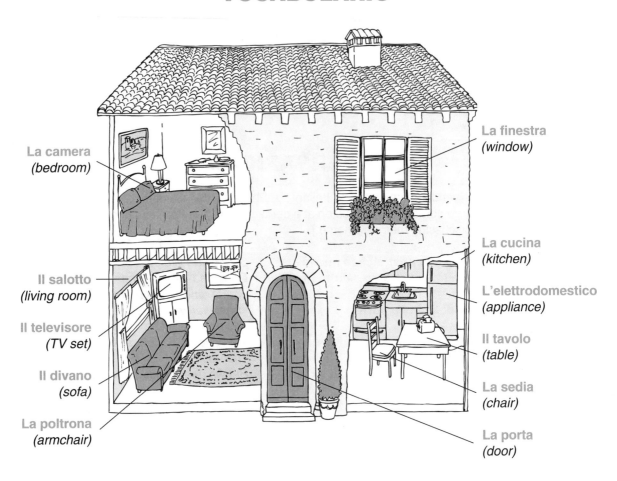

La camera
(bedroom)

La finestra
(window)

Il salotto
(living room)

La cucina
(kitchen)

Il televisore
(TV set)

L'elettrodomestico
(appliance)

Il divano
(sofa)

Il tavolo
(table)

La poltrona
(armchair)

La sedia
(chair)

La porta
(door)

PAROLE NUOVE

adesso	now
allora	so, therefore
la camera (kAh-meh-rah)	bedroom
la cucina (kooh-chEEh-nah)	kitchen
il divano	sofa
l'elettrodomestico	appliance
la finestra	window
il frigorifero (freeh-goh-rEEh-feh-roh)	refrigerator
la mobilia (moh-bEEh-leeh-ah)	furniture
nuovo	new
piacere	to be pleasing to, to like
la poltrona	armchair
la porta	door
salotto	living room
sedia	chair
spazioso (spah-tsyOh-zoh)	spacious
specialmente	especially
tavolo (tAh-voh-loh)	table
televisore	TV set

STRUTTURE VERBALI

mi piace / mi piacciono (pyAh-choh-noh)	I like
ti piace / ti piacciono	you like (familiar)

ATTIVITÀ

B. Comunicazione! Say or ask the following things.

Say that …

1. you like Carla's new house

_____

2. the house has a large living room

_____

3. the kitchen is beautiful

_____

4. the house has some beautiful windows and doors

_____

5. your new house has very spacious bedrooms

_____

6. you need furniture and some appliances

_____

7. you especially need a table for now

_____

8. you want to buy a new sofa and a new TV set

_____

9. you need some chairs and a new refrigerator

_____

Ask Alessandro…

10. if he likes your new house

_____

11. if he knows where to go to buy everything

_____

12. if he wants to buy a new house

_____

C. Questions and answers. First, ask a friend if he or she likes the indicated thing. Then, provide his or her answer following the model. If you are using this book in a classroom situation, do this activity with a partner—one of you asks the question, the other answers it.

> _Model:_ the new house
> —_Allora, ti piace la casa nuova?_
> —_Sì, mi piace._

> **Rule of Thumb**
>
> If the noun (or noun phrase) is singular, use the singular form of the verb:
>
> Ti piace la camera? / Do you like the bedroom?
> Sì mi piace. / Yes, I like it.
>
> If the noun (or noun phrase) is plural, use the plural form of the verb:
> Ti piacciono le camere? / Do you like the bedrooms?
> Sì mi piacciono. / Yes, I like them.

1. those bedrooms

2. the new kitchen

3. the new doors

4. this table

5. those chairs

6. that spacious living room

7. the new furniture

8. that sofa

9. our new refrigerator

10. the armchairs

D. Domande personali. Answer the questions.

1. Com'è la tua casa?

2. Com'è la mobilia della tua casa?

3. Che tipo di *(type of)* casa ti piace?

E. Write a TV commercial similar to the one on page 197. If you are using this book in a classroom situation, do this activity with a partner.

La nostra casa nuova!

_____

_____

_____

_____

_____

_____

_____

LINGUA

The Adjective bello: Part 2

In Unit 7 the singular forms of bello (before a noun) were introduced. Its plural forms are charted below:

Singular		Plural	
Before a masculine singular noun beginning with any consonant except *z* or *s + consonant*			
bel bel giorno	*nice day*	bei bei giorni	*nice days*
Before a masculine singular noun beginning with *z* or *s + consonant*			
bello bello studente	*nice student*	begli begli studenti	*nice students*
Before a feminine singular noun beginning with any consonant			
bella bella giornata	*nice day*	belle belle giornate	*nice days*
Before any singular noun, masculine or feminine, beginning with any vowel			
bell' bell'amico bell'amica	*handsome friend* *beautiful friend*	begli *(masculine)* / belle *(feminine)* begli amici belle amiche	*handsome friends* *beautiful friends*

Che bella casa, no?

This adjective can occur before or after the noun it modifies. The forms on page 201 are used only when the adjective occurs before the noun. When it occurs after, just change the final vowel of bello according to the gender and number of the noun it modifies:

Before	After
il bel giorno	il giorno bello
il bello studente	lo studente bello
la bella giornata	la giornata bella
il bell'amico	l'amico bello
la bell'amica	l'amica bella
i bei giorni	i giorni belli
i begli studenti	gli studenti belli
le belle giornate	le giornate belle
i begli amici	gli amici belli
le belle amiche	le amiche belle

The Verb piacere: Part 1

The verb piacere is a tricky one in Italian because it is translated generally as *to like* but it really means *to be pleasing to*.

Singular	Plural
Mi piace il tavolo.	Mi piacciono i tavoli.
The table is pleasing to me.	*The tables are pleasing to me.*
(I like the table.)	*(I like the tables.)*
Ti piace quella casa?	Ti piacciono quelle case?
Is that house pleasing to you?	*Are those houses pleasing to you?*
(Do you like that house?)	*(Do you like those houses?)*

Ti piace la mia casa?

The chart below summarizes the two most commonly used present indicative forms of **piacere**. In subsequent chapters other forms of this difficult verb are introduced in manageable stages. Note: **piacciono** = (pyAh-choh-noh):

I like	
With Singular Nouns	**With Plural Nouns**
Mi piace la casa.	Mi piacciono le case.
I like the house.	*I like the houses.*
Mi piace il divano.	Mi piacciono le sedie.
I like the sofa.	*I like the chairs.*
You like **(familiar, singular)**	
With Singular Nouns	**With Plural Nouns**
Ti piace la casa?	Ti piacciono le case?
Do you like the house?	*Do you like the houses?*
Ti piace il divano?	Ti piacciono le sedie?
Do you like the sofa?	*Do you like the chairs?*

Descriptive Adjectives

As you already know, adjectives agree in gender (masculine or feminine) and number (singular or plural) with the nouns they modify. Regular descriptive adjectives end in either -o or -e, and they generally follow the noun they modify:

With Masculine Singular Nouns		With Masculine Plural Nouns	
nuovo		nuovi	
il divano nuovo	the new sofa	i divani nuovi	the new sofas
il televisore nuovo	the new TV set	i televisori nuovi	the new TV sets
grande		grandi	
il divano grande	the large sofa	i divani grandi	the large sofas
il televisore grande	the big TV set	i televisori grandi	the big TV sets
With Feminine Singular Nouns		**With Feminine Plural Nouns**	
nuova		nuove	
la sedia nuova	the new chair	le sedie nuove	the new chairs
la stazione nuova	the new station	le stazioni nuove	the new stations
grande		grandi	
la sedia grande	the big chair	le sedie grandi	the big chairs
la stazione grande	the big station	le stazioni grandi	the big stations

Some adjectives can also be put in front of the noun to give emphasis to the meaning.

Before
È una casa nuova. / *It's a new house.*
Ha una casa grande. / *He has a big house.*

After
È una nuova casa. / *It's a <u>new</u> house.*
Ha una grande casa. / *He has a <u>big</u> house.*

ATTIVITÀ

F. First, ask a friend if he or she likes the indicated item, changing the position of the adjective bello to before the noun. Then provide an answer, following the model. If you are using this book in a classroom situation, do this activity with a partner—one of you asks the question, the other answers it.

> *Model:* il nostro frigorifero bello
> —*Ti piace il nostro bel frigorifero?*
> —*Certo che mi piace.*

1. la nostra casa bella

_____

2. le nostre poltrone belle

_____

3. il nostro elettrodomestico bello

_____

4. la nostra amica bella

_____

5. i nostri elettrodomestici belli

_____

6. le nostre amiche belle

_____

7. il nostro zio bello

_____

8. i nostri zii belli

_____

9. il nostro televisore bello

_____

10. i nostri tavoli belli

_____

G. Say that you like the indicated persons or things.

> _Model:_ a spacious house
> _Mi piace una casa spaziosa._

1. those spacious houses

_____

2. his new table

_____

3. her new chairs

_____

4. your _(familiar)_ new armchair

_____

5. their new appliances

_____

6. that spacious bedroom

_____

7. that humble man

_____

8. those humble men

_____

9. that kind woman

_____

10. those kind women

_____

11. her big shoes

_____

12. his big pants

_____

H. Cruciverba!

Horizontal	**Vertical**

Horizontal

3 Tu hai dei … orecchini.
5 Io ho un … zio.
6 La nostra casa ha un salotto …
8 Voi avete dei … zii.
10 Voglio comprare delle sedie …
11 Quei due tavoli sono …
13 Non … piace la tua casa.
14 Sì, è un … divano.
18 Lui è un … uomo.
19 so
20 chair
21 window
23 door
24 sofa
25 Sì, mi … la tua casa.
27 table
28 Mi … molto quel tavolo.
29 especially
30 living room
31 La loro casa ha un salotto …
33 Mi … la Sua mobilia.
34 Ti … la mia cucina?
35 Non mi … quelle scarpe.
36 Ti … questi orecchini?

Vertical

1 refrigerator
2 appliance
3 Tu hai dei … divani.
4 La tua casa ha delle finestre …
5 Mi piacciono i tuoi … pantaloni.
7 Ti piace il … frigorifero?
8 La nostra casa ha due … camere.
9 Abbiamo bisogno di una poltrona …
12 kitchen
13 Abbiamo bisogno di … nuova.
15 furniture
16 now
17 bedroom
22 to like
23 armchair
26 TV set
32 Ti … i miei pantaloni?

NOTA CULTURALE

Una villa

Una palazzina

Italian Housing

Notice that the word casa in Italian means both *house* and *home*. A very large home, usually in the countryside, is called a villa. The word appartamento refers to the actual apartment suite in a building. The word for *apartment building* is edificio, although the word palazzina is used if it is a relatively small building.

I. Use each of the previous words in sentences that will make their meaning clear.

> *Model:* appartamento
> *Mio zio abita (lives) in un appartamento nell'edificio vicino a via Nazionale.*

1. casa

_____

2. palazzina

_____

3. villa

_____

4. appartamento

_____

5. edificio

_____

Review Part 3

1. Excuse me *(polite)*!

_____

2. You are very kind *(polite, singular)*.

_____

3. You are very humble *(familiar, singular)*.

_____

4. They do not speak Italian.

_____

5. The clerk says that she understands and writes English.

_____

6. Your *(familiar, singular)* friends say that they are coming to the party.

_____

7. Your *(plural)* brother knows your friends very well.

_____

8. Alessandro always sleeps till late *(tardi)* on Saturdays.

_____

9. They want to go to Italy.

_____

10. We want to eat meat, but we can't.

_____

B. Comunicazione!

Say that …

1. unfortunately you and your friend do not speak Italian

_____

2. to get to Garibaldi street someone has to go right and then left

_____

3. your friends are at the traffic light

_____

4. you understand, speak, and write Italian very well

_____

5. you have been studying Italian for five years

_____

6. you need some bread, oil, sugar, spaghetti, and meat

_____

7. you want to buy pants, shoes, and earrings

_____

8. you are going shopping downtown tomorrow

_____

9. you would like some sugar

_____

10. you like their new house

_____

11. the house has a large living room and a beautiful kitchen

_____

12. you have a new refrigerator and a beautiful TV set

_____

Tell Sara to...

13. go straight ahead for one block

_____

14. turn right at the traffic light

_____

15. study Italian

_____

16. finish at 5:15

_____

17. buy the earrings

_____

Tell Mrs. Martini to...

18. go straight ahead for one block

_____

19. turn right at the traffic light

_____

20. study English

_____

21. finish at 5:15

_____

Ask …

22. someone if he or she can tell you where the train station is

_____

23. Mr. Martini if he speaks English

_____

24. who speaks Italian really well

_____

25. Mark and Paul if they have a mailing address here in Italy

_____

26. Professoressa Giusti if she can help you find Nazionale Street

_____

27. Alessandro what he wants

_____

28. Sara what you should buy

_____

29. Dina if she liked the new chairs

_____

30. Carla if she liked the spacious living room

_____

C. Domande personali. Answer the questions.

1. Come si chiamano i tuoi cugini?

_____

2. Tu parli altre lingue *(other languages)*?

_____

3. Che cosa vuoi per il tuo compleanno?

_____

4. Chi fa la spesa nella tua famiglia?

_____

5. Che tipo *(type)* di caffè preferisci?

_____

D. Tell a friend to do 10 things *(go downtown, study Italian, etc.)*. List them below.

1. _____

2. _____

3. _____

4. _____

5. _____

6. _____

7. _____

8. _____

9. _____

10. _____

E. There are 20 words hidden in the word search puzzle below: 10 can be read from left to right (horizontally) and 10 in a top-down direction (vertically). Can you find them? The clues given below will help you look for them. The numbers of the clues do not reflect any particular order or arrangement to the hidden words.

V	E	R	A	M	E	N	T	E	X	X	X	D	I	R	E	C	A	D	S
C	A	D	D	A	C	A	A	C	A	D	D	A	C	A	A	X	X	X	A
S	T	U	D	I	O	D	S	E	M	A	F	O	R	O	C	D	X	A	D
C	A	D	D	A	C	A	A	C	A	D	D	A	C	A	A	X	X	X	E
S	T	A	Z	I	O	N	E	S	D	I	R	I	T	T	O	S	S	S	S
V	V	B	N	M	J	K	L	L	C	V	C	A	D	D	A	C	A	A	S
X	M	B	N	M	J	K	L	L	C	P	C	A	D	D	A	C	A	A	O
C	P	B	N	M	J	K	L	L	C	I	C	A	D	D	A	C	A	A	A
S	I	B	N	M	J	K	L	L	C	A	C	A	D	D	A	C	A	A	G
N	A	B	N	M	J	K	L	L	C	C	C	D	F	G	H	J	K	J	R
B	C	P	P	P	X	X	X	S	S	C	B	N	M	K	L	K	L	Y	A
V	E	A	S	D	F	C	A	D	D	I	A	C	C	B	B	B	C	C	N
X	X	X	C	C	C	A	D	D	D	O	A	A	A	I	X	X	X	D	E
L	K	J	H	G	F	P	D	S	A	N	Q	E	R	T	S	Y	U	I	E
Q	W	E	R	T	Y	I	U	I	O	O	P	L	K	J	O	H	G	F	V
P	A	R	L	A	N	S	M	L	C	A	D	C	S	L	G	M	C	D	S
A	V	B	N	Q	C	C	D	D	E	A	A	A	P	B	N	E	A	R	O
G	E	N	T	I	L	E	S	D	R	Q	T	R	E	P	O	J	S	K	N
Q	E	R	T	Y	U	I	U	Y	T	Z	C	V	S	C	A	D	A	A	O
D	E	S	T	R	A	A	A	M	O	G	L	I	E	A	S	D	F	G	H

Horizontal

1 Scusi, Lei … inglese?
2 Lei è molto …
3 Mia … parla italiano molto bene.
4 Subito a … c'è via Nazionale.
5 Lei lo parla … bene!
6 Sono due anni che lo …
7 Scusi, mi sa … dov'è via Carducci?
8 Al … giri a destra.
9 A due passi c'è la …
10 Vada … per due isolati.

Vertical

11 Scusi, signore, Lei … l'italiano?
12 … che lo capisco.
13 Marcello, … io, Lucia.
14 A che ora torni a …?
15 Faccio delle … in centro.
16 Ho … del pane.
17 Mi … molto le camere.
18 Ma non mi … la cucina.
19 Abbiamo una casa … e bella.
20 Basta, per …!

Part 4: Daily Life

Certo!

Unit 16

La settimana scorsa!

CONVERSAZIONE

[Needing some extra money to stay in Perugia a little longer, Dina has decided to take on a part-time job at a software company that hires English-speaking students on a part-time basis. She is talking to one of the employees, il signor Marchi, whom she just met.]

Dina	Quanto tempo è che lavori qui?	How long have you been working here?
Marchi	Due anni, e tu?	Two years, and you?
Dina	Ho cominciato la settimana scorsa.	I began last week.
Marchi	Ti piace lavorare qui?	Do you like working here?
Dina	Sì, mi piace molto. È la prima volta che lavoro per una ditta d'informatica.	Yes, I like it a lot. It's the first time that I work for a computer firm.
Marchi	Conosci Marco Pisani che lavora al secondo piano?	Do you know Marco Pisani who works on the second floor?
Dina	No, ma ho conosciuto alcune persone al terzo, al quarto, al quinto, al sesto e al settimo piano ieri.	No, but I met several people on the third, fourth, fifth, sixth, and seventh floors yesterday.
Marchi	Sei mai andata all'ottavo, al nono e al decimo?	Have you ever been to the eighth, ninth, and tenth floors?
Dina	Sì, ma non conosco ancora nessuno lì. Allora andiamo a prendere un caffè a mezzogiorno?	Yes, but I don't know anyone there yet. So, shall we go and get a coffee at noon?
Marchi	D'accordo! Lo dico anche a Marco e ad altri, va bene?	Yes (I agree)! I'll tell (invite) Marco and others, OK?
Dina	Certo!	Of course!

[Note: In Italy, the ground floor is not the first floor. Il primo piano is the floor above the ground floor. Therefore, it corresponds to the second floor in the U.S. and Canada.]

COMPRENSIONE

A. Vero o falso?

_____ 1. Sono due anni che Marchi lavora in quella ditta d'informatica.

_____ 2. Dina ha cominciato la settimana scorsa.

_____ 3. A Dina piace lavorare in quella ditta.

_____ 4. Dina non conosce Marco Pisani.

_____ 5. Marco Pisani lavora al secondo piano.

_____ 6. Dina ha conosciuto alcune persone solo *(only)* al primo piano.

_____ 7. Dina, Marchi, Pisani e altri vanno a prendere un caffè a mezzogiorno.

VOCABOLARIO

Vuole un caffè, signorina?

PAROLE NUOVE

alcuni / alcune	*some, several (masculine / feminine plural)*
ancora	*yet, still*
che	*that, which, who (relative pronoun)*
cominciare (koh-meehn-chAh-reh)	*to begin, to start*
conoscere	*to know someone, to meet (for the first time)*
ieri	*yesterday*
il caffè	*coffee*
il piano	*floor*
il tempo	*time (in general)*
l'informatica (eehn-fohr-mAh-teeh-kah)	*computer science*
la ditta	*firm, company*
la persona	*person*
la volta	*time (as in: first time, second time, …)*
lavorare	*to work*
mai (mAh-eeh)	*ever*
molto	*a lot*
nessuno	*no one*
prendere (prEhn-deh-reh)	*to get, to take*
quanto (kwAhn-toh)	*how much / many*
scorso	*last (previous)*

ESPRESSIONI E MODI DI DIRE

D'accordo!	*I agree! / OK!*
non…nessuno	*no one*

NUMERI ORDINALI **(ORDINAL NUMBERS)**

primo	*first*
secondo	*second*
terzo (tEhr-tsoh)	*third*
quarto (kwAhr-toh)	*fourth*
quinto (kwEEhn-toh)	*fifth*
sesto	*sixth*
settimo (sEh-tteeh-moh)	*seventh*
ottavo	*eighth*
nono	*ninth*
decimo (dEh-cheeh-moh)	*tenth*

STRUTTURE VERBALI

(io) ho cominciato (koh-meehn-chAh-toh)	*I started, I began*
(io) ho conosciuto (koh-noh-shOOh-toh)	*I met*
(tu) sei andata	*you have gone (familiar, feminine)*

ATTIVITÀ

B. Comunicazione! Say or ask the following things.

Say that …

1. you have been working here for two years

_____

2. you started last month

_____

3. you really like working here

_____

4. it's the first time that you work for a computer firm

_____

5. you met some people on the sixth floor last week

_____

6. you know no one there yet

_____

7. you agree

_____

Ask …

8. Dina how long she has been working here

_____

9. Claudio if he likes to work here

_____

10. Mr. Marchi if he knows Mrs. Di Nardo who works on the tenth floor

_____

11. Dina if she has ever gone to the eighth floor

_____

12. Alessandro and Claudio if they want to get a coffee at noon with you

_____

C. Say the following things.

First, say that you worked on the indicated floors for the suggested period of time.

Ho lavorato…

1. on the first floor for two years

_____

2. on the second floor for several years

_____

3. on the third floor for many years

_____

4. on the fourth floor for six years

_____

5. on the fifth floor for a year

_____

6. on the sixth floor for eight years

_____

7. on the seventh floor for too many years

_____

8. on the eighth floor for seven years

_____

9. on the ninth floor for so many years

_____

10. on the tenth floor for nine years

_____

Now, say that you met the indicated person(s) at the suggested time/period/…

Ho conosciuto…

11. Marco Pisani last week

_____

12. Dina yesterday

_____

13. her brother last month

_____

14. her sister last year

_____

15. that person yesterday

_____

D. Domande personali. Answer the questions.

1. Tu lavori? Se sì, per quale *(which)* ditta?

_____

2. Ti piace lavorare? Perché sì / no?

_____

3. Quanto tempo è che lavori?

_____

E. Descrizione! Write an imaginary description of about 6–7 lines based on the picture you see. If you are using this book in a classroom situation, do this activity with a partner.

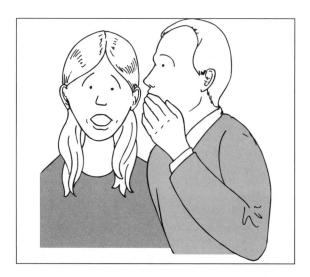

_____

_____

_____

_____

_____

_____

_____

LINGUA

Ordinal Numbers

You have learned the first ten ordinal numbers. The ordinal numbers from 11 on are formed by: (1) dropping the final vowel of the corresponding cardinal number (Unit 5) and (2) adding the ending -esimo:

11th	(undici	+	-esimo)	undicesimo
12th	(dodici	+	-esimo)	dodicesimo
13th	(tredici	+	-esimo)	tredicesimo

The accent mark is removed from cardinal numbers ending in -tré and the vowel is retained:

23rd	(ventitré	+	-esimo)	ventitreesimo
33rd	(trentatré	+	-esimo)	trentatreesimo
43rd	(quarantatré	+	-esimo)	quarantatreesimo

The final vowel is retained, moreover, in the case of cardinal numbers ending in -sei:

36th	(trentasei	+	-esimo)	trentaseiesimo
86th	(ottantasei	+	-esimo)	ottatantaseiesimo
96th	(novantasei	+	-esimo)	novantaseiesimo

Ordinal numbers are adjectives. Hence, they must agree in gender and number with the nouns they modify:

il primo piano	*the first floor*
i primi piani	*the first floors*
la quinta giornata	*the fifth day*
le quinte giornate	*the fifth days*

The Relative Pronoun che

You have encountered the word che in previous units as an interrogative: Che (cosa) è? / *What is it?* It is also a relative pronoun that corresponds to the English *that, which,* or *who*:

Questa è la casa che ho comprato l'anno scorso.
This is the house that I bought last year.
Lui è la persona che lavora per IBM.
He's the person who works for IBM.

Spelling Peculiarities of First Conjugation Verbs

In the case of first conjugation verbs ending in -ciare, pronounced "chAh-reh," or -giare, pronounced "jAh-reh," you write only one -i when attaching the tu (second person singular) or noi (first person plural) endings, which also begin with -i. Below are two verbs fully conjugated for you:

cominciare → cominci- *to begin*	
(io) comincio	*I begin, I am beginning*
(tu) cominci	*you begin, you are beginning (familiar)*
(Lei) comincia	*you begin, you are beginning (polite)*
(lui / lei) comincia	*he / she begins, he / she is beginning*
(noi) cominciamo	*we begin, we are beginning*
(voi) cominciate	*you begin, you are beginning (plural)*
(loro) cominciano (koh-mEEhn-chah-noh)	*they begin, they are beginning*

mangiare → mangi- *to eat*	
(io) mangio	*I eat, I am eating*
(tu) mangi	*you eat, you are eating (familiar)*
(Lei) mangia	*you eat, you are eating (polite)*
(lui / lei) mangia	*he / she eats, he / she is eating*
(noi) mangiamo	*we eat, we are eating*
(voi) mangiate	*you eat, you are eating (plural)*
(loro) mangiano (mAhn-jah-noh)	*they eat, they are eating*

In the case of first conjugation verbs ending in -care, pronounced "kAh-reh," or -gare, pronounced "gAh-reh," you must add an -h before the tu and noi endings, since they begin with an -i. This indicates that the hard c and g sounds are to be retained. Below are two verbs fully conjugated for you:

cercare → cerc- *to search for, to look for*	
(io) cerco	*I search, I am searching*
(tu) cerchi (chEhr-keeh)	*you search, you are searching (familiar)*
(Lei) cerca	*you search, you are searching (polite)*
(lui / lei) cerca	*he / she searches, he / she is searching*
(noi) cerchiamo (cherh-kyAh-moh)	*we search, we are searching*
(voi) cercate	*you search, you are searching (plural)*
(loro) cercano (chEhr-kah-noh)	*they search, they are searching*

pagare → pag- *to pay*	
(io) pago	*I pay, I am paying*
(tu) paghi (pAh-geeh)	*you pay, you are paying (familiar)*
(Lei) paga	*you pay, you are paying (polite)*
(lui / lei) paga	*he / she pays, he / she is paying*
(noi) paghiamo (pah-gyAh-moh)	*we pay, we are paying*
(voi) pagate	*you pay, you are paying (plural)*
(loro) pagano (pAh-gah-noh)	*they pay, they are paying*

The Present Perfect of First Conjugation Verbs

The *present perfect* is a tense that allows you to refer to completed actions in the past: *I have gone, I ate,* and so on. It is a *compound tense*. This means that it is made up of two separate parts: (1) the present indicative of the auxiliary verb avere or essere followed by (2) the past participle of the verb. The present indicative of avere and essere were presented in Unit 9. The past participle ending of first conjugation verbs is -ato:

Infinitive Ending	Past Participle Ending	
-are	-ato	
parlare	parlato	*spoken*
cominciare	cominciato	*begun*
mangiare	mangiato	*eaten*
cercare	cercato	*searched*
pagare	pagato	*paid*

The verb avere is the more commonly used auxiliary verb. Here is the verb cominciare / *to begin* fully conjugated for you:

(io) ho cominciato	*I have begun, I began*
(tu) hai cominciato	*you have begun, you began (familiar)*
(Lei) ha cominciato	*you have begun, you began (polite)*
(lui / lei) ha cominciato	*he / she has begun, he / she began*
(noi) abbiamo cominciato	*we have begun, we began*
(voi) avete cominciato	*you have begun, you began (plural)*
(loro) hanno cominciato	*they have begun, they began*

Some verbs are conjugated with essere rather than avere. From this unit on, such verbs will be identified with an asterisk (andare*) when they are first introduced. The verb andare / *to go* is one such verb. It is conjugated in the present perfect as follows:

(io) sono andato / andata	*I have gone, I went*
(tu) sei andato / andata	*you have gone / you went (familiar)*
(Lei) è andato / andata	*you have gone, you went (polite)*
(lui) è andato	*he has gone, he went*
(lei) è andata	*she has gone, she went*
(noi) siamo andati / andate	*we have gone, we went*
(voi) siete andati / andate	*you have gone, you went (plural)*
(loro) sono andati / andate	*they have gone, they went*

In the case of verbs conjugated with essere the past participle agrees in gender and number with the subject of the sentence. In other words, treat it as you would a descriptive adjective:

Marco è andato in Italia.	*Marco went to Italy.*
Maria è andata in Italia.	*Mary went to Italy.*
Gli uomini sono andati in Italia.	*The men went to Italy.*
Le donne sono andate in Italia.	*The women went to Italy.*

Other -are verbs introduced in previous chapters that are conjugated with essere are:

arrivare	*to arrive*
tornare	*to return*

The following expressions usually require or imply that the present perfect is to be used:

scorso	*last* (as in *last week*)
fa	*ago*
ieri	*yesterday*
già	*already*

Sono arrivati la settimana scorsa.	*They arrived last week.*
È arrivata due minuti fa.	*She arrived a few minutes ago.*
Sono tornati ieri.	*They returned yesterday.*
Io ho già mangiato.	*I have already eaten.*

ATTIVITÀ

F. Comunicazione.

First, say that the indicated person has been working on a certain floor for a suggested period of time.

>*Model:* Dina/ 23rd floor / three weeks
>*Sono tre settimane che Dina lavora al ventitreesimo piano.*

1. Mark / 19th floor / three months

_____

2. Mr. Martini / 18th floor / six weeks

_____

3. Mrs. Di Nardo / 12th floor / one year

_____

4. Alessandro / 15th floor / a long time

_____

5. Sara / 21st floor / several years

_____

Now, simply indicate how to say the following things in Italian. Again, follow the model.

>Model: 16th person
>la sedicesima persona

6. 11th coffee

_____

7. 13th woman

_____

8. 14th man

_____

9. 17th day

_____

10. 36th time (occasion)

_____

11. 48th minute

_____

12. 53rd number

_____

13. 69th day

_____

14. 77th time (occasion)

_____

15. 83rd floor

_____

16. 96th birthday

_____

Finally, say that the indicated persons are doing the suggested things.

> *Model:* Io…
> *Io mangio sempre gli spaghetti.*
> *Io comincio alle sette a lavorare.*
> *Io cerco la sua casa.*
> *Io pago domani.*

Tu…

17. _____ sempre gli spaghetti.

18. _____ alle sette a lavorare.

19. _____ la sua casa.

20. _____ domani.

Lei *(polite)*…

21. _____ sempre gli spaghetti.

22. _____ alle sette a lavorare.

23. _____ la sua casa.

24. _____ domani.

Noi…

25. _____ sempre gli spaghetti.

26. _____ alle sette a lavorare.

27. _____ la sua casa.

28. _____ domani.

Voi...

29. _____ sempre gli spaghetti.

30. _____ alle sette a lavorare.

31. _____ la sua casa.

32. _____ domani.

Lui / Lei

33. _____ sempre gli spaghetti.

34. _____ alle sette a lavorare.

35. _____ la sua casa.

36. _____ domani.

Loro...

37. _____ sempre gli spaghetti.

38. _____ alle sette a lavorare.

39. _____ la sua casa.

40. _____ domani.

G. Make complete sentences with the given words, using the present perfect of the verb.

     Model: Dina...mangiare / già
             Dina ha già mangiato.

Io...

1. parlare / già / al professore

_____

2. mangiare / già / gli spaghetti

_____

3. andare / già / in Italia

_____

4. tornare / già / a casa

_____

5. arrivare / alle sei e mezzo

_____

6. pagare / già / tutto

_____

7. non / trovare / la sua casa

_____

Tu...

8. parlare / al professore / la settimana scorsa

_____

9. mangiare / gli spaghetti / ieri

_____

10. andare / in Italia / l'anno scorso

_____

11. tornare / a casa / alcuni minuti fa

_____

12. arrivare / due minuti fa

_____

13. pagare / ieri

_____

14. non / trovare / la sua casa

_____

Lui / Lei...

15. parlare / al professore / ieri

_____

16. mangiare / gli spaghetti / ieri

_____

17. andare / in Italia / tre anni fa

_____

18. tornare / a casa / alcuni minuti fa

_____

19. arrivare / già

_____

20. pagare / ieri / tutto

_____

21. non / trovare / la sua casa

_____

Noi...

22. parlare / già / alla professoressa

_____

23. mangiare / già / gli spaghetti

_____

24. andare / in Italia / l'anno scorso

_____

25. tornare / a casa / un'ora fa

_____

26. arrivare / ieri

_____

27. pagare / già / tutto

_____

28. non / trovare / la sua casa

_____

Voi...

29. parlare / alla professoressa / ieri

_____

30. mangiare / già / gli spaghetti

_____

31. andare / già / in Italia

_____

32. tornare / a casa / due minuti fa

_____

33. arrivare / alcuni giorni fa

_____

34. pagare / già / tutto

_____

35. non / trovare / la sua casa

_____

Loro...

36. parlare / già / alla signora Martini

_____

37. mangiare / già / la carne

_____

38. andare / in Italia / ieri

_____

39. tornare / già / a casa

_____

40. arrivare / alcuni minuti fa

_____

41. pagare / già / tutto

_____

42. non / trovare / la sua casa

_____

H. Cruciverba!

Horizontal

5   Io *(male)* sono … in Italia l'anno scorso.
7   Le mie amiche sono … l'anno scorso.
11 Anche noi siamo … in Italia l'anno scorso.
12 La signora Martini è … l'anno scorso.
13 Lui lavora al … piano.
15 Anche voi avete … con Marco, vero?
16 le *eighth* persone
18 le dodici
19 la *third* volta
21 Non ho mai lavorato al *second* piano.
24 Non sono mai andato al *seventh* piano.
26 Mi piace … lavorare per questa ditta.
28 OK, I agree!
33 Questa è la terza … che lavoro per questa ditta.
34 Allora, … un caffè con me a mezzogiorno?
35 Prendiamo un … a mezzogiorno, va bene?
36 Chi è quella …?
37 Non conosco … nessuno al terzo piano.
38 Loro hanno cominciato a lavorare il mese …

Vertical

1   Mia sorella è … in Italia l'anno scorso.
2   Io lavoro al *first* piano.
3   Anch'io ho … tutto!
4   le ventiquattro
6   A che ora sei *(male)* … a casa?
7   I miei parenti sono … l'anno scorso.
8   Le tue amiche sono … in Italia, vero?
9   Quando hai … a lavorare per quella ditta?
10 Loro hanno … tutto!
14 le *fourth* settimane
17 Non conosco … nessuno al dodicesimo piano.
20 Sei mai andato al *fifth* piano?
21 Chi lavora al … piano?
22 Anche lei lavora al *tenth* piano?
23 È la prima volta … lavoro per questa ditta.
25 Tu sei … andato al quindicesimo piano?
27 Anche noi abbiamo … per quella ditta due anni fa.
29 Ho conosciuto … persone al ventiseiesimo piano.
30 Allora, … tempo è che lavori qui?
31 Non è molto … che lavoro qui.
32 Questa è una … d'informatica.
34 Non sono mai andato al sedicesimo …

NOTA CULTURALE

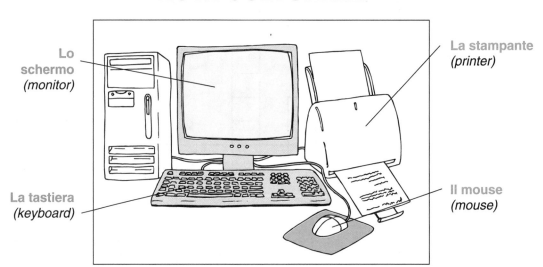

Lo schermo *(monitor)*

La stampante *(printer)*

La tastiera *(keyboard)*

Il mouse *(mouse)*

Computer Terms in Italian

In the Italian workplace today, computers dominate, as elsewhere. Many English terms have not been translated but are used as they are. Here are the most common ones:

il computer	*computer*
il software	*software*
l'hardware	*hardware*
il CD-ROM	*CD-ROM*

I. Say that you bought the following things as indicated.

       Model: computer / last week
              Ho comprato un computer la settimana scorsa.

1. software for your computer / last week

_____

2. a monitor and a keyboard for your computer / last month

_____

3. a printer for your computer / last year

_____

4. a CD-ROM and a DVD / last week

_____

Ha mai lavorato in un ufficio?

Unit 17

Cosa faceva?

CONVERSAZIONE

[At her part-time job yesterday, Dina was walking toward her desk when, passing by the interview office for new employees, she overheard a conversation between an employee and a man who was being interviewed for a job. As always, she couldn't help but listen in.]

Uomo	**Vorrei lavorare per questa ditta.**	*I would like to work for this company.*
Impiegato	**Ha mai lavorato in un ufficio?**	*Have you ever worked in an office?*
Uomo	**Sì, per una banca quattro anni fa. Ma la banca era troppo lontana da casa mia.**	*Yes, for a bank four years ago. But the bank was too far from my house.*
Impiegato	**Che cosa faceva nella banca?**	*What did you do in the bank?*
Uomo	**Ero un impiegato.**	*I was a clerk.*
Impiegato	**Qual è il Suo indirizzo?**	*What's your address?*
Uomo	**Abito in via del Corso, numero quindici.**	*I live on 15 Corso Street.*
Impiegato	**Quanti anni ha?**	*How old are you?*
Uomo	**Ho ventotto anni.**	*I'm twenty-eight years old.*
Impiegato	**Qual è il Suo stato civile?**	*What's your marital status?*
Uomo	**Sono sposato, ma non ho figli.**	*I'm married, but I do not have children.*
Impiegato	**Va bene così. Per adesso, ho finito. La chiamo tra una settimana.**	*OK. For now, I'm finished. I'll call you in a week.*

COMPRENSIONE

A. Which response, a or b, is the correct or appropriate one?

1. L'uomo vuole lavorare…
   a. per una banca.
   b. per la ditta d'informatica dove lavora anche Dina.

2. La banca dove lavorava l'uomo era…
   a. vicino a casa sua.
   b. lontana da casa sua.

3. L'uomo ha lavorato per una banca…
   a. due anni fa.
   b. quattro anni fa.

4. Nella banca lui faceva…
   a. tutto.
   b. l'impiegato.

5. L'uomo abita…
   a. in via del Corso, numero quindici.
   b. in via del Corso, numero ventuno.

6. L'uomo ha…
   a. ventotto anni.
   b. quaranta anni.

7. L'uomo è sposato…
   a. e ha due figli.
   b. ma non ha figli.

8. L'impiegato chiama l'uomo tra…
   a. un mese.
   b. una settimana.

VOCABOLARIO

PAROLE NUOVE

abitare	*to live, to dwell*
la banca	*bank*
chiamare	*to call*
così	*so, like this*
fa	*ago*
finire (isc)	*to finish*
l'impiegato / l'impiegata	*employee, clerk (male / female)*
lontano	*far*
quale (kwAh-leh)	*which, what*
sposato / sposata	*married (male / female)*
l'ufficio (ooh-fEEh-choh)	*office*

ESPRESSIONI E MODI DI DIRE

avere…anni	*to be…years old*
Ho ventotto anni.	*I'm twenty-eight years old.*
Quanti anni ha?	*How old are you (polite)?*
lo stato civile	*marital status*

PREPOSIZIONE ARTICOLATA

nella = (in + la): nella banca	*in the bank*

STRUTTURE VERBALI

(io) ero	*I was*
era	*it was*
(Lei) faceva	*you used to do (polite)*
(io) ho finito	*I have finished*

Quanti anni   Troppi!
hai, nonno?

ATTIVITÀ

B. Comunicazione!

Say that …

1. you would like to work for this company

_____

2. you worked for a bank two years ago

_____

3. the bank was too far from your house

_____

4. you were an employee of that bank

_____

5. you live on 72 Boccaccio Street

_____

6. you are twenty-two years old

_____

7. Claudio is married with three children

_____

8. for now you are finished

_____

Tell...

9. Mrs. Di Nardo that you will call her in a few weeks.

_____

Ask ...

10. Dina if she has ever worked in another office

_____

11. Mr. Marchi what he used to do in the bank

_____

12. Mrs. Di Nardo what her address is

_____

13. Miss Nardini how old she is

_____

14. Mr. Marchi what his marital status is

_____

C. You are interviewing someone for a job at your company.

Ask him or her...

1. where he or she lives

_____

2. what his or her address is

_____

3. if he or she ever worked for another company

_____

4. what he or she used to do in the bank

_____

5. what his or her marital status is

_____

D. Domande personali. Answer the questions.

1. Qual è il tuo indirizzo?

_____

2. Quanti anni hai?

_____

3. Qual è il tuo stato civile?

_____

E. Descrizione! Write an imaginary description of about 6–7 lines based on the picture you see. If you are using this book in a classroom situation, do this activity with a partner.

_____

_____

_____

_____

_____

_____

_____

_____

_____

LINGUA

The Present Perfect of Second and Third Conjugation Verbs

As discussed in the previous unit, the *present perfect* is made up of two separate parts: (1) the present indicative of the auxiliary verb, and (2) the past participle of the verb. The past participles of regular second conjugation (-ere) and third conjugation (-ire) verbs are -uto and -ito respectively:

Infinitive Ending	Past Participle Ending	
-ere	-uto	
piovere	piovuto	*rained*
potere	potuto	*was able*
conoscere	conosciuto	*known, met*

Infinitive Ending	Past Participle Ending	
-ire	-ito	
partire	partito	*left*
capire	capito	*understood*
finire	finito	*finished*

The verbs conoscere / *to know* and finire / *to finish* are conjugated with avere. These are fully conjugated for you below:

(io) ho conosciuto	*I have known / met, I knew / met*
(tu) hai conosciuto	*you have known / met, you knew / met (familiar)*
(Lei) ha conosciuto	*you have known / met, you knew / met (polite)*
(lui / lei) ha conosciuto	*he / she has known / met, he / she knew / met*
(noi) abbiamo conosciuto	*we have known / met, we knew / met*
(voi) avete conosciuto	*you have known / met, you knew / met (plural)*
(loro) hanno conosciuto	*they have known / met, they knew / met*

(io) ho finito	*I have finished, I finished*
(tu) hai finito	*you have finished, you finished (familiar)*
(Lei) ha finito	*you have finished, you finished (polite)*
(lui / lei) ha finito	*he / she has finished, he / she finished*
(noi) abbiamo finito	*we have finished, we finished*
(voi) avete finito	*you have finished, you finished (plural)*
(loro) hanno finito	*they have finished, they finished*

Non ho ancora finito!

The verb partire / *to leave* is conjugated instead with essere:

(io) sono partito / a	*I have left, I left*
(tu) sei partito / a	*you have left, you left (familiar)*
(Lei) è partito / a	*you have left, you left (polite)*
(lui) è partito	*he has left, he left*
(lei) è partita	*she has left, she left*
(noi) siamo partiti / e	*we have left, we left*
(voi) siete partiti / e	*you have left, you left (plural)*
(loro) sono partiti / e	*they have left, they left*

Other second and third conjugation verbs introduced so far that are conjugated with essere are:

essere	*to be*
piacere	*to like*
venire	*to come*

The verbs piovere / *to rain* and nevicare / *to snow* can be conjugated with either avere or essere:

Ha piovuto / È piovuto ieri	*It rained yesterday*
Ha nevicato / È nevicato ieri	*It snowed yesterday*

Verbs with Irregular Past Participles

Of the verbs introduced so far, the following have irregular past participles (Note: verbs conjugated with essere are identified with an asterisk):

Verb	Irregular Past Participle	
dare	dato	*given*
decidere	deciso	*decided*
dire	detto	*told, said*
essere*	stato	*been*
fare	fatto	*did, made*
perdere	perso	*lost*
prendere	preso	*taken, had*
scrivere	scritto	*written*
vedere	visto (also: veduto)	*seen*
venire*	venuto	*come*

The verb vedere / *to see* has both regular and irregular forms. These are used alternatively:

vedere	veduto	*or*	visto	*seen*

The Imperfect of essere and fare

In the conversation above, the verbs essere and fare were used in the *imperfect* tense. This is a verb tense that allows you to refer to unfinished or repeating actions in the past: *I used to be, I was, I used to do*, etc.

The imperfect of these two verbs is irregular:

essere	*to be*
(io) ero	*I was, I used to be*
(tu) eri	*you were, you used to be (familiar)*
(Lei) era	*you were, you used to be (polite)*
(lui / lei) era	*he / she was, he / she used to be*
(noi) eravamo	*we were, we used to be*
(voi) eravate	*you were, you used to be (plural)*
(loro) erano (Eh-rah-noh)	*they were, they used to be*

Ah, quando ero bambino ... !

fare	*to do, to make*
(io) facevo	*I was doing, I used to do*
(tu) facevi	*you were doing, you used to do (familiar)*
(Lei) faceva	*you were doing, you used to do (polite)*
(lui / lei) faceva	*he / she was doing, he / she used to do*
(noi) facevamo	*we were doing, we used to do*
(voi) facevate	*you were doing, you used to do (plural)*
(loro) facevano (fah-chEh-vah-noh)	*they were doing, they used to do*

ATTIVITÀ

F. Make complete sentences with the given words, using the present perfect of the verb.

> *Model:* Dina...volere /mangiare / tutti gli spaghetti
> *Dina ha voluto mangiare tutti gli spaghetti.*

Io...

1. volere / mangiare / tutti gli spaghetti

_____

2. dormire / tutta la giornata ieri

_____

3. conoscere / la professoressa / alcune settimane fa

_____

4. finire / già / di studiare

_____

5. partire / per l'Italia / ieri

_____

Tu...

6. volere / mangiare / tutti gli spaghetti

_____

7. dormire / tutta la giornata ieri

_____

8. conoscere / la professoressa / alcune settimane fa

_____

9. finire / già / di studiare

_____

10. partire / per l'Italia / ieri

_____

Lui / Lei

11. volere / mangiare / tutti gli spaghetti

_____

12. dormire / tutta la giornata ieri

_____

13. conoscere / la professoressa / alcune settimane fa

_____

14. finire / già / di studiare

_____

15. partire / per l'Italia / ieri

_____

Noi…

16. volere / mangiare / tutti gli spaghetti

_____

17. dormire / tutta la giornata ieri

_____

18. conoscere / la professoressa / alcune settimane fa

_____

19. finire / già / di studiare

_____

20. partire / per l'Italia / ieri

_____

Voi…

21. volere / mangiare / tutti gli spaghetti

_____

22. dormire / tutta la giornata ieri

_____

23. conoscere / la professoressa / alcune settimane fa

_____

24. finire / già / di studiare

_____

25. partire / per l'Italia / ieri

_____

Loro…

26. volere / mangiare / tutti gli spaghetti

_____

27. dormire / tutta la giornata ieri

_____

28. conoscere / la professoressa / alcune settimane fa

_____

29. finire / già / di studiare

_____

30. partire / per l'Italia / ieri

_____

G. Polite and Informal. Give the corresponding polite form of each question. Follow the model.

> _Model:_ (Tu) Quando sei venuto, tu?
> (Lei) _Quando è venuto, Lei?_
>
> (Voi) Quando siete venuti, voi?
> (Loro) _Quando sono venuti, Loro_

Tu / Lei...

1. Che cosa hai dato alla professoressa?

_____

2. Che cosa hai deciso di fare ieri?

_____

3. Che cosa hai detto ieri?

_____

4. Dove sei stata ieri?

_____

5. Che cosa hai fatto la settimana scorsa?

_____

6. Che cosa hai perso ieri?

_____

7. Che cosa hai preso?

_____

8. A chi hai scritto ieri?

_____

9. Chi hai visto ieri?

_____

10. A che ora sei venuto ieri?

_____

Voi / Loro...

11. Che cosa avete dato alla professoressa?

_____

12. Che cosa avete deciso di fare ieri?

_____

13. Che cosa avete detto ieri?

_____

14. Dove siete state ieri?

_____

15. Che cosa avete fatto la settimana scorsa?

_____

16. Che cosa avete perso ieri?

_____

17. Che cosa avete preso?

_____

18. A chi avete scritto ieri?

_____

19. Chi avete visto ieri?

_____

20. A che ora siete venuti ieri?

_____

H. Comunicazione. Say that each person was tired yesterday because he or she was doing too much. Follow the model.

     Model: Dina
     Dina era stanca ieri perché faceva troppo.

NOTE	
Singular	Plural
stanco	stanchi
Il ragazzo è stanco.	I ragazzi sono stanchi.
stanca	stanche
La ragazza è stanca.	Le ragazze sono stanche.

1. Io

_____

2. Tu

_____

3. Alessandro

_____

4. Sara

_____

5. Noi

_____

6. Voi

_____

7. I bambini

_____

I. Cruciverba!

Horizontal

1 they were doing
3 Mio fratello La … tra un giorno o due.
4 you were *(familiar)*
9 I was
10 we used to do
11 Lui non è mai … in Italia.
14 Loro non hanno … nessuno lì.
15 Chi … quell'uomo che ti ha chiamato ieri?
16 Non ho ancora … di lavorare.
20 Voi non avete mai … ai parenti, vero?
22 you used to do *(plural)*
26 La … era troppo lontana da casa mia.
27 Signor Martini, ha già … di lavorare?
28 Ho già … delle spese in centro.
30 Qual è il Suo stato …?
31 Ero un … in quella banca.
32 married

Vertical

1 I was making
2 Anche tu, Mark, sei … alla festa?
3 Va bene …
4 you were *(plural)*
5 Sì, … solo venticinque anni.
6 Che cosa ha … Maria?
7 Quanti anni … Lei?
8 Dina, hai … la testa?
10 Anche voi avete … di lavorare?
12 they were
13 office
17 we were
18 Abbiamo *taken*
19 E tu cosa … nella banca?
21 Quando sono … i tuoi genitori?
22 Cosa … tuo fratello in quella banca?
23 Le mie amiche sono già … per l'Italia.
24 Lui abita troppo … da casa mia.
25 Allora, … indirizzo è il Suo?
28 Loro sono arrivati venti minuti …
29 Quando hai … di lavorare?

NOTA CULTURALE

Italy and Banking

Modern banking began to develop during the 1200s in Italy. The word "bank" comes from the Italian word **banco**, meaning *bench*. Early Italian bankers conducted their business on benches in the street. Large banking firms were established in Florence, Rome, Venice, and other Italian cities, and banking activities slowly spread throughout Europe. By the 1600s, London bankers had developed many of the features of modern banking. They paid interest to attract deposits and loaned out a portion of their deposits to earn interest themselves. By the same date, individuals and businesses in England began to make payments with written drafts on their bank balances, similar to modern checks.

J. Find the names of various current Italian banks: la Banca Nazionale del Lavoro is an example. Look these up in a reference source or on the Internet. If you are using this book in a classroom situation, do this activity with a partner.

_____

_____

_____

_____

_____

_____

_____

_____

_____

Deve studiare di più, va bene?

Unit 18

Non ho capito!

CONVERSAZIONE

[At the *Università per Stranieri*, we find Mark Cardelli speaking to one of his instructors after class.]

Mark	Scusi, professore, ma non ho capito la lezione. Cosa devo fare?	*Excuse me, Professor, but I didn't understand the lesson. What should I do?*
Professore	Lei deve studiare di più. Legga anche questo libro.	*You must study more. Read this book as well.*
Mark	Altro?	*Anything else?*
Professore	Sì, scriva le domande che ha sulla grammatica che abbiamo studiato oggi e le consegni domani dopo la lezione.	*Yes, write the questions you have on the grammar we studied today and hand them in tomorrow after class.*
Mark	Va bene!	*OK!*
Professore	La lezione di oggi era difficile, ma molto importante.	*Today's class was hard, but very important.*
Mark	Sono d'accordo!	*I agree!*

COMPRENSIONE

A. Complete each statement or question in an appropriate fashion with the missing word or expression.

1. Scusi, professore, ma non _____ la lezione.

2. _____ anche questo libro.

3. Lei _____ studiare di più.

4. Scriva le domande che ha sulla grammatica che _____ oggi.

5. Le _____ domani dopo la lezione.

6. La lezione di oggi _____ difficile, ma molto importante.

7. Cosa _____ fare?

8. _____ d'accordo!

VOCABOLARIO

La grammatica è molto difficile!

PAROLE NUOVE

consegnare	*to hand in*
difficile (deeh-fEEh-cheeh-leh)	*difficult*
la domanda	*question*
dovere	*to have to*
la grammatica (grah-mmAh-teeh-kah)	*grammar*
importante	*important*
leggere (lEh-jjeh-reh)	*to read*
la lezione (leh-tsyOh-neh)	*lesson, class*
il libro	*book*
su	*on*
il tema	*composition (written)*

ESPRESSIONI E MODI DI DIRE

di più (pyOOh)	*more*
Sono d'accordo!	*I agree!*

STRUTTURE VERBALI

(io) devo	*I must*
(Lei) deve	*you must (polite)*

IRREGOLARITÀ

[Starting with this unit, irregular forms will be indicated in this section.]

- The noun il tema is masculine, even though it ends in -a, and its plural form is i temi *(compositions)*
- The past participle of leggere is letto *(read)*

ATTIVITÀ

B. Comunicazione!

Tell …

1. your professor / teacher that you did not understand the lesson

_____

2. Mr. Marchi to read this book too

_____

3. Mrs. Di Nardo to write the questions she has on the grammar that she studied today

_____

4. Mrs. Di Nardo to hand them in tomorrow after class

_____

Say that…

5. today's lesson was difficult

_____

6. today's lesson was very important

_____

7. you agree

_____

Ask your professor /teacher …

8. what you should do

_____

9. what you should read

_____

C. Say that you did the following things yesterday.

> _Model:_ bought a book
> _Ieri ho comprato un libro._

1. handed in your compositions

_____

2. read a book

_____

3. ate some meat

_____

4. studied the lesson

_____

5. read a book of grammar

_____

D. Domande personali. Answer the questions.

1. È difficile per te la grammatica italiana?

_____

2. Ti piace studiare la lingua italiana? Perché sì / no?

_____

3. Quali sono le domande che tu hai sulla grammatica italiana?

_____

E. Descrizione! Write an imaginary description of about 6–7 lines based on the picture you see. If you are using this book in a classroom situation, do this activity with a partner.

_____

_____

_____

_____

_____

_____

_____

LINGUA

Il professor Marchi

Titles: Part 2

The title **professore / professoressa** applies to both high school and university instructors. The title **dottore / dottoressa** applies not only to medical doctors, but also to anyone with a university degree. As mentioned in Unit 2, the final **-e** of masculine titles is dropped before a name:

Masculine		Feminine	
il professor Marchi	*Prof. Marchi*	la professoressa Dini	*Prof. Dini*
il dottor Brunetti	*Dr. Brunetti*	la dottoressa Mirri	*Dr. Mirri*

The definite article is used with titles, but it is dropped when talking to the person directly:

Talking about...	Talking to...
Il professor Marchi è italiano	"Buongiorno, professor Marchi"
Professor Marchi is Italian	*"Hello, Professor Marchi"*
La dottoressa Dini è italiana	"Buonasera, dottoressa Dini"
Dr. Dini is Italian	*"Good afternoon, Dr. Dini"*

Contractions: A Summary

The following chart summarizes the main prepositional contractions, many of which you have already encountered and used:

+	il	i	lo	l'	gli	la	le
a	al	ai	allo	all'	agli	alla	alle
da	dal	dai	dallo	dall'	dagli	dalla	dalle
di	del	dei	dello	dell'	degli	della	delle
in	nel	nei	nello	nell'	negli	nella	nelle
su	sul	sui	sullo	sull'	sugli	sulla	sulle

The Imperfect of First Conjugation Verbs

As mentioned in the previous unit, the imperfect tense allows you to indicate that a past action was incomplete, repetitive, or continuous: *I used to eat, I was watching,* and so on. It also allows you describe certain features in the past: *She used to have blond hair, I was skinny as a child,* and so on.

The following expressions usually indicate or imply that the verb is to be used in the imperfect:

spesso	*often*
di solito	*usually*
generalmente	*generally*
mentre	*while*
da bambino / da bambina	*as a child*
da giovane	*as a young person*

Loro spesso facevano la spesa in centro	*They often shopped downtown*
Noi di solito andavamo in Italia d'estate	*We usually went to Italy in the summer*

The imperfect of first conjugation (-are) verbs is formed by dropping the -are and adding the following endings to the resulting stem:

Singular	
1st person	-avo
2nd person	-avi
3rd person	-ava

Plural	
1st person	-avamo
2nd person	-avate
3rd person	-avano

Below is the verb parlare / *to speak* fully conjugated for you:

parlare → parl- *to speak*	
(io) parlavo	*I was speaking, I used to speak*
(tu) parlavi	*you were speaking, you used to speak (familiar)*
(Lei) parlava	*you were speaking, you used to speak (polite)*
(lui / lei) parlava	*he / she was speaking, he / she used to speak*
(noi) parlavamo	*we were speaking, we used to speak*
(voi) parlavate	*you were speaking, you used to speak (plural)*
(loro) parlavano (pahr-lAh-vah-noh)	*they were speaking, they used to speak*

The Verb dovere

The verb dovere / *to have to* is the last of the modal verbs. You have already learned to use volere / *to want,* and potere / *to be able to* (see Units 13 and 14). It also has irregular forms in the present indicative:

(io) devo	*I have to, I must*
(tu) devi	*you have to, you must (familiar)*
(Lei) deve	*you have to, you must (polite)*
(lui / lei) deve	*he / she has to, he / she must*
(noi) dobbiamo	*we have to, we must*
(voi) dovete	*you have to, you must (plural)*
(loro) devono (dEh-voh-noh)	*they have to, they must*

In the present perfect the auxiliary used with modal verbs depends on the verb that they accompany. If the verb is conjugated with avere, then the whole modal construction is conjugated with avere; likewise, if the verb is conjugated with essere, then the whole modal construction is conjugated with essere:

With avere

Dina ha potuto lavorare per due settimane	*Dina was able to work for two weeks*
Dina ha voluto lavorare per due settimane	*Dina wanted to work for two weeks*
Dina ha dovuto lavorare per due settimane	*Dina had to work for two weeks*

With essere

Dina è potuta andare in Italia	*Dina was able to go to Italy*
Dina è voluta andare in Italia	*Dina wanted to go to Italy*
Dina è dovuta andare in Italia	*Dina had to go to Italy*

In colloquial Italian, however, only avere tends to be used:

Dina è voluta andare in Italia   =   Dina ha voluto andare in Italia

ATTIVITÀ

F. Comunicazione. First, say that the indicated person went downtown yesterday. Then ask him or her if it is true. If you are using this book in a classroom situation, do this activity with a partner. Follow the model.

> *Model:* Prof. Giusti (a male)
> —*Il professor Giusti è andato in centro ieri.*
> —*Professor Giusti, è vero che Lei è andato in centro ieri?*

1. Prof. Mirri (a female)

_____

2. Dr. Nardini (a male)

_____

3. Mr. Gardini

_____

4. Mrs. Gardini

_____

5. Dr. Giusti (a female)

_____

G. Come si dice in italiano?

> _Model:_ on the tenth floor
> _sul decimo piano_

1. mother of the boy

_____

2. mother of the girl

_____

3. shoes of the uncle

_____

4. shoes of the friend (female)

_____

5. mother of the boys

_____

6. mother of the girls

_____

7. from downtown

_____

8. from the tables

_____

9. from the uncle

_____

10. from the uncles

_____

11. from the girl

_____

12. from the friends (female)

_____

13. at the traffic light

_____

14. to the instructors (male)

_____

15. to the uncle

_____

16. to the uncles

_____

17. to the boys

_____

18. to the girl

_____

19. to the girls

_____

20. in the bus

_____

21. in the bank

_____

22. in the banks

_____

23. in the train

_____

24. in the spaghetti

_____

25. on the spaghetti

_____

26. on the meat

_____

27. on the bread

_____

28. on the tables

_____

H. Make complete sentences with the given words, using the imperfect of the verb.

> _Model:_ Dina...abitare / in centro / da bambina
> _Dina abitava in centro da bambina._

Io...

1. abitare / in centro / da bambino / da bambina

_____

2. arrivare / spesso / in ritardo _(late)_ / mentre il professore faceva lezione _(was teaching)_

_____

3. mangiare / spesso / gli spaghetti / da giovane

_____

4. pagare / tutto / da giovane

_____

Tu...

5. abitare / in centro / da bambino / da bambina

_____

6. arrivare / spesso / in ritardo *(late)* / mentre il professore faceva lezione

_____

7. mangiare / spesso / gli spaghetti / da giovane

_____

8. pagare / tutto / da giovane

_____

Lui / Lei...

9. abitare / in centro / da bambino / da bambina

_____

10. arrivare / spesso / in ritardo *(late)* / mentre il professore faceva lezione

_____

11. mangiare / spesso / gli spaghetti / da giovane

_____

12. pagare / tutto / da giovane

_____

Noi...

13. abitare / in centro / da bambini / da bambine

_____

14. arrivare / spesso / in ritardo *(late)* / mentre il professore faceva lezione

_____

15. mangiare / spesso / gli spaghetti / da giovani

_____

16. pagare / tutto / da giovani

_____

Voi...

17. abitare / in centro / da bambini / da bambine

_____

18. arrivare / spesso / in ritardo *(late)* / mentre il professore faceva lezione

_____

19. mangiare / spesso / gli spaghetti / da giovani

_____

20. pagare / tutto / da giovani

_____

Loro...

21. abitare / in centro / da bambini / da bambine

_____

22. arrivare / spesso / in ritardo *(late)* / mentre il professore faceva lezione

_____

23. mangiare / spesso / gli spaghetti / da giovani

_____

24. pagare / tutto / da giovani

_____

I. First, make up three modal constructions for each given verb in the present indicative. Also, translate each one into English.

> *Model:* Io / andare
> *Io devo andare (I have to go)*
> *Io posso andare (I can go)*
> *Io voglio andare (I want to go)*

1. Io / partire

_____

_____

_____

2. Tu / mangiare

_____

_____

_____

3. Dina / parlare italiano

_____

_____

_____

4. Noi / comprare gli orecchini

_____

_____

_____

5. Voi / lavorare

_____

_____

_____

6. I ragazzi / venire alla festa

_____

_____

_____

Now, give the present perfect of the above constructions. Again, translate them into English.

> _Model:_ Io / andare
> _Io sono dovuto / dovuta andare (I had to go)_
> _Io sono potuto / potuta andare (I was able to go)_
> _Io sono voluto / voluta andare (I wanted to go)_

7. Io / partire

_____

_____

_____

8. Tu / mangiare

_____

_____

_____

9. Dina / parlare italiano

_____

_____

_____

10. Noi / comprare gli orecchini

_____

_____

_____

11. Voi / lavorare

_____

_____

_____

12. I ragazzi / venire alla festa

_____

_____

_____

J. Cruciverba!

Horizontal	Vertical

Horizontal

3 Lei deve studiare di …

5 Lui è il … Marchi.

8 Consegni il Suo tema … la lezione, va bene?

10 Anche tu … studiare di più.

11 Lo consegni domani dopo la …

13 … mesi di estate vado sempre in Italia.

14 Il professore non ha ancora finito la …

15 Hai parlato … ragazzi?

16 Avete letto quei …?

19 Le presento la … Rossi.

22 Ho scritto già … zii.

23 you used to study *(familiar)*

24 Ho scritto un tema … miei fratelli.

25 Loro … molto quando erano bambini.

27 you used to study *(plural)*

32 Anche voi … studiare di più.

33 Siamo … salotto.

35 Sono tornato … amici.

36 Faccio delle spese due volte … settimana.

Vertical

1 Dr. *(male)*

2 Le presento il … Rossi.

4 Ho già … il tema due giorni fa.

6 Scriva un … sulla grammatica!

7 Non ho mai capito la … italiana.

8 Io … studiare di più.

9 Io dormo sempre … divano.

12 Non ho mai … quel libro.

14 Alessandro, hai mai letto quel …?

17 the plural of *tema* …

18 Anche loro … studiare di più.

20 Io … molto quando ero bambina.

21 Anche lui … molto quando era bambino.

26 Lui … studiare di più.

28 Noi … studiare di più.

29 Hai parlato … mie amiche, vero?

30 Hai parlato … uomo?

31 Oggi è il primo giorno … settimana.

32 Sono tornato … zio.

34 Anche lui ha dormito … divano.

NOTA CULTURALE

La professoressa insegna la grammatica

Italian Grammar

As you may have noticed, there are a few general features about Italian grammar. First, there is the fact that most of its nouns end in a vowel. This makes it easy to construct poetry with rhyme. The most difficult things to master about the grammar for a student such as yourself are: the verbal conjugations, the articles, and the object pronouns.

Here are a few grammatical terms in Italian:

il nome	noun
l'aggettivo	adjective
il verbo	verb
l'avverbio	adverb
la preposizione	preposition
l'articolo	article

K. Identify each word grammatically (if it is a noun, verb, etc.).

1. un

_____

2. di

_____

3. generalmente

_____

4. parlare

_____

5. casa

_____

6. bello

_____

Desidera?

Unit 19

Desidera?

CONVERSAZIONE

[Dina is browsing around in the clothing section of a department store. She overhears a man talking to a sales clerk wanting to buy clothes for himself. As always, she listens in on the conversation so that she can learn from it.]

Commesso	Desidera, signore?	*May I help you, sir?*
Cliente	Vorrei comprare una giacca, una camicia, una cravatta e forse anche un paio di pantaloni.	*I would like to buy a jacket, a shirt, a tie, and maybe also a pair of pants.*
Commesso	Che taglie porta?	*What sizes do you wear?*
Cliente	Non sono sicuro.	*I'm not sure.*
Commesso	Quali colori preferisce?	*Which colors do you prefer?*
Cliente	Mi piace l'azzurro, il rosso, il verde, il nero e anche il bianco.	*I like blue, red, green, black, and even white.*
Commesso	Allora, va bene una giacca nera, una camicia bianca, una cravatta rossa, e i pantaloni verdi?	*OK, then, how about a black jacket, a white shirt, a red tie, and green pants?*
Cliente	Lei scherza, vero?	*You're joking, aren't you?*
Commesso	Sì.	*Yes.*

[In another part of the clothing section Dina overhears a female customer talking to another salesclerk.]

Commessa	Desidera, signora?	*May I help you, madam?*
Cliente	Ci devo pensare!	*I have to think about it!*
Commessa	Oggi tutto è in saldo!	*Today everything is on sale!*
Cliente	Vorrei comprare una gonna, una camicetta e un vestito da sera	*I would like to buy a skirt, a blouse, and an evening dress.*
Commessa	Quali colori preferisce?	*Which colors do you prefer?*
Cliente	I colori che generalmente mi piacciono sono l'arancione, il marrone, il giallo, il grigio, il rosa e il viola.	*The colors that I generally like are orange, brown, yellow, gray, pink, and purple.*
Commessa	Che taglie porta?	*What sizes do you wear?*
Cliente	Non sono sicura.	*I'm not sure.*
Commessa	Non c'è problema. Prendiamo le misure.	*No problem. We'll take your measurements.*

COMPRENSIONE

A. Rispondi alle seguenti domande con frasi intere.

1. Che cosa vuole comprare il primo cliente?

_____

2. Che cosa vuole comprare la seconda cliente?

_____

3. Quali colori preferisce il primo cliente?

_____

4. Quali colori preferisce la seconda cliente?

_____

5. Che cosa fa il primo commesso?

_____

6. Che cosa fa la seconda commessa?

_____

VOCABOLARIO

PAROLE NUOVE

la camicetta (kah-meeh-chEh-ttah)	*blouse*
la camicia (kah-mEEh-chah)	*shirt*
il cliente / la cliente	*customer (male / female)*
il colore	*color*
il commesso / la commessa	*salesclerk (male / female)*
la cravatta	*tie*
la giacca (jAh-kkah)	*jacket*
la gonna	*skirt*
la misura	*measurement*
il paio	*pair*
pensare	*to think*
portare	*to wear, to carry*
preferire (isc)	*to prefer*
il problema	*problem*
il saldo	*sale*
sicuro	*sure*
la taglia (tAh-lyah)	*size (of clothes)*
tanto	*much, many*
il vestito	*dress, suit*

ESPRESSIONI E MODI DI DIRE

Ci devo pensare!	*I have to think about it!*
Desidera? (deh-zEEh-deh-rah)	*May I help you? (polite)*
in saldo	*on sale*
Non c'e problema!	*No problem!*

Non c'è problema!   Prego, signora?

I COLORI

arancione	*orange (invariable)*
azzurro (ah-dsdsOOh-rroh)	*blue*
bianco	*white*
giallo (jAh-lloh)	*yellow*
grigio (grEEh-joh)	*gray*
marrone	*brown (invariable)*
nero	*black*
rosa	*pink (invariable)*
rosso	*red*
verde	*green*
viola	*purple (invariable)*

IRREGOLARITÀ

- The plural of il paio is le paia *(pairs).* Note that it changes from the masculine to the feminine gender: il nuovo paio – le nuove paia *(the new pairs)*
- The adjectives arancione, marrone, rosa, and viola are invariable (that is, they do not change in form): i vestiti arancione / *the orange suits*, i pantaloni marrone / *the brown pants*, le camicette rosa / *the pink blouses*, il vestito viola / *the purple suit*
- The noun il problema is masculine, even though it ends in -a. Its plural form is i problemi
- The plural of la camicia is le camicie

ATTIVITÀ

B. Comunicazione!

Say that …

1. you would like to buy a black jacket

_____

2. your friend needs a white shirt

_____

3. your brother needs a tie and maybe a pair of black pants

_____

4. you are not sure what size you wear

_____

5. you would like green pants and a red tie

_____

6. your sister wants a pair of white pants

_____

7. your brother wants a blue shirt

_____

8. you'll have to think about it

_____

9. everything is on sale today

_____

10. your mother bought a yellow blouse last week

_____

11. your sister bought a brown blouse last week

_____

12. your mother also bought a pink evening dress

_____

13. your sister also bought a purple skirt and a gray blouse

_____

14. there is no problem

_____

Ask a customer …

15. if you can help him or her

_____

16. what size he or she wears

_____

17. what color he or she prefers

_____

18. if he or she is joking

_____

19. if you can take his or her measurements

_____

20. which colors he or she usually prefers

_____

C. Say that you like the following things.

> *Model:* the green blouse
> *Sì, mi piace la camicetta verde.*

1. those white shirts

_____

2. that orange blouse

_____

3. those brown ties

_____

4. that yellow jacket

_____

5. that pair of black pants

_____

6. those pairs of red pants

_____

7. the green evening dress

_____

8. the pink blouses

_____

9. the purple shoes

_____

D. Domande personali.

1. Che taglia di pantaloni porti?

_____

2. Che taglia di camicia / camicetta porti?

_____

3. Quali colori preferisci?

_____

4. Di che cosa hai bisogno *(What do you need)*?

_____

E. Descrizione! Write an imaginary description of about 6–7 lines based on the picture you see. If you are using this book in a classroom situation, do this activity with a partner.

_____

_____

_____

_____

_____

_____

_____

_____

_____

_____

_____

LINGUA

Interrogative Forms

The interrogative adjective quale / *which* changes in form according to the gender and number of the noun:

Singular	Plural
Quale vestito vuole? *Which dress do you want?*	Quali vestiti vuole? *Which dresses do you want?*
Quale camicia preferisce? *Which shirt do you prefer?*	Quali camicie preferisce? *Which shirts do you prefer?*

Quale vestito vuole?

Note that the -e may be dropped before the verb form è:

Quale è il tuo amico? *Which one is your friend?*	Qual è il tuo amico? *Which one is your friend?*
Quale è il suo libro? *Which one is his / her book?*	Qual è il suo libro? *Which one is his / her book?*

Summarized below are other common interrogative forms, most of which you have been using throughout the previous units:

Che / Cosa / Che cosa?	*What?*
Chi?	*Who?*
Come?	*How?*
Quando?	*When?*
Perché?	*Why?*
Dove?	*Where?*
Quanto?	*How much?*

Note that quanto, like quale, is an adjective and, thus, must agree with the gender and number of the noun:

Singular	Plural
Quanto zucchero vuole? *How much sugar do you want?*	Quanti spaghetti vuole? *How many spaghetti do you want?*
Quanta carne preferisce? *How much meat do you prefer?*	Quante camicie preferisce? *How many shirts do you prefer?*

The Imperfect of Second Conjugation Verbs

The imperfect of second conjugation (-ere) verbs is formed by dropping the -ere and adding the following endings to the resulting stem:

Singular		Plural	
1st person	-evo	1st person	-evamo
2nd person	-evi	2nd person	-evate
3rd person	-eva	3rd person	-evano

Below is the verb leggere / *to read,* fully conjugated for you:

leggere → legg- *to read*	
(io) leggevo	*I was reading, I used to read*
(tu) leggevi	*you were reading, you used to read (familiar)*
(Lei) leggeva	*you were reading, you used to read (polite)*
(lui / lei) leggeva	*he / she was reading, he / she used to read*
(noi) leggevamo	*we were reading, we used to read*
(voi) leggevate	*you were reading, you used to read (plural)*
(loro) leggevano (leh-jEh-vah-noh)	*they were reading, they used to read*

The Verb piacere: Part 2

To use the verb piacere, you will have to learn the indirect object forms first. They are listed below:

Singular			Plural		
1st person	mi	*to me*	1st person	ci	*to us*
2nd person	ti	*to you (familiar)*	2nd person	vi	*to you*
3rd person	gli	*to him*	3rd person	gli	*to them*
	le	*to her*			
	Le	*to you (polite)*			

271

With Singular Nouns	With Plural Nouns
I like	
Mi piace la camicia *I like the shirt*	Mi piacciono le camicie *I like the shirts*
You like (familiar)	
Ti piace il vestito azzurro *You like the blue dress*	Ti piacciono i vestiti azzurri *You like the blue dresses*
You like (polite)	
Le piace la giacca rossa *You like the red jacket*	Le piacciono le giacche rosse *You like the red jackets*
He likes	
Gli piace il libro italiano *He likes the Italian book*	Gli piacciono i libri italiani *He likes the Italian books*
She likes	
Le piace il libro italiano *She likes the Italian book*	Le piacciono i libri italiani *She likes the Italian books*
We like	
Ci piace la lezione *We like the class*	Ci piacciono le lezioni *We like the classes*
You like (plural)	
Vi piace la cravatta gialla *You like the yellow tie*	Vi piacciono le cravatte gialle *You like the yellow ties*
They like	
Gli piace la camicetta *They like the blouse*	Gli piacciono le camicette *They like the blouses*

The indirect object pronouns are necessary because the verb piacere literally means *to be pleasing to someone.* Thus when a name or noun phrase is used, the preposition a / *to* is required:

Singular	Plural
A Marco piace quel libro *Mark likes that book =* *That book is pleasing to Mark*	A Marco piacciono quei libri *Mark likes those books =* *Those books are pleasing to Mark*
Alla ragazza piace la camicetta gialla *The girl likes the yellow blouse =* *The yellow blouse is pleasing to the girl*	Alla ragazza piacciono le camicette gialle *The girl likes the yellow blouses =* *The yellow blouses are pleasing to the girl*

ATTIVITÀ

F. You are given the responses of a customer to the questions of a salesclerk. Provide the clerk's questions.

> *Model:* La camicetta rosa è lì.
> *Dov'è la camicetta rosa?*

1. Preferisco quella giacca lì.

2. Voglio quei pantaloni lì.

3. Preferisco quelle scarpe lì.

4. Voglio tanta carne.

5. Voglio tanti spaghetti.

6. Voglio due giacche.

7. È un libro.

8. Quella persona è mio marito.

9. Mi chiamo Sofia Di Nardo.

10. Ho comprato quel vestito due giorni fa.

11. Ho comprato quel vestito perché era in saldo.

12. Ho comprato quel vestito in centro.

G. Make complete sentences with the given words, using the imperfect of the verb.

> *Model:* Dina...conoscere / Franco / da bambina
> *Dina conosceva Franco da bambina.*

Io...

1. conoscere / Franco / da bambino

_____

2. leggere / tanti libri / da giovane

_____

3. avere / molti amici / da giovane

_____

Tu...

4. conoscere / Franco / da bambino

_____

5. leggere / tanti libri / da giovane

_____

6. avere / molti amici / da giovane

_____

Dina…

7. conoscere / Franco / da bambina

8. leggere / tanti libri / da giovane

9. avere / molti amici / da giovane

Noi…

10. conoscere / Franco / da bambini

11. leggere / tanti libri / da giovani

12. avere / molti amici / da giovani

Voi…

13. conoscere / Franco / da bambini

14. leggere / tanti libri / da giovani

15. avere / molti amici / da giovani

Le tue amiche…

16. conoscere / Franco / da bambine

17. leggere / tanti libri / da giovani

18. avere / molti amici / da giovani

H. Say that the indicated persons like the suggested thing(s).

> *Model:* quella camicia…I like
> *Mi piace quella camicia.*

quella camicia…

1. I like

2. you *(familiar)* like

_____

3. he likes

_____

4. she likes

_____

5. we like

_____

6. you *(polite)* like

_____

7. you *(plural)* like

_____

8. they like

_____

9. the woman likes

_____

10. the men like

_____

quei pantaloni…

11. I like…

_____

12. you *(familiar)* like

_____

13. he likes

_____

14. she likes

_____

15. we like

_____

16. you *(polite)* like

_____

17. you *(plural)* like

_____

18. they like

_____

19. the woman likes

_____

20. the men like

_____

I. Cruciverba!

Horizontal

5 Mi piace molto la tua … grigia.
8 customer
10 Non mi piace quella … gialla.
12 Lei porta sempre la … lunga.
13 Vorrei due … di scarpe.
14 A lui piace la cravatta …
15 Non sono …
18 clerk *(female)*
20 Mi piace solo il vestito …
22 In … colori preferisce la giacca e i pantaloni?
24 Preferisco il vestito …
28 Signora, … piacciono questi pantaloni?
29 Sì, … piacciono molto.
30 Lei porta sempre la camicetta …
31 Quando eri bambina, tu… molto ai tuoi amici.
35 Anche noi … molto quando eravamo bambini.
36 they used to write
38 Voi … molto quando eravate bambini, vero?
41 Anche a noi … piace il tuo vestito.
42 Maria, … piace la mia cravatta?

Vertical

1 Sì, … piace molto il tuo vestito.
2 Anch'io … di andare in Italia in estate.
3 Quando lei era giovane … sempre la gonna rosa.
4 Mi piace la tua cravatta …
5 Lui porta sempre la … bianca.
6 Quale … preferisce?
7 Di solito io mangio … carne.
9 Che … porta, Lei?
11 Il tuo … è veramente molto bello.
12 Le piace questa … azzurra?
13 Quale colore … Lei?
14 purple
16 pink
17 Allora, … colori preferisce?
18 A noi … piace molto la tua giacca.
19 Vorrei comprare anche quella giacca …
21 Qualche giorno fa ho comprato una cravatta …
23 Ti piacciono quei pantaloni …?
25 Quando ero bambino, … tanti libri.
26 Ti … quella gonna?
27 Vorrei comprare quella gonna …
32 Anche tuo fratello … molto quando era bambino.
33 Gli … molto quei pantaloni.
34 Anche a lei … piace molto quella giacca.
35 Signora, … piace questa camicetta?
37 Alessandro e Dina, … piace la mia camicia?
39 Anche a Franco … piace quella giacca.
40 Claudia e Maria … piace la mia camicetta?

NOTA CULTURALE

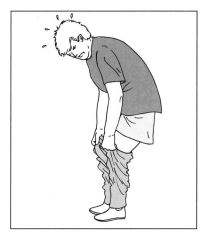

La moda!

Italian Fashion

With designers such as Armani, Gucci, Prada, Benetton, Fendi, Inghirami, Valentino, Missoni, and many others, Italy is world famous for its fashion design. Most Italians, however, are content to buy clothes at department stores, the two most popular being UPIM and Standa.

Here is a comparison of sizes for clothes (**abbigliamento**) and shoes (**scarpe**):

Abbigliamento				Scarpe	
Uomini		Donne			
U.S.	Italia	U.S.	Italia	U.S.	Italia
S	46	8	42	7	37
M	48	10	44	8	38
L	50	12	46	9	39
XL	52	14	48	11	41

J. You are given a U.S. size. Give its Italian equivalent.

> *Model:* size 8 clothes
> *il quarantasei*

size…

1. 10 clothes

_____

2. 14 clothes

_____

3. 7 shoe

_____

4. 8 shoe

_____

5. 11 shoe

_____

Un caffè lungo, per favore.

Unit 20

Vorrei un caffè lungo!

CONVERSAZIONE

[Dina and Alessandro have decided to take a break at a café, relaxing after a long day of classes.]

Dina	Io vorrei un caffè lungo, per favore.	I would like a long (diluted) coffee, please.
Barista	E Lei signore, cosa desidera?	And you sir, what would you like?
Alessandro	Per me, un caffè ristretto.	For me, a strong coffee.
Barista	Prego.	Fine.
Dina	Ma non hai appena finito di bere un cappuccino?	But haven't you just finished drinking a cappuccino?
Alessandro	Sì, ma io amo il caffè. Mi è sempre piaciuto molto!	Yes, but I love coffee! I have always liked it a lot!
Dina	Prendiamo anche qualcosa da mangiare?	Shall we also have something to eat?
Alessandro	Sì, io prendo una focaccia e poi un dolce.	Yes, I'll have a focaccia sandwich and then a sweet pastry.
Dina	E io solo un panino.	And I only a sandwich.
Alessandro	Oggi pago io.	I'll pay today.
Dina	Tu sei sempre così gentile!	You're always so kind!

[Note: If you decide to stand at an espresso bar, you must first pay the cashier, who will give you a scontrino (*receipt*). You then give the receipt to the server at the counter, requesting what you have paid for. If you sit at a table at a café, a waiter will serve you and bring you the bill.]

COMPRENSIONE

A. Match the items in the two columns in an appropriate fashion.

1. Chi vuole il caffé lungo?   a. Alessandro

2. Chi vuole il caffé ristretto?   b. Il caffé

3. Che cosa ama molto Alessandro?   c. Una focaccia e un dolce

4. Che cosa prende Alessandro da mangiare? d. Solo un panino.

5. Che cosa prende Dina da mangiare?   e. Dina

VOCABOLARIO

Mi piace molto il
caffè ristretto!

A me, invece, piace
il cappuccino!

PAROLE NUOVE

amare	*to love*
appena	*just, barely*
il barista / la barista	*bartender (male / female)*
bere	*to drink*
il cappuccino	*cappuccino coffee*
desiderare	*to want*
il dolce (dOhl-cheh)	*sweet pastry*
la focaccia (foh-kAh-cchah)	*focaccia (sandwich)*
il panino	*sandwich (bun style)*
prendere	*to take, to have something to eat / drink*
ristretto	*strong, short (coffee)*
lo scontrino	*cash register tape, receipt*

ESPRESSIONI E MODI DI DIRE

il caffè lungo	*long coffee (not strong)*
il caffè ristretto	*strong coffee*
per favore	*please*

IRREGOLARITÀ

- Nouns ending in -ista can be masculine or feminine:

il barista	*male bartender*	i baristi	*male bartenders*
la barista	*female bartender*	le bariste	*female bartenders*

- The verb bere / *to drink* is irregular in the present indicative and imperative and it has an irregular past participle:

Pres. Ind.   (io) bevo, (tu) bevi, (lui / lei / Lei) beve, (noi) beviamo, (voi) bevete, (loro) bevono

Imperative   (io) —, (tu) bevi, (lui / lei / Lei) beva, (noi) beviamo, (voi) bevete, (loro) bevano

Past Participle: bevuto

281

ATTIVITÀ

B. Comunicazione!

Say that …

1. you would like a long coffee, please

_____

2. you would like a strong coffee, please.

_____

3. you really love coffee

_____

4. you have always liked it

_____

5. you'll have a focaccia sandwich

_____

6. after, you'll also have a sweet pastry

_____

7. maybe you'll have a sandwich

_____

8. today you will pay

_____

Tell Dina that…

9. she is always so kind

_____

Ask …

10. a young lady what she would like

_____

11. Dina if she hasn't just finished drinking a cappuccino

_____

12. Dina if the two of you should also have something to eat

_____

C. Come si dice in italiano?

First, say that each person is drinking cappuccino.

> *Model:* Dina
> *Dina beve il cappuccino.*

1. Io

_____

2. Tu

_____

3. Quel barista

_____

4. Quelle bariste

_____

5. Noi

_____

6. Voi

_____

Now, say that they drank it yesterday too.

> *Model:* Dina
> *Dina ha bevuto il cappuccino anche ieri.*

7. Io

_____

8. Tu

_____

9. Quel barista

_____

10. Quelle bariste

_____

11. Noi

_____

12. Voi

_____

Finally, order each of the indicated persons to drink a long coffee.

> *Model:* Dina
> *Dina, bevi il caffè lungo!*

13. Alessandro

_____

14. Signora Martini

_____

15. Dina e Alessandro

_____

16. Signora Martini e signor Giusti

_____

17. Noi

_____

D. Domande personali.

1. Tu bevi il caffè?

_____

2. Ti piace?

_____

3. Ti piacciono le focacce?

_____

4. Che tipo di panino ti piace?

_____

Tipi di Panino	
panino al prosciutto	ham sandwich
panino al formaggio	cheese sandwich
panino al salame	salami sandwich

E. Descrizione! Write an imaginary description of about 6–7 lines based on the picture you see. If you are using this book in a classroom situation, do this activity with a partner.

_____

_____

_____

_____

_____

_____

_____

_____

_____

LINGUA

The Imperfect of Third Conjugation Verbs

The imperfect of third conjugation (-ire) verbs is formed by dropping the -ire and adding the following endings to the resulting stem:

Singular	
1st person	-ivo
2nd person	-ivi
3rd person	-iva

Plural	
1st person	-ivamo
2nd person	-ivate
3rd person	-ivano

Below is the verb finire / to finish fully conjugated for you:

finire → fin- to finish	
(io) finivo	I was finishing, I used to finish
(tu) finivi	you were finishing, you used to finish (familiar)
(Lei) finiva	you were finishing, you used to finish (polite)
(lui / lei) finiva	he / she was finishing, he / she used to finish
(noi) finivamo	we were finishing, we used to finish
(voi) finivate	you were finishing, you used to finish (plural)
(loro) finivano (feeh-nEEh-vah-noh)	they were finishing, they used to finish

Irregular Verbs in the Imperfect

There are very few irregular verbs in the imperfect. You have already learned the imperfect forms of **essere** and **fare** (Unit 17). Of the other verbs you have encountered so far, the following are irregular in the imperfect:

bere to drink	
(io) bevevo	I was drinking, I used to drink
(tu) bevevi	you were drinking, you used to drink (familiar)
(Lei) beveva	you were drinking, you used to drink (polite)
(lui / lei) beveva	he / she was drinking, he / she used to drink
(noi) bevevamo	we were drinking, we used to drink
(voi) bevevate	you were drinking, you used to drink (plural)
(loro) bevevano (beh-vEh-vah-noh)	they were drinking, they used to drink

dare to give	
(io) davo	I was giving, I used to give
(tu) davi	you were giving, you used to give (familiar)
(Lei) dava	you were giving, you used to give (polite)
(lui / lei) dava	he / she was giving, he / she used to give
(noi) davamo	we were giving, we used to give
(voi) davate	you were giving, you used to give (plural)
(loro) davano (dAh-vah-noh)	they were giving, they used to give

dire to say, to tell	
(io) dicevo	I was saying, I used to say
(tu) dicevi	you were saying, you used to say (familiar)
(Lei) diceva	you were saying, you used to say (polite)
(lui / lei) diceva	he / she was saying, he / she used to say
(noi) dicevamo	we were saying, we used to say
(voi) dicevate	you were saying, you used to say (plural)
(loro) dicevano (deeh-chEh-vah-noh)	they were saying, they used to say

Da bambino, mi piacevano i dolci!

The Verb piacere: Part 3

The verb piacere is conjugated with essere in the present perfect. Here are common present perfect and imperfect forms of this verb:

I liked / I used to like	
With Singular Nouns	With Plural Nouns
Mi è piaciuto il caffè *I liked the coffee*	Mi sono piaciuti i caffè *I liked the coffees*
Mi piaceva il caffè *I used to like coffee*	Mi piacevano i dolci *I used to like sweets*

You liked / You used to like (familiar)	
With Singular Nouns	With Plural Nouns
Ti è piaciuta la focaccia *You liked the focaccia sandwich*	Ti sono piaciute le focacce *You liked the focaccia sandwiches*
Ti piaceva il pane *You used to like bread*	Ti piacevano gli spaghetti *You used to like spaghetti*

You liked / You used to like (polite)	
With Singular Nouns	With Plural Nouns
Le è piaciuto il cappuccino *You liked the cappuccino*	Le sono piaciuti i cappuccini *You liked the cappuccinos*
Le piaceva la carne *You used to like meat*	Le piacevano gli spaghetti *You used to like spaghetti*

He liked / He used to like

With Singular Nouns	With Plural Nouns
Gli è piaciuta la focaccia *He liked the focaccia sandwich*	Gli sono piaciute le focacce *He liked the focaccia sandwiches*
Gli piaceva il caffè *He used to like coffee*	Gli piacevano i dolci *He used to like sweets*

She liked / She used to like

With Singular Nouns	With Plural Nouns
Le è piaciuta la focaccia *She liked the focaccia sandwich*	Le sono piaciute le focacce *She liked the focaccia sandwiches*
Le piaceva il caffè *She used to like coffee*	Le piacevano i dolci *She used to like sweets*

We liked / We used to like

With Singular Nouns	With Plural Nouns
Ci è piaciuto il panino *We liked the sandwich*	Ci sono piaciuti i panini *We liked the sandwiches*
Ci piaceva il caffè *We used to like coffee*	Ci piacevano gli spaghetti *We used to like spaghetti*

You liked / You used to like (plural)

With Singular Nouns	With Plural Nouns
Vi è piaciuta la pizza *You liked the pizza*	Vi sono piaciute le pizze *You liked the pizzas*
Vi piaceva la pizza *You used to like pizza*	Vi piacevano i dolci *You used to like sweets*

They liked / They used to like

With Singular Nouns	With Plural Nouns
Gli è piaciuto il panino *They liked the sandwich*	Gli sono piaciuti i panini *They liked the sandwiches*
Gli piaceva il caffè *They used to like coffee*	Gli piacevano i dolci *They used to like sweets*

Nouns Ending in an Accented Vowel

The plural of **caffè**, and of all nouns ending in an accented vowel, is invariable:

Singular	Plural
il caffè / *the coffee*	i caffè / *the coffees*
il lunedì / *Monday*	i lunedì / *Mondays*
la città / *the city*	le città / *the cities*
l'università / *the university*	le università / *the universities*

ATTIVITÀ

F. Make complete sentences with the given words, using the imperfect form of the verb.

> *Model:* Dina...dormire / molto / da bambina
> *Dina dormiva molto da bambina.*

Io...

1. dormire / molto / da bambino

_____

2. preferire / l'inverno / da giovane

_____

3. dare / spesso / i miei euro / alla famiglia

_____

4. dire / sempre / tutto / alla mamma

_____

5. non bere / mai / il caffè

_____

Tu...

6. dormire / molto / da bambino

_____

7. preferire / l'inverno / da giovane

_____

8. dare / spesso / i tuoi euro / alla famiglia

_____

9. dire / sempre / tutto / alla mamma

_____

10. non bere / mai / il caffè

_____

Dina...

11. dormire / molto / da bambina

_____

12. preferire / l'inverno / da giovane

_____

13. dare / spesso / i suoi euro / alla famiglia

_____

14. dire / sempre / tutto / alla mamma

_____

15. non bere / mai / il caffè

_____

Noi...

16. dormire / molto / da bambini

_____

17. preferire / l'inverno / da giovani

_____

18. dare / spesso / i nostri euro / alla famiglia

_____

19. dire / sempre / tutto / alla mamma

_____

20. non bere / mai / il caffè

_____

Voi...

21. dormire / molto / da bambini

_____

22. preferire / l'inverno / da giovani

_____

23. dare / spesso / i vostri euro / alla famiglia

_____

24. dire / sempre / tutto / alla mamma

_____

25. non bere / mai / il caffè

_____

Gli amici di Alessandro…

26. dormire / molto / da bambini

_____

27. preferire / l'inverno / da giovani

_____

28. dare / spesso / i loro euro / alla famiglia

_____

29. dire / sempre / tutto / alla mamma

_____

30. non bere / mai / il caffè

_____

G. Comunicazione. If you are using this book in a classroom situation, do this activity with a partner.

First, say that the indicated person liked the item in question. Then say that he or she didn't like it as a youth. Follow the model.

> *Model:* il cappuccino…he
> —*Gli è piaciuto il cappuccino.*
> —*Ma da giovane non gli piaceva.*

cappuccino…

1. I

_____

2. you *(familiar)*

_____

3. you *(polite)*

_____

4. he

_____

5. she

_____

6. we

_____

7. you *(plural)*

_____

8. they

_____

quelle città…

9. I

_____

10. you *(familiar)*

_____

11. you *(polite)*

_____

12. he

_____

13. she

_____

14. we

_____

15. you *(plural)*

_____

16. they

_____

H. Cruciverba!

Horizontal

1 Cosa … voi, un caffè lungo o un cappuccino?
2 Noi non … mai il caffè ristretto.
3 Ma non hai … finito di bere un cappuccino?
6 Quando erano bambini, loro non … mai il caffè.
7 Ah, …, un caffè, per favore!
9 Al mattino mi piace bere il …
11 No, preferisco un …, non un panino.
13 you used to understand *(familiar)*
14 Prendo un …, non un dolce.
16 she used to finish
17 Per me, un cappuccino, per …
18 Vado io a prendere lo …
20 Quando eravamo bambini, ci … molto i dolci.
21 you used to finish *(plural)*
23 they used to understand
24 Non mi è mai … la carne.
25 Ti sono … quelle focacce?

Vertical

1 Alessandro, e tu cosa …, un caffè ristretto o lungo?
2 Mio fratello non … mai il cappuccino.
3 Quando erano bambini, loro … andare in Italia.
4 Per me, un … lungo.
5 Io ho già mangiato una …
6 Anch'io … sempre il caffè ristretto.
8 Mi piace il caffè …, non lungo.
10 Quando era bambina, a lei … molto il cappuccino.
12 Vorrei un caffè …, per favore.
13 I used to understand
15 we used to understand
19 Non gli è mai … il caffè espresso.
22 Vi sono … quei panini?

NOTA CULTURALE

L'espresso

Il cappuccino

Italian Coffee

Italians love their coffee! Espresso bars are everywhere. So, here are the ways to have Italian coffee.

un caffellatte	coffee and steamed milk in equal portions/a "latte"
un cappuccino	cappuccino (espresso coffee with steamed milk)
corretto	with a dash of liqueur
decaffeinato	decaffeinated
doppio	double
un espresso	an espresso coffee
lungo	less concentrated/long
macchiato	with a drop of milk
ristretto	strong/short

I. Now, order coffee, Italian style! Follow the model.

> *Model:* an espresso coffee
> *Vorrei un espresso, per favore.*

1. coffee and steamed milk

_____

2. cappuccino

_____

3. a coffee with a dash of liqueur

_____

4. a decaffeinated coffee

_____

5. a double espresso

_____

6. a long coffee

_____

7. an espresso with a drop of milk

_____

8. a short coffee

_____

Review Part 4

A. Comunicazione!

Say that …

1. you have been working for a computer firm for several years

_____

2. you started working last year

_____

3. it's not the first time that you work for a computer firm

_____

4. you met some people who work there a few weeks ago

_____

5. you worked for that bank several years ago

_____

6. your friend lives at 123 Verdi Street

_____

7. your brother is married with four children

_____

8. today's lesson was difficult, but it was very important

_____

9. you would like to buy a new jacket and white shirt

_____

10. your brother bought a beautiful new tie two weeks ago

_____

11. everything is on sale today, but you do not know what to buy

_____

12. you like strong coffee

_____

13. you like only focaccia sandwiches

_____

Ask a customer …

14. if you can help him or her and what size he or she wears

_____

15. what colors he or she prefers for the evening dress

_____

Tell …

16. your professor / teacher that you did not understand last week's lessons

_____

17. Mr. Marchi to read this book and to write down the questions he has

_____

18. Mrs. Di Nardo to write the questions she has on the grammar that she studied today

_____

Ask …

19. Sarah how long she has been working for that firm

_____

20. Mrs. Marchi if she has met Mr. Pasquali who works on the sixth floor

_____

21. Dina if she has ever worked for another company

_____

22. Sarah what her address is

_____

23. Alessandro how old he is

_____

24. your professor / teacher what you should do to learn grammar

_____

25. your brother what size he wears

_____

26. your sister what colors she prefers

_____

27. Dina if she wants a cappuccino

_____

B. Come si dice?

1. I worked on the tenth floor for six years.

_____

2. My brother met Dina two years ago.

_____

3. They read a book on Italian grammar yesterday.

_____

4. We didn't hand in our composition to the professor / teacher.

_____

C. Domande personali. Answer the questions.

1. Lavori per una ditta? Quale?

_____

2. Ti piace lavorare per la ditta? Perché?

_____

3. Qual è l'indirizzo del tuo miglior amico / la tua miglior amica?

_____

4. Quanti anni ha il tuo amico? / la tua amica?

_____

5. Quali aspetti *(aspects)* della lingua italiana trovi difficili?

_____

6. Che taglie porti?

_____

7. Quali sono i tuoi colori preferiti *(favorite)*?

_____

D. Make a list of all the clothes you want to buy, describing them (color, size, etc.) according to your preferences.

_____

_____

_____

_____

_____

_____

_____

_____

_____

_____

_____

_____

_____

_____

_____

_____

E. There are 20 words hidden in the word search puzzle below: 10 can be read from left to right (horizontally) and 10 in a top-down direction (vertically). Can you find them? The clues given below will help you look for them. The numbers of the clues do not reflect any particular order or arrangement to the hidden words.

A	A	N	D	A	T	A	A	P	A	D	P	P	D	S	T	A	T	O	X
T	X	X	X	C	C	B	I	B	A	R	P	D	E	R	T	P	X	X	X
A	X	X	X	C	C	C	N	A	N	D	O	O	S	R	T	Y	L	X	X
G	X	X	X	C	C	F	M	C	M	A	F	I	A	T	Y	V	K	X	M
L	X	X	X	C	C	I	K	C	K	D	E	U	D	Y	U	O	J	L	A
I	Q	E	D	R	T	N	L	I	L	C	S	Y	E	Q	I	R	K	E	R
A	Q	E	D	R	T	I	M	O	G	C	S	T	S	Q	P	R	L	G	C
Q	W	E	R	T	Y	T	V	N	H	C	O	R	I	A	L	E	G	G	A
N	E	S	S	U	N	O	B	O	S	A	R	A	D	D	Q	I	M	E	M
S	D	F	G	H	J	K	K	M	G	N	B	V	E	C	P	G	N	V	N
S	D	F	G	H	J	K	L	M	E	N	B	V	R	Q	I	L	P	O	I
C	A	P	I	T	O	M	N	J	N	J	K	L	A	V	A	Q	E	D	S
Q	E	D	X	X	X	A	A	C	T	C	B	V	N	T	C	Q	E	D	P
Q	E	D	X	X	X	A	A	C	I	C	B	V	N	T	E	Q	E	D	I
Q	E	D	X	X	X	A	A	C	L	C	B	V	N	T	V	R	E	D	A
Q	E	D	X	X	X	A	A	C	E	C	B	V	N	T	A	R	E	D	C
A	N	N	I	A	D	C	B	N	L	C	B	V	N	T	N	R	E	D	I
Q	E	D	X	X	X	A	A	B	I	T	O	X	X	X	O	R	E	D	U
Q	E	D	X	X	X	A	A	C	D	C	B	V	N	T	D	Q	E	D	T
P	I	A	C	E	Q	L	A	V	O	R	A	T	O	Q	P	I	A	N	O

Horizontal

1 Ti ... lavorare qui?
2 Non conosco nessuno al ventesimo ...
3 Signora Verdi, Lei è mai ... al dodicesimo piano?
4 Non conosco ... al settimo piano.
5 ... in via Dante, 45.
6 Quanti ... hai, Giovanni?
7 Non ho mai ... per quella ditta.
8 Qual è il Suo ... civile?
9 Scusi, ma non ho ... la lezione.
10 Signorina, ... questo libro!

Vertical

11 Quando ero bambino, io ... molti libri.
12 Le presento il ... Giusti.
13 Signore, ...?
14 Che ... porta, Lei?
15 Quali colori Le ...?
16 Non hai appena ... di bere un caffè?
17 Mi è sempre ... il caffè!
18 Tu sei sempre così ...
19 Quando ero bambino mi ... molto i dolci.
20 Ti ... il caffè

Part 5: Getting Around

Questi stivali Le stanno proprio bene!

Unit 21

Ne abbiamo molti!

CONVERSAZIONE

[Yesterday, Dina went shopping. First she went to the same bookstore where she had bought Dante's masterful *Divine Comedy* a few days before.]

Libraia	Desidera signorina?	*May I help you, young lady?*
Dina	Cercavo un romanzo da leggere.	*I was looking for a novel to read.*
Libraia	Ne abbiamo molti.	*We have many.*
Dina	Mi piace quello che ha in vetrina.	*I like the one that you have in the window.*
Libraia	Quello di fantascienza?	*The science fiction one?*
Dina	Sì.	*Yes.*
Libraia	Altro?	*Anything else?*
Dina	Ha riviste di moda?	*Do you have any fashion magazines?*
Libraia	Abbiamo solo queste due.	*We have only these two.*
Dina	Va bene, le prendo. Ha il giornale di oggi?	*OK, I'll take them. Do you have today's newspaper?*
Libraia	Il giornale lo deve comprare a quel chiosco là all'angolo.	*You'll have to buy the newspaper at that kiosk over there at the corner.*
Dina	Grazie.	*Thank you.*
Libraia	A Lei.	*And to you.*

[A bit later, she went to a shoe store.]

Commesso	Cosa Le serve, signorina?	*What do you need, Miss?*
Dina	Mi serve un paio di stivali neri come quelli in vetrina.	*I need a pair of black boots like the ones in the window.*
Commesso	Che numero porta?	*What's your shoe size?*
Dina	Di solito il trentotto e mezzo.	*Usually 38½ (= 8½ in US/Canadian sizes)*
Commesso	Si provi questi! Le stanno perfettamente bene!	*Try these ones on! They look perfectly good on you!*
Dina	È vero. Quanto costano?	*It's true. How much are they?*
Commesso	Sono in saldo.	*They're on sale.*
Dina	Va bene. Li prendo.	*OK. I'll take them.*
Commesso	Ottima scelta! Anche le nostre scarpe sono in saldo oggi.	*Excellent choice! Our shoes are also on sale today.*
Dina	No, grazie. Va bene così!	*No, thanks. I'm fine!*

COMPRENSIONE

A. Vero o falso?

_____ 1. Ieri Dina cercava un romanzo da leggere.

_____ 2. La libraia non aveva nessun romanzo.

_____ 3. Dina voleva il romanzo di fantascienza che era in vetrina.

_____ 4. Dina voleva anche qualche rivista di moda.

_____ 5. Dina voleva comprare il giornale.

_____ 6. Dina porta il numero trentotto e mezzo.

_____ 7. Gli stivali erano in saldo.

_____ 8. Dina non ha preso gli stivali perché non le stavano bene.

VOCABOLARIO

PAROLE NUOVE

l'angolo (Ahn-goh-loh)	corner
la calzoleria	shoe store
il chiosco	kiosk
costare*	to cost
la fantascienza	science fiction
il giornale (johr-nAh-leh)	newspaper
là	over there
il libraio / la libraia	book vendor (male / female)
la libreria	bookstore
mezzo	half
la moda	fashion
ne	of it, of them
ottimo	great, wonderful, excellent
perfettamente	perfectly
provarsi	to try on
la rivista	magazine
il romanzo	novel
la scelta (shEhl-tah)	choice
servire a	to need
solo	only
stare*	to stay, to be (in some expressions)
lo stivale	boot
vero	true
la vetrina	shop window

ESPRESSIONI E MODI DI DIRE

il numero (di scarpa)	size (of shoe)
pensare di sì / no	to think so / not
stare* bene a	to look good on

Come mi sta?

STRUTTURE VERBALI

mi serve / mi servono (sEhr-voh-noh)	*I need*
Le serve / Le servono	*you need (polite)*
Le stanno bene	*They look good on you (polite)*
Si provi…!	*Try on…! (polite)*

ATTIVITÀ

B. Scegli la risposta adatta.

_____ 1. No, grazie. Va bene …
         a. molto.
         b. così.

_____ 2. Ottima …!
         a. saldo
         b. scelta

_____ 3. Quanto costano?
         a. È vero.
         b. Sono in saldo.

_____ 4. Si … questi!
         a. prova
         b. provi

_____ 5. Questi Le … perfettamente bene!
         a. stanno
         b. sta

_____ 6. Che numero porta?
         a. Non importa.
         b. Il trentadue.

_____ 7. Ha il giornale di oggi?
       a. Altro.
       b. Penso di sì.

_____ 8. Desidera?
       a. Vorrei una rivista di moda.
       b. Grazie.

_____ 9. Preferisco un libro di …
       a. fantascienza
       b. oggi

_____ 10. Il giornale lo deve comprare …
       a. all'angolo dove c'è il chiosco.
       b. nella calzoleria.

_____ 11. Quanto … quel romanzo?
       a. ti sta bene
       b. costa

_____ 12. Vede quelle scarpe …?
       a. là
       b. mezze

_____ 13. Penso proprio di …
       a. no
       b. ne

_____ 14. Mi … anche gli stivali.
       a. serve
       b. servono

C. Domande personali!

1. Che tipo di libro preferisci?

_____

2. Perché?

_____

3. Leggi il giornale? Quale?

_____

4. Quale rivista ti piace?

_____

5. Perché?

_____

6. Che numero di scarpa porti?

_____

7. Ti serve qualcosa? Che cosa?

_____

D. Come si dice in italiano?

1. I'm looking for a novel, newspaper, or even a magazine.

_____

2. We've got lots of them.

_____

3. I like the science fiction one in the window.

_____

4. Would you like anything else?

_____

5. We have only these two.

_____

6. OK, I'll take them.

_____

7. I think so.

_____

8. Here's the newspaper!

_____

9. I need a pair of black boots.

_____

10. These look very good on you!

_____

E. Attività creativa. Describe in your own words the kind of wardrobe you think is ideal. Use a dictionary if necessary. If you are using this book in a classroom situation, do this activity with a partner.

_____

_____

_____

_____

_____

_____

_____

_____

LINGUA

TheVerb stare

The verb stare / *to stay, to be* is a very important one. It is used in progressive tenses, as you will see below. It is irregular in all tenses.

Present Indicative	
(io) sto	*I stay, I am staying*
(tu) stai	*you stay, you are staying*
(Lei) sta	*you stay, you are staying (polite)*
(lui / lei) sta	*he / she stays, he / she is staying*
(noi) stiamo	*we stay, we are staying*
(voi) state	*you stay, you are staying (plural)*
(loro) stanno	*they stay, they are staying*

Imperative	
(io) —	
(tu) sta'	*stay, be (familiar)*
(Lei) stia	*stay, be (polite)*
(noi) stiamo	*let's stay, let's be*
(voi) state	*stay, be (familiar)*
(loro) stiano	*stay, be (polite)*

Present Perfect	
(io) sono stato / stata	*I have stayed, I stayed*
(tu) sei stato / stata	*you have stayed, you stayed (familiar)*
(Lei) è stato / stata	*you have stayed, you stayed (polite)*
(lui) è stato	*he has stayed, he stayed*
(lei) è stata	*she has stayed, she stayed*
(noi) siami stati / state	*we have stayed, we stayed*
(voi) siete stati / state	*you have stayed, you stayed (plural)*
(loro) sono stati / state	*they have stayed, they stayed*

Imperfect	
(io) stavo	*I used to stay*
(tu) stavi	*you used to stay (familiar)*
(Lei) stava	*you used to stay (polite)*
(lui) stava	*he used to stay*
(lei) stava	*she used to stay*
(noi) stavamo	*we used to stay*
(voi) stavate	*you used to stay(plural)*
(loro) stavano	*they used to stay*

The expression *stare bene a* renders the idea of *to look good on*. Indirect object pronouns are used frequently with this verbal expression. These were introduced in Unit 19. Go back to that unit if you have forgotten them.

La camicia mi sta bene	*The shirt looks good on me*
Le camicie ti stanno bene	*The shirts look good on you (familiar)*
Il vestito Le sta bene	*The dress looks good on you (polite)*
Quei vestiti Le stanno bene	*Those dresses look good on you (polite)*
Gli stivali ci stanno bene	*Boots look good on us*
Gli stivali vi stanno bene	*Boots look good on you (plural)*
Quelle scarpe gli stanno bene	*Those shoes look good on him*
Quella camicetta le sta bene	*That blouse looks good on her*
Quelle scarpe gli stanno bene	*Those shoes look good on them*

Quelle scarpe Le stanno molto bene!

Use the preposition *a* to introduce indirect objects:

La camicia sta bene a Mark.	*The shirt looks good on Mark.*
La gonna sta bene alla donna.	*The skirt looks good on the woman.*

The Present Progressive

The *present progressive* is a tense that allows you to zero in on ongoing actions: *she is reading, you are watching TV,* etc. The present progressive is made up of two separate parts: (1) the present indicative of the verb *stare*, and (2) the gerund of the verb. The gerund endings are as follows:

Infinitive Ending	Gerund Ending	
-are	-ando	*-ing*
-ere	-endo	*-ing*
-ire	-endo	*-ing*
comprare	comprando	*buying*
leggere	leggendo	*reading*
finire	finendo	*finishing*

Below are three verbs in the present progressive fully conjugated for you:

(io) sto comprando / leggendo / finendo	*I am buying / reading / finishing*
(tu) stai comprando / leggendo / finendo	*you are buying / reading / finishing (familiar)*
(Lei) sta comprando / leggendo / finendo	*you are buying / reading / finishing (polite)*
(lui / lei) sta comprando / leggendo / finendo	*he / she is buying / reading / finishing*
(noi) stiamo comprando / leggendo / finendo	*we are buying / reading / finishing*
(voi) state comprando / leggendo / finendo	*you are buying / reading / finishing (plural)*
(loro) stanno comprando / leggendo / finendo	*they are buying / reading / finishing*

Of the verbs introduced so far, the following have irregular gerunds:

bere	bevendo	*drinking*
dare	dando	*giving*
dire	dicendo	*saying, telling*
fare	facendo	*doing, making*
stare	stando	*staying*
venire	venendo	*coming*

In actual practice, the present progressive is used alternatively with the present indicative:

Present Indicative	**Present Progressive**
Di solito bevo solo l'espresso	Ma in questo momento sto bevendo il cappuccino
I usually drink only espresso	*But at this moment I am drinking cappuccino*
Lui beve un caffè	Mentre lui sta bevendo un caffè, io sto leggendo
He is drinking a coffee	*While he drinks a coffee, I am reading*

The Partitive: Part 2

The forms alcuni / alcune can be used in place of the plural partitives dei, degli, and delle (Unit 14). These forms render the idea of *several* more than of *some*:

Voglio dei libri.	Voglio alcuni libri.
I want some books.	*I want several books.*
Ci sono degli studenti qui.	Ci sono alcuni studenti qui.
There are some students here.	*There are several students here.*
Ho comprato delle cravatte.	Ho comprato alcune cravatte.
I bought some ties.	*I bought several ties.*

The form qualche is also a partitive structure that can be used in place of the plural partitives dei, degli, and delle. It too renders the idea of *several* more than of *some*. In this case, you must be careful because the noun form is singular, even though the meaning is plural (in English):

Voglio dei libri.	Voglio qualche libro.
I want some books.	*I want several books.*
Ci sono degli studenti qui.	C'è qualche studente qui.
There are some students here.	*There are several students here.*
Ho comprato delle cravatte.	Ho comprato qualche cravatta.
I bought some ties.	*I bought several ties.*

The expression **un po' di** means literally *a bit of*:

Voglio della carne.
I want some meat.

Voglio un po' di carne.
I want a bit of meat.

Vorrei dello zucchero.
I would like some sugar.

Vorrei un po' di zucchero.
I would like a bit of sugar.

The Particle ne

The particle **ne** replaces partitive expressions; it means *some, of them, a few*, etc.

Desidera della carne?	*Would you like some meat?*
Sì, ne vorrei un po'.	*Yes, I would like a bit.*
Sì, ne vorrei due chili.	*Yes, I would like two kg.*
Desidera dei libri?	*Would you like some books?*
Sì, ne vorrei cinque.	*Yes, I would like five (of them).*

In compound tenses, the past participle agrees with **ne** in gender and number:

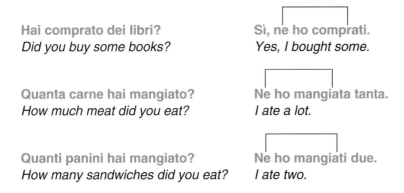

Hai comprato dei libri?
Did you buy some books?

Sì, ne ho comprati.
Yes, I bought some.

Quanta carne hai mangiato?
How much meat did you eat?

Ne ho mangiata tanta.
I ate a lot.

Quanti panini hai mangiato?
How many sandwiches did you eat?

Ne ho mangiati due.
I ate two.

Demonstrative Pronouns

Demonstrative pronouns—*this one, those ones*, etc.—are derived from their corresponding adjective forms as shown below:

This one / These ones			
Demonstrative Adjective Forms		**Demonstrative Pronoun Forms**	
questo / quest'		questo	
questi		questi	
questa / quest'		questa	
queste		queste	
questo romanzo	*this novel*	questo	*this one*
questi stivali	*these boots*	questi	*these ones*
questa scarpa	*this shoe*	questa	*this one*
queste scarpe	*these shoes*	queste	*these ones*

That one / Those ones			
Demonstrative Adjective Forms		**Demonstrative Pronoun Forms**	
Masculine Forms			
quel		quello	
quello		quello	
quell'		quello	
quei		quelli	
quegli		quelli	
Feminine Forms			
quella / quell'		quella	
quelle		quelle	
quel libro	*that book*	quello	*that one*
quei libri	*those books*	quelli	*those ones*
quello stivale	*that boot*	quello	*that one*
quegli stivali	*those boots*	quelli	*those ones*
quell'orecchino	*that earring*	quello	*that one*
quella camicia	*that shirt*	quella	*that one*
quelle camicie	*those shirts*	quelle	*those ones*

The Expression servire a

Like piacere and stare bene a, the expression servire a requires an indirect object or an indirect object pronoun:

With Singular Nouns	**With Plural Nouns**
I need	
Mi serve un romanzo	Mi servono alcuni romanzi
I need a novel	*I need several novels*
you need (familiar)	
Ti serve una camicia	Ti servono alcune camicie
You need a shirt	*You need several shirts*
you need (polite)	
Le serve una camicia	Le servono alcune camicie
You need a shirt	*You need several shirts*
he needs	
Gli serve della carne	Gli servono gli stivali
He needs some meat	*He needs boots*
she needs	
Le serve della carne	Le servono gli stivali
She needs some meat	*She needs boots*

With Singular Nouns	With Plural Nouns
we need	
Ci serve del pane	**Ci servono degli spaghetti**
We need some bread	*We need spaghetti*
you need (plural)	
Vi serve del caffè	**Vi servono degli spaghetti**
You need some coffee	*You need spaghetti*
they need	
Gli serve del caffè	**Gli servono degli spaghetti**
They need some coffee	*They need spaghetti*

ATTIVITÀ

F. Do the following:

First, give the gerund of the following verbs:

1. parlare _____

2. mangiare _____

3. prendere _____

4. scrivere _____

5. capire _____

6. preferire _____

7. dare _____

8. stare _____

9. venire _____

10. essere _____

Now, say the following things in Italian.

Note	
stare zitto	*to be quiet*
Claudio non sta mai zitto.	**Dina non sta mai zitta.**
Loro non stanno mai zitti.	**Le ragazze non stanno mai zitte.**
non più	*not anymore*
in Italia	*to Italy*

11. That shirt looks good on you *(familiar)*.

_____

12. That shirt used to look good on you *(polite)*, but not anymore.

_____

13. Dina, be quiet!

_____

14. Mrs. Martini, be quiet!

_____

15. Carla and Claudio, be quiet!

_____

16. Ladies and gentlemen, be quiet!

_____

17. We have been to Italy!

_____

18. They have also been in Italy!

_____

19. Let's be quiet!

_____

20. Have you ever been to Italy, Bill?

_____

G. Answer the questions as indicated, using the present progressive form of the verb.

> *Model:* Cosa sta facendo Dina?/mangiare
> *Dina sta mangiando.*

1. Cosa stai facendo tu?/leggere

_____

2. Cosa state facendo voi?/bere un caffè

_____

3. Cosa stanno facendo loro?/dormire

_____

4. Cosa sta facendo Alessandro?/dormire

_____

5. Cosa sta facendo Sara?/andare in centro con un'amica

_____

6. Cosa stanno facendo i tuoi genitori?/bere il caffè

_____

7. Cosa state facendo, tu e tua sorella?/parlare

_____

8. Cosa sta facendo Mark?/dire tutto al professore

_____

9. Cosa sta facendo Carla?/dire qualcosa a sua cugina

_____

10. Cosa sta facendo Lei, professoressa?/leggere un bel libro

_____

H. Say that the shirt / blouse looks good on…

     Model: Dina
              La camicetta sta bene a Dina.

1. Marco

_____

2. that man there

_____

3. you _(familiar)_

_____

4. your friend

_____

5. those boys

_____

6. them

_____

7. you _(polite)_

_____

8. me

_____

Now, say that the boots look good on…

9. you _(plural)_

_____

10. that woman there

_____

11. us

_____

12. her

_____

I. Say that the indicated person(s) need(s) the following things in three ways, following the model.

> *Model:* I / apples
> *Mi servono delle mele/Mi servono alcune mele/Mi serve qualche mela*

1. you *(familiar)* / books

_____

2. he / boots

_____

3. she / shoes

_____

4. we / shirts

_____

5. you *(plural)* photos

_____

6. I / tables

_____

7. you *(familiar)* earrings

_____

8. they / chairs

_____

9. they / armchairs

_____

J. Answer the following questions, as indicated:

> *Model:* Vuoi della carne?
> *No, ne ho mangiata troppa.*

1. Vuoi un po' di carne?

_____

2. Vuoi degli spaghetti?

_____

3. Vuoi un po' di panettone?

_____

4. Vuoi delle caramelle *(candies)*?

_____

5. Vuoi dei dolci?

_____

K. Use demonstrative pronouns, following the model.

> *Model:* Vorrei quella camicia.
> *Vorrei quella.*

1. Telefono a quell'amica stasera.

_____

2. Ieri ho parlato a quegli uomini.

_____

3. Anche la settimana scorsa hai mangiate queste caramelle.

_____

4. Hai visto quell'amico ieri.

_____

5. Hai visto quell'amica la settimana scorsa.

_____

6. Non ho mai mangiati quei dolci.

_____

7. Tutti hanno letto questi libri.

_____

8. Domani vado a quella città.

_____

L. Cruciverba!

Horizontal

3 Mi piace ... camicia, non questa.
4 Rosella è andata a fare delle spese ...
5 Mi ... gli stivali.
7 Prego, ... servono dei libri, signore?
10 Mi ... una rivista di moda.
11 Quali riviste vuole? Queste o ...?
12 Quanti romanzi vuole? ... voglio tre.
13 Quante riviste legge al giorno? ... leggo due.
14 ... servono questi libri? *(plural)*
17 Quali stivali mi stanno bene, questi o ...?
19 Cosa fai? ... leggendo un libro.
21 Di solito, porto il trentacinque e ...
23 Alessandro, questa camicia ... sta bene.
24 Quale rivista ti serve, ... o quella?
25 Questa camicetta Le ... veramente bene.
26 Quali scarpe preferisce, ... o quelle?
28 Non ... sta bene quella giacca.
29 Lui sta ... ai suoi amici in questo momento.
30 Questo vestito Le ... molto bene.
31 Che cosa serve a lui? ... serve un paio di stivali.
32 Anche voi ... mangiando in questo momento?
33 Stay! *(polite)*
36 Quella camicia ti sta bene. Sì, è ...
37 Queste scarpe mi ... bene.
39 Quel vestito Le sta molto ...
40 Stay! *(familiar)*
41 Marco ... a destra; lì c'è il negozio.
43 to try on
44 boot
46 Ottima ...
47 Vorrei comprare un ... di fantascienza.
48 science fiction

Vertical

1 Ha il ... di oggi?
2 Cosa ... serve, signora?
3 Quale romanzo vuole? Questo o ...?
5 Le ... anche gli orecchini, signora?
6 Vuole delle scarpe? Sì, ... vorrei un paio.
8 Che ... di scarpa porta, Lei?
9 Vuole della carne? Sì, ... voglio.
10 Ti ... questo vestito?
11 Quale vestito vuole? Questo o ...?
15 Quale libro Le serve? ... o quello?
16 Sì, ... servono gli stivali?
18 Cosa stai ...?
19 Maria, cosa ... leggendo?
20 Anche noi ... leggendo il giornale.
21 Mi serve quella rivista di ...
22 Quali libri preferisci, ... o quelli?
27 Io sto ... di leggere il libro in questo momento.
30 Anche lui è ... molto male ieri.
31 Cosa serve a loro? ... servono libri nuovi.
33 Loro ... mangiando in questo momento, vero?
34 only
35 Voi ... bene, vero?
36 Vorrei gli stivali che ha in ...
38 magazine
42 Desidera? Sì, ... un romanzo
45 Quanto ... questa camicia? Solo trenta euro.

NOTA CULTURALE

Dante Alighieri (1265–1321)

Dante: il padre della lingua italiana

In the dialogue it is mentioned that Dina bought Dante's *Divine Comedy* a few days before. The great medieval poet is considered to be the "father" of the Italian language.

GLOSSARIO

il poeta	*poet*
infatti	*in fact*
l'opera	*work*
stabilire	*to establish*
quindi	*thus*
va il merito	*goes the merit*
il volgare	*vulgar (spoken) language*
trattare di	*to deal with*
allegorico	*allegorical*
il simbolo	*symbol*
la ragione	*reason*

[Look up any other word you cannot figure out.]

Il poeta italiano Dante Alighieri (Firenze, 1265—Ravenna, 1321) è considerato il "padre" della lingua italiana. Infatti, la sua *Divina Commedia* è considerata l'opera che stabilisce la lingua toscana come la lingua letteraria di tutti gli italiani, e quindi a Dante va il merito di aver dato al volgare italiano la dignità di lingua d'arte.

La *Commedia* (completata nel 1321) tratta del viaggio allegorico di Dante nell'Inferno, nel Purgatorio e nel Paradiso, accompagnato dal poeta romano Virgilio, il simbolo della ragione, nell'Inferno. È invece Beatrice, la donna che Dante ama, che lo accompagna in Paradiso.

M. Answer the following questions with complete sentences.

1. Che cosa è considerato Dante Alighieri?

_____

2. Che cosa è considerata la *Divina Commedia*?

_____

3. Che merito va a Dante?

_____

4. Quando è stata completata la *Divina Commedia?*

_____

5. Che cosa significa *(means)* l'Inferno, il Purgatorio e il Paradiso in inglese?

_____

6. Chi accompagna Dante nell'Inferno?

_____

7. Chi accompagna Dante in Paradiso?

_____

Vorrei depositare dei soldi!

Unit 22

Lei ha un conto, vero?

CONVERSAZIONE

[Dina is at a bank taking out some money because she is going on an excursion in a few days to see an opera at Milan's La Scala theater. As always she is curious to find out how certain things are said in Italian, so she listens in on a transaction between another customer and a teller.]

Cliente	Scusi, vorrei depositare quest'assegno.	Excuse me, I would like to deposit this check.
Impiegato	Prego. Lei ha un conto in questa banca, vero?	Certainly. You have an account in this bank, don't you?
Cliente	Sì. Lo aprì mia moglie molti anni fa.	My wife opened it many years ago.
Impiegato	Mi deve dare il Suo libretto e deve anche compilare questo modulo.	You must give me your bankbook and you must also fill out this slip.
Cliente	Ecco il mio libretto e il modulo di versamento.	Here's my bankbook and the deposit slip.
Impiegato	Altro?	Anything else?
Cliente	Sì, vorrei riscuotere in contanti quest'altro assegno.	Yes, I would like to cash this other check.
Impiegato	In biglietti di taglio grosso o piccolo?	In large or small bills?
Cliente	Di taglio grosso e, se possibile, pochi spiccioli. Infine, vorrei prelevare un po' di soldi da quest'altro conto.	In large bills and, if possible, little loose change. Finally, I would like to withdraw a bit of money from this other account.
Impiegato	Va bene! [A little later] Ecco tutto fatto!	OK! All done!
Cliente	Grazie!	Thank you!
Impiegato	Non c'è di che! Buona giornata!	No need to thank me! Have a nice day!

COMPRENSIONE

A. Which response, a or b, is the correct or appropriate one?

1. Il cliente vuole depositare…
   a. un assegno.
   b. un libretto.

2. La moglie dell'uomo aprì un conto nella banca…
   a. molti anni fa.
   b. due anni fa.

3. Il cliente deve compilare…
   a. il suo libretto.
   b. un modulo di versamento.

4. Il cliente vorrebbe anche…
   a. compilare un altro modulo
   b. riscuotere in contanti un altro assegno.

5. Il cliente preferisce i biglietti…
   a. di taglio grosso.
   b. di taglio piccolo.

6. Infine, il cliente vorrebbe…
   a. il suo libretto.
   b. prelevare un po' di soldi da un altro conto.

VOCABOLARIO

Vorrei fare un versamento!

PAROLE NUOVE

aprire	*to open*
l'assegno (ah-ssEh-nyoh)	*check*
il biglietto (beeh-lyEh-ttoh)	*bill*
buono	*good*
compilare	*to fill out*
i contanti	*cash*
il conto	*account*
depositare	*to deposit*
grosso	*big, large*
infine	*finally*
il libretto	*bankbook*
il modulo	*form (to fill out), slip*
poco	*little, few*
possibile	*possible*
prelevare	*to withdraw*
riscuotere (reehs-kwOh-the-reh)	*to cash*
i soldi	*money*
gli spiccioli (spEEh-choh-leeh)	*coins, loose change*
il taglio	*size, cut*
il versamento	*deposit*

ESPRESSIONI E MODI DI DIRE

il biglietto di taglio grosso / piccolo	*large / small bill*
Buona giornata!	*Have a nice day!*
Non c'è di che!	*Don't mention it! No need to thank me!*
tutto fatto	*all done*
un po' di	*a bit of, a little*
vorrei	*I would like*

IRREGOLARITÀ

- The verb aprire has an irregular past participle: aperto / *opened*
- The verb riscuotere also has an irregular past participle: riscosso / *cashed*

ATTIVITÀ

B. Comunicazione.

Say that …

1. you would like to deposit a check in your bank account

_____

2. your mother opened an account many years ago

_____

3. you would like to cash another check

_____

4. you would like large bills, not small ones

_____

5. you do not have any loose change

_____

6. you would like to withdraw a bit of money from another account

_____

7. all is done

_____

Tell a customer that he or she…

8. has to give you his or her bankbook

_____

9. has to fill out this slip

_____

Ask …

10. a customer if he or she has an account in this bank

_____

C. Ask the indicated persons when they did the suggested things. Follow the model. If you are using this book in a classroom situation, then a partner should provide an appropriate answer.

> *Model:* Signor Giusti / aprire / un conto
> —*Signor Giusti, quando ha aperto un conto?*
> —*L'ho aperto ieri.*

1. Signora Martini / aprire / un conto

_____

2. Signor Nardini / riscuotere / quell'assegno

_____

3. Dottor Marchi / compilare / quel modulo

_____

4. Dottoressa Di Nardo / riscuotere / i soldi in contanti

_____

5. Dina / depositare / i soldi

_____

6. Dina / perdere / il tuo libretto

_____

7. Alessandro / prelevare / i soldi

_____

8. Signora Martini / compilare / il modulo di versamento

_____

D. Domande personali.

1. Hai mai aperto un conto in banca? Quando?

_____

2. Vai mai in banca? Per quali ragioni?

_____

3. Quanti soldi vuoi avere?

_____

E. Give a list of activities that someone can carry out in a bank. If you are using this book in a classroom situation, then do this activity with a partner.

_____

_____

_____

_____

_____

_____

_____

_____

LINGUA

The Adjective buono

Like bello, the adjective buono can come before or after the noun it modifies. If it comes after, it is inflected in the regular way. If it comes before the noun it is inflected in a manner that is similar to the indefinite article:

Modifying a masculine noun beginning with z or s + consonant			
Before		After	
buono	(singular)	buono	(singular)
buoni	(plural)	buoni	(plural)
(un) buono zio	a good uncle	(uno) zio buono	
(dei) buoni zii	some good uncles	(degli) zii buoni	

Modifying a masculine noun beginning with any other consonant or any vowel			
Before		After	
buon	(singular)	buono	(singular)
buoni	(plural)	buoni	(plural)
(un) buon libro	a good book	(un) libro buono	
(un) buon amico	a good friend	(un) amico buono	
(dei) buoni libri	some good books	(dei) libri buoni	
(dei) buoni amici	some good friends	(degli) amici buoni	

Modifying a feminine noun beginning with any consonant			
Before		After	
buona	(singular)	buona	(singular)
buone	(plural)	buone	(plural)
(una) buona zia	a good aunt	(una) zia buona	
(delle) buone zie	some good aunts	(delle) zie buone	

Modifying a feminine noun beginning with any vowel			
Before		After	
buon'	(singular)	buona	(singular)
buone	(plural)	buone	(plural)
(una) buon'amica	a good friend	(un') amica buona	
(delle) buone amiche	some good friends	(delle) amiche buone	

When used in certain social expressions or in wish expressions, the adjective always comes before the noun:

Buona giornata!	*Have a nice day!*
Buon anno!	*Happy New Year!*
Buona fortuna!	*Good luck!*
Buon compleanno!	*Happy birthday!*
Buon giorno!	*Good day!*
Buona sera!	*Good evening!*
Buona notte!	*Good night!*

Buona
fortuna!

Object Pronouns: Part 1

In previous units you have been using *indirect object pronouns* such as mi / *to me* and ti / *to you*. There are, of course, also *direct object pronouns*. Like the indirect ones, these are placed right before the verb:

Singular	**Indirect**		**Direct**	
1st person	mi	*to me*	mi	*me*
2nd person	ti	*to you (familiar)*	ti	*you (familiar)*
3rd person	gli	*to him*	lo	*him, it (masculine)*
	le	*to her*	la	*her, it (feminine)*
	Le	*to you (polite)*	La	*you (polite)*
Plural				
1st person	ci	*to us*	ci	*us*
2nd person	vi	*to you*	vi	*you*
3rd person	gli	*to them*	li	*them (masculine)*
			le	*them (feminine)*

Here are examples of direct object pronouns used in simple sentences:

mi	*me*
Maria mi ama	*Mary loves me*
Marco non mi ama	*Marco doesn't love me*

ti	*you (familiar)*
Lui ti conosce	*He knows you*
Noi non ti conosciamo	*We do not know you*

La	you (polite)
Lui La conosce	He knows you
Noi non La conosciamo	We do not know you

lo	him
Io lo chiamo ogni giorno	I call him every day
Noi non lo chiamiamo mai	We never call him

la	her
Loro la conoscono	They know her
Voi invece non la conoscete	You, however, do not know her

ci	us
L'insegnante ci preferisce	The teacher prefers us
Il signor Nardini non ci preferisce	Mr. Nardini does not prefer us

vi	you (plural)
L'insegnante vi chiama	The teacher is calling you
La signora Nardini non vi chiama	Mrs. Nardini is not calling you

li	them (masculine)
Io li chiamo ogni giorno	I call them every day
Noi non li vediamo mai	We never see them

le	them (feminine)
Loro le conoscono	They know them
Voi non le conoscete	You do not know them

Note that lo and la can also mean *it*, and li / le, *them*:

lo replaces a masculine singular direct object	
Maria vuole il panino	Mary wants the sandwich
Maria lo vuole	Mary wants it

la replaces a feminine singular direct object	
Maria vuole la carne	Mary wants the meat
Maria la vuole	Mary wants it

li replaces a masculine plural direct object	
Maria vuole i panini	Mary wants the sandwiches
Maria li vuole	Mary wants them

le replaces a feminine plural direct object	
Maria vuole le scarpe	Mary wants the shoes
Maria le vuole	Mary wants them

When the verb is in the present perfect, there is agreement in gender and number between lo, la, li, le and the past participle. In effect, treat the past participle like an adjective:

Io ho mangiato il panino	*I ate the sandwich*
Io lo ho (l'ho) mangiato	*I ate it*
Io ho mangiato la pizza	*I ate the pizza*
Io la ho (l'ho) mangiata	*I ate it*
Io ho mangiato i panini	*I ate the sandwiches*
Io li ho mangiati	*I ate them*
Io ho mangiato le pizze	*I ate the pizzas*
Io le ho mangiate	*I ate them*

The Past Absolute of Regular Verbs

The past absolute corresponds to English *I spoke, you came, he ate, she bought,* and so on. As you learned in Unit 16, these are usually rendered in Italian with the present perfect:

Ho parlato	*I spoke / I have spoken*
Sei venuto	*You came / You have come*
Ha mangiato	*He ate / He has eaten*
Ha comprato	*She bought / She has bought*

The past absolute can be used in place of the present perfect, but only for "remote" actions, that is for actions that occurred relatively long ago. It is thus used mainly to refer to historical events and dates:

Loro **emigrarono** trent'anni fa. / *They emigrated thirty years ago.*
Galileo **inventò** il telescopio. / *Galileo invented the telescope.*

The past absolute cannot be used with temporal adverbs such as già / *already*, poco fa / *a little while ago*, etc., which limit the action to the immediate past (occurring within less than twenty-four hours). Only the present perfect can be used in such cases.

The past absolute of regular verbs is formed by dropping the infinitive ending of the verbs and adding the following endings to the resulting stem:

First Conjugation		Second Conjugation		Third Conjugation	
Singular		**Singular**		**Singular**	
1st person	-ai	*1st person*	-ei (-etti)	*1st person*	-ii
2nd person	-asti	*2nd person*	-esti	*2nd person*	-isti
3rd person	-ò	*3rd person*	-é (-ette)	*3rd person*	-ì
Plural		**Plural**		**Plural**	
1st person	-ammo	*1st person*	-emmo	*1st person*	-immo
2nd person	-aste	*2nd person*	-este	*2nd person*	-iste
3rd person	-arono	*3rd person*	-erono (-ettero)	*3rd person*	-irono

Below are three verbs fully conjugated for you.

amare → am- *to love*	
(io) amai	*I loved*
(tu) amasti	*you loved (familiar)*
(Lei) amò	*you loved (polite)*
(lui / lei) amò	*he / she loved*
(noi) amammo	*we loved*
(voi) amaste	*you loved (plural)*
(loro) amarono (ah-mAh-roh-noh)	*they loved*

dovere → dov- *to have to*	
(io) dovei / dovetti	*I had to*
(tu) dovesti	*you had to (familiar)*
(Lei) dové / dovette	*you had to (polite)*
(lui / lei) dové / dovette	*he / she had to*
(noi) dovemmo	*we had to*
(voi) doveste	*you had to (plural)*
(loro) doverono / dovettero	*they had to*

finire → fin- *to finish*	
(io) finii	*I finished*
(tu) finisti	*you finished (familiar)*
(Lei) finì	*you finished (polite)*
(lui / lei) finì	*he / she finished*
(noi) finimmo	*we finished*
(voi) finiste	*you finished (plural)*
(loro) finirono (feeh-nEEh-roh-noh)	*they finished*

The Past Absolute of Irregular Verbs

Of the verbs introduced so far, the following have irregular past absolute forms. Notice that in the first set, only the first person singular and the third person singular and plural are irregular. The other persons are formed in the usual way:

avere *to have*	
(io) ebbi	*I had*
(tu) avesti	*you had (familiar)*
(Lei) ebbe	*you had (polite)*
(lui / lei) ebbe	*he / she had*
(noi) avemmo	*we had*
(voi) aveste	*you had (plural)*
(loro) ebbero (Ehb-beh-roh)	*they had*

conoscere *to know, to meet someone (for the first time)*	
(io) conobbi	*I knew, met*
(tu) conoscesti	*you knew, met (familiar)*
(Lei) conobbe	*you knew, met (polite)*
(lui / lei) conobbe	*he / she knew, met*
(noi) conoscemmo	*we knew, met*
(voi) conosceste	*you knew, met (plural)*
(loro) conobbero (koh-nOhb-beh-roh)	*they knew, met*

decidere *to decide*	
(io) decisi	*I decided*
(tu) decidesti	*you decided (familiar)*
(Lei) decise	*you decided (polite)*
(lui / lei) decise	*he / she decided*
(noi) decidemmo	*we decided*
(voi) decideste	*you decided (plural)*
(loro) decisero (deh-chEEh-zeh-roh)	*they decided*

prendere *to take*	
(io) presi	*I took*
(tu) prendesti	*you took (familiar)*
(Lei) prese	*you took (polite)*
(lui / lei) prese	*he / she took*
(noi) prendemmo	*we took*
(voi) prendeste	*you took (plural)*
(loro) presero (prEh-zeh-roh)	*they took*

riscuotere *to cash*	
(io) riscossi	*I cashed*
(tu) riscotesti	*you cashed (familiar)*
(Lei) riscosse	*you cashed (polite)*
(lui / lei) riscosse	*he / she cashed*
(noi) riscuotemmo	*we cashed*
(voi) riscoteste	*you cashed (plural)*
(loro) riscossero (reehs-kOhs-seh-roh)	*they cashed*

scrivere *to write*	
(io) scrissi	*I wrote*
(tu) scrivesti	*you wrote (familiar)*
(Lei) scrisse	*you wrote (polite)*
(lui / lei) scrisse	*he / she wrote*
(noi) scrivemmo	*we wrote*
(voi) scriveste	*you wrote (plural)*
(loro) scrissero (skEEhs-seh-roh)	*they wrote*

venire	to come	
(io) venni	I came	
(tu) venisti	you came (familiar)	
(Lei) venne	you came (polite)	
(lui / lei) venne	he / she came	
(noi) venimmo	we came	
(voi) veniste	you came (plural)	
(loro) vennero (vEhn-neh-roh)	they came	

volere	to want	
(io) volli	I wanted	
(tu) volesti	you wanted (familiar)	
(Lei) volle	you wanted (polite)	
(lui / lei) volle	he / she wanted	
(noi) volemmo	we wanted	
(voi) voleste	you wanted (plural)	
(loro) vollero (vohl-leh-roh)	they wanted	

The following verbs are irregular throughout the conjugation:

bere	to drink	
(io) bevvi / bevetti	I drank	
(tu) bevesti	you drank (familiar)	
(Lei) bevve / bevette	you drank (polite)	
(lui / lei) bevve / bevette	he / she drank	
(noi) bevemmo	we drank	
(voi) beveste	you drank (plural)	
(loro) bevvero (bEhv-veh-roh)/ bevettero	they drank	

dare	to give	
(io) diedi	I gave	
(tu) desti	you gave (familiar)	
(Lei) diede	you gave (polite)	
(lui / lei) diede	he / she gave	
(noi) demmo	we gave	
(voi) deste	you gave (plural)	
(loro) diedero (dyEh-deh-roh)	they gave	

dire *to say, to tell*	
(io) dissi	*I said*
(tu) dicesti	*you said (familiar)*
(Lei) disse	*you said (polite)*
(lui / lei) disse	*he / she said*
(noi) dicemmo	*we said*
(voi) diceste	*you said (plural)*
(loro) dissero (dEEhs-seh-roh)	*they said*

essere *to be*	
(io) fui	*I was*
(tu) fosti	*you were (familiar)*
(Lei) fu	*you were (polite)*
(lui / lei) fu	*he / she was*
(noi) fummo	*we were*
(voi) foste	*you were (plural)*
(loro) furono (fOOh-roh-noh)	*they were*

fare *to do, to make*	
(io) feci	*I did*
(tu) facesti	*you did (familiar)*
(Lei) fece	*you did (polite)*
(lui / lei) fece	*he / she did*
(noi) facemmo	*we did*
(voi) faceste	*you did (plural)*
(loro) fecero (fEh-cheh-roh)	*they did*

stare *to stay*	
(io) stetti	*I stayed*
(tu) stesti	*you stayed (familiar)*
(Lei) stette	*you stayed (polite)*
(lui / lei) stette	*he / she stayed*
(noi) stemmo	*we stayed*
(voi) steste	*you stayed (plural)*
(loro) stettero (stEht-teh-roh)	*they stayed*

ATTIVITÀ

F. Tell your friend to have a nice day, to have a nice evening, etc. Follow the model.

> *Model:* giornata
> *Buona giornata!*

Parole Nuove	
l'annata	*year (all year)*
il divertimento	*enjoyment, fun*
la notte	*night*
la serata	*evening (all evening)*
la vacanza	*vacation*
il viaggio	*trip*

1. viaggio

_____

2. notte

_____

3. serata

_____

4. vacanze

_____

5. divertimento

_____

6. scelta

_____

7. anno

_____

8. annata

_____

G. Say that Dina calls the following people every day.

> *Model:* me
> *Dina mi chiama ogni giorno.*

1. me

_____

2. you *(familiar, singular)*

_____

3. you *(polite, singular)*

_____

4. us

_____

5. you *(plural)*

_____

6. them *(females)*

_____

7. them *(males)*

_____

H. First, ask a friend if he or she wants the indicated item. Then, answer for your friend by saying that you (the friend) do not want it because you bought it already. Follow the model. If you are using this book in a classroom situation, do this activity with a partner.

> *Model:* la carne
> —*Vuoi la carne?*
> —*No, non la voglio perché l'ho comprata già.*

1. la camicia

_____

2. il cellulare

_____

3. le cravatte

_____

4. i dolci

_____

5. gli elettrodomestici

_____

6. quella giacca

_____

7. quelle gonne

_____

8. quei libri

_____

9. quegli orecchini

_____

10. quelle scarpe

_____

I. Come si dice in italiano? Use the past absolute throughout.

> *Model:* I...went to Italy to a long time ago
> *Io andai in Italia molto tempo fa.*

Parole Nuove	
gli Stati Uniti	*the United States*
traslocare	*to move (from one place to another)*

I...

1. went to Italy a long time ago

_____

2. had to work many years ago

_____

3. left for the United States in 1996

_____

4. met Dina in 1995

_____

5. had a house in that city a long time ago

_____

6. decided to move to another city a long time ago

_____

7. took a holiday in 1990

_____

8. came to the United States in 1999

_____

You *(familiar, singular)*...

9. went to Italy a long time ago

_____

10. had to work many years ago

_____

11. left for the United States in 1996

_____

12. met Dina in 1995

_____

13. had a house in that city a long time ago

_____

14. decided to move to another city a long time ago

_____

15. took a holiday in 1990

_____

16. came to the United States in 1999

_____

He / She...

17. went to Italy a long time ago

_____

18. had to work many years ago

_____

19. left for the United States in 1996

_____

20. met Dina in 1995

_____

21. had a house in that city a long time ago

_____

22. decided to move to another city a long time ago

_____

23. took a holiday in 1990

_____

24. came to the United States in 1999

_____

We...

25. went to Italy a long time ago

_____

26. had to work many years ago

_____

27. left for the United States in 1996

_____

28. met Dina in 1995

_____

29. had a house in that city a long time ago

_____

30. decided to move to another city a long time ago

_____

31. took a holiday in 1990

_____

32. came to the United States in 1999

_____

You *(plural)*...

33. went to Italy a long time ago

_____

34. had to work many years ago

_____

35. left for the United States in 1996

_____

36. met Dina in 1995

_____

37. had a house in that city a long time ago

_____

38. decided to move to another city a long time ago

_____

39. took a holiday in 1990

_____

40. came to the United States in 1999

_____

They...

41. went to Italy a long time ago

_____

42. had to work many years ago

_____

43. left for the United States in 1996

_____

44. met Dina in 1995

_____

45. had a house in that city a long time ago

_____

46. decided to move to another city a long time ago

_____

47. took a holiday in 1990

_____

48. came to the United States in 1999

_____

J. Give the corresponding past absolute forms of the following.

      Model: ho mangiato
              mangiai

1. ha scritto

_____

2. hanno voluto

_____

3. ho riscosso

_____

4. abbiamo bevuto

_____

5. avete dato

_____

6. ha detto

_____

7. è stato

_____

8. ha fatto

_____

9. siamo stati

_____

K. Cruciverba!

Horizontal	**Vertical**

Horizontal

1 he gives
5 you give *(familiar)*
6 loose change
7 you give *(plural)*
10 Chi ti ha … tutti quei soldi?
11 Ti piacciono quelle scarpe? Sì, …
   voglio comprare.
12 they give
13 Ha il libretto? Sì, … ho.
14 Vorrei prelevare un po' … soldi.
16 Vuoi questo panino? No, non … voglio.
17 you give *(plural)*
18 Ho … un conto in questa banca un
   anno fa.
19 Lui conosce noi? Sì, lui … conosce.
20 Vorrei biglietti di … piccolo.
22 Anche lui … tanti soldi di solito.
23 Lei deve compilare questo …
26 Vorrei depositare quest'…
27 Mi deve dare il Suo …
28 Ha un … in questa banca?
34 Ho … quei soldi ieri.
35 Questo dolce è molto …
36 Ho già … quel modulo.
38 Questi sono dolci molto …
39 Hai mangiato il dolce? Sì, lo ho …
41 Hai comprate quelle scarpe? Sì, …
   ho comprate
42 Hai mangiato quei panini? Sì, li ho …
44 Hai comprato le scarpe? Sì, le ho … ieri.
45 Hai comprato la carne? Sì, la ho … ieri.

Vertical

1 we give
2 Io ho … quell'assegno in contanti.
3 Vorrei prelevare un po' di … dal mio conto.
4 Vuoi questi soldi? Sì, … voglio.
5 I give
6 Prego, … possibile, non vorrei spiccioli.
8 Se …, vorrei biglietti di taglio grosso.
9 Ho … quei soldi due giorni fa.
12 Give! *(polite)*
15 Ho bisogno di un modulo di …
17 Give! *(familiar)*
21 Signore, … anno!
24 Ti piacciono queste scarpe? Sì, … voglio.
25 Marco e Maria, … chiamo stasera,
   va bene?
29 Signora, … giornata!
30 Vorrei riscuotere in … quest'altro assegno.
31 Quando … hai chiamato?
32 Hai mangiato la carne? Sì, … ho mangiata.
33 Hai comprato quel libro? Sì, … ho comprato.
34 Give! *(polite)*
37 Queste pizze sono molto …
39 Hai mangiato la carne? Sì, la ho …
40 Ti ha chiamato Marco? Sì, lui … ha chiamato.
43 Mi hai chiamato ieri? Sì, … ho chiamato.

NOTA CULTURALE

Dina is going to Milan's La Scala. The opera house was opened in 1778 and has remained symbolic of Italian opera as an art of great appeal to all kinds of people ever since.

L'opera
[Look up any words you cannot figure out].

L'opera nasce *(is born)* in Italia nel tardo sedicesimo secolo *(century)* dagli sforzi *(efforts)* di un gruppo di musicisti e studiosi chiamato Camerata. La Camerata aveva due obiettivi principali: (1) rianimare *(revive)* lo stile musicale degli Antichi Greci, che essi usavano nel loro teatro e

(2) sviluppare *(develop)* un'alternativa alla musica sacra e polifonica del tardo Rinascimento. I membri di Camerata volevano che i compositori trattassero *(treat)* il testo *(text)* su cui era basata la musica in modo realistico, frase per frase.

I più grandi compositori italiani d'opera sono, indubbiamente, i seguenti:

Compositore	Opere principali
Gioacchino Rossini (1792–1868)	*Il Barbiere di Siviglia* (1816)
	Guglielmo Tell (1829)
Gaetano Donizetti (1797–1848)	*L'Elisir d'amore* (1832)
	Lucia di Lamermoor (1835)
Vincenzo Bellini (1801–1835)	*La Sonnambula* (1831)
	Norma (1831)
Giuseppe Verdi (1813–1901)	*La Traviata* (1853)
	Aida (1871)
Giacomo Puccini (1858–1924)	*La Bohème* (1896)
	Madama Butterfly (1904)

L. Identify the composer of the opera and the date when it was first performed.

1. *Guglielmo Tell*

_____

2. *Madama Butterfly*

_____

3. *La Bohème*

_____

4. *Aida*

_____

5. *La Traviata*

_____

6. *Norma*

_____

7. *La Sonnambula*

_____

8. *Il Barbiere di Siviglia*

_____

9. *L'Elisir d'amore*

_____

10. *Lucia di Lamermoor*

_____

Che bel ristorante, vero?

Unit 23

Che bel ristorante!

CONVERSAZIONE

[Dina and Alessandro are at an elegant restaurant one evening, after visiting the famous Uffizi Gallery in Florence earlier in the day.]

Dina	Che bel ristorante!	*What a nice restaurant!*
Alessandro	Io ho molta fame e sete, e tu?	*I'm very hungry and thirsty, and you?*
Dina	Anch'io.	*Me too.*
Alessandro	Cameriere, il menù per favore!	*Waiter, the menu, please!*
Cameriere	Prego!	*Here you are!*
Dina	Per me l'antipasto di melone e prosciutto.	*I'll have (for me) the cantaloupe and ham appetizer.*
Alessandro	Anche per me.	*So will I.*
Cameriere	Va bene. Per il primo piatto, un po' di pasta, minestra?	*OK. For a first dish (would you like) some pasta, soup?*
Dina	A me generalmente piacciono di più i secondi piatti. Io prendo una bistecca alla fiorentina.	*I generally like second dishes more. I'll have a steak in the Florentine style.*
Alessandro	Anch'io.	*So will I.*
Cameriere	Qualcosa da bere? Una bottiglia di vino rosso?	*Something to drink? A bottle of red wine?*
Alessandro	No, siamo troppo giovani. Una bottiglia di acqua minerale.	*No, we are too young. A bottle of mineral water.*
Dina	Buon appetito!	*Eat up! (Have a good appetite!)*
Alessandro	Grazie. Buon appetito!	*Thank you! Eat up!*

[Near the end of the meal]

Dina	Prendiamo un po' di frutta e di caffè espresso?	*Shall we have some fruit and coffee?*
Alessandro	Sì, e forse anche un po' di formaggio. Poi chiederò il conto.	*Yes, and maybe a little bit of cheese. Then I'll ask for the check.*
Dina	E non dimenticare di lasciare una bella mancia!	*And don't forget to leave a nice tip!*
Alessandro	Non è sempre necessario in Italia!	*It is not always necessary in Italy.*

COMPRENSIONE

A. Complete each statement in an appropriate fashion with the missing word(s) or expression.

1. Che _____ ristorante!

2. In Italia, non è sempre necessario lasciare la _____.

3. Alla fine della cena *(At the end of the dinner)* Dina vuole prendere _____.

4. Alla fine Alessandro preferisce _____.

5. Alessandro chiede _____.

6. Dina e Alessandro hanno molta _____.

7. Per l'antipasto, Dina e Alessandro prendono _____.

8. Dina prende una bistecca _____.

9. Da bere prendono _____.

VOCABOLARIO

PAROLE NUOVE

l'acqua (Ah-kkwah)	water
l'antipasto	appetizer
l'appetito	appetite
la bistecca	steak
la bottiglia (boh-ttEEh-lyah)	bottle
il cameriere	waiter
chiedere a (kyEh-deh-reh)	to ask for
il conto	check, bill
dimenticare	to forget
l'espresso	espresso coffee
la fame	hunger
fiorentino	Florentine
il formaggio (fohr-mAh-jjoh)	cheese
la frutta	fruit
lasciare (lah-shAh-reh)	to leave (behind)
la mancia (mAhn-chah)	tip
il melone	cantaloupe
il menù	menu
minerale	mineral
la minestra	soup
necessario	necessary
la pasta	pasta
il piatto	dish
il prosciutto (proh-shOOh-ttoh)	ham (cured)
il ristorante	restaurant
la sete	thirst
il vino	wine

Buon appetito!

ESPRESSIONI E MODI DI DIRE

alla fiorentina	*in the Florentine style / way*
avere fame	*to be hungry*
avere sete	*to be thirsty*
Buon appetito!	*Eat up! (literally: May you have a good appetite!)*

IRREGOLARITÀ

- The past participle of chiedere is chiesto *(asked)*. This verb is also irregular in the past absolute:

Past absolute: (io) chiesi, (tu) chiedesti, (lui / lei / Lei) chiese, (noi) chiedemmo, (voi) chiedeste, (loro) chiesero

- Recall that nouns ending in an accented vowel are invariable: il menù / *the menu*, i menù / *the menus*

ATTIVITÀ

B. Comunicazione.

Say that …

1. you are hungry and thirsty

_____

2. you'll have the cantaloupe and ham appetizer

_____

3. for a first dish, you'll have a plate of pasta

_____

4. you generally like spaghetti for a second dish

_____

5. you'll take a steak in the Florentine style for a second dish today

_____

6. your parents will have a bottle of red wine

_____

7. you and your friend are too young

_____

8. you'll have a bottle of mineral water

_____

9. you and your friend will have a bit of fruit

_____

10. you would also like a bit of cheese

_____

11. you will ask for the check (bill)

_____

12. it is not always necessary to leave a tip in Italy

_____

13. your father asked your mother to come to the United States many years ago

_____

14. you asked your mother why we came to the United States a long time ago

_____

Tell Alessandro…

15. not to forget to leave a nice tip

_____

Ask …

16. a waiter for the menu

_____

17. Dina if she is also hungry and thirsty

_____

18. Alessandro if he wants a bit of soup for a first dish

_____

19. Dina if she'll have something to drink

_____

20. Mrs. Martini if she likes cheese

_____

C. Come si dice in italiano?

Note
To express *What a nice / beautiful …!* use **bello** before the noun:
Che bella giornata! *What a beautiful day!* **Che bella gonna!** *What a nice skirt!*

1. What a nice restaurant!

_____

2. What a nice steak!

_____

3. What a nice dress!

_____

4. What nice pants!

_____

5. What nice books!

_____

6. What a nice city!

_____

7. What beautiful weather!

_____

8. Eat up!

_____

9. What nice menus!

_____

10. I want a steak in the Florentine style

_____

D. Order the following dishes, drinks, etc. at a restaurant. Follow the model.

> *Model:* a plate of spaghetti
> *Vorrei un piatto di spaghetti.*

1. a bottle of mineral water

_____

2. a steak

_____

3. an appetizer of ham and cantaloupe

_____

4. an espresso

_____

5. some cheese

_____

6. some fruit

_____

7. a bowl of soup

_____

8. a plate of pasta

_____

E. Domande personali.

1. Qual è il tuo piatto preferito *(favorite)*?

_____

2. Ti piace l'espresso?

_____

3. Cosa prendi di solito per antipasto?

_____

4. Cosa prendi di solito per primo piatto?

_____

5. Cosa prendi di solito per dessert?

_____

F. Write a brief composition on any experience you have had eating at an Italian restaurant.

Parole Utili *(useful)*	
il bicchiere	glass (drinking)
il coltello	knife
il cucchiaio	spoon
il dessert	dessert
la forchetta	fork
preferito	favorite
succedere (past participle: successo)	to happen
è successo	it happened
la trattoria	family restaurant

_____

_____

_____

_____

_____

_____

_____

_____

LINGUA

Object Pronouns: Part 2

A *stressed object pronoun* is one that follows the verb. It is used for emphasis, for avoiding ambiguity, and after prepositions. Here is a summary of the stressed object pronouns:

Singular	Indirect		Direct	
1st person	a me	to me	me	me
2nd person	a te	to you (familiar)	te	you (familiar)
3rd person	a lui	to him	lui	him
	a lei	to her	lei	her
	a Lei	to you (polite)	Lei	you (polite)
Plural				
1st person	a noi	to us	noi	us
2nd person	a voi	to you	voi	you
3rd person	a loro	to them	loro	them

me Maria ama me, non te	me Mary loves me, not you
te Io vengo con te in centro	you (familiar) I'm coming with you downtown
Lei Io vengo con Lei in centro	you (polite) I'm coming with you downtown
lui Mio zio preferisce lui, non me	him My uncle prefers him, not me
lei Voi conoscete solo lei, vero?	her You know only her, right?
noi Anche Maria viene con noi	us Maria is also coming with us
voi Lei parla sempre di voi	you (plural) She always speaks of you
loro Marco parla sempre di loro	them Marco always speaks about them

Maria ama me, non te!

The Uses of molto

The word molto has several meanings and functions. As an adjective it means *much, many*, agreeing with the noun it modifies in gender and number. As an adverb it means *very*. There is no agreement in the latter case:

As an Adjective	As an Adverb
Lei mangia molto formaggio *She eats a lot of cheese*	Il formaggio è molto buono *The cheese is very good*
Lui mangia molta carne *He eats a lot of meat*	La carne è molto buona *The meat is very good*
Qui ci sono molti ristoranti buoni *Here there are many good restaurants*	Quei ristoranti sono molto buoni *Those restaurants are very good*
Maria ha molte amiche *Mary has many friends*	Le sue amiche sono molto belle *Her friends are very beautiful*

Note: when modifying nouns found in idiomatic expressions such as avere fame, avere sete, etc., molto still agrees with the noun, no matter what its meaning is when translated into English:

> Sandra ha molta sete   *Sandra is very thirsty*
> Umberto ha molta fame   *Umberto is very hungry*

The opposite of molto is poco:

As an Adjective	As an Adverb
Lei mangia poco formaggio *She eats little cheese*	Il formaggio è poco buono *The cheese is not so great*
Lui mangia poca carne *He eats little meat*	La carne è poco buona *The meat is not so good*
Qui ci sono pochi ristoranti buoni *Here there are few good restaurants*	Quei ristoranti sono poco buoni *Those restaurants are not so good*
Maria ha poche amiche *Mary has few friends*	Le sue amiche sono poco interessanti *Her friends are not so interesting*

Food Preparations

The prepositional contraction a + *definite article* is used to convey the type of food preparation used:

la bistecca alla fiorentina	*steak in the Florentine style*
il panino al formaggio	*cheese sandwich*
gli spaghetti all'olio	*spaghetti with oil*

The Negative Imperative

As is the case with all verbal tenses, the negative imperative is formed by adding **non** before the predicate. However, you must make one change in this case. In the second-person singular (**tu** form) you must use the infinitive of the verb:

Familiar Forms	
Affirmative Imperative	Negative Imperative
Umberto, mangia la pasta! *Umberto, eat the pasta!*	Umberto, non mangiare la pasta! *Umberto, don't eat the pasta!*
Sandra, bevi l'acqua! *Sandra, drink the water!*	Sandra, non bere l'acqua! *Sandra, don't drink the water!*
Polite Forms	
Affirmative Imperative	Negative Imperative
Signor Marchi, mangi la pasta! *Mr. Marchi, eat the pasta!*	Signor Marchi, non mangi la pasta! *Mr. Marchi, don't eat the pasta!*
Signora Marchi, beva l'acqua! *Mrs. Marchi, drink the water!*	Signora Marchi, non beva l'acqua! *Mrs. Marchi, don't drink the water!*
Plural Forms	
Affirmative Imperative	Negative Imperative
Signori, mangino la pasta! *Gentlemen, eat the pasta!*	Signori, non mangino la pasta! *Gentlemen, don't eat the pasta!*
Marco e Mina, bevete l'acqua! *Marco and Mina, drink the water!*	Marco e Mina, non bevete l'acqua! *Marco and Mina, don't drink the water!*

ATTIVITÀ

G. Tell the following people to do certain things, as in the model.

> *Model:* Dina...come with me!
> *Dina, vieni con me!*

Parola Nuova	
senza	without

Dina...

1. come with me

_____

2. don't eat the pasta, without him

_____

3. speak to us, not to them

_____

4. go with them to the restaurant

_____

5. don't say that I never come with you

_____

Signora Marchi...

6. eat a lot of soup

_____

7. don't eat too many sweets

_____

8. drink a lot of mineral water

_____

9. don't speak to him and don't call her

_____

Mark and Paul...

10. eat that ham sandwich

_____

11. don't eat the cheese pastry

_____

12. eat that steak in the Florentine style

_____

H. Make each command negative.

>*Model:* Parla a lui!
>*Non parlare a lui!*

1. Andiamo in centro!

_____

2. Va' in centro!

_____

3. Beva l'acqua!

_____

4. Bevi l'acqua!

_____

5. Di' tutto a loro!

_____

6. Dica tutto a loro!

_____

I. Say the following things about Dina and Alessandro, following the model. Use *molto* and *poco* as shown.

>*Model:* stanco
>*Dina è molto stanca.*
>*Alessandro, invece, è poco stanco.*
>
>fame
>*Dina ha molta fame.*
>*Alessandro, invece, ha poca fame.*

1. sete

_____

2. amici

_____

3. sonno

_____

4. soldi

_____

J. Cruciverba!

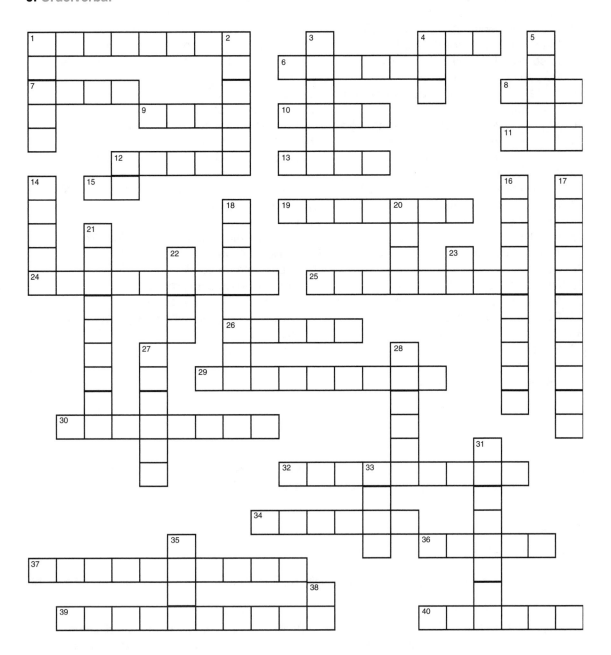

Horizontal	**Vertical**

Horizontal

1 Marco, non … tutta la pasta!
4 Io vado in centro con …, non con lei.
6 Marco, non … in centro oggi!
7 Io sono andata con … in centro.
8 Ho parlato a …, non a lui.
9 Maria, non andare a … delle spese oggi! Fa brutto tempo.
10 Signora Balducci, non … in centro oggi!
11 Il professore ha parlato a … ieri.
12 Ti ho detto questo … volte.
13 Marco, non … troppo vino!
15 Lui ha chiamato …, vero? *(familiar)*
19 Hai … ancora il conto?
24 Vorrei l'… di melone e prosciutto.
25 to ask for
26 Adesso chiederò il …
29 waiter
30 Hai … una mancia?
32 Mi piacciono i panini al …
34 Per antipasto prendo il … e prosciutto.
36 Per primo piatto prendo la …
37 Preferisco i panini al …
39 restaurant
40 Per secondo …, prendo una bistecca.

Vertical

1 Lei mangia … formaggio.
2 Angela, non … sempre così umile!
3 Roberto, Angela, non … in centro!
4 Tu sei andata in centro con …, non con lui, vero?
5 May I help you?
12 Lui ha chiamato …. non te.
14 Prendiamo anche una bottiglia di … minerale.
16 Mi dia una bistecca alla …
17 Non … di lasciare una bella mancia!
18 No, non mi piace la … alla fiorentina.
20 Hai …? Allora, prendiamo l'acqua minerale.
21 Prendiamo una … di vino rosso.
22 Ho molta ….
23 Chi è andato in centro con …, Maria?
27 Hai lasciato la … al cameriere?
28 Prendiamo un po' di … e di caffè?
31 Per primo piatto, io prendo la …
33 Cameriere, il …, per favore!
35 Da bere prendiamo una bottiglia di … rosso.
38 Vieni con …!

NOTA CULTURALE

Dina and Alessandro visited the famous Uffizi Gallery in Florence, which is symbolic of the importance that the visual arts play, and have always played, in Italian culture.

L'arte
[Look up any words you cannot figure out.]

L'arte italiana è storicamente *(historically)* una delle più importanti del mondo. Eccone alcuni esempi:

Artista	*Opere*	*Importanza*
Giotto (1267?–1337)	*Cristo e la Vergine* (1305) *La Madonna degli Ognissanti* (1310)	È importante per la sua dipintura del corpo umano in termini naturali, diventando così il primo artista "realistico."
Leonardo da Vinci (1452–1519)	*L'Ultima Cena* (1495) *La Gioconda/Mona Lisa* (1503)	Da Vinci era un grande artista, ingegnere, musicista e scienziato. Era il più versatile genio del Rinascimento.
Michelangelo Buonarroti (1475–1564)	*Il Davide* (1501) *La Pietà* (1498–1500)	Michelangelo è probabilmente il più grande artista della storia, famoso sia per i suoi dipinti che per le sue sculture.
Giorgio de Chirico (1888–1978)	*Ariadne* (1933) *Piazza Italiana* (1955)	Artista italiano nato in Grecia, egli fondò lo stile metafisico con i suoi contrasti di chiaro e di scuro.

K. Now, in your own words give a summary of the accomplishments of each artist. Do not copy the comments above directly. Use them as a basis.

1. Giotto

_____

_____

_____

_____

_____

2. Leonardo da Vinci

_____

_____

_____

_____

_____

3. Michelangelo

_____

_____

_____

_____

_____

4. Giorgio de Chirico

_____

_____

_____

_____

_____

Vuoi uscire, Dina?

Unit 24

Vuoi uscire stasera?

CONVERSAZIONE

[Alessandro phones Dina to ask her out that evening. He suggests going first to a lecture at the university on the works of Alberto Moravia, a famous twentieth-century writer, and then to a movie or disco.]

Alessandro	Pronto, Dina, sono io, Alessandro. Vuoi uscire stasera? Pago tutto io!	Hello, Dina, it's me, Alessandro. Do you want to go out tonight? I'll pay for everything!
Dina	Tu sei sempre così ironico, Alessandro! Dove andiamo?	You're always so ironic, Alessandro! Where shall we go?
Alessandro	Prima c'è una conferenza all'università. Dopo possiamo andare a ballare o al cinema. Che ne pensi?	First, there's a lecture at the university. Then we can go dancing or to the movies. What do you think?
Dina	Preferirei andare a un concerto o a un locale notturno.	I would prefer to go to a concert or to a nightclub.
Alessandro	Va bene, vedremo. Ti telefono più tardi. Verso le venti, va bene?	OK, we'll see. I'll call you later. Around 8:00 P.M., OK?
Dina	D'accordo. Aspetto la tua telefonata.	OK. I'll wait for your call.
Alessandro	A presto!	Talk to you soon!

COMPRENSIONE

A. Rispondi alle seguenti domande con frasi intere.

1. Che cosa chiede Alessandro a Dina?

_____

2. Chi pagherà tutto?

_____

3. Che cosa è sempre Alessandro, secondo Dina?

_____

4. Dove vuole andare prima Alessandro?

_____

5. Dove vuole andare Alessandro dopo?

_____

6. Dove preferirebbe andare Dina?

_____

7. A che ora telefonerà Alessandro a Dina?

VOCABOLARIO

PAROLE NUOVE

aspettare	to wait for
ballare	to dance
il cinema (chEEh-neh-mah)	movies
il concerto	concert
la conferenza	lecture
ironico (eeh-rOh-neeh-koh)	ironic
l'opera	work (literary, artistic, etc.)
prima	first, at first
tardi	late
telefonare	to phone
la telefonata	phone call
uscire (ooh-shEEh-reh)	to go out
verso	towards, around

ESPRESSIONI E MODI DI DIRE

Che ne pensi?	What do you think about it?
locale notturno	nightclub
più tardi	later

Che ne pensi?

IRREGOLARITÀ

- Notice that il cinema is masculine, even though it ends in -a. The reason is that the word is an abbreviation of il cinematografo. It is invariable: i cinema / the movies
- The verb uscire has the following irregular forms:

Pres. Ind.   (io) esco, (tu) esci, (lui / lei / Lei) esce, (noi) usciamo, (voi) uscite, (loro) escono (Ehs-koh-noh)

Imperative   (io)—, (tu) esci, (Lei) esca, (noi) usciamo, (voi) uscite, (Loro) escano

Note that it is conjugated with essere in compound tenses: (io) sono uscito / uscita, etc.

ATTIVITÀ

B. Comunicazione.

Say that…

1. it is you on the phone

_____

2. you will pay for everything

_____

3. there is a lecture at the university

_____

4. afterwards you (two) can go dancing

_____

5. you would prefer going to the movies

_____

6. or you would prefer going to a concert or nightclub

_____

Tell a friend that…

7. you'll phone him or her later

_____

8. you'll phone him or her around five P.M.

_____

9. you'll wait for his or her phone call

_____

Ask …

10. Dina if she wants to go out

_____

11. Alessandro why he is always so ironic

_____

12. Alessandro where the two of you will be going

_____

13. Dina what she thinks

_____

14. Dina at what time she wishes to go out

_____

C. Indicate who is going out with whom. Follow the model, using uscire in the present indicative first and then in the present perfect (as shown).

> *Model:* Io / with you
> *Io esco con te stasera.*
> *Sono uscito / uscita con te anche ieri sera* (last night).

1. Io / with them

_____

2. Tu / with her

_____

3. Lui / with us

_____

4. Noi / with them

_____

5. Voi / with him

_____

6. Loro / with us

_____

D. Tell the following people to come out with you to the movies.

> *Model:* Dina
> *Dina esci con me al cinema!*

1. Alessandro

_____

2. Signor Martini

_____

3. Mark e Paul

_____

4. Signor e signora Martini

_____

E. Domande personali

1. Ti piace uscire la sera?

_____

2. Con chi esci generalmente?

_____

3. Dove vai?

_____

F. Write a brief composition about any Italian movie you have seen. If you have not seen an Italian movie, then write about your favorite movie.

Parole Utili	
il film (i film)	movie (movies)
il regista / la regista	the movie director (male / female)
l'attore / l'attrice	actor / actress

_____

_____

_____

_____

_____

_____

_____

_____

LINGUA

Chi ha mangiato la carne?

Lui l'ha mangiata tutta!

Object Pronouns: Part 3

You have learned to use indirect and direct object pronouns in previous units. You also learned that there is agreement in gender and number between the direct object pronoun and the past participle of verbs in compound tenses:

Lui ha mangiato tutta la carne
He ate all the meat

Lui l'ha mangiata tutta
He ate it all

Lei ha mangiato tutti gli spaghetti
She ate all the spaghetti

Lei li ha mangiati tutti
She ate them all

However, do not assume that past participles agree with indirect object pronouns as well. There is, in fact, no agreement between indirect object pronouns and past participles:

mi	*to me*
(Tu) mi hai dato il menù, vero?	*You gave the menu to me, right?*
ti	*to you (familiar)*
Sì, io ti ho dato il menù	*Yes, I gave you the menu*
Le	*to you (polite)*
Le ho detto tutto!	*I said everything to you!*
gli	*to him*
Gli ho parlato ieri	*I spoke to him yesterday*
le	*to her*
Le ho parlato ieri	*I spoke to her yesterday*
ci	*to us*
(Loro) ci hanno detto tutto	*They told everything to us*
vi	*to you (plural)*
(Loro) vi hanno detto tutto	*They told everything to you*
gli	*to them*
Alessandro gli ha parlato ieri	*Alessandro spoke to them yesterday*

Recall as well that stressed pronouns (Unit 23) can be used in place of unstressed indirect object pronouns after a to convey emphasis. These come after the verb:

a me	*to me*
Tu hai dato il menù a me, vero?	*You gave the menu to me, right?*
a te	*to you (familiar)*
Sì, ho dato il menù a te	*Yes, I gave the menu to you*
a Lei	*to you (polite)*
Ho detto tutto a Lei	*I told everything to you*
a lui	*to him*
Ho parlato a lui ieri	*I spoke to him yesterday*
a lei	*to her*
Ho parlato a lei ieri	*I spoke to her yesterday*
a noi	*to us*
(Loro) hanno detto tutto a noi	*They told everything to us*
a voi	*to you (plural)*
(Loro) hanno detto tutto a voi	*They told everything to you*
a loro	*to them*
Alessandro ha parlato a loro ieri	*Alessandro spoke to them yesterday*

Peculiar Verb Uses

Note that aspettare means *to wait for.* Thus, do not translate *for* in Italian in this case:

Io aspetto Maria	*I'm waiting for Mary*
Chi ha aspettato il tuo amico?	*Who waited for your friend?*

The same applies to cercare and pagare:

Maria cerca la sua amica	*Mary is looking for her friend*
Ho pagato tutto io!	*I paid for everything!*

On the other hand, unlike English *to phone,* the verb telefonare requires the preposition a:

Maria sta telefonando alla sua amica	*Mary is phoning her friend*
Ho già telefonato a lei!	*I already phoned her!*

Therefore, only indirect object pronouns are used with this verb:

Maria le telefona ogni giorno	*Mary phones her every day*
Gli ho già telefonato!	*I have already phoned him!*

ATTIVITÀ

G. Indicate who Dina phones and waits for often. Then say that she phoned and waited for the indicated persons even yesterday. Follow the model.

> *Model:* telefonare… "me"
> *Dina mi telefona spesso.*
> *Dina mi ha telefonato anche ieri.*
>
> aspettare… "me"
> *Dina mi aspetta spesso.*
> *Dina mi ha aspettato anche ieri.*

telefonare…

1. "me"

_____

2. "you" *(familiar, singular)*

_____

3. "you" *(familiar, polite)*

_____

4. "us"

5. "you" *(plural)*

6. "them" *(masculine)*

7. "them" *(feminine)*

aspettare…

8. "me"

9. "you" *(familiar, singular)*

10. "you" *(familiar, polite)*

11. "us"

12. "you" *(plural)*

13. "them" *(masculine)*

14. "them" *(feminine)*

H. Come si dice in italiano?

1. Who paid those bills? Alessandro paid for them.

2. Who looked for Dina? They looked for her.

3. They said everything to me, not to her.

4. To whom did you give the menù? Did you give it to him or to her?

5. I saw those two movies. I saw them yesterday.

I. Cruciverba!

Horizontal

3 Ho … la tua telefonata tutta la giornata ieri.
7 Possiamo andare al …, va bene?
10 Hai telefonato a Claudio? Sì, … ho già telefonato.
12 Dina, che cosa …?
15 Ti telefono più …, va bene?
16 Perché non andiamo a un … notturno?
17 Lui ha telefonato a …, non a te.
20 Lei non ha mai telefonato a …
21 Preferirei andare a un …
23 Di solito quando usciamo, … noi.
24 Hai parlato a Claudio? Sì, ho parlato a … ieri
27 Hai dato il libro a Claudio? Sì, … ho dato il libro.
28 A che ora … i tuoi amici stasera?
30 Go out! *(plural)*
32 Dina, perché non … mai la carne?

Vertical

1 Carla, … telefono più tardi, va bene?
2 Hai telefonato a Dina? Sì … ho telefonato.
4 Chi paga oggi? … tu, va bene?
5 Quando mi hai …?
6 D'accordo. Aspetto la tua …
7 Quando vi ha telefonato? … ha telefonato ieri.
8 Quando … hai telefonato?
9 Ti telefono … le diciotto.
11 Mia sorella … molto bene.
13 Il sabato sera, di solito … con gli amici.
14 Claudio, quando … di solito a lavorare?
18 Mark, Dina, … ho detto tutto.
19 Hai parlato ai miei amici? Sì, ho già parlato a …
22 Alessandro, a che ora … stasera?
23 Loro non … mai quando escono.
24 Hai parlato a Carla? Sì, ho parlato a … ieri.
25 A che ora … noi stasera?
26 Mark, … con me!
28 A che ora … tua sorella stasera?
29 Loro sono già …
31 Signora Marchi, … con me!

NOTA CULTURALE

Alessandro asks Dina to go with him to a lecture on the works of the late Alberto Moravia (1907–1990), just one of the great names in the history of Italian literature.

Le origini della letteratura italiana

Il Medioevo

[Look up any word you cannot figure out.]

La letteratura italiana traccia *(traces)* le sue radici *(roots)* all'inizio del Duecento *(twelve hundreds)*, promuovendo *(promoting)* attraverso i secoli *(centuries)* molti movimenti che hanno avuto grande impatto *(impact)* sulle altre letterature nazionali, anche se l'italiano non diventò una lingua ufficiale fino al 1870.

Tuttavia *(nevertheless)*, la caratteristica principale della letteratura italiana è l'uniformità della sua lingua—uniformità che inizia con le opere di tre grandi scrittori toscani medioevali, Dante Alighieri (1265–1321), l'autore della *Divina Commedia* (Unit 21), Francesco Petrarca (1304–1374), l'autore del *Canzoniere*, una collezione di 366 poesie che trattano dell'amore di Petrarca per una donna chiamata Laura, e Giovanni Boccaccio (1313–1375), l'autore del *Decamerone*, una collezione di cento novelle che trattano della vita quotidiana *(daily life)* medioevale dal punto di vista psicologico. Questi lavori stabiliscono il toscano come la lingua letteraria di tutta l'Italia.

J. Answer the following questions.

1. Dove traccia le sue radici la letteratura italiana?

_____

2. Che cosa promuove attraverso i secoli?

_____

3. Quando diventò una lingua ufficiale l'italiano?

_____

4. Che cosa scrisse Dante?

_____

5. Che cosa scrisse Petrarca?

_____

6. Che cosa scrisse Boccaccio?

_____

Dottoressa, ho un forte mal di testa!

Mi fa male la gola!

CONVERSAZIONE

[After having gone out to the movies the night before with Alessandro, Dina wakes up this morning feeling rather sick. She decides to go and see a doctor. Fortunately, she gets an appointment right away.]

Dina	Dottoressa, mi fa male la gola.	*Doctor, my throat hurts.*
Dottoressa	Ha la febbre?	*Do you have a fever?*
Dina	Sì, e ho un forte mal di testa.	*Yes, and I have a bad (strong) headache.*
Dottoressa	Ha anche mal di stomaco?	*Do you also have a stomachache?*
Dina	No, ma mi sento veramente male.	*No, but I feel really bad.*
Dottoressa	[After examining Dina] Lei ha un forte raffreddore che potrebbe diventare influenza se non lo curiamo.	*You have a bad cold, which could turn into the flu, if we don't look after it.*
Dina	Che cosa devo fare?	*What should I do?*
Dottoressa	Stia a casa e beva molti liquidi!	*Stay at home and drink plenty of liquids!*
Dina	E se peggiora?	*And if it gets worse?*
Dottoressa	Torni da me e Le prescriverò degli antibiotici.	*Come back to me and I will prescribe some antibiotics.*
Dina	Grazie, dottoressa!	*Thank you, doctor.*

COMPRENSIONE

A. Match the items in the two columns in an appropriate fashion.

1. A Dina fa male …	a. degli antibiotici.
2. Ha anche la …	b. liquidi.
3. E un forte …	c. casa.
4. Non ha il …	d. influenza.
5. Dina si sente veramente …	e. raffreddore.
6. Dina ha un forte …	f. male.
7. Potrebbe diventare …	g. mal di stomaco.
8. Dina deve stare a …	h. mal di testa.
9. Deve bere molti …	i. febbre.
10. Se peggiora, la dotteressa le prescriverà…	j. la gola.

VOCABOLARIO

PAROLE NUOVE

l'antibiotico	*antibiotic*
curare	*to look after, to cure*
diventare*	*to become*
la febbre	*fever, temperature*
forte	*strong*
la gola	*throat*
l'influenza	*flu*
il liquido (IEEh-kweeh-doh)	*liquid*
male	*bad*
prescrivere (preh-skrEEh-veh-reh)	*to prescribe*
il raffreddore	*common cold*
sentirsi	*to feel*
lo stomaco (stOh-mah-koh)	*stomach*
la testa	*head*

ESPRESSIONI E MODI DI DIRE

fare male a	*to hurt*
mal di (mal di testa, stomaco...)	*ache (headache, stomachache, ...)*
potrebbe	*it could*

Mi fa male la testa!

NOTA

- The verb prescrivere is made up of pre and the verb scrivere. So it is conjugated exactly like scrivere.

ATTIVITÀ

B. Comunicazione.

Tell your doctor that …

1. your throat hurts

_____

2. you have a fever

_____

3. you have a bad headache

_____

4. you also have a stomachache

_____

5. you feel really bad

_____

6. you have a bad cold

_____

Ask the doctor …

7. if you have the flu

_____

8. what you must do to look after your cold

_____

9. if you should stay at home

_____

10. if you should drink liquids

_____

11. what you should do if it gets worse

_____

12. if you should go back to him or her

_____

13. if he or she will prescribe antibiotics

_____

C. Your brother is feeling bad. First, give his symptoms.

> *Model:* stomachache
> *Mio fratello ha mal di stomaco.*

1. fever

_____

2. sore throat

_____

3. bad headache

_____

4. stomachache

_____

Now, after going to the doctor say the following.

> *Model:* that he has a cold
> *Mio fratello ha il raffreddore.*

Say that he…

5. might have the flu

_____

6. has to take antibiotics

_____

7. has to take plenty of liquids

_____

8. has to stay at home

_____

D. Domande personali.

Parole Utili / Espressioni	
il medico (mEh-deeh-koh)	medical doctor
lo studio medico	doctor's office
da + place	
dal medico	at the doctor's
da Dina	at Dina's house

1. Hai un medico di famiglia? Come si chiama?

_____

2. Dove ha il suo studio?

_____

3. Quante volte all'anno vai dal medico?

_____

4. Come ti senti in questo momento?

_____

5. Che cosa fai quando hai il raffreddore?

_____

E. Your sister just caught a bad cold. Describe her symptoms and then write down what the doctor told her.

_____

_____

_____

_____

_____

_____

_____

_____

_____

_____

_____

_____

_____

LINGUA

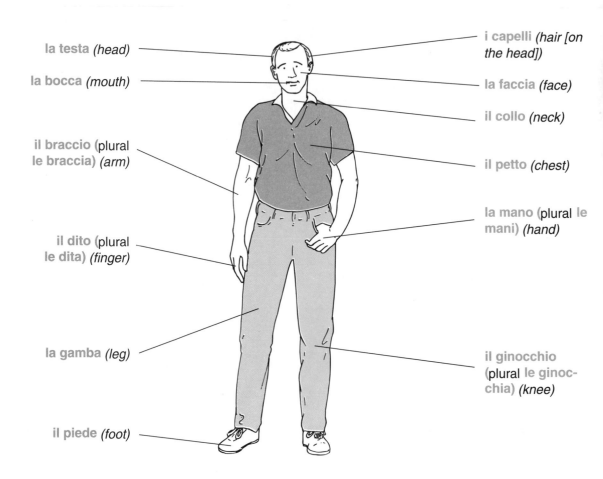

la testa *(head)*

la bocca *(mouth)*

il braccio (plural le braccia) *(arm)*

il dito (plural le dita) *(finger)*

la gamba *(leg)*

il piede *(foot)*

i capelli *(hair [on the head])*

la faccia *(face)*

il collo *(neck)*

il petto *(chest)*

la mano (plural le mani) *(hand)*

il ginocchio (plural le ginocchia) *(knee)*

The Human Body

The following words and expressions will come in handy when talking about the human body:

il corpo	body
la fronte	forehead
il gomito	elbow
la guancia	cheek
il labbro (plural le labbra)	lip
la lingua	tongue
il naso	nose
l'occhio	eye
l'orecchio	ear
la spalla	shoulder
l'unghia	fingernail

Notice that some nouns have irregular plurals ending in -a. And in the plural, the gender of these nouns changes to the feminine:

Singular (Masculine)		Plural (Feminine)	
il braccio lungo	*the long arm*	le braccia lunghe	*the long arms*
il dito lungo	*the long finger*	le dita lunghe	*the long fingers*
il ginocchio grosso	*the huge knee*	le ginocchia grosse	*the huge knees*
il labbro grosso	*the large lip*	le labbra grosse	*the large lips*

Notice that the expression fare male a is translated as *to hurt,* but it literally means *"to make hurt to":*

With Singular Nouns	With Plural Nouns
Mi fa male la testa	Mi fanno male i piedi
My head hurts	*My feet hurt*
Ti fa male la gola?	Ti fanno male le ginocchia?
Does your throat hurt? (familiar)	*Do your knees hurt? (familiar)*
Le fa male il dito?	Le fanno male le dita?
Does your finger hurt? (polite)	*Do your fingers hurt? (polite)*
Gli fa male la testa	Gli fanno male i piedi
His head hurts	*His feet hurt*
Le fa male la gola	Le fanno male le labbra
Her throat hurts	*Her lips hurt*
Ci fa male la testa	Ci fanno male le braccia
Our heads hurt	*Our arms hurt*
Vi fa male la gola?	Vi fanno male le gambe?
Does your throat hurt? (plural)	*Do your legs hurt?*
Gli fa male la gola	Gli fanno male le gambe
Their throats hurt	*Their legs hurt*

Spelling Changes in Plural Formation

As you know, masculine nouns ending in -o are made plural by changing the -o to -i:

Singular		Plural	
libro	*book*	libri	*books*
tavolo	*table*	tavoli	*tables*

If the noun or adjective ends in -co, the hard sound is retained if the preceding sound is a consonant. The hard c sound is indicated with ch:

Singular		Plural	
stanco	tired	stanchi (stAhn-keeh)	tired
bianco	white	bianchi (byAhn-keeh)	white

If the preceding sound is a, o, or u, the tendency is to maintain the hard c sound. This is a tendency, not a hard and fast rule. There are exceptions to it:

Singular		Plural	
buco	hole	buchi (bOOh-keeh)	holes
baco	silkworm	bachi (bAh-keeh)	silkworms
fuoco	fire	fuochi (fwOh-keeh)	fires

If the preceding sound is e or i, the tendency is instead to make the plural -ci, which represents a soft c sound. Again, this is a tendency, not a hard and fast rule. There are exceptions to it:

Singular		Plural	
amico	friend	amici (ah-mEEh-cheeh)	friends
medico	doctor	medici (mEh-deeh-cheeh)	doctors

This "dual plural system" does not apply to feminine nouns and adjectives ending in -ca. In this case the hard c sound is always retained:

Singular		Plural	
amica	friend	amiche (ah-mEEh-keeh)	friends (female)
stanca	tired	stanche (stAhn-keh)	tired

In the case of -go the hard sound is normally retained unless the ending is -logo and refers to a profession or job:

Singular		Plural	
lago	lake	laghi (lAh-geeh)	lakes
albergo	hotel	alberghi (ahl-bEhr-geeh)	hotels
but			
biologo	biologist	biologi (beeh-Oh-loh-jeeh)	biologists

Object Pronouns: Part 4

When the indirect and direct object pronouns come together, changes are made to the indirect object pronouns as follows:

1. mi is changed to me (Note: the agreement pattern between past participles and direct object pronouns still holds):

me lo, me la	it to me
me li, me le	them to me
Gianni mi dà il menù	Gianni me lo dà
John gives the menu to me	John gives it to me
Gianni mi ha comprato quella camicia	Gianni me l'ha comprata
John bought me that shirt	John bought it for me
Gianni mi dà i menù	Gianni me li dà
John gives the menus to me	John gives them to me
Gianni mi ha comprato quelle camicie	Gianni me le ha comprate
John bought me those shirts	John bought them for me

2. ti is changed to te:

te lo, te la	it to you (familiar)
te li, te le	them to you (familiar)
Claudia ti ha dato quel libro	Claudia te l'ha dato
Claudia gave that book to you	Claudia gave it to you
Claudia ti ha scritto quella lettera	Claudia te l'ha scritta
Claudia wrote that letter to you	Claudia wrote it to you
Claudia ti ha dato quei libri	Claudia te li ha dati
Claudia gave those books to you	Claudia gave them to you
Claudia ti ha scritto quelle lettere	Claudia te le ha scritte
Claudia wrote those letters to you	Claudia wrote them to you

3. **La** is changed to **glie** and the two pronouns are written as one word:

glielo, gliela	*it to you (polite)*
glieli, gliele	*them to you (polite)*
La signora Dini Le ha dato quel libro	**La signora Dini gliel'ha dato**
Mrs. Dini gave that book to you	*Mrs. Dini gave it to you*
La signora Dini Le ha scritto la lettera	**La signora Dini gliel'ha scritta**
Mrs. Dini wrote the letter to you	*Mrs. Dini wrote it to you*
La signora Dini Le ha dato quei libri	**La signora Dini glieli ha dati**
Mrs. Dini gave those books to you	*Mrs. Dini gave them to you*
La signora Dini Le ha scritto le lettere	**La signora Dini gliele ha scritte**
Mrs. Dini wrote the letters to you	*Mrs. Dini wrote them to you*

4. **gli** and **le** are changed to **glie** and the two pronouns are written as one word:

glielo, gliela	*it to him / her / them*
glieli, gliele	*them to him / her / them*
Lei gli ha insegnato l'italiano	**Lei gliel'ha insegnato**
She taught him Italian	*She taught it to him*
Lei le ha insegnato l'italiano	**Lei gliel'ha insegnato**
She taught her Italian	*She taught it to her*
Lei gli insegna la grammatica	**Lei gliela insegna**
She teaches them grammar	*She teaches it to them*
Lei le insegna la grammatica	**Lei gliela insegna**
She teaches her grammar	*She teaches it to her*

5. **ci** is changed to **ce**:

ce lo, ce la	*it to us*
ce li, ce le	*them to us*
Il cameriere ci porta il menù	**Il cameriere ce lo porta**
The waiter brings the menu to us	*The waiter brings it to us*
La commessa ci ha dato la camicia	**La commessa ce l'ha data**
The salesclerk gave us the shirt	*The salesclerk gave it to us*
Il cameriere ci porta i menù	**Il cameriere ce li porta**
The waiter brings the menus to us	*The waiter brings them to us*
La commessa ci ha dato le camicie	**La commessa ce le ha date**
The salesclerk gave us the shirts	*The salesclerk gave them to us*

6. **vi** is changed to **ve**:

ve lo, ve la	*it to you (plural)*
ve li, ve le	*them to you (plural)*
Il cameriere vi porta il menù	**Il cameriere ve lo porta**
The waiter brings the menu to you	*The waiter brings it to you*
La commessa vi ha dato la camicia	**La commessa ve l'ha data**
The salesclerk gave you the shirt	*The salesclerk gave it to you*
Il cameriere vi porta i menù	**Il cameriere ve li porta**
The waiter brings the menus to you	*The waiter brings them to you*
La commessa vi ha dato le camicie	**La commessa ve le ha date**
The salesclerk gave you the shirts	*The salesclerk gave them to you*

ATTIVITÀ

F. Imagine being at the doctor's. First, he or she asks you if your ear, lip, etc. hurts. You answer that your ears, lips, etc. hurt. Provide both the doctor's question and your answer, as in the model. If you are using this book in a classroom situation, do this activity with a partner.

Model: ear
   —*Le fa male l'orecchio?*
   —*Mi fanno male gli orecchi!*

1. arm

_____

2. finger

_____

3. leg

_____

4. knee

_____

5. elbow

_____

6. cheek

_____

7. lip

_____

8. hand

_____

9. eye

_____

10. foot

_____

11. shoulder

_____

12. fingernail

_____

G. *Come si dice in italiano?* Follow the model.

> *Model:* His mouth hurts.
> *Gli fa male la bocca.*

1. Her neck hurts.

_____

2. Her hair is very long.

_____

3. Your *(familiar, singular)* body hurts.

_____

4. You *(familiar, singular)* have a long face!

_____

5. She has a large forehead.

_____

6. My tongue hurts.

_____

7. You *(familiar, singular)* have a small nose.

_____

8. Our chest hurts.

_____

9. My head hurts.

_____

H. Make the following plural.

Parole Nuove	
l'albergo	hotel
l'antropologo	anthropologist
il baco	silkworm
il biologo	biologist
il buco	hole
il fuoco	fire
il lago	lake

1. l'amica

_____

2. l'amico

_____

3. l'antibiotico

_____

4. la bocca

_____

5. il chiosco

_____

6. l'antropologo

_____

7. l'elettrodomestico

_____

8. la grammatica

_____

9. il medico

_____

10. il fuoco

_____

11. il baco

_____

12. il buco

_____

13. il lago

_____

14. l'albergo

_____

15. il biologo

_____

I. Indicate that the following things were given to certain people. Use double pronouns. Follow the model.

> *Model:* to me...il bicchiere
> *Me lo ha dato.*

to me...

1. il bicchiere

_____

2. gli stivali

_____

3. la bottiglia

_____

4. le scarpe

_____

to you *(familiar, singular)*...

5. il bicchiere

_____

6. gli stivali

_____

7. la bottiglia

_____

8. le scarpe

_____

to him...

9. il bicchiere

_____

10. gli stivali

_____

11. la bottiglia

_____

12. le scarpe

_____

to her...

13. il bicchiere

_____

14. gli stivali

_____

15. la bottiglia

_____

16. le scarpe

_____

to us...

17. il bicchiere

_____

18. gli stivali

_____

19. la bottiglia

_____

20. le scarpe

_____

to you *(plural)* ...

21. il bicchiere

_____

22. gli stivali

_____

23. la bottiglia

_____

24. le scarpe

_____

to them...

25. il bicchiere

_____

26. gli stivali

_____

27. la bottiglia

_____

28. le scarpe

_____

J. Cruciverba!

Horizontal

3 Chi ha dato il libro a lei? Io … ho dato.
4 Chi ti ha dato la camicia? … la ha data Dina.
5 Ci hai dato i libri? Sì, … li ho dati ieri.
6 Mi hai dato le riviste? Sì, … le ho date.
7 Hai dato I libri a lui? Sì, … ho dati.
8 Vi ho dato il libro? Sì, … lo hai dato.
11 Hai dato le scarpe a lei? Sì, … ho date.
12 Ti … male le mani?
14 Vi ho dato il libro? Sì, … lo hai dato.
15 fingernail
19 Hai dato il libro a loro? Sì, … ho dato.
20 Mi fa male un … della mano destra.
21 hair
24 arms
25 body
30 knee
32 elbow
33 Ho un forte … di gola.
34 shoulder
36 Mi … veramente male.
37 foot
38 Mi fa male lo …
40 Lei ha l'influenza o un forte …
42 flu

Vertical

1 Lui ha dato la mancia al cameriere, no? Sì … ha data.
2 Ci hai dato il libro? Sì … lo ho dato ieri.
3 Chi ha dato la mancia a lui? Io … ho data.
4 Chi ti ha dato il libro? … lo ha dato Carlo.
6 Mi hai dato le scarpe? Sì, … le ho date.
7 Hai dato le riviste a lei? Sì, … ho date.
9 cheeks
10 Dottore, mi … male lo stomaco.
11 Hai dato i libri a lei? Sì, … ho dati.
12 Mi … male i piedi.
13 nose
16 forehead
17 Allora, apra la …, per favore!
18 neck
22 face
23 lip
26 eye
27 tongue
28 hands
29 Dottoressa, ho un forte mal di …
31 ears
35 Ho mal di … e di testa.
39 Ha la …?
41 Lei ha un … raffreddore.

NOTA CULTURALE

As we found out in this unit, Dina and Alessandro ended up going to the movies last night. No doubt, as a student of Italian language and culture, Dina must have found the experience rather memorable.

Fellini e il cinema italiano
[Look up any words you cannot figure out.]

Considerato uno dei più grandi registi *(directors)* del cinema italiano, Federico Fellini è distinto dal fatto *(distinguished by the fact)* che combina elementi satirici con elementi di fantasia in film come *La Dolce Vita* (1960) e *Amarcord* (1973).

Il suo primo film, *Città Aperta* (1945) fu fatto *(was made)* in collaborazione con Roberto Rossellini (1906–1977), un altro grande regista del cinema italiano. Fu il film *I Vitelloni* (1953) che stabilì la sua fama internazionale. Quattro dei suoi film hanno infatti vinto *(won)* premi internazionali: *La Strada* (1954), *Le Notti di Cabiria* (1957), *8½* (1963) e *Amarcord*.

K. Answer the questions.

1. Che cosa è considerato Federico Fellini?

_____

2. Che cosa combina Fellini?

_____

3. Quale fu il suo primo film?

_____

4. Con chi lo fece?

_____

5. Quale film stabilì la sua fama internazionale?

_____

6. Quali dei suoi film hanno vinto premi internazionali?

_____

Review Part 5

A. Comunicazione!

Say that…

1. the boots look really well on you

_____

2. you'll take them (the boots)

_____

3. it is an excellent choice

_____

4. you are reading, while your sister is eating

_____

5. those boots used to look good on you

_____

6. you ate a bit of meat yesterday

_____

7. you deposited a check in your bank account yesterday

_____

8. your father opened an account many years ago

_____

9. you'll have the cantaloupe and ham appetizer and then pasta and a steak

_____

10. you would also like a bit of cheese, because you are still very hungry

_____

11. you would like to go to a lecture at the university

_____

12. you would like to go dancing at a nightclub tonight

_____

13. you prefer going to the movies on Fridays

_____

Tell your doctor …

14. that your throat and stomach hurt and that you have a fever

_____

Ask…

15. your doctor what you must do to look after your flu

_____

16. a young female customer what she needs

_____

17. a customer what his or her shoe size is

_____

18. a customer what size jacket he or she wears

_____

19. how much the boots cost

_____

20. a customer if he or she opened an account in this bank

_____

21. Mrs. Martini if she is hungry and thirsty

_____

22. Professoressa Giusti if she wants a bit of soup for a first dish

_____

23. Dina if she wants to go to the movies

_____

24. Alessandro what he thinks

_____

25. your doctor if you should take antibiotics

_____

B. Come si dice in italiano?

1. You can buy the newspaper at the kiosk at the corner.

_____

2. I bought a magazine yesterday. I bought it because I like to read.

_____

3. Leave a nice tip, Alessandro!

_____

4. What a beautiful day!

_____

5. They came to America in 1956.

_____

6. Our family bought that house in 1990.

_____

7. They always came to the movies with me when we were young.

_____

8. Yesterday he was very hungry.

_____

9. He gave the books to them, right? Yes, he gave them to them.

_____

C. Domande personali.

1. Che tipo di libro leggi di solito? Perché?

_____

2. Ti piace leggere il giornale? Perché sì / no?

_____

3. Quale rivista leggi di solito? Perché?

_____

4. Chi ha un conto in banca nella tua famiglia?

_____

5. Ti piace andare al ristorante o alla trattoria? Perché?

_____

6. Che cosa preferisci mangiare per antipasto, primo piatto, secondo piatto e dessert?

_____

7. Preferisci andare al cinema o a ballare quando vuoi uscire?

_____

8. Per quali ragioni _(reasons)_ vai dal medico?

_____

D. Write a brief imaginary story about the things you did last week. Include the fact that you went shopping for clothes, ate out at an elegant restaurant, went to the bank, went to the movies, and went to the doctor's.

_____

_____

_____

_____

_____

_____

_____

_____

_____

_____

_____

_____

E. There are 20 words hidden in the word search puzzle below: 10 can be read from left to right (horizontally) and 10 in a top-down direction (vertically). Can you find them? The clues given below will help you look for them. The numbers of the clues do not reflect any particular order or arrangement to the hidden words.

R	O	M	A	N	Z	O	B	V	B	V	F	V	S	G	L	G	F	G	G
A	D	F	G	H	J	K	I	B	O	B	O	B	P	H	I	H	A	H	I
R	I	V	I	S	T	A	L	M	T	M	R	M	I	N	B	N	N	N	O
A	D	F	G	H	J	K	P	N	T	N	M	N	C	X	R	X	T	X	R
A	S	S	E	G	N	O	N	L	I	L	A	L	C	R	E	R	A	R	N
A	D	F	G	H	J	K	D	O	G	O	G	O	I	C	T	C	S	C	A
C	O	N	T	O	D	D	F	P	L	P	G	P	O	D	T	D	C	D	L
A	D	F	G	H	J	K	G	L	I	L	I	L	L	B	O	B	I	B	E
M	A	N	C	I	A	D	H	J	A	J	O	J	I	A	D	X	E	V	B
A	D	F	G	H	J	K	J	Y	B	Y	S	Y	A	T	V	B	N	X	I
B	I	S	T	E	C	C	A	L	G	H	J	K	L	E	K	J	Z	L	N
A	D	F	G	H	J	K	T	K	B	N	B	S	D	L	C	V	A	B	F
C	I	N	E	M	A	K	T	K	B	N	A	D	E	E	C	V	B	N	L
K	T	K	B	N	Q	K	T	K	B	N	L	A	D	F	X	X	X	V	U
U	S	C	I	R	E	N	M	J	K	I	L	A	D	O	M	M	M	M	E
N	M	J	K	I	O	N	M	J	K	I	A	A	D	N	L	A	L	L	N
P	I	E	D	E	X	X	X	A	A	R	A	S	A	T	N	T	T	Z	
N	M	J	K	I	O	N	M	J	K	I	E	B	N	T	O	O	O	O	A
N	M	J	K	I	O	N	M	J	K	I	P	H	D	A	I	V	I	I	D
R	A	F	F	R	E	D	D	O	R	E	M	E	D	A	U	M	U	U	D

Horizontal

1 Non ho mai letto quel …
2 Ti piace questa … di moda?
3 Vorrei depositare quest' …
4 Ha un … in questa banca?
5 Hai dato una … al cameriere?
6 Mi piace molto la carne della …
7 Mi piace molto il … italiano.
8 Stasera vorrei … con te, va bene?
9 Ho mal di gola e di testa. Forse ho un …
10 Mi fa molto male un …

Vertical

11 Preferisco i romanzi di …
12 Generalmente non leggo il …
13 Ha un … di banca?
14 Vorrei pagare questo conto con gli …, va bene?
15 Non mi piacciono i panini al …
16 In quella … non c'è più vino.
17 Mi piace molto andare a … il sabato sera.
18 Aspetto la tua …, e poi usciamo, va bene?
19 Sto veramente male. Forse ho l'…
20 La mia … destra mi fa male.

Part 6: Hobbies and Vacations

Devo fare il pieno!

Unit 26

Il pieno, per favore!

CONVERSAZIONE

[Alessandro has decided to take Dina for an excursion into the beautiful Umbrian countryside. Running low on gas, he pulls into a gas station.]

Alessandro	Il pieno, per favore! Può anche controllare l'olio e l'acqua?	Fill it up, please! Can you also check the oil and water?
Benzinaio	Certo! Vedo che le Sue gomme hanno bisogno di un po' d'aria.	Certainly! I see that your tires need some air.
Alessandro	Va bene, ci metta l'aria. Può anche pulire il parabrezza?	OK, put in some air. Can you also clean the windshield?
Benzinaio	Sì, certo. Le piace guidare una macchina giapponese?	Yes, certainly. Do you like driving a Japanese car?
Alessandro	Sì. La mia è un'automobile economica e efficiente. Si guida con grande facilità.	Yes. Mine is an economical and efficient automobile. It drives easily (literally: One drives it with great facility.)
Benzinaio	Ecco, tutto fatto! Ha bisogno d'altro?	All done! Do you need anything else?
Alessandro	Dovrei cambiare l'olio, ma tornerò la prossima settimana.	I should change the oil, but I'll come back next week.
Benzinaio	Molto bene. Buona giornata!	Fine. Have a nice day!
Alessandro	Anche a Lei!	And you too!

COMPRENSIONE

A. Vero o falso?

_____ 1. Alessandro ha bisogno di fare il pieno.

_____ 2. Deve anche controllare l'olio e l'acqua.

_____ 3. Le sue gomme hanno bisogno di un po' d'aria.

_____ 4. Il benzinaio pulisce il parabrezza.

_____ 5. Alessandro guida una macchina giapponese.

_____ 6. La macchina di Alessandro è economica e efficiente.

_____ 7. Si guida con grande facilità.

_____ 8. Alessandro non ha bisogno di cambiare l'olio.

_____ 9. Alessandro tornerà la prossima settimana.

VOCABOLARIO

PAROLE NUOVE

l'aria	*air*
l'automobile (ah-ooh-toh-mOh-beeh-leh)	*automobile*
il benzinaio	*gas attendant*
cambiare	*to change*
controllare	*to check*
economico (eh-koh-nOh-meeh-koh)	*economical*
efficiente (eh-ffeeh-chEhn-teh)	*efficient*
la facilità (fah-cheeh-leeh-tAh)	*ease, facility*
giapponese	*Japanese*
la gomma	*tire*
guidare (gweeh-dAh-reh)	*to drive*
la macchina (mAh-kkeeh-nah)	*car*
mettere (mEh-tteh-reh)	*to put*
il parabrezza	*windshield*
pieno (pyEh-noh)	*full*
prossimo (prOh-sseeh-moh)	*next (as in: next week)*
pulire (isc)	*to clean*

Ho fatto il pieno!

IRREGOLARITÀ

• The verb mettere has an irregular past participle: messo. It is also irregular in the past absolute:

Past Absolute: (io) misi, (tu) mettesti, (lui / lei / Lei) mise, (noi) mettemmo, (voi) metteste, (loro) misero.

ATTIVITÀ

B. Comunicazione.

Say that ...

1. your tires need a bit of air

_____

2. your car is an economical and efficient one

_____

3. your car can be driven with great facility

_____

4. you should change your oil

_____

5. you will come back next week

_____

Tell a gas attendant...

6. to fill up your car, please

_____

7. to put in some air

_____

Ask ...

8. a gas attendant if he or she can check your oil and water

_____

9. a gas attendant if he or she can also clean your windshield

_____

10. someone if he or she likes to drive a Japanese car

_____

C. Match the words in the left column to their meanings or exemplifications in the right column.

Parola Nuova	
la benzina	*gas, petrol*

1. guidare

2. il benzinaio

3. una macchina giapponese

4. una macchina italiana

5. una macchina americana

6. le gomme

7. il pieno

8. pulire

a. la Honda

b. la FIAT

c. la Cadillac

d. usare l'automobile

e. mettere la benzina nella macchina

f. il parabrezza

g. controlla l'olio, l'acqua, …

h. hanno bisogno d'aria

D. Say that someone (as indicated) put gas in the car yesterday and that someone else (as indicated) put it in a long time ago. Follow the model.

> *Model:* tu / io
>
> *Tu hai messo la benzina nella macchina ieri, e io,*
> *invece, la misi nella macchina la settimana scorsa.*

1. io / lui

_____

2. noi / tu

_____

3. voi / io

_____

4. loro / noi

_____

5. io / voi

_____

6. lei / loro

_____

E. Domande personali.

Parola Nuova	
il meccanico	mechanic

1. Quante volte all'anno si dovrebbe *(one should)* portare la macchina dal meccanico?

_____

2. Hai la macchina?

_____

3. Che macchina è?

_____

4. Com'è?

_____

5. Che macchina ti piacerebbe *(you would like)* avere?

_____

F. Write a brief composition about taking the car to the gas station yesterday and what happened there.

_____

_____

_____

_____

_____

_____

_____

_____

_____

_____

_____

_____

_____

_____

LINGUA

The Particle ci

The particle ci, as used in the conversation, means *there*. It is placed before verbs in the same manner as the unstressed object pronouns:

Place Expression	Replacement with ci
Metta l'aria nella macchina! *Put air in the car!*	Ci metta l'aria! *Put air in it (= there)!*
Vado in Italia fra un anno *I'm going to Italy in a year*	Ci vado fra un anno *I'm going there in a year*
Lei è andata a casa due minuti fa *She went home two minutes ago*	Lei ci è andata due minuti fa *She went there two minutes ago*

The Impersonal si

The conversation also contains an example of si, meaning *one, people, they (in general)*. Notice the agreement pattern of the verb with singular and plural nouns:

With Singular Nouns	With Plural Nouns
Si parla italiano qui *One speaks / They speak Italian here*	Si parlano molte lingue qui *One speaks / They speak many languages here*
Si mangia la pasta in Italia *One eats / They eat pasta in Italy*	Si mangiano gli spaghetti in Italia *One eats / They eat spaghetti in Italy*

The Simple Future

The future tense allows you to refer to actions that will take place in the future:

> Finirò di studiare stasera   *I will finish studying tonight*
> Parlerò con Dina dopo   *I will speak to Dina later*

The future of regular verbs is formed by:

1. dropping the final -e from the -are, -ere, and -ire endings of the infinitive, changing the a in the first conjugation to e:

guidare	*to drive*	→	guider- [Note the change of a to e]
chiedere	*to ask for*	→	chieder-
finire	*to finish*	→	finir-

2. adding the following endings to the stems.

Singular	
1st person	-ò
2nd person	-ai
3rd person	-à

Plural	
1st person	-emo
2nd person	-ete
3rd person	-anno

Quando sarò grande, guiderò la Ferrari!

Below are the verbs guidare, chiedere, and finire fully conjugated:

guidare *to drive,* chiedere *to ask for,* finire *to finish*	
(io) guiderò	*I will drive*
(io) chiederò	*I will ask*
(io) finirò	*I will finish*
(tu) guiderai	*you will drive (familiar)*
(tu) chiederai	*you will ask (familiar)*
(tu) finirai	*you will finish (familiar)*
(Lei) guiderà	*you will drive (polite)*
(Lei) chiederà	*you will ask (polite)*
(Lei) finirà	*you will finish (polite)*
(lui / lei) guiderà	*he / she will drive*
(lui / lei) chiederà	*he / she will ask*
(lui / lei) finirà	*he / she will finish*
(noi) guideremo	*we will drive*
(noi) chiederemo	*we will ask*
(noi) finiremo	*we will finish*
(voi) guiderete	*you will drive (plural)*
(voi) chiederete	*you will ask (plural)*
(voi) finirete	*you will finish (plural)*
(loro) guideranno	*they will drive*
(loro) chiederanno	*they will ask*
(loro) finiranno	*they will finish*

With verbs ending in -ciare and -giare the "i" is dropped when the change is made from -are to -er. Here are the verbs cominciare / *to begin,* and mangiare / *to eat,* fully conjugated:

cominciare → comincer- *to begin,* mangiare → manger- *to eat*	
(io) comincerò	*I will begin*
(io) mangerò	*I will eat*
(tu) comincerai	*you will begin (familiar)*
(tu) mangerai	*you will eat (familiar)*
(Lei) comincerà	*you will begin (polite)*
(Lei) mangerà	*you will eat (polite)*
(lui / lei) comincerà	*he / she will begin*
(lui / lei) mangerà	*he / she will eat*
(noi) cominceremo	*we will begin*
(noi) mangeremo	*we will eat*
(voi) comincerete	*you will begin (plural)*
(voi) mangerete	*you will eat (plural)*
(loro) cominceranno	*they will begin*
(loro) mangeranno	*they will eat*

With verbs ending in -care and -gare the hard sound is retained when the change is made from -are to -er. This is shown by adding an h. Here are the verbs cercare / *to search for*, and pagare / *to pay*, fully conjugated:

cercare → cercher- *to search for*, pagare → pagher- *to pay*	
(io) cercherò (io) pagherò	*I will search for* *I will pay*
(tu) cercherai (tu) pagherai	*you will search for (familiar)* *you will pay (familiar)*
(Lei) cercherà (Lei) pagherà	*you will search for (polite)* *you will pay (polite)*
(lui / lei) cercherà (lui / lei) pagherà	*he / she will search for* *he / she will pay*
(noi) cercheremo (noi) pagheremo	*we will search for* *we will pay*
(voi) cercherete (voi) pagherete	*you will search for (plural)* *you will pay (plural)*
(loro) cercheranno (loro) pagheranno	*they will search for* *they will pay*

The Conditional

The conditional is a tense that allows you to express conditions:

> Dovrei cambiare l'olio, ma non ho tempo
> *I should change the oil, but I don't have time*

> Mangerei la pizza, ma non ho fame
> *I would eat pizza, but I'm not hungry.*

The conditional of regular verbs is formed in exactly the same manner as the future; namely, by:

1. dropping the final -e from the -are, -ere, and -ire suffixes and, at the same time, changing the a in the first conjugation suffix to e:

guidare	*to drive*	→	guider- [Note again the change of a to e]
chiedere	*to ask for*	→	chieder-
finire	*to finish*	→	finir-

2. adding the following endings to the stems.

Singular	
1st person	*-ei*
2nd person	*-esti*
3rd person	*-ebbe*

Plural	
1st person	*-emmo*
2nd person	*-este*
3rd person	*-ebbero*

Below are the verb **guidare**, **chiedere**, and **finire** fully conjugated:

guidare *to drive,* chiedere *to ask for,* finire *to finish*	
(io) guiderei	*I would drive*
(io) chiederei	*I would ask for*
(io) finirei	*I would finish*
(tu) guideresti	*you would drive (familiar)*
(tu) chiederesti	*you would ask for (familiar)*
(tu) finiresti	*you would finish (familiar)*
(Lei) guiderebbe	*you would drive (polite)*
(Lei) chiederebbe	*you would ask for (polite)*
(Lei) finirebbe	*you would finish (polite)*
(lui / lei) guiderebbe	*he / she would drive*
(lui / lei) chiederebbe	*he / she would ask for*
(lui / lei) finirebbe	*he / she would finish*
(noi) guideremmo	*we would drive*
(noi) chiederemmo	*we would ask for*
(noi) finiremmo	*we would finish*
(voi) guidereste	*you would drive (plural)*
(voi) chiedereste	*you would ask for (plural)*
(voi) finireste	*you would finish (plural)*
(loro) guiderebbero	*they would drive*
(loro) chiederebbero	*they would ask for*
(loro) finirebbero	*they would finish*

Once again, with verbs ending in **-ciare** and **-giare** the "i" is not necessary when the change is made from **-are** to **-er**. Here are the verbs **cominciare** / *to begin,* and **mangiare** / *to eat,* fully conjugated:

cominciare *to begin,* mangiare *to eat*	
(io) comincerei	*I would begin*
(io) mangerei	*I would eat*
(tu) cominceresti	*you would begin (familiar)*
(tu) mangeresti	*you would eat (familiar)*
(Lei) comincerebbe	*you would begin (polite)*
(Lei) mangerebbe	*you would eat (polite)*
(lui / lei) comincerebbe	*he / she would begin*
(lui / lei) mangerebbe	*he / she would eat*
(noi) cominceremmo	*we would begin*
(noi) mangeremmo	*we would eat*
(voi) comincereste	*you would begin (plural)*
(voi) mangereste	*you would eat (plural)*
(loro) comincerebbero	*they would begin*
(loro) mangerebbero	*they would eat*

With verbs ending in -care and -gare the hard sound is retained when the change is made from -are to -er. This is shown, again, by adding an h. Here are the verbs cercare / *to search,* and pagare / *to pay,* fully conjugated:

cercare *to search,* pagare *to pay*	
(io) cercherei	*I would search*
(io) pagherei	*I would pay*
(tu) cercheresti	*you would search (familiar)*
(tu) pagheresti	*you would pay (familiar)*
(Lei) cercherebbe	*you would search (polite)*
(Lei) pagherebbe	*you would pay (polite)*
(lui / lei) cercherebbe	*he / she would search*
(lui / lei) pagherebbe	*he / she would pay*
(noi) cercheremmo	*we would search*
(noi) pagheremmo	*we would pay*
(voi) cerchereste	*you would search (plural)*
(voi) paghereste	*you would pay (plural)*
(loro) cercherebbero	*they would search*
(loro) pagherebbero	*they would pay*

ATTIVITÀ

G. Pose the questions as indicated in the model and then answer them, using the particle ci. If you are using this book in a classroom situation, do this activity with a partner.

> *Model:* Italy / in a year's time
> —*Quando vai in Italia?*
> —*Ci vado tra un anno.*

Note	
to a country or region:	
in Italia	to Italy
in Toscana	to Tuscany
to a city:	
a Firenze	to Florence
a Roma	to Rome

Quando…

1. downtown / tomorrow

_____

2. the doctor's / in an hour

_____

3. Florence (Firenze) / in a few days

_____

4. Rome / in a little while

_____

5. Calabria / in a month

_____

Now, do the same activity in the past tense.

> _Model:_ Italy / two days ago
> —_Quando sei andato / andata in Italia?_
> —_Ci sono andato / andata due giorni fa._

6. Tuscany/ yesterday

_____

7. the doctor's / an hour ago

_____

8. Pisa / several days ago

_____

9. Milan / a little while ago

_____

10. Sicily / a month ago

_____

H. Pose an appropriate question as in the model. Use the impersonal si as shown.

> _Model:_ mangiare / la pasta
> _Dove si mangia la pasta?_

1. guidare / le macchine giapponesi

_____

2. studiare / l'italiano

_____

3. mangiare / gli spaghetti alla bolognese

_____

4. bere / un buon espresso

_____

5. stare / veramente bene

I. Come si dice in italiano? Use the simple future and conditional tenses of the given verbs throughout, as shown in the model. Finish off the conditional sentence freely in any appropriate way.

> *Model:* I will / would ... arrive tomorrow
> *Io arriverò domani.*
> *io arriverei domani, ma ...*

I will / would ...

1. arrive tomorrow

_____

2. have an espresso coffee

_____

3. go out tonight

_____

4. move in a week

_____

5. pay for everything

_____

6. begin working next week

_____

7. eat the spaghetti

_____

You *(familiar, singular)* will / would ...

8. arrive tomorrow

_____

9. have an espresso coffee

_____

10. go out tonight

_____

11. move in a week

_____

12. pay for everything

_____

13. begin working next week

_____

14. eat the spaghetti

_____

He / She will / would …

15. arrive tomorrow

_____

16. have an espresso coffee

_____

17. go out tonight

_____

18. move in a week

_____

19. pay for everything

_____

20. begin working next week

_____

21. eat the spaghetti

_____

We will / would …

22. arrive tomorrow

_____

23. have an espresso coffee

_____

24. go out tonight

_____

25. move in a week

_____

26. pay for everything

_____

27. begin working next week

_____

28. eat the spaghetti

_____

You *(plural)* will / would ...

29. arrive tomorrow

_____

30. have an espresso coffee

_____

31. go out tonight

_____

32. move in a week

_____

33. pay for everything

_____

34. begin working next week

_____

35. eat the spaghetti

_____

They will / would ...

36. arrive tomorrow

_____

37. have an espresso coffee

_____

38. go out tonight

_____

39. move in a week

_____

40. pay for everything

_____

41. begin working next week

_____

42. eat the spaghetti

_____

J. Cruciverba!

Horizontal

2 Vai in Italia? Sì … vado quest'anno.
3 Io … una FIAT in Italia.
5 Mio fratello … una Lancia in Italia.
6 we will ask
7 Noi … una Maserati in Italia.
10 they will finish
11 Che cosa hai messo nella gomma? … ho messo l'aria.
12 she will finish
14 we will finish
16 I will ask
19 you will ask *(familiar)*
20 Ho già … l'aria nelle gomme.
22 Dovrei cambiare l'olio, ma tornerò il … mese
24 Io guido una … giapponese.
26 La mia macchina è molto …
28 macchina
30 La mia macchina è …

Vertical

1 Quale macchina … in Italia? *(familiar)*
2 you will ask *(plural)*
4 Come sono quelle macchine? … guidano con facilità.
5 Quale macchina … voi in Italia?
7 Loro … una Ferrari in Italia.
8 A che ora … di lavorare oggi, Francesco?
9 they will ask
10 I will finish
11 you will ask *(polite)*
12 you will finish *(plural)*
13 Cosa … mangia di solito in Italia?
15 Cosa fa? … il parabrezza della Sua macchina.
17 Anche in America … mangiano gli spaghetti.
18 Può anche pulire il …?
19 Quando vai in centro? … vado fra qualche ora.
21 Vedo che le Sue gomme hanno bisogno di …
22 Il …, per favore!
23 La mia macchina è …
25 Dina, quando … l'olio?
27 Le Sue … hanno bisogno di un po' d'aria.
29 Si guida con grande …

NOTA CULTURALE

Although Alessandro drives a trendy Japanese car, the "national" car of Italy is the FIAT, which stands for *Fabbrica* (Factory) *Italiana di Automobili di Torino*.

La FIAT

[Look up any words you cannot figure out.]

La FIAT fu fondata nel 1899 da alcuni industriali, tra cui *(among whom)* Giovanni Agnelli. Nel 1969 la FIAT acquistò *(acquired)* il capitale sociale della Lancia e una partecipazione del 50% nel capitale della Ferrari. Nel 1986 acquistò l'Alfa Romeo, confluita *(merging)* poi nella nuova società *(company)* Alfa-Lancia.

Nel 1995 completò una joint venture con la Chrysler per la produzione di jeep. Nel 1997 la FIAT e la francese Lohr firmarono *(signed)* un accordo per lo sviluppo delle loro attività nel settore dei trasporti urbani.

K. Answer the questions.

1. Quando fu fondata la FIAT?

_____

2. Chi ha fondato la FIAT?

_____

3. Quando acquistò la Lancia?

_____

4. Quando acquistò l'Alfa Romeo?

_____

5. Quando completò una joint venture con la Chrysler?

_____

6. Che cosa firmò con la francese Lohr?

_____

Preferirei un posto al corridoio!

Unit 27

Il biglietto, per favore!

CONVERSAZIONE

[Mark has decided to go back home to the United States. He's at the airport, at a check-in counter.]

Impiegato	Prego, il Suo biglietto per favore?	Excuse me, may I have your ticket, please?
Mark	Ecco il mio biglietto e passaporto.	Here is my ticket and passport.
Impiegato	Desidera un posto al corridoio o al finestrino?	Would you like an aisle or window seat?
Mark	Lo preferirei al corridoio.	I would prefer an aisle seat.
Impiegato	Ecco la Sua carta d'imbarco. Il Suo aereo partirà dall'uscita numero A15.	Here's your boarding pass. Your plane will depart from gate number A15.

[Before going into the waiting room Mark runs into Sarah, an old friend from back home who has also come to Italy to study Italian.]

Mark	Ciao, Sara, come va? È tanto tempo che non ci vediamo.	Hi, Sarah, how's it going? We haven't seen each other in a long time.
Sarah	Mark, che piacere! Infatti, sai, sono due anni che non ci vediamo!	Mark, what a pleasure! In fact, you know, we haven't seen each other for two years!
Mark	Devo andare, purtroppo! Hanno annunciato il mio volo! Ciao!	I must go, unfortunately! They have announced my flight! Bye!
Sarah	Buon viaggio!	Have a nice trip!

COMPRENSIONE

A. Which response, a or b, is the correct or appropriate one?

1. Prego, il Suo … per favore.
   - a. biglietto
   - b. posto

2. Ecco il mio biglietto e …
   - a. passaporto
   - b. posto

3. Mark preferisce un posto…
   - a. al corridoio
   - b. al finestrino

4. Il suo aereo partirà … numero A15.
      a. dall'uscita
      b. dalla carta

5. Sara, è … che non ci vediamo.
      a. tanto tempo
      b. vero

6. Mark, sono due anni che …
      a. piacere
      b. non ci vediamo

7. Devo andare! Hanno annunciato …
      a. il mio volo
      b. la mia amica

VOCABOLARIO

La carta
d'imbarco,
per favore!

Ahi!
Dov'è?

PAROLE NUOVE

l'aereo	airplane
annunciare	to announce
la carta	card, pass
il corridoio (koh-rreeh-dOh-yoh)	aisle
il finestrino	window (of a vehicle)
infatti	in fact
il passaporto	passport
il posto	place, seat
sapere	to know (in general)
l'uscita (ooh-shEEh-tah)	gate, exit
il volo	flight

ESPRESSIONE

la carta d'imbarco	boarding pass

IRREGOLARITÀ

• The verb **sapere** is irregular. It will be taken up in detail later in this unit.

414

ATTIVITÀ

B. Comunicazione.

Say that …

1. you are looking for your ticket and passport

_____

2. you would like an aisle seat

_____

3. you would not prefer a window seat

_____

4. your plane will be leaving from gate S21

_____

Tell Sarah that…

5. you haven't seen each other in a long time

_____

6. unfortunately you have to go, because they have announced your flight

_____

Ask …

7. someone for his or her ticket

_____

8. your friend if he or she has your boarding pass

_____

Wish Mark…

9. a nice trip

_____

C. Come si dice in italiano?

1. My plane will be leaving in an hour.

_____

2. They will announce your _(familiar, singular)_ flight shortly.

_____

3. Here is your _(polite, singular)_ boarding pass.

_____

4. He would prefer an aisle seat, because he doesn't like window seats.

_____

5. Where is the gate?

_____

D. Domande personali.

Parole Nuove	
avere paura	to be afraid
viaggiare	to travel
visitare	to visit
volare	to fly

1. Ti piace viaggiare?

_____

2. Quali paesi e città vorresti visitare?

_____

3. Perché?

_____

4. Ti piace volare?

_____

5. Hai paura di volare?

_____

E. Write a brief composition about any incident that may have happened to you at an airport.

_____

_____

_____

_____

_____

_____

_____

_____

_____

_____

_____

_____

LINGUA

The Expression fare il biglietto

As you know, the verb comprare means *to buy*. However, the expression fare il biglietto *(literally: to make the ticket)* is used when buying travel tickets:

Buying (in general)	Buying a ticket for travel
Ho comprato il biglietto del cinema *I bought the movie ticket*	Ho fatto il biglietto per l'Italia *I bought the ticket for Italy*
Domani comprerò quel romanzo *Tomorrow I will buy that novel*	Domani farò il biglietto *Tomorrow I will buy the travel ticket*

Dal mio finestrino vedo un UFO!

Different Words for "Window"

The word il finestrino refers to a window in a vehicle; la finestra to a window in a house or building; and la vetrina to a shop window.

Vorrei un posto al finestrino.   *I would like a window seat.*
Quella casa ha le finestre grandi.   *That house has large windows.*
Preferirei quella camicia in vetrina.   *I would prefer the shirt in the window.*

Irregular Verbs in the Future and Conditional

Of the verbs introduced so far, the following have irregular future and conditional conjugations. For a set of such verbs, drop both vowels in the infinitive ending and then add the usual endings (Unit 26):

andare	→	andr-
avere	→	avr-
dovere	→	dovr-
potere	→	potr-
vedere	→	vedr-

andare	to go
Future	(io) andrò, (tu) andrai, (Lei) andrà, (lui / lei) andrà, (noi) andremo, (voi) andrete, (loro) andranno
Cond.	(io) andrei, (tu) andresti, (Lei) andrebbe, (lui / lei) andrebbe, (noi) andremmo, (voi) andreste, (loro) andrebbero

avere	to have
Future	(io) avrò, (tu) avrai, (Lei) avrà, (lui / lei) avrà, (noi) avremo, (voi) avrete, (loro) avranno
Cond.	(io) avrei, (tu) avresti, (Lei) avrebbe, (lui / lei) avrebbe, (noi) avremmo, (voi) avreste, (loro) avrebbero

bere	to drink
Future	(io) berrò, (tu) berrai, (Lei) berrà, (lui / lei) berrà, (noi) berremo, (voi) berrete, (loro) berranno
Cond.	(io) berrei, (tu) berresti, (Lei) berebbe, (lui / lei) berebbe, (noi) berremmo, (voi) berreste, (loro) berrebbero

dare	to give
Future	(io) darò, (tu) darai, (Lei) darà, (lui / lei) darà, (noi) daremo, (voi) darete, (loro) daranno
Cond.	(io) darei, (tu) daresti, (Lei) darebbe, (lui / lei) darebbe, (noi) daremmo, (voi) dareste, (loro) darebbero

dire	to say, tell
Future	(io) dirò, (tu) dirai, (Lei) dirà, (lui / lei) dirà, (noi) diremo, (voi) direte, (loro) diranno
Cond.	(io) direi, (tu) diresti, (Lei) direbbe, (lui / lei) direbbe, (noi) diremmo, (voi) direste, (loro) direbbero

dovere	to have to
Future	(io) dovrò, (tu) dovrai, (Lei) dovrà, (lui / lei) dovrà, (noi) dovremo, (voi) dovrete, (loro) dovranno
Cond.	(io) dovrei, (tu) dovresti, (Lei) dovrebbe, (lui / lei) dovrebbe, (noi) dovremmo, (voi) dovreste, (loro) dovrebbero

essere	to be
Future	(io) sarò, (tu) sarai, (Lei) sarà, (lui / lei) sarà, (noi) saremo, (voi) sarete, (loro) saranno
Cond.	(io) sarei, (tu) saresti, (Lei) sarebbe, (lui / lei) sarebbe, (noi) saremmo, (voi) sareste, (loro) sarebbero

fare	*to do, to make*
Future	(io) farò, (tu) farai, (Lei) farà, (lui / lei) farà, (noi) faremo, (voi) farete, (loro) faranno
Cond.	(io) farei, (tu) faresti, (Lei) farebbe, (lui / lei) farebbe, (noi) faremmo, (voi) fareste, (loro) farebbero

potere	*to be able to*
Future	(io) potrò, (tu) potrai, (Lei) potrà, (lui / lei) potrà, (noi) potremo, (voi) potrete, (loro) potranno
Cond.	(io) potrei, (tu) potresti, (Lei) potrebbe, (lui / lei) potrebbe, (noi) potremmo, (voi) potreste, (loro) potrebbero

stare	*to stay*
Future	(io) starò, (tu) starai, (Lei) starà, (lui / lei) starà, (noi) staremo, (voi) starete, (loro) staranno
Cond.	(io) starei, (tu) staresti, (Lei) starebbe, (lui / lei) starebbe, (noi) staremmo, (voi) stareste, (loro) starebbero

vedere	*to see*
Future	(io) vedrò, (tu) vedrai, (Lei) vedrà, (lui / lei) vedrà, (noi) vedremo, (voi) vedrete, (loro) vedranno
Cond.	(io) vedrei, (tu) vedresti, (Lei) vedrebbe, (lui / lei) vedrebbe, (noi) vedremmo, (voi) vedreste, (loro) vedrebbero

venire	*to come*
Future	(io) verrò, (tu) verrai, (Lei) verrà, (lui / lei) verrà, (noi) verremo, (voi) verrete, (loro) verranno
Cond.	(io) verrei, (tu) verresti, (Lei) verrebbe, (lui / lei) verrebbe, (noi) verremmo, (voi) verreste, (loro) verrebbero

volere	*to want to*
Future	(io) vorrò, (tu) vorrai, (Lei) vorrà, (lui / lei) vorrà, (noi) vorremo, (voi) vorrete, (loro) vorranno
Cond.	(io) vorrei, (tu) vorresti, (Lei) vorrebbe, (lui / lei) vorrebbe, (noi) vorremmo, (voi) vorreste, (loro) vorrebbero

The Verb piacere: Part 4

The most common forms of this verb in the future and conditional are given below.

With Singular Nouns	With Plural Nouns
I will like / I would like	
Mi piacerà la pasta italiana *I will like Italian pasta* **Mi piacerebbe la pasta italiana** *I would like Italian pasta*	**Mi piaceranno gli spaghetti alla bolognese** *I will like spaghetti in the Bolognese style* **Mi piacerebbero gli spaghetti alla bolognese** *I would like spaghetti in the Bolognese style*
You will like / You would like (familiar)	
Ti piacerà la pasta italiana *You will like Italian pasta (fam.)* **Ti piacerebbe la pasta italiana** *You would like Italian pasta (fam.)*	**Ti piaceranno gli spaghetti alla bolognese** *You will like spaghetti in the Bolognese style (fam.)* **Ti piacerebbero gli spaghetti alla bolognese** *You would like spaghetti in the Bolognese style (fam.)*
You will like / You would like (polite)	
Le piacerà la pasta italiana *You will like Italian pasta (pol.)* **Le piacerebbe la pasta italiana** *You would like Italian pasta (pol.)*	**Le piaceranno gli spaghetti alla bolognese** *You will like spaghetti in the Bolognese style (pol.)* **Le piacerebbero gli spaghetti alla bolognese** *You would like spaghetti in the Bolognese style (pol.)*
He / They will like / He / They would like	
Gli piacerà la pasta italiana *He / They will like Italian pasta* **Gli piacerebbe la pasta italiana** *He / They would like Italian pasta*	**Gli piaceranno gli spaghetti alla bolognese** *He / They will like spaghetti in the Bolognese style* **Gli piacerebbero gli spaghetti alla bolognese** *He / They would like spaghetti in the Bolognese style*
She will like / She would like	
Le piacerà la pasta italiana *She will like Italian pasta* **Le piacerebbe la pasta italiana** *She would like Italian pasta*	**Le piaceranno gli spaghetti alla bolognese** *She will like spaghetti in the Bolognese style* **Le piacerebbero gli spaghetti alla bolognese** *She would like spaghetti in the Bolognese style*
We will like / We would like	
Ci piacerà la pasta italiana *We will like Italian pasta* **Ci piacerebbe la pasta italiana** *We would like Italian pasta*	**Ci piaceranno gli spaghetti alla bolognese** *We will like spaghetti in the Bolognese style* **Ci piacerebbero gli spaghetti alla bolognese** *We would like spaghetti in the Bolognese style*
You will like / You would like (plural)	
Vi piacerà la pasta italiana *You will like Italian pasta (pl.)* **Vi piacerebbe la pasta italiana** *You would like Italian pasta (pl.)*	**Vi piaceranno gli spaghetti alla bolognese** *You will like spaghetti in the Bolognese style (pl.)* **Vi piacerebbero gli spaghetti alla bolognese** *You would like spaghetti in the Bolognese style (pl.)*

The Verbs sapere and conoscere

Both these verbs mean *to know*, but they suggest different nuances of knowing as follows:

sapere	to know something (in general), to know how to
conoscere	to know / meet someone, to be familiar with

Alessandro sa tante cose	Alessandro conosce Maddalena
Alessandro knows many things	*Alessandro knows Maddalena*
Alessandro sa parlare l'italiano	Alessandro conosce Firenze molto bene
Alessandro knows how to speak Italian	*Alessandro knows (is familiar with)*
quite well	*Florence*
Sai come si chiama?	Conosci la sua amica?
Do you know his / her name?	*Do you know his / her friend?*

The verb sapere has irregular present indicative, imperative, past absolute, future, and conditional conjugations:

sapere	to know something (in general), to know how to
Present Indicative	
(io) so	*I know*
(tu) sai	*you know (familiar)*
(Lei) sa	*you know (polite)*
(lui / lei) sa	*he / she knows*
(noi) sappiamo	*we know*
(voi) sapete	*you know (plural)*
(loro) sanno	*they know*
Imperative	
(tu) sappi	*know (familiar, singular)*
(Lei) sappia	*know (polite, singular)*
(noi) sappiamo	*let's know*
(voi) sappiate	*know (familiar, plural)*
(Loro) sappiano	*know (polite, plural)*
Future	
(io) saprò	*I will know*
(tu) saprai	*you will know (familiar)*
(Lei) saprà	*you will know (polite)*
(lui / lei) saprà	*he / she will know*
(noi) sapremo	*we will know*
(voi) saprete	*you will know (plural)*
(loro) sapranno	*they will know*

Conditional	
(io) saprei	*I would know*
(tu) sapresti	*you would know (familiar)*
(Lei) saprebbe	*you would know (polite)*
(noi) sapremmo	*we would know*
(voi) sapreste	*you would know (plural)*
(loro) saprebbero	*they would know*
Past Absolute	
(io) seppi	*I knew*
(tu) sapesti	*you knew (familiar)*
(Lei) seppe	*you knew (polite)*
(noi) sapemmo	*we knew*
(voi) sapeste	*you knew (plural)*
(loro) seppero	*they knew*

ATTIVITÀ

F. Choose the appropriate or correct response.

1. Quando hai … il biglietto per l'Italia?
      a. fatto
      b. comprato

2. Chi … il biglietto per il concerto?
      a. comprerà
      b. farà

3. Vorrei un posto …
      a. alla finestra
      b. al finestrino

4. Ho visto quella giacca…
      a. nella finestra
      b. in vetrina

5. Quando hai … Dina?
      a. saputo
      b. conosciuto

6. Alessandro … parlare molto bene.
      a. sa
      b. conosce

7. Noi … un bel ristorante qui vicino.
  a. conosciamo
  b. sappiamo

8. … che cosa faranno alla festa?
  a. Sai
  b. Conosci

G. Futuro o condizionale? Now give the appropriate future or conditional form of the verb.

  Model: io / andare / in Italia tra un mese
    Io andrò in Italia tra un mese.

    io / andare / in Italia, ma non ho soldi
    Io andrei in italia, ma non ho soldi.

1. tu / andare / in centro domani

_____

2. tu / andare / in centro domani, ma non hai tempo

_____

3. lui / avere / tempo domani

_____

4. lei / bere / il cappuccino, ma non le piace

_____

5. noi / dare / quel libro a Carla, ma lo abbiamo perso

_____

6. voi / dire / tutto alla professoressa domani

_____

7. loro / dovere / andare in Italia, ma non hanno soldi

_____

8. lei / essere / molto stanca, dopo che ha lavorato

_____

9. io / fare / il biglietto domani

_____

10. loro / non potere / venire al cinema perché lavorano

_____

H. Verb Game! If you are given a future form, provide the corresponding conditional form. If you are given a conditional form, provide the corresponding future form.

Future	*Conditional*
1. vi piaceranno	1. _____
2. _____	2. ci piacerebbe
3. vi piacerà	3. _____
4. _____	4. gli piacerebbe
5. le piacerà	5. _____
6. _____	6. ti piacerebbe
7. mi piacerà	7. _____
8. loro vorranno	8. _____
9. _____	9. io verrei
10. _____	10. noi vedremmo
11. tu starai	11. _____
12. _____	12. io saprei

I. Cruciverba!

Horizontal	**Vertical**

Horizontal

1 Loro … parlare molto bene.
2 Io … che tu sei italiano.
3 Lei … mio fratello, vero?
6 Noi non … dov'è via Nazionale.
8 Know! *(polite)*
10 He knows
12 Io … il biglietto domani.
13 Carla, … che ore sono?
14 I will drink
15 Vi piaceranno quelle macchine? Sì, ci …
16 I will have
17 Piacerà quel libro a Dina? Sì, le …
19 Io … in Italia l'anno prossimo.
20 Anche a loro … quelle macchine nuove.
21 he will be
22 I will have to
24 I will want
25 I will be able to
27 L'… partirà dall'uscita numero A15.
29 I will stay
31 Desidera un posto al corridoio o al …?
33 window
34 Dovremo andare. Hanno … il nostro volo
38 Ha la … d'imbarco?
39 Avete il …?
40 Buon …!

Vertical

1 Voi … parlare l'italiano, vero?
2 Know! *(familiar)*
3 Tu … mio fratello, vero
4 Lei … dov'è via Boccaccio?
5 Lui … tutto!
6 Tu … dov'è mia sorella?
7 Piaceranno i dolci a Marco? Sì, gli …
9 Ti piacerà andare in Italia? Sì, mi …
11 I will give
15 Signora, Le piacerà quel libro. Sì, anch'io penso che mi …
18 I will say
23 I will see
24 Io … alla festa sabato prossimo.
26 shop window
28 Hai fatto il …?
30 Felice di fare la tua …
32 … di fare la Sua conoscenza
35 Dove desidera il posto, al finestrino o al …?
36 Desidera un … al finestrino o al corridoio?
37 Andiamo! Hanno annunciato il nostro …

NOTA CULTURALE

Mark is at the airport in Pisa. As you may know, Italy's national airline is called *Alitalia*, which is a clever contraction of ali *wings* and Italia *Italy*.

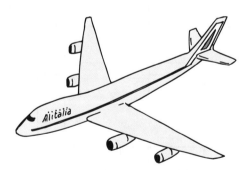

Alitalia
[Look up any words you cannot figure out.]

L'Alitalia è stata costituita *(was founded)* nel 1946 dallo Stato contemporaneamente alla L.A.I. (Linee Aeree Italiane). Nel 1957 diventò l'unica compagnia aerea nazionale. La base della compagnia è a Roma, ma dispone di sedi *(branches)* in tutto il mondo.

Gli anni Novanta *(1990s)* sono stati caratterizzati da numerosi accordi di collaborazione con compagnie straniere. Nel 1996, l'Alitalia ha costituito la nuova società operativa *Alitalia Team* per collegamenti *(connections)* a medio e lungo raggio *(medium and short range)* a basso costo. Nel 1998, ha stabilito un'alleanza con KLM (Paesi Bassi) e Continental (Stati Uniti), insieme ad Air France (Francia) e all'altra compagnia statunitense Northwest.

J. Write a brief composition on *Alitalia*, adding to the information above anything else you know about it. If you are using this book in a classroom situation, do this activity with a partner.

_____

_____

_____

_____

_____

_____

_____

_____

_____

_____

_____

_____

_____

_____

_____

_____

_____

_____

_____

_____

_____

Voglio andare all'estero!

Unit 28

Buon divertimento!

CONVERSAZIONE

[Carla is planning a holiday. She asks Dina to accompany her to a travel agency.]

Carla	Voglio andare all'estero. Dove, secondo Lei, mi divertirò di più? Voglio fare una vacanza indimenticabile!	I want to go abroad. Where, in your opinion, will I enjoy myself the most? I want to have an unforgettable vacation!
Impiegato	Ci sono tanti bei paesi e tante belle città da vedere.	There are many nice countries and cities to see.
Carla	Mi piacciono solo gli alberghi di prima categoria. E voglio noleggiare la macchina.	I only like first-class hotels. I also want to rent a car.
Impiegato	Ci penso io! Mi dia la Sua carta di credito, per favore.	I'll take care of it! Give me your credit card, please.

[At the check-in desk of a hotel in Paris a few weeks later. Fortunately for Carla the desk clerk speaks Italian.]

Carla	Ha ricevuto la mia prenotazione?	Did you receive my reservation?
Impiegata	Sì, l'abbiamo ricevuta. Ha tanto bagaglio? Ha bisogno di aiuto?	Yes, we received it. Do you have a lot of baggage? Do you need help?
Carla	No, ho solo due valige.	No, I have only two suitcases.
Impiegata	Ecco a Lei la chiave per la camera numero cinquecento cinquantacinque.	Here's your key for room number 555.
Carla	Grazie.	Thank you!
Impiegata	Buon divertimento a Parigi!	Have fun in Paris!

COMPRENSIONE

A. Complete each statement or question in an appropriate fashion with the missing word(s) or expression.

1. Voglio andare _____.

2. Voglio fare una vacanza _____!

3. Buon _____ a Parigi!

4. Ci sono tanti bei paesi e tante belle città _____.

5. Ecco a Lei _____ per la sua camera.

6. Mi piacciono solo _____ di prima categoria.

7. Voglio _____ la macchina.

8. Mi dia la Sua _____, per favore.

9. No, ho solo _____.

VOCABOLARIO

Ho perso la valigia!

PAROLE NUOVE

l'aiuto	*help*
l'albergo	*hotel*
il bagaglio (bah-gAh-lyoh)	*baggage*
la camera (kAh-meh-rah)	*hotel room*
la categoria (kah-teh-goh-rEEh-ah)	*category, class*
la chiave (kyAh-veh)	*key*
divertirsi	*to enjoy oneself*
l'estero (Ehs-teh-roh)	*abroad*
indimenticabile	*unforgettable*
noleggiare	*to rent (a vehicle)*
la prenotazione	*reservation*
ricevere (reeh-chEh-veh-reh)	*to receive*
secondo	*according to*
la valigia (vah-lEEh-jah)	*suitcase*

ESPRESSIONI E MODI DI DIRE

la carta di credito (krEh-deeh-toh)	*credit card*
pensarci / Ci penso io!	*to take care of / I'll take care of it!*
secondo Lei	*in your opinion*

ATTIVITÀ

B. Comuncazione.

Say that …

1. you want to go abroad

_____

2. you will enjoy yourself more in Italy

_____

3. you want to have an unforgettable holiday

_____

4. you want to visit many beautiful countries and cities

_____

5. you like only first-class hotels

_____

6. you would like to rent a car

_____

7. you'll take care of it

_____

8. you do not have lots of baggage

_____

9. you have only two suitcases

_____

10. you do not need any help

_____

Ask …

11. someone for his or her credit card (politely)

_____

12. a hotel desk clerk if he or she has received your reservation

_____

13. a hotel desk clerk if you could have two keys for your room

_____

C. Choose the appropriate or correct response.

1. Ha bisogno di…?
      a. aiuto
      b. categoria

2. Preferisco solo … di prima categoria.
      a. le camere
      b. gli alberghi

3. Quanto … ha?
      a. bagaglio
      b. valige

4. Ecco la … della Sua camera.
      a. valigia
      b. chiave

5. Vorrei andare … a vedere molti bei paesi.
      a. all'estero
      b. a Parigi

6. Vorrei … una macchina.
      a. indimenticabile
      b. noleggiare

7. … in Italia.
      a. Mi divertirò
      b. Riceverò

8. … me, l'Italia è un bel paese.
      a. Ci penso
      b. Secondo

D. Domande personali.

1. Ti piace viaggiare?

_____

2. Dove vorresti andare?

_____

3. Quali città vorresti vedere e perché?

_____

E. Plan a trip with a friend. Write out the imaginary dialogue the two of you will have. If you are using this book in a classroom situation, do this activity with a partner.

_____

_____

_____

_____

_____

_____

_____

_____

_____

_____

_____

_____

LINGUA

The Future and Conditional Perfect

Like the present perfect (Unit 16), the future perfect is a compound tense.

It is a formed with the future of the auxiliary verb plus the past participle of the verb, in that order.

avrò mangiato	*I will have eaten*
sarò andato/andata	*I will have gone*

You already know how to form the past participle (Unit 16) and you know the future forms of both avere and essere (Unit 27). So, here are mangiare / *to eat* (conjugated with avere), and andare / *to go* (conjugated with essere), fully conjugated:

(io) avrò mangiato	*I will have eaten*
(tu) avrai mangiato	*you will have eaten (familiar)*
(Lei) avrà mangiato	*you will have eaten (polite)*
(lui / lei) avrà mangiato	*he / she will have eaten*
(noi) avremo mangiato	*we will have eaten*
(voi) avrete mangiato	*you will have eaten (plural)*
(loro) avranno mangiato	*they will have eaten*

(io) sarò andato / a	I will have gone
(tu) sarai andato / a	you will have gone (familiar)
(Lei) sarà andato / a	you will have gone (polite)
(lui) sarà andato	he will have gone
(lei) sarà andata	she will have gone
(noi) saremo andati / e	we will have gone
(voi) sarete andati / e	you will have gone (plural)
(loro) saranno andati / e	they will have gone

Generally, this tense corresponds to the English future perfect. It is used to refer to actions that occurred before simple future actions.

> Andremo al cinema, appena avrai finito di lavorare.
> *We will go to the movies as soon as you (will) have finished work.*

> Usciremo, dopo che avremo mangiato.
> *We will go out after we (will) have finished eating.*

Thus, it is used primarily in clauses starting with words and expressions such as:

| appena | *as soon as* |
| dopo che | *after* |

However, in conversational Italian, the simple future can often be used instead:

> Andremo al cinema, appena finirai di lavorare.
> *We will go to the movies as soon as you finish work.*

The conditional perfect is also a compound tense. It is a formed with the conditional of the auxiliary verb plus the past participle of the verb, in that order.

| avrei mangiato | *I would have eaten* |
| sarei andato/andata | *I would have gone* |

Again, you already know how to form the past participle (Unit 16) and you know the conditional forms of both avere and essere (Unit 27). So, here are mangiare / *to eat* (conjugated with avere), and andare / *to go* (conjugated with essere), fully conjugated:

(io) avrei mangiato	I would have eaten
(tu) avresti mangiato	you would have eaten (familiar)
(Lei) avrebbe mangiato	you would have eaten (polite)
(lui / lei) avrebbe mangiato	he / she would have eaten
(noi) avremmo mangiato	we would have eaten
(voi) avreste mangiato	you would have eaten (plural)
(loro) avrebbero mangiato	they would have eaten

(io) sarei andato / andata	*I would have gone*
(tu) saresti andato / andata	*you would have gone (familiar)*
(Lei) sarebbe andato / andata	*you would have gone (polite)*
(lui) sarebbe andato	*he would have gone*
(lei) sarebbe andata	*she would have gone*
(noi) saremmo andati / andate	*we would have gone*
(voi) sareste andati / andate	*you would have gone (plural)*
(loro) sarebbero andati / andate	*they would have gone*

Generally, this tense corresponds to the English conditional perfect (*I would have...; You would have ...;* etc.). It is used to refer to actions that occurred before other actions:

Mi ha detto che sarebbe venuto.	*He told me that he would (would have) come.*
Sapeva che io avrei capito.	*He knew I would have understood.*

Reflexive Verbs

Reflexive verbs allow you to refer to actions that are "reflected" back on the subject: *I wash myself, you enjoy yourself.* Reflexive verbs are conjugated in exactly the same way as nonreflexive ones, but with the addition of reflexive pronouns:

mi	*myself*
ti	*yourself (familiar)*
si	*himself / herself / yourself (polite)*
ci	*ourselves*
vi	*yourselves (plural)*
si	*themselves*

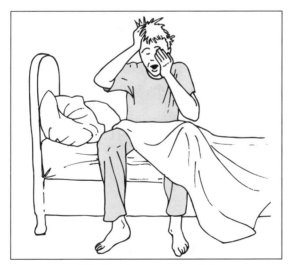

Mi alzo troppo presto!

Reflexive verbs are identified by the suffix -si / *oneself* on the infinitive:

alzare	+	-si	alzarsi	*to get up*
mettere	+	-si	mettersi	*to put on*
divertire	+	-si	divertirsi	*to enjoy oneself*

435

Below are examples of these three reflexive verbs conjugated in the present indicative:

Present Indicative			
alzare	→	alz-	*to get up*
mettere	→	mett-	*to put on*
divertire	→	divert-	*to enjoy oneself*

(io) mi alzo	*I get up (= I get myself up), I am getting up*
(io) mi metto	*I put on (= I put on myself), I am putting on*
(io) mi diverto	*I enjoy myself, I am enjoying myself*
(tu) ti alzi	*you get up, you are getting up (familiar)*
(tu) ti metti	*you put on, you are putting on (familiar)*
(tu) ti diverti	*you enjoy yourself, you are enjoying yourself (familiar)*
(Lei) si alza	*you get up, you are getting up (polite)*
(Lei) si mette	*you put on, you are putting on (polite)*
(Lei) si diverte	*you enjoy yourself, you are enjoying yourself (polite)*
(lui / lei) si alza	*he / she gets up, he / she is getting up*
(lui / lei) si mette	*he / she puts on, he /she is putting on*
(lui / lei) si diverte	*he / she enjoys himself / herself, he /she is enjoying himself / herself*
(noi) ci alziamo	*we get up, we are getting up*
(noi) ci mettiamo	*we put on, we are putting on*
(noi) ci divertiamo	*we enjoy ourselves, we are enjoying ourselves*
(voi) vi alzate	*you get up, you are getting up (plural)*
(voi) vi mettete	*you put on, you are putting on (plural)*
(voi) vi divertite	*you enjoy yourselves, you are enjoying yourselves (plural)*
(loro) si alzano	*they get up, they are getting up*
(loro) si mettono	*they put on, they are putting on*
(loro) si divertono	*they enjoy themselves, they are enjoying themselves*

To form the imperfect, past absolute, future, and conditional of reflexive verbs, do the same thing:

(1) conjugate the reflexive verb in the usual fashion
(2) use reflexive pronouns

Here are a few examples:

Imperfect
Da bambino io mi alzavo sempre tardi. / *As a child, I always used to get up late.*
Da giovani, ci divertivamo molto. / *As young people, we used to have a lot of fun.*

Past Absolute
Lui si divertì molto in Italia. / *He really enjoyed himself in Italy.*
Anch'io mi divertii molto. / *I also really enjoyed myself.*

Future

Tu ti metterai un nuovo vestito per la festa.
You are going to put on a new dress for the party.

Loro si divertiranno in Italia.
They will enjoy themselves in Italy.

Conditional

Lei si alzerebbe presto, ma ha sempre sonno.
She would get up early, but she is always tired.

Io mi divertirei di più in Italia.
I would enjoy myself more in Italy.

In compound tenses (the present perfect, the future perfect, the conditional perfect) reflexive verbs are conjugated only with **essere**. The verb **alzarsi** is conjugated below in the present perfect:

(io) mi sono alzato / a	*I have gotten up, I got up*
(tu) ti sei alzato / a	*you have gotten up, you got up (familiar)*
(Lei) si è alzato / a	*you have gotten up, you got up (polite)*
(lui /lei) si è alzato / a	*he / she has gotten up, he / she got up*
(noi) ci siamo alzati / e	*we have gotten up, we got up*
(voi) vi siete alzati / e	*you have gotten up, you got up (plural)*
(loro) si sono alzati / e	*they have gotten up, they got up*

Examples of verbs used in compound tenses are as follows:

Ieri lei si è divertita in centro.
Yesterday she enjoyed herself downtown.

Appena si saranno alzati, usciranno.
As soon as they will have gotten up, they will go out.

Mi sarei alzato prima, ma ero stanco.
I would have gotten up earlier, but I was tired.

In the imperative, the reflexive pronoun is attached to the familiar forms of the verb:

Familiar		**Polite**	
alzarsi	*to get up*		
(tu) Alzati!	*Get up!*	(Lei) Si alzi!	*Get up!*
(voi) Alzatevi!	*Get up!*	(Loro) Si alzino!	*Get up!*
(noi) Alziamoci!	*Let's get up!*		
mettersi	*to put on*		
(tu) Mettiti!	*Put on!*	(Lei) Si metta!	*Put on!*
(voi) Mettetevi!	*Put on!*	(Loro) Si mettano!	*Put on!*
(noi) Mettiamoci!	*Let's put on!*		
divertirsi	*to enjoy oneself*		
(tu) Divertiti!	*Enjoy yourself!*	(Lei) Si diverta!	*Enjoy yourself!*
(voi) Divertitevi!	*Enjoy yourselves!*	(Loro) Si divertano!	*Enjoy yourselves!*
(noi) Divertiamoci!	*Let's enjoy ourselves!*		

Here are some examples of the uses of such imperative forms:

alzarsi	
Marco, alzati! Signor Dini, si alzi! Marco e Sandra, alzatevi!	Mark, get up! (familiar) Mr. Dini, get up! (polite) Mark and Sandra, get up! (plural)
mettersi	
Claudia, mettiti la giacca! Signora, si metta la giacca! Ragazzi, mettetevi la giacca!	Claudia, put on a jacket! (familiar) Madam, put on a jacket! (polite) Boys, put on a jacket! (plural)
divertirsi	
Alessandro divertiti! Signor Rossi, si diverta! Ragazzi, divertitevi!	Alessandro, enjoy yourself! (familiar) Mr. Rossi, enjoy yourself! (polite) Boys, enjoy yourselves! (plural)

ATTIVITÀ

F. Come si dice in italiano? Follow the model.

Model: Loro andranno al cinema, appena che … I have finished working
Loro andranno al cinema, appena che io avrò finito di lavorare.

Loro andranno al cinema, appena che …

1. I have finished working

_____

2. you *(familiar, singular)* will have arrived

_____

3. he will have come

_____

4. we will have eaten

_____

5. you *(plural)* will have gotten up

_____

6. my friends will have gotten up

_____

G. Now, say the following things.

1. I would have finished working earlier, but …

_____

2. You *(familiar, singular)* would have arrived earlier, but …

_____

3. He would have come earlier, but …

_____

4. We would have eaten earlier, but …

_____

5. You *(plural)* would have gotten up earlier, but …

_____

6. My friends would have gotten up earlier, but …

_____

H. Say that the indicated people do, used to do, and will always do certain things. Follow the model.

> *Model:* alzarsi presto … Io
> *Io mi alzo sempre presto. Anche da giovane mi*
> *alzavo sempre presto. E mi alzerò sempre presto.*
>
> mettersi la giacca … Io
> *Io mi metto sempre la giacca. Anche da giovane*
> *me la mettevo sempre. E me la metterò sempre.*
>
> divertirsi … Io
> *Io mi diverto sempre. Anche da giovane mi divertivo*
> *sempre. E mi divertirò sempre.*

Parole Nuove	
presto	early
tardi	late

alzarsi presto…

1. Io

_____

2. Tu

_____

3. Lui / Lei

_____

4. Noi

_____

5. Voi

_____

6. Loro

_____

mettersi la giacca...

7. Io

_____

8. Tu

_____

9. Lui / Lei

_____

10. Noi

_____

11. Voi

_____

12. Loro

_____

divertirsi...

13. Io

_____

14. Tu

_____

15. Lui / Lei

_____

16. Noi

_____

17. Voi

_____

18. Loro

_____

I. Tell the following people to do the indicated things.

>*Model:* Tell Dina...to enjoy herself
>*Dina, divertiti!*

Tell Dina...

  1. to get up early

_____

  2. to put on a new pair of pants

_____

  3. to enjoy herself

_____

Tell Mrs. Martini...

  4. to get up early

_____

  5. to put on a new pair of pants

_____

  6. to enjoy herself

_____

Tell Dina and Alessandro...

  7. to get up early

_____

  8. to put on a new pair of pants

_____

  9. to enjoy themselves

_____

Tell Mr. and Mrs. Martini...

10. to get up early

_____

11. to put on a new pair of pants

_____

12. to enjoy themselves

_____

J. Cruciverba!

Horizontal	**Vertical**

Horizontal

2 Noi ci siamo ... molto in Italia.
4 Avete bisogno di ...?
5 A che ora ... alza Lei di solito?
6 Io ... alzo sempre alle sei.
7 Le mie sorelle si sono ... la giacca
    perché fa freddo.
8 Dina si è ... tardi.
9 Cosa vi ... voi per uscire?
10 A che ora ti ... di solito?
11 A che ora vi ... il sabato?
13 Sono sicuro che voi vi ... in Italia.
14 Noi ... siamo divertiti molto in Italia.
17 Vogliamo prenotare un ... di prima
     categoria.
18 Domani mi ... alle cinque e mezzo.
19 Anche voi ... siete divertiti in Italia, vero?
23 Loro si ... molto alla festa sabato prossimo.
24 Voglio andare all'... per una vacanza.
25 Ci sono tante belle ... da vedere.
26 Ecco a Lei la ... della Sua camera.
27 Ci ... io!
28 Ho fatto la ... alcuni mesi fa.
29 Questo è un albergo di prima ...
30 Buon ...!
31 Voglio fare una ... all'estero.

Vertical

1 Domani ... alzerò alle sei del mattino.
2 Tu ti ... molto in centro, vero?
3 Cosa ... metti per uscire?
4 Lui si è ... tardi.
6 Lei cosa si ... per uscire stasera?
12 Cosa ti ... per la festa sabato prossimo?
14 Ha una carta di ...?
15 Avete tanto ...?
16 Vogliamo anche ... una macchina.
20 La vostra ... è il numero 15 al terzo piano.
21 Loro ... sono divertiti molto in Italia.
22 Abbiamo solo due ...
26 A me piacciono solo gli alberghi di prima ...

NOTA CULTURALE

Carla is on vacation. In Italy there are so many wonderful places to see that it would be hard to decide where to go. One city that cannot be missed is Pisa. The leaning tower is truly an enigma.

Pisa

[Look up any words you cannot figure out.]

Collocata *(located)* sulle due rive *(banks)* dell'Arno, Pisa è importante per industrie varie. Il turismo è attratto dalla *(is attracted by)* sua storia artistica, accentrata *(centered)* nella Piazza dei Miracoli, con il duomo, iniziato nel 1063 e finito nel tredicesimo secolo, il famoso campanile *(bell tower)*, più noto con il nome di torre pendente (dodicesimo secolo), il battistero (secoli dodicesimo-quattordicesimo), il camposanto *(cemetery)*.

Tra gli altri edifici notevoli, le chiese di Santa Maria della Spina, di San Paolo a Ripa d'Arno, di Santo Stefano dei Cavalieri, i palazzi dell'Orologio, Toscanelli, dei Cavalieri e numerosi edifici caratteristici dei quattordicesimo-quindicesimo secoli. Glorie di Pisa sono anche l'università e la Scuola normale superiore.

La Torre di Pisa

K. Write a brief composition on Pisa, adding to the information given anything else you know about it. If you are using this book in a classroom situation, do this activity with a partner.

_____

_____

_____

_____

_____

_____

_____

_____

_____

_____

_____

_____

_____

_____

_____

_____

_____

_____

_____

_____

C'è un partita importante in televisione stasera!

Una partita importante!

CONVERSAZIONE

[Dina is watching TV with Paul in the residence where they are staying. They are arguing over which TV program to watch.]

Dina	Stasera c'è un bel programma di pattinaggio in televisione!	*Tonight there's a nice skating program on TV!*
Paul	No, no! C'è una partita importante di calcio e poi una di pallacanestro.	*No way! There's an important soccer match on and then a basketball game.*
Dina	Va bene, ma domani voglio guardare l'incontro di tennis!	*OK, but tomorrow I want to watch the tennis match!*
Paul	D'accordo. Ma la sera dopo c'è il pugilato e una gara di bicicletta!	*OK. But the evening after there's boxing and a bicycle race!*
Dina	Adesso esco per fare un po' di ginnastica. Anche tu dovresti praticare di più lo sport.	*I'm going out now to work out. You should practice sports more, too.*
Paul	Hai ragione. Domani comincerò a fare il footing. Divertiti!	*You're right. Tomorrow I'll start jogging. Enjoy yourself!*
Dina	Ciao!	*Bye!*

COMPRENSIONE

A. Rispondi alle seguenti domande con frasi intere.

1. Che cosa vuole guardare stasera Dina in televisione?

_____

2. Che cosa vuole guardare invece Alessandro?

_____

3. Che cosa vuole guardare domani Dina?

_____

4. E che cosa vuole guardare Alessandro la sera dopo?

_____

5. Dove va Dina?

_____

6. Chi dovrebbe praticare di più lo sport, secondo Dina?

_____

7. Che cosa comincerà a fare domani Alessandro?

_____

VOCABOLARIO

Fare ginnastica!

PAROLE NUOVE

la bicicletta	*bicycle*
il calcio (kAhl-choh)	*soccer*
la gara	*competition*
la ginnastica (jeeh-nnAhs-teeh-kah)	*gymnastics*
guardare	*to watch*
l'incontro	*match, encounter*
la pallacanestro	*basketball*
la partita	*match, game*
il pattinaggio (pah-tteeh-nAh-jjoh)	*skating*
praticare	*to practice*
il programma	*program*
il pugilato	*boxing*
lo sport	*sport*
la televisione	*television*
il tennis	*tennis*

ESPRESSIONI E MODI DI DIRE

fare il footing	*to jog*
fare ginnastica	*to work out*

IRREGOLARITÀ

- **Il programma** is masculine, even though it ends in -a. Its plural form is: **i programmi** / *the programs.*

ATTIVITÀ

B. Comunicazione.

Say that …

1. tonight there's a nice skating program on TV

_____

2. there's an important soccer match on TV later

_____

3. there will be a basketball game on TV tomorrow

_____

4. you want to watch a tennis match tomorrow

_____

5. the night after there's boxing on TV

_____

6. every Tuesday evening there is a bicycle race on TV in the summer

_____

7. you are going out to work out a little bit

_____

8. you should practice sports more

_____

9. tomorrow you will start jogging

_____

Tell Dina to…

10. enjoy herself

_____

C. Say if you would or would not like to try out the following sports.

> _Model:_ calcio
> _Sì, mi piacerebbe praticare il calcio. / No, non mi piacerebbe praticare il calcio._

1. calcio

_____

2. ginnastica

_____

3. pallacanestro

_____

4. pattinaggio

_____

5. pugilato

_____

6. tennis

_____

7. footing

_____

D. Domande personali.

1. Quale sport ti piace di più?

_____

2. Perché?

_____

3. Quale sport non ti piace?

_____

4. Perché?

_____

5. Fai il footing o la ginnastica? Quante volte alla settimana?

_____

E. Give a list of several sports you would like to do. Use a dictionary if necessary. Explain briefly the reason for each one.

_____

_____

_____

_____

_____

_____

_____

_____

_____

_____

LINGUA

English and Greek Words in Italian

Lo sport is a word that Italians have borrowed from English. All such words are invariable:

Singular		Plural	
lo sport	*sport*	gli sport	*sports*
il film	*movie*	i film	*movies*

As pointed out above, **il programma** is a masculine noun. Those nouns ending in **-amma** and **-ema** are all masculine because they are of Greek origin. In the plural they have the normal masculine plural ending **-i**:

Singular		Plural	
il programma	*program*	i programmi	*programs*
il problema	*problem*	i problemi	*problems*

Nervoso   Calma

Adjectives Referring to Physical and Social Traits

The following adjectives are arranged in terms of "opposite traits":

Trait		Opposite Trait	
alto	*tall*	basso	*short*
calmo	*calm*	nervoso	*nervous*
energico	*energetic*	pigro	*lazy*
giovane	*young*	vecchio	*old*
grande	*big*	piccolo	*small*
intelligente	*intelligent*	stupido	*stupid*
magro	*skinny*	grasso	*fat*
ricco	*rich*	povero	*poor*
simpatico	*nice*	antipatico	*unpleasant*

The Imperative with Unstressed Object Pronouns

Recall from the previous unit that reflexive pronouns are attached to familiar forms of reflexive verbs in the imperative. The same pattern applies to the conjugation of any verb in the imperative with unstressed object pronouns:

Imperative Tu Forms	With Unstressed Object Pronouns
Alessandro, mangia il panino! *Alessandro, eat the sandwich!*	Alessandro, mangialo! *Alessandro, eat it!*
Claudia, parla al professore! *Claudia, speak to the professor!*	Claudia, parlagli! *Claudia, speak to him!*

Imperative Lei Forms	With Unstressed Object Pronouns
Signor Rossi, mangi il panino! *Mr. Rossi, eat the sandwich!*	Signor Rossi, lo mangi! *Mr. Rossi, eat it!*
Signora Verdi, parli al professore! *Mrs. Verdi, speak to the professor!*	Signora Verdi, gli parli! *Mrs. Verdi, speak to him!*

Imperative Voi Forms	With Unstressed Object Pronouns
Ragazzi, mangiate i panini! *Boys, eat the sandwiches!*	Ragazzi, mangiateli! *Boys, eat them!*
Ragazzi, parlate al professore! *Boys, speak to the professor!*	Ragazzi, parlategli! *Boys, speak to him!*

Imperative Loro Forms	With Unstressed Object Pronouns
Signori, mangino i panini! *Gentlemen, eat the sandwiches!*	Signori, li mangino! *Gentlemen, eat them!*
Signorine, parlino al professore! *Young ladies, speak to the professor!*	Signorine, gli parlino! *Young ladies, speak to him!*

Imperative noi Forms	With Unstressed Object Pronouns
Mangiamo i panini! *Let's eat the sandwiches!*	Mangiamoli! *Let's eat them!*
Parliamo al professore! *Let's speak to the professor!*	Parliamogli! *Let's speak to him!*

Reciprocal Forms

The reflexive pronouns si, ci, and vi are also used to convey "reciprocity"—*to each other, to one another*, etc.

Loro non si parlano da un anno.	*They haven't spoken to each other for a year.*
Lui e io ci telefoniamo ogni sera.	*He and I phone each other every evening.*
Voi due vi telefonate spesso, no?	*The two of you phone each other often, don't you?*

The Pluperfect

The pluperfect is a compound tense. It is conjugated with an auxiliary verb, either avere or essere, and the past participle of the verb. In this case the auxiliary verb is in the imperfect tense.

avevo mangiato	*I had eaten*
ero andato / andata	*I had gone*

You already know how to form the past participle, and you know the imperfect forms of both avere and essere. So, here are mangiare / *to eat* (conjugated with avere), and andare / *to go* (conjugated with essere), fully conjugated:

(io) avevo mangiato	*I had eaten*
(tu) avevi mangiato	*you had eaten (familiar)*
(Lei) aveva mangiato	*you had eaten (polite)*
(lui / lei) aveva mangiato	*he / she had eaten*
(noi) avevamo mangiato	*we had eaten*
(voi) avevate mangiato	*you had eaten (plural)*
(loro) avevano mangiato	*they had eaten*

(io) ero andato / andata	*I had gone*
(tu) eri andato / andata	*you had gone (familiar)*
(Lei) era andato / andata	*you had gone (polite)*
(lui) era andato	*he had gone*
(lei) era andata	*she had gone*
(noi) eravamo andati / andate	*we had gone*
(voi) eravate andati / andate	*you had gone (plural)*
(loro) erano andati / andate	*they had gone*

The pluperfect tense (literally, "more than perfect" or "more than past") allows you to express an action that occurred *before* a simple past action as expressed by the present perfect, the imperfect, or the past absolute:

Dopo che era arrivata, mi ha telefonato.
After she had arrived, she phoned me.

Lui mi ha detto che le aveva già parlato.
He told me that he had already talked to her.

Essentially, this tense corresponds to the English pluperfect (*had* + past participle). But be careful! Sometimes the pluperfect is only implied in English colloquial usage.

Sono andati in Italia dopo che avevano finito gli esami.
They went to Italy after they finished (= had finished) their exams.

ATTIVITÀ

F. Give the indicated word in Italian and then make it plural. Follow the model.

> *Model:* sport
> *lo sport / gli sport*

1. movie

_____

2. program

_____

3. problem

_____

4. composition, theme

_____

G. You are very opinionated! First, say that your sister has the indicated trait, but that your brother has the opposite trait. Then say that this is true of all your female friends with respect to your male friends. Finally, say that you always phone each other. Follow the model.

> *Model:* tall
> *Mia sorella è alta, ma mio fratello è basso.*
> *Infatti, tutte le mie amiche sono alte, ma i miei amici sono bassi.*
> *Ci telefoniamo spesso!*

1. calm

_____

2. energetic

_____

3. young

_____

4. small

_____

5. intelligent

_____

6. skinny

_____

7. rich

_____

8. nice

_____

H. Tell the following people to do the indicated things.

> *Model:* Dina...speak to him
> *Dina, parlagli!*

Tell Dina to...

1. speak to him

_____

2. eat them (the spaghetti)

_____

3. call us

_____

4. drink it (the coffee)

_____

5. speak to her

_____

Tell Mrs. Martini to...

6. speak to him

_____

7. eat them (the spaghetti)

_____

8. call us

_____

9. drink it (the coffee)

_____

10. speak to her

_____

Tell Dina and Alessandro to...

11. speak to him

_____

12. eat them (the spaghetti)

_____

13. call us

_____

14. drink it (the coffee)

_____

15. speak to her

_____

Tell Mr. and Mrs. Martini to...

16. speak to him

_____

17. eat them (the spaghetti)

_____

18. call us

_____

19. drink it (the coffee)

_____

20. speak to her

_____

I. Come si dice in italiano?

> *Model:* Io...had spoken to him already
> *Io gli avevo già parlato.*

Io...

1. had spoken to him already

_____

2. had gotten up early yesterday

_____

3. had come late

_____

Tu...

4. had spoken to him already

_____

5. had gotten up early yesterday

_____

6. had come late

_____

Lui...

7. had spoken to him already

_____

8. had gotten up early yesterday

_____

9. had come late

_____

Lei...

10. had spoken to him already

_____

11. had gotten up early yesterday

_____

12. had come late

_____

Noi...

13. had spoken to him already

_____

14. had gotten up early yesterday

_____

15. had come late

_____

Voi...

16. had spoken to him already

_____

17. had gotten up early yesterday

_____

18. had come late

_____

Loro...

19. had spoken to him already

_____

20. had gotten up early yesterday

_____

21. had come late

_____

J. Cruciverba!

Horizontal	**Vertical**

Horizontal

4 Alessandro, fa freddo. … la giacca!
6 La sera dopo c'è una gara di …
8 Signora Giusti, non ha parlato a lui?
   Allora, gli …!
9 Call me! *(familiar)*
12 Alessandro, …! Sono già le dieci e
   mezzo.
15 Non le hai portato il libro? Allora, …
   il libro!
16 Claudio, Carla, …! Sono già le dieci
   e mezzo.
17 non povero
20 Ho veduto tutti i … di Fellini.
21 non antipatico
22 Anche tu … il footing, vero?
23 Stasera c'è una … di bicicletta.
24 Mi piacciono tutti i … di sport in
   televisione.
27 Stasera in televisione c'è una partita …
   di calcio.
28 Voglio vedere l'… di tennis, va bene?
30 TV
31 Questa … c'è un programma importante.

Vertical

1 Loro … telefonano ogni sera.
2 Alessandro, Dina, … alla festa!
3 Signor Carducci, … metta questa giacca!
4 Alessandro, ecco il panino che volevi. …!
5 Non hai parlato a Maria? Allora, …!
7 non alti
8 Non hai parlato a Claudio? Allora, …!
9 Non hai comprato quei libri? Allora, …!
10 non grassa
11 non energico
13 non nervoso
14 non giovani
15 non grande *(feminine)*
18 C'è una partita importante di …
19 Mi piacciono tutti gli …
25 A che ora comincia la … di calcio?
26 Lei ha tanti …
29 tennis

NOTA CULTURALE

As you read in the dialogue, Paul has obviously become interested in Italy's favorite sport: soccer.

Il calcio
[Look up any words you cannot figure out.]

Il calcio si è sviluppato dal "football" che veniva giocato nei college inglesi nel secolo scorso, gioco dal quale è derivato anche il rugby. Il primo codice calcistico (le *quattordici regole di Cambridge*) risale al *(goes back to)* 1848; nel 1863, per unificare le regole del gioco, venne costituita la *Football Association*. Altri organi internazionali *(international bodies)* del calcio sono la *Fédération Internationale de Football Association* (F.I.F.A.), con sede a Zurigo, costituita nel 1904 a Parigi con lo scopo di organizzare la diffusione del calcio nel mondo, e l'*International Board* che dal 1886 è incaricato di far osservare il Regolamento Ufficiale. Le regole fondamentali del calcio sono 17, ciascuna eventualmente integrata da disposizioni delle singole federazioni.

K. Write a brief composition on soccer, adding to the information above anything else you know about it. If you are using this book in a classroom situation, do this activity with a partner.

_____

_____

_____

_____

_____

_____

_____

_____

_____

_____

_____

_____

_____

_____

_____

_____

_____

_____

_____

_____

Stasera vorrei guardare il telefilm, va bene?

Unit 30

Dov'è il telecomando?

CONVERSAZIONE

[Alessandro and Dina are watching TV after dinner one evening at Alessandro's house. Dina has come to finally meet his parents for the first time.]

Alessandro	Dina, stasera vorrei guardare il telefilm. È l'ultima puntata.	Dina, tonight I would like to watch the TV movie. It's the last episode.
Dina	Va bene. Ma dopo voglio guardare il telequiz su RAI Uno.	OK. But then I want to watch the quiz show on RAI One.
Alessandro	A me piace più la cronaca che i programmi popolari che guardi tu!	I like documentaries more than the programs that you watch!
Dina	Non essere cattivo! Dov'è il telecomando?	Don't be mean! Where's the remote control?
Alessandro	L'ho io!	I have it!
Dina	Allora cambia canale! Sono stufa del tuo telefilm! Non lo voglio guardare più!	Then change the channel! I'm fed up with your TV movie! I don't want to watch it anymore!
Alessandro	Perché, sarebbe un film difficile per te?	Why, is it a difficult film for you (to understand)?
Dina	Ma che difficile! È anzi troppo «facile»!	What, difficult! As a matter of fact, it's too «easy».
Alessandro	Hai ragione. Non vale niente!	You're right. It's not worth anything!
Dina	Finalmente, capisci qualcosa!	Finally, you understand something!

COMPRENSIONE

A. Match the items in the two columns in an appropriate fashion.

1. Dina, stasera vorrei ….   a. vale

2. È l'ultima …   b. difficile

3. Non … niente!   c. puntata

4. Sarebbe un film … per te?   d. guardare il telefilm

5. Allora … canale!   e. telecomando

6. Dov'è il …?   f. cronaca

7. A me piace più la … che programmi popolari   g. cambia

VOCABOLARIO

Dammi il telecomando!   No!

PAROLE NUOVE

anzi	*as a matter of fact*
il canale	*channel*
cattivo	*bad, mischievous*
la cronaca (krOh-nah-kah)	*documentary, special interest show*
difficile (deeh-fEEh-cheeh-leh)	*difficult*
facile (fAh-chEEh-leh)	*easy*
il film	*film, movie*
finalmente	*finally, at last*
niente	*nothing*
popolare	*popular*
la puntata	*episode*
stufo	*fed up*
il telecomando	*remote control*
il telefilm	*TV movie*
il telequiz	*TV game show*
ultimo (Oohl-teeh-moh)	*last*
valere	*to be worth*

ESPRESSIONI E MODI DI DIRE

non...niente	*nothing*
non...più	*no longer, no more*

IRREGOLARITÀ

• The verb **valere** has the following irregular forms:

Pres. Ind.:   **(io) valgo, (tu) vali, (lui / lei / Lei) vale, (noi) valiamo, (voi) valete, (loro) valgono (vAhl-goh-noh)**

Past Part.:   **valso** (conjugated with **essere**)

Past Absolute: **(io) valsi, (tu) valesti, (lui / lei / Lei) valse, (noi) valemmo, (voi) valeste, (loro) valsero**

Future: (io) varrò, (tu) varrai, (lui / lei / Lei) varrà, (noi) varremo, (voi) varrete, (loro) varranno

Conditional: (io) varrei, (tu) varresti, (lui / lei / Lei) varrebbe, (noi) varremmo, (voi) varreste, (loro) varrebbero

- Negative adverbs in Italian require non: **non voglio niente** / *I do not want anything,* **non lo guardo più** / *I am not going to watch it anymore,* and so on

ATTIVITÀ

B. Comunicazione.

Say that …

1. tonight you would like to watch the last episode of the TV movie

_____

2. after you want to watch the quiz show on RAI One

_____

3. you like documentaries more than popular programs

_____

4. you have the remote control

_____

5. you're fed up with popular programs

_____

6. you do not want to watch them anymore

_____

7. documentaries in Italian are a little too difficult for you

_____

8. popular programs in Italian, as a matter of fact, are easy for you

_____

9. the TV movie is not worth anything

_____

Tell Alessandro …

10. not to be mean

_____

11. to change the channel

_____

12. finally, he understands something

_____

C. Choose the appropriate or correct response.

1. ..., è molto facile.
        a. Anzi
        b. Finalmente

2. Cambia ... per favore!
        a. il canale
        b. niente

3. Dov'è il ... ?
        a. telecomando
        b. popolare

4. Non è ... niente!
        a. valso
        b. stufo

5. È ... puntata del telefilm.
        a. l'ultima
        b. facile

6. Sono ... di guardare quel programma.
        a. stufa
        b. difficile

7. Non ... cattivo!
        a. vale
        b. essere

D. Say that the movie...

1. is worth nothing

_____

2. was not worth anything

_____

3. will be worth it

_____

4. would be worth seeing, but you have no time

_____

E. Domande personali.

1. Ti piace guardare la televisione?

_____

2. Quando la guardi?

_____

3. Quali sono i programmi che odi *(hate)* di più?

_____

4. Perché?

_____

F. Make a list of your favorite TV programs, explaining briefly why you like each one. Use a dictionary if necessary.

_____

_____

_____

_____

_____

_____

_____

_____

_____

_____

_____

_____

_____

_____

_____

_____

_____

_____

_____

_____

LINGUA

Gianni è alto   Marco è più alto

Comparison

To compare adjectives, adverbs, and other structures, simply use **più** for *more* (comparison of majority) and **meno** for *less* (comparison of minority):

Gianni è alto *Gianni is tall*	**Marco è più alto** *Marco is taller*
Claudia è ricca *Claudia is rich*	**Mia cugina è più ricca** *My cousin is richer*
I miei amici sono simpatici *My friends are nice*	**I tuoi amici sono più simpatici** *Your friends are nicer*
Le mie zie sono ricche *My aunts are rich*	**Le tue zie sono più ricche** *Your aunts are richer*
Gianni è magro *Gianni is skinny*	**Marco è meno magro** *Marco is less skinny*
Loro sono intelligenti *They are intelligent*	**Noi siamo meno intelligenti** *We are less intelligent*

When two people or things are compared in terms of one attribute, the following structures are used:

più...di	*more...than*
meno...di	*less...than*

Marco è più alto di Gianni	*Marco is taller than Gianni*
Mia cugina è più ricca di Claudia	*My cousin is richer than Claudia*
Loro sono più simpatici di noi	*They are nicer than we*
Marco è meno magro di Gianni	*Marco is less skinny than Gianni*

466

When two attributes apply to the same person or things, the following structures are used instead:

più...che	*more...than*
meno...che	*less...than*

Marco è più nervoso che calmo	*Marco is more nervous than calm*
Lei è più nervosa che calma	*She is more nervous than calm*
Loro sono meno nervosi che calmi	*They are less nervous than calm*

The following structures are used to compare people or things in terms of equality:

così...come	*as...as*
tanto...quanto	*as...as*

Marco è così alto come Gianni	*Marco is as tall as Gianni*
Mia cugina è tanto ricca quanto lui	*My cousin is as rich as he is*

The Superlative

The superlative *(the most, the least)* is expressed by simply putting the appropriate form of the definite article in front of the comparative form:

Gianni è alto	Marco è il più alto
Gianni is tall	*Marco is the tallest*
Claudia è ricca	Mia cugina è la più ricca
Claudia is rich	*My cousin is the richest*
I miei amici sono simpatici	I tuoi amici sono i più simpatici
My friends are nice	*Your friends are the nicest*
Le mie zie sono ricche	Le tue zie sono le più ricche
My aunts are rich	*Your aunts are the richest*
Gianni è magro	Marco è il meno magro
Gianni is skinny	*Marco is the least skinny*
Loro sono intelligenti	Noi siamo i meno intelligenti
They are intelligent	*We are the least intelligent*

When followed by a relevant phrase—*in the class, of the family*—the preposition di (also in contracted form) is used:

Gianni è il più alto della classe	*Gianni is the tallest in the class*
Lei è la più bella della città	*She is the most beautiful in the city*
Quei panini sono i più buoni del bar	*Those sandwiches are the best in the bar*
Quelle sono le più belle	*Those are the most beautiful ones*
Lui è il meno ricco della famiglia	*He is the least rich of the family*
Io sono la meno calma della famiglia	*I'm the least calm one of my family*

Adverbs of Manner

Adverbs of manner *(finally, clearly, ...)* are formed by adding -mente to the adjective as follows:

Adjectives ending in -o		→	-o is changed to -a	
energico	*energetic*		energicamente	*energetically*
calmo	*calm*		calmamente	*calmly*
alto	*high*		altamente	*highly*

Adjectives ending in -e		→	No change	
intelligente	*intelligent*		intelligentemente	*intelligently*
forte	*strong*		fortemente	*strongly*

Adjectives ending in -le or -re		→	-e is dropped	
facile	*easy*		facilmente	*easily*
difficile	*difficult*		difficilmente	*with difficulty*
popolare	*popular*		popolarmente	*popularly*

Adjectives of Nationality

The following adjectives can also be used as nouns:

Adjectives	**Nouns**
Lui è di origine africana	Lui è africano
He is of African origin	*He is African*
Lei è di origine italiana	Lei parla italiano molto bene
She is of Italian origin	*She speaks Italian very well*

africano	*African*
americano	*American*
australiano	*Australian*
canadese	*Canadian*
cinese	*Chinese*
danese	*Danish*
francese	*French*
giapponese	*Japanese*
greco	*Greek*
inglese	*English*
italiano	*Italian*
messicano	*Mexican*
norvegese	*Norwegian*
olandese	*Dutch*
polacco	*Polish*
portoghese	*Portuguese*
russo	*Russian*
spagnolo	*Spanish*
svedese	*Swedish*
svizzero (zvEEh-tseh-roh)	*Swiss*
tedesco	*German*

The Verb piacere: An Overview

You have been using the most common forms of piacere throughout this book. Now it is time to get a general (albeit not complete) picture of this pesky verb! You will learn more about it as you go on to higher levels of study.

First, note that it has irregular present indicative forms:

piacere a *to be pleasing to*	
(io) piaccio a	*I am pleasing to*
(tu) piaci a	*you are pleasing to (familiar)*
(Lei) piace a	*you are pleasing to (polite)*
(lui / lei) piace a	*he / she is pleasing to*
(noi) piacciamo a	*we are pleasing to*
(voi) piacete a	*you are pleasing to*
(loro) piacciono a	*they are pleasing to*

When saying that you or someone else likes something, translate the English expression in your mind as *to be pleasing to*:

I like that skirt

Mi	piace	quella gonna.
↓	↓	↓
To me	*is pleasing*	*that skirt.*

I like those skirts

Mi	piacciono	quelle gonne.
↓	↓	↓
To me	*are pleasing*	*those skirts.*

If you think this way, you will always be correct. Notice that the real subject is usually put at the end (although this is not necessary). Here are other examples for you to study carefully:

Mary likes John

A Maria	piace	Giovanni.
↓	↓	↓
To Mary	*is pleasing*	*John.*

She likes her friends

Le	piacciono	i suoi amici.
↓	↓	↓
To her	*are pleasing*	*her friends.*

Her friends like her

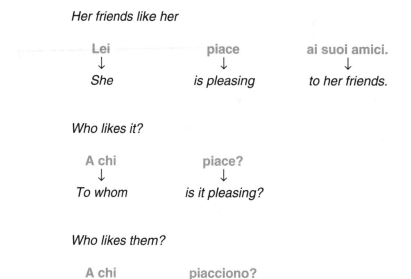

Lei	piace	ai suoi amici.
↓	↓	↓
She	is pleasing	to her friends.

Who likes it?

A chi	piace?
↓	↓
To whom	is it pleasing?

Who likes them?

A chi	piacciono?
↓	↓
To whom	are they pleasing?

In compound tenses, **piacere** is conjugated with **essere**. This means, of course, that the past participle agrees with the subject—no matter where it occurs in the sentence.

I didn't like her.

Non mi	è piaciuta	(lei).
↓	↓	↓
Not to me	was pleasing	she.

She didn't like us.

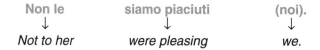

Non le	siamo piaciuti	(noi).
↓	↓	↓
Not to her	were pleasing	we.

And do not forget that you might need to use those object pronouns that come after the verb for reasons of emphasis or clarity.

> **La musica piace a me, non a te!**
> *I like the music, not you (The music is pleasing to me, not to you)!*

To say that you do not like something, simply put **non** before the predicate in the normal fashion:

| **Non mi piace quella rivista.** | *I do not like that magazine.* |
| **Non le piacciono i ravioli.** | *She doesn't like ravioli.* |

ATTIVITÀ

G. Compare yourself to others in your family. First, say that your brother has a certain trait or exemplifies a certain state but that your sister has more of it. Then, compare yourself to him (less) and to her (more). Follow the model.

> *Model:* alto
> *Mio fratello è alto, ma mia sorella è più alta.*
> *Io sono meno alto / alta di lui, ma più alto / alta di lei.*

Parole Nuove	
felice	happy
triste	sad

1. stanco

_____

2. simpatico

_____

3. intelligente

_____

4. grande

_____

5. ironico

_____

6. umile

_____

7. felice

_____

8. triste

_____

H. Now, say that your brother is more one thing (trait characteristics) than another and that your sister is the opposite. Also say that you are like your brother. Finally, say that your mother exemplifies the trait the most. Follow the model.

> *Model:* nervoso / calmo
> —*Mio fratello è più nervoso che calmo, ma mia sorella è meno nervosa che calma.*
> —*Io sono così nervoso / nervosa come lui.*
> —*Ma nostra madre è la più nervosa della famiglia.*

1. grande / piccolo

_____

2. simpatico / gentile

_____

3. energico / umile

_____

4. forte / energico

_____

I. Turn each of the following adjectives into an adverb of manner.

     Model: alto
            altamente

  1. facile

_____

  2. calmo

_____

  3. certo

_____

  4. efficiente

_____

  5. economico

_____

  6. difficile

_____

  7. differente

_____

  8. felice

_____

  9. forte

_____

10. gentile

_____

11. umile

_____

12. sicuro

_____

J. Say that a certain man is one nationality and a woman another (as indicated). Follow the model.

     Model: German / Canadian
           Quell'uomo è tedesco e quella donna è canadese.

  1. Swiss / Swedish

_____

  2. Spanish / Russian

_____

3. Portuguese / Dutch

_____

4. Polish / Norwegian

_____

5. Mexican / Italian

_____

6. English / Greek

_____

7. Japanese / French

_____

8. Danish / Chinese

_____

9. African / Australian

_____

10. American / German

_____

K. Come si dice in italiano?

1. I like her, but she doesn't like me.

_____

2. She used to like us, but she only likes you *(familiar, plural)* now.

_____

3. They will like him a lot.

_____

4. I would like to go to Italy, but I do not have enough money.

_____

5. We didn't like the spaghetti, but she liked it a lot.

_____

6. Do you *(plural)* like me?

_____

7. He likes her, and she likes him too.

_____

8. Alessandro likes Dina, and Dina likes him.

_____

9. Did you *(familiar, singular)* like the meat?

_____

10. No, I didn't like it.

_____

L. Cruciverba!

Horizontal

2 Lui è … simpatico di lei.
5 as a matter of fact
6 Lui è più ricco … voi.
7 Canadian
8 German *(masculine)*
9 Marco è … pigro di me.
11 English
12 Australian *(masculine)*
13 Russian *(masculine)*
15 Portuguese
18 easily
22 Alessandro è più energico … pigro.
23 French
26 Dov'è il …?
27 Mi piace più la … che i programmi
   popolari.
28 Sono … del tuo telefilm.

Vertical

1 Io sono più calmo … voi.
2 Marco è … alto di Nicola.
3 Danish
4 Mexican *(masculine)*
5 American *(masculine)*
7 Chinese
10 calmly
14 Spanish *(masculine)*
15 Lui è … simpatico che intelligente.
16 Maria è … alta quanto Sandra.
17 Swiss *(masculine)*
19 Sono stufa del telefilm. Cambia …!
20 Lui è … grande come suo fratello.
21 Lui è il più simpatico … film.
24 È l'ultima … del telefilm.
25 Non vale …

NOTA CULTURALE

Dina and Alessandro are watching TV. In Italy there are three public, state-run channels: RAI Uno, RAI Due, RAI Tre. There are also many private channels.

La RAI

[Look up any words you cannot figure out.]

La RAI, sigla *(abbreviation)* di Radio Audizione Italiana, sta per la radiotelevisione pubblica italiana, la sua organizzazione, e i suoi programmi. Sorta *(born)* nel 1924 come URI (Unione radiofonica italiana), nel 1928 assunse *(took on)* il nome di EIAR (Ente italiano audizioni radiofoniche) e nel 1944 quello di RAI. Nel 1975 la RAI fu riformata con la creazione di tre reti—RAI 1, RAI 2 e RAI 3—dotate di ampia autonomia.

Nei primi anni Ottanta *(1980s)* le televisioni private diventarono un centinaio e assunsero grande importanza. Messo in crisi il monopolio della RAI, il sistema televisivo italiano fu riorganizzato secondo la regolamentazione di una nuova legge *(law)*, il 6 agosto 1990. Questa riconobbe *(recognized)* l'esistenza di un sistema misto *(mixed)*, costituito da canali privati e pubblici.

M. Write a brief composition on Italian television, adding to the information above anything else you know about it. If you are using this book in a classroom situation, do this activity with a partner.

_____

_____

_____

_____

_____

_____

_____

_____

_____

_____

Review Part 6

Say that …

1. your tires need a bit of air and that you should change the oil

_____

2. your car can be driven with great facility, because it is economical and efficient

_____

3. you forgot your ticket and passport in the car

_____

4. you would prefer an aisle seat

_____

5. you would like to go abroad for an unforgettable holiday

_____

6. you would like to rent a car to visit many beautiful countries

_____

7. you always have lots of baggage and, thus, you always need help

_____

8. tonight there's a soccer match on TV and later a tennis match

_____

9. you work out a little bit two days every week

_____

10. everyone should practice sports more

_____

11. tonight you would like to watch the last episode of a TV movie, not the game show

_____

12. you like Italian documentaries more than popular programs, because you understand them better

_____

Tell …

13. Dina not to be mean and to change the channel

_____

14. a gas attendant to fill up your car with gas and to put some air in the tires

_____

Ask …

15. a gas attendant if he or she can check your oil and water and then clean your windshield

_____

16. Sarah if she has seen your boarding pass

_____

17. a hotel desk clerk why he or she has not yet received your reservation

_____

B. Come si dice in italiano?

1. Dina's friends will be going to Italy in a month's time.

_____

2. Alessandro would eat the meat, but he is not too hungry.

_____

3. The plane will be leaving in an hour from gate A1521.

_____

4. I would prefer an aisle seat, but if there isn't one left, I will take a window seat.

_____

5. Do you (familiar, singular) know Mark? Do you know if he will be coming to the movies with us?

_____

6. He will enjoy himself in Italy, because he likes beautiful weather.

_____

7. Miss, try these shoes on!

_____

8. After they had arrived yesterday, we decided to go to the movies.

_____

9. I didn't eat the meat, because I really didn't like it.

_____

C. Domande personali.

1. Che tipo di macchina vorresti guidare?

_____

2. Perché?

_____

3. Hai paura di volare?

_____

4. Dove vorresti andare in vacanza?

_____

5. Quali paesi vorresti visitare?

_____

6. Quali città vorresti visitare?

_____

7. Quali programmi guardi regolarmente *(regularly)* in televisione? Perché?

_____

8. Quali programmi non ti piacciono? Perché?

_____

9. Quali sport pratichi?

_____

D. Write a brief account of what you will be doing next week. Include in your account the fact that you will be going for an oil change, that you will be engaging in a few sports, watching some TV, going to a travel agent to plan a trip abroad, and finally, going to the airport to leave for your holiday.

_____

_____

_____

_____

_____

_____

_____

_____

_____

_____

_____

_____

_____

_____

_____

_____

E. There are 20 words hidden in the word search puzzle below: 10 can be read from left to right (horizontally) and 10 in a top-down direction (vertically). Can you find them? The clues given below will help you look for them. The numbers of the clues do not reflect any particular order or arrangement to the hidden words.

A	C	O	N	T	R	O	L	L	A	R	E	X	X	X	B	U	O	N	C
Z	A	S	D	F	G	H	J	K	L	M	N	M	K	L	O	P	P	H	D
P	A	R	A	B	R	E	Z	Z	A	A	M	A	C	C	H	I	N	A	A
K	A	S	D	F	G	H	J	K	L	M	P	H	D	P	H	D	A	D	P
T	O	R	N	E	R	O	A	U	S	C	I	T	A	X	P	Q	P	N	A
J	A	S	D	F	G	H	J	K	L	M	D	F	L	X	I	W	R	M	E
C	O	N	O	S	C	E	N	Z	A	L	H	J	T	X	G	E	I	L	S
G	A	S	D	F	G	H	J	K	L	M	N	M	O	X	R	R	M	S	I
V	O	L	O	A	E	S	T	E	R	O	O	F	T	X	A	T	A	D	I
S	A	S	D	F	G	H	J	K	L	M	Q	A	G	C	B	Y	S	P	O
N	O	L	E	G	G	I	A	R	E	S	P	I	B	A	N	D	D	D	H
A	S	D	F	G	H	J	K	L	M	P	S	O	F	L	M	E	T	I	K
A	S	D	F	G	H	J	K	L	M	I	U	C	G	C	O	L	F	H	L
A	S	D	F	G	H	J	K	L	M	U	T	H	J	I	P	L	V	N	M
A	D	F	G	H	J	K	L	B	M	H	H	E	H	O	H	A	H	H	H
A	S	D	E	G	D	X	X	X	A	D	C	Q	E	D	A	C	X	X	X
A	S	D	E	G	D	X	X	X	A	D	C	Q	E	D	A	C	X	X	X
A	S	D	E	G	D	X	X	X	A	D	C	Q	E	D	A	C	X	X	X
A	S	D	E	G	D	X	X	X	A	D	C	Q	E	D	A	C	X	X	X
A	S	D	E	G	D	X	X	X	A	D	C	Q	E	D	A	C	X	X	X

Horizontal

1 Può … l'olio e l'acqua?
2 Signori, … viaggio!
3 Può anche pulire il …?
4 Le piace guidare una … economica?
5 Io … la prossima settimana.
6 Da quale … si deve prendere l'aereo?
7 Felice di fare la Sua …!
8 Hanno annunciato il nostro …!
9 Vorrei andare all'… per una vacanza.
10 Vogliamo … una macchina.

Vertical

11 Ci sono tanti bei … da vedere.
12 Voglio un albergo di … categoria.
13 Mia sorella non è energica! Lei è …
14 Lui non è basso; è molto …
15 Anche tu … il footing, vero?
16 Preferisco le partite di …
17 Mi piace … studiare che lavorare.
18 Lui è più simpatico … intelligente.
19 Lui è il ragazzo più simpatico … famiglia.
20 Lei è più alta … me.

Irregular Verbs

* = conjugated with essere in compound tenses

andare* / to go

Pres. Ind.	(io) vado, (tu) vai, (lui / lei / Lei) va, (noi) andiamo, (voi) andate, (loro) vanno
Imperative	(io) —, (tu) va', (Lei) vada, (noi) andiamo, (voi) andate, (Loro) vadano
Future	(io) andrò, (tu) andrai, (lui / lei / Lei) andrà, (noi) andremo, (voi) andrete, (loro) andranno
Conditional	(io) andrei, (tu) andresti, (lui / lei / Lei) andrebbe, (noi) andremmo, (voi) andreste, (loro) andrebbero

aprire / to open

Past Part.	aperto

avere / to have

Pres. Ind.	(io) ho, (tu) hai, (lui / lei / Lei) ha, (noi) abbiamo, (voi) avete, (loro) hanno
Imperative	(io) —, (tu) abbi, (Lei) abbia, (noi) abbiamo, (voi) abbiate, (Loro) abbiano
Past Abs.	(io) ebbi, (tu) avesti, (lui / lei / Lei) ebbe, (noi) avemmo, (voi) aveste, (loro) ebbero
Future	(io) avrò, (tu) avrai, (lui / lei / Lei) avrà, (noi) avremo, (voi) avrete, (loro) avranno
Conditional	(io) avrei, (tu) avresti, (lui / lei / Lei) avrebbe, (noi) avremmo, (voi) avreste, (loro) avrebbero

bere / to drink

Pres. Ind.	(io) bevo, (tu) bevi, (lui / lei / Lei) beve, (noi) beviamo, (voi) bevete, (loro) bevono
Imperative	(io) —, (tu) bevi, (Lei) beva, (noi) beviamo, (voi) bevete, (Loro) bevano
Past Part.	bevuto
Imperfect	(io) bevevo, (tu) bevevi, (lui / lei / Lei) beveva, (noi) bevevamo, (voi) bevevate, (loro) bevevano
Past Abs.	(io) bevvi (bevetti), (tu) bevesti, (lui / lei / Lei) bevve (bevette), (noi) bevemmo, (voi) beveste, (loro) bevvero (bevettero)
Future	(io) berrò, (tu) berrai, (lui / lei / Lei) berrà, (noi) berremo, (voi) berrete, (loro) berranno
Conditional	(io) berrei, (tu) berresti, (lui / lei / Lei) berrebbe, (noi) berremmo, (voi) berreste, (loro) berrebbero

chiedere / to ask for

Past Part.	chiesto
Past Abs.	(io) chiesi, (tu) chiedesti, (lui / lei / Lei) chiese, (noi) chiedemmo, (voi) chiedeste, (loro) chiesero

conoscere / to know (someone)

Past Abs.	(io) conobbi, (tu) conoscesti, (lui / lei / Lei) conobbe, (noi) conoscemmo, (voi) conosceste, (loro) conobbero

dare / to give

Pres. Ind.	(io) do, (tu) dai, (lui / lei / Lei) dà, (noi) diamo, (voi) date, (loro) danno
Imperative	(io) —, (tu) da', (Lei) dia, (noi) diamo, (voi) date, (Loro) diano
Past Part.	dato
Imperfect	(io) davo, (tu) davi, (lui / lei / Lei) dava, (noi) davamo, (voi) davate, (loro) davano
Past Abs.	(io) diedi, (tu) desti, (lui / lei / Lei) diede, (noi) demmo, (voi) deste, (loro) diedero

Future	(io) darò, (tu) darai, (lui / lei / Lei) darà, (noi) daremo, (voi) darete, (loro) daranno
Conditional	(io) darei, (tu) daresti, (lui / lei / Lei) darebbe, (noi) daremmo, (voi) dareste, (loro) darebbero

decidere / *to decide*

Past Part.	deciso
Past Abs.	(io) decisi, (tu) decidesti, (lui / lei / Lei) decise, (noi) decidemmo, (voi) decideste, (loro) decisero

dire / *to say, to tell*

Pres. Ind.	(io) dico, (tu) dici, (lui / lei / Lei) dice, (noi) diciamo, (voi) dite, (loro) dicono
Imperative	(io) —, (tu) di', (Lei) dica, (noi) diciamo, (voi) dite, (Loro) dicano
Past Part.	detto
Imperfect	(io) dicevo, (tu) dicevi, (lui / lei / Lei) diceva, (noi) dicevamo, (voi) dicevate, (loro) dicevano
Past Abs.	(io) dissi, (tu) dicesti, (lui / lei / Lei) disse, (noi) dicemmo, (voi) diceste, (loro) dissero
Future	(io) dirò, (tu) dirai, (lui / lei / Lei) dirà, (noi) diremo, (voi) direte, (loro) diranno
Conditional	(io) direi, (tu) diresti, (lui / lei / Lei) direbbe, (noi) diremmo, (voi) direste, (loro) direbbero

dovere / *to have to*

Pres. Ind.	(io) devo, (tu) devi, (lui / lei / Lei) deve, (noi) dobbiamo, (voi) dovete, (loro) devono
Future	(io) dovrò, (tu) dovrai, (lui / lei / Lei) dovrà, (noi) dovremo, (voi) dovrete, (loro) dovranno
Conditional	(io) dovrei, (tu) dovresti, (lui / lei / Lei) dovrebbe, (noi) dovremmo, (voi) dovreste, (loro) dovrebbero

essere* / *to be*

Pres. Ind.	(io) sono, (tu) sei, (lui / lei / Lei) è, (noi) siamo, (voi) siete, (loro) sono
Imperative	(io) —, (tu) sii, (Lei) sia, (noi) siamo, (voi) siate, (Loro) siano
Past Part.	stato
Imperfect	(io) ero, (tu) eri, (lui / lei / Lei) era, (noi) eravamo, (voi) eravate, (loro) erano
Past Abs.	(io) fui, (tu) fosti, (lui / lei / Lei) fu, (noi) fummo, (voi) foste, (loro) furono
Future	(io) sarò, (tu) sarai, (lui / lei / Lei) sarà, (noi) saremo, (voi) sarete, (loro) saranno
Conditional	(io) sarei, (tu) saresti, (lui / lei / Lei) sarebbe, (noi) saremmo, (voi) sareste, (loro) sarebbero

fare / *to do, to make*

Pres. Ind.	(io) faccio, (tu) fai, (lui / lei / Lei) fa, (noi) facciamo, (voi) fate, (loro) fanno
Imperative	(io) —, (tu) fa', (Lei) faccia, (noi) facciamo, (voi) fate, (Loro) facciano
Past Part.	fatto
Imperfect	(io) facevo, (tu) facevi, (lui / lei / Lei) faceva, (noi) facevamo, (voi) facevate, (loro) facevano
Past Abs.	(io) feci, (tu) facesti, (lui / lei / Lei) fece, (noi) facemmo, (voi) faceste, (loro) fecero
Future	(io) farò, (tu) farai, (lui / lei / Lei) farà, (noi) faremo, (voi) farete, (loro) faranno
Conditional	(io) farei, (tu) faresti, (lui / lei / Lei) farebbe, (noi) faremmo, (voi) fareste, (loro) farebbero

leggere / *to read*

Past Part.	letto
Past Abs.	(io) lessi, (tu) leggesti, (lui / lei / Lei) lesse, (noi) leggemmo, (voi) leggeste, (loro) lessero

mettere / *to put*
Past Part.	messo
Past Abs.	(io) misi, (tu) mettesti, (lui / lei / Lei) mise, (noi) mettemmo, (voi) metteste, (loro) misero

mettersi / *to put on*
[conjugated like mettere]

perdere / *to lose*
Past Part.	perso
Past Abs.	(io) persi (perdetti), (tu) perdesti, (lui / lei / Lei) perse (perdette), (noi) perdemmo, (voi) perdeste, (loro) persero (perdettero)

piacere* / *to be pleasing to, to like*
Pres. Ind.	(io) piaccio, (tu) piaci, (lui / lei / Lei) piace, (noi) piacciamo, (voi) piacete, (loro) piacciono
Past Abs.	(io) piacqui, (tu) piacesti, (lui / lei / Lei) piacque, (noi) piacemmo, (voi) piaceste, (loro) piacquero

piovere / *to rain*
Past Abs.	piovve

potere / *to be able to*
Pres. Ind.	(io) posso, (tu) puoi, (lui / lei / Lei) può, (noi) possiamo, (voi) potete, (loro) possono
Future	(io) potrò, (tu) potrai, (lui / lei / Lei) potrà, (noi) potremo, (voi) potrete, (loro) potranno
Conditional	(io) potrei, (tu) potresti, (lui / lei / Lei) potrebbe, (noi) potremmo, (voi) potreste, (loro) potrebbero

prendere / *to take, to get, to have something to eat or drink*
Past Part.	preso
Past Abs.	(io) presi, (tu) prendesti, (lui / lei / Lei) prese, (noi) prendemmo, (voi) prendeste, (loro) presero

prescrivere / *to prescribe*
[conjugated like scrivere]

riscuotere / *to cash*
Past Part.	riscosso
Past Abs.	(io) riscossi, (tu) riscotesti, (lui / lei / Lei) riscosse, (noi) riscotemmo, (voi) riscoteste, (loro) riscossero

sapere / *to know (in general)*
Pres. Ind.	(io) so, (tu) sai, (lui / lei / Lei) sa, (noi) sappiamo, (voi) sapete, (loro) sanno
Imperative	(io) —, (tu) sappi, (Lei) sappia, (noi) sappiamo, (voi) sappiate, (Loro) sappiano
Past Abs.	(io) seppi, (tu) sapesti, (lui / lei / Lei) seppe, (noi) sapemmo, (voi) sapeste, (loro) seppero
Future	(io) saprò, (tu) saprai, (lui / lei / Lei) saprà, (noi) sapremo, (voi) saprete, (loro) sapranno
Conditional	(io) saprei, (tu) sapresti, (lui / lei / Lei) saprebbe, (noi) sapremmo, (voi) sapreste, (loro) saprebbero

scrivere / *to write*
Past Part.	scritto
Past Abs.	(io) scrissi, (tu) scrivesti, (lui / lei / Lei) scrisse, (noi) scrivemmo, (voi) scriveste, (loro) scrissero

stare* / *to stay, to be*
Pres. Ind.	(io) sto, (tu) stai, (lui / lei / Lei) sta, (noi) stiamo, (voi) state, (loro) stanno
Past Part.	stato
Imperfect	(io) stavo, (tu) stavi, (lui / lei / Lei) stava, (noi) stavamo, (voi) stavate, (loro) stavano
Past Abs.	(io) stetti, (tu) stesti, (lui / lei / Lei) stette, (noi) stemmo, (voi) steste, (loro) stettero
Future	(io) starò, (tu) starai, (lui / lei / Lei) starà, (noi) staremo, (voi) starete, (loro) staranno
Conditional	(io) starei, (tu) staresti, (lui / lei / Lei) starebbe, (noi) staremmo, (voi) stareste, (loro) starebbero

succedere* / *to happen*
Past Part.	successo
Past Abs.	successe, successero

uscire* / *to go out*
Pres. Ind.	(io) esco, (tu) esci, (lui / lei / Lei) esce, (noi) usciamo, (voi) uscite, (loro) escono
Imperative	(io) —, (tu) esci, (Lei) esca, (noi) usciamo, (voi) uscite, (Loro) escano

valere* / *to be worth*
Pres. Ind.	(io) valgo, (tu) vali, (lui / lei / Lei) vale, (noi) valiamo, (voi) valete, (loro) valgono
Past Part.	valso
Past Abs.	(io) valsi, (tu) valesti, (lui / lei / Lei) valse, (noi) valemmo, (voi) valeste, (loro) valsero
Future	(io) varrò, (tu) varrai, (lui / lei / Lei) varrà, (noi) varremo, (voi) varrete, (loro) varranno
Conditional	(io) varrei, (tu) varresti, (lui / lei / Lei) varrebbe, (noi) varremmo, (voi) varreste, (loro) varrebbero

vedere / *to see*
Past Part.	visto / veduto
Past Abs.	(io) vidi, (tu) vedesti, (lui / lei / Lei) vide, (noi) vedemmo, (voi) vedeste, (loro) videro
Future	(io) vedrò, (tu) vedrai, (lui / lei / Lei) vedrà, (noi) vedremo, (voi) vedrete, (loro) vedranno
Conditional	(io) vedrei, (tu) vedresti, (lui / lei / Lei) vedrebbe, (noi) vedremmo, (voi) vedreste, (loro) vedrebbero

venire* / *to come*
Pres. Ind.	(io) vengo, (tu) vieni, (lui / lei / Lei) viene, (noi) veniamo, (voi) venite, (loro) vengono
Imperative	(io) —, (tu) vieni, (Lei) venga, (noi) veniamo, (voi) venite, (Loro) vengano
Past Part.	venuto
Past Abs.	(io) venni, (tu) venisti, (lui / lei / Lei) venne, (noi) venimmo, (voi) veniste, (loro) vennero
Future	(io) verrò, (tu) verrai, (lui / lei / Lei) verrà, (noi) verremo, (voi) verrete, (loro) verranno
Conditional	(io) verrei, (tu) verresti, (lui / lei / Lei) verrebbe, (noi) verremmo, (voi) verreste, (loro) verrebbero

volere / *to want*
Pres. Ind.	(io) voglio, (tu) vuoi, (lui / lei / Lei) vuole, (noi) vogliamo, (voi) volete, (loro) vogliono
Past Abs.	(io) volli, (tu) volesti, (lui / lei / Lei) volle, (noi) volemmo, (voi) voleste, (loro) vollero
Future	(io) vorrò, (tu) vorrai, (lui / lei / Lei) vorrà, (noi) vorremo, (voi) vorrete, (loro) vorranno
Conditional	(io) vorrei, (tu) vorresti, (lui / lei / Lei) vorrebbe, (noi) vorremmo, (voi) vorreste, (loro) vorrebbero

Italian-English Glossary

Adjectives (descriptive, demonstrative, possessive, etc.) and nouns are listed in their masculine singular forms.

Verbs with **isc** in parentheses are those that require this affix when they are conjugated in the present tense and in the imperative.

Verbs with an asterisk * are those that are conjugated with **essere** in compound tenses.

Nouns ending in **-e** will be specified as either *masculine* or *feminine*.

A

a   *to, at, in*
a destra   *to the right*
A presto!   *See you soon!*
a sinistra   *to the left*
abbastanza   *quite, enough*
Abbastanza bene!   *Quite well!*
abitare   *to live, to dwell*
acqua   *water*
adesso   *now*
aereo   *airplane*
africano   *African*
agosto   *August*
aiutare   *to help*
aiuto   *help*
albergo   *hotel*
alcuni   *some, several*
allora   *so, therefore*
alto   *tall*
altrimenti   *otherwise*
altro   *other*
alzarsi   *to get up*
amare   *to love*
americano / americana   *American (male / female)*
amico / amica   *friend (male / female)*
anche   *also, too*
ancora   *yet, still*
andare*   *to go*
angolo   *corner*
annata   *year (all year)*
anno   *year*
annunciare   *to announce*
antibiotico   *antibiotic*
antipasto   *appetizer*
antipatico   *unpleasant*
antropologo   *anthropologist*
anzi   *as a matter of fact*
appena   *just, barely, as soon as*
appetito   *appetite*

appuntamento   *appointment, date*
aprile   *April*
aprire   *to open*
arancione   *orange (invariable)*
aria   *air*
arrivare*   *to arrive*
ArrivederLa! / Arrivederci!   *Good-bye! (polite / familiar)*
aspettare   *to wait for*
assai   *quite*
assegno   *check*
attore / attrice   *actor (male / female)*
australiano   *Australian*
autobus *(masculine)*   *bus*
automobile *(feminine)*   *automobile*
autunno   *fall / autumn*
avere   *to have*
avere bisogno di   *to need*
avere fame   *to be hungry*
avere paura   *to be afraid*
avere ragione   *to be right*
avere sete   *to be thirsty*
avere sonno   *to be sleepy*
avere...anni   *to be...years old*
azzurro   *blue*

B

baco   *silkworm*
bagaglio   *baggage*
ballare   *to dance*
bambino / bambina   *child (male / female)*
banca   *bank*
barista   *bartender (male / female)*
basso   *short*
Basta!   *That's enough!*
bello   *beautiful, nice*
bene   *well*
benzina   *gas, petrol*
benzinaio   *gas attendant*
bere   *to drink*

bianco   *white*

bicchiere *(masculine)*   glass (drinking)

bicicletta   *bicycle*

biglietto   *bill, ticket*

biologo   *biologist*

bistecca   *steak*

bocca   *mouth*

bottiglia   *bottle*

braccio   *arm*

brutto   *ugly, awful*

buco   *hole*

Buon appetito!   *Eat up! (literally: Have a good appetite!)*

Buon pomeriggio   *Good afternoon!*

Buonanotte!   *Good night!*

Buonasera!   *Good afternoon! / Good evening!*

Buongiorno!   *Hello! / Good day! / Good morning!*

buono   *good*

C

caffè *(masculine)*   coffee

calcio   *soccer*

caldo   *hot, warm*

calmo   *calm*

calzoleria   *shoe store*

cambiare   *to change*

camera   *bedroom, hotel room*

cameriere *(masculine)*   waiter

camicetta   *blouse*

camicia   *shirt*

canadese   *Canadian*

canale *(masculine)*   channel

capelli *(masculine, plural)*   hair (on the head)

capire (isc)   *to understand*

cappuccino   *cappuccino coffee*

carne *(feminine)*   meat

carta   *card, pass*

carta d'imbarco   *boarding pass*

carta di credito   *credit card*

casa   *house, home*

categoria   *category, class*

cattivo   *bad, mischievous*

cellulare *(masculine)*   cellphone

cento   *hundred*

centro   *downtown*

cercare   *to look for, to search for*

certo   *of course, certainly*

che   *what, that, which, who (relative pronoun)*

Che c'è?   *What's up?*

che cosa   *what*

Che giorno è oggi?   *What day is it today?*

Che tempo fa?   *How's the weather?*

chi   *who / whom*

chiamare   *to call*

chiamarsi   *to be called*

chiave *(feminine)*   key

chiedere   *to ask for*

chiosco   *kiosk*

ci   *us, to us, ourselves*

Ci vediamo!   *See you!*

Ciao!   *Hi! / Bye!*

cinema *(masculine)*   movies

cinese   *Chinese*

cinquanta   *fifty*

cinque   *five*

città *(feminine)*   city

cliente   *customer (male / female)*

collo   *neck*

colore   *color*

coltello   *knife*

come   *how (what), like*

Come si chiama? / Come ti chiami?   *What's your name? (polite / familiar)*

Come sta? / Come stai?   *How are you? (polite / familiar)*

Come va?   *How's it going?*

cominciare   *to begin, to start*

commesso / commessa   *store clerk (male / female)*

compilare   *to fill out*

compleanno   *birthday*

comprare   *to buy*

con   *with*

concerto   *concert*

conferenza   *lecture*

conoscere   *to know (someone), to meet (for the first time)*

consegnare   *to hand in*

contanti   *cash*

contare   *to count*

conto   *check, bill, account*

controllare   *to check*

corpo   *body*

corridoio   *aisle*

così   *so, thus, like this*

così, così   *so-so*

costare*   *to cost*

cravatta   *tie*

cronaca   *documentary, special interest show*

cucchiaio   *spoon*

cucina   *kitchen*

cugino / cugina   *cousin (male / female)*

curare   *to look after, to cure*

D

da   *from*

danese   *Danish*

dare   *to give*

data   *date*

decidere   *to decide*

decimo   *tenth*
depositare   *to deposit*
desiderare   *to desire, to want*
dessert *(masculine)*   *dessert*
destra   *right*
di   *of, from*
Di dove è? / Di dove sei?   *Where are you from? (polite / familiar)*
di più   *more*
di solito   *usually*
dicembre   *December*
diciannove   *nineteen*
diciassette   *seventeen*
diciotto   *eighteen*
dieci   *ten*
differente   *different*
difficile   *difficult*
dimenticare   *to forget*
dire   *to say, to tell*
diritto   *straight*
dito   *finger*
ditta   *firm, company*
divano   *sofa*
diventare*   *to become*
divertimento   *enjoyment, fun*
divertirsi   *to enjoy oneself*
dodici   *twelve*
dolce   *sweet pastry*
domanda   *question*
domani   *tomorrow*
domenica   *Sunday*
donna   *woman*
dopo   *after*
dormire   *to sleep*
dottore / dottoressa   *doctor, Dr. (male / female)*
dove   *where*
dovere   *to have to*
due   *two*
duecento   *two hundred*
duemila   *two thousand*
dunque   *so, therefore*

E

e   *and*
ecco   *here is / here are*
economico   *economical*
efficiente   *efficient*
elettrodomestico   *appliance*
energico   *energetic*
espresso   *espresso coffee*
esserci*   *to be here / there*
essere*   *to be*
estate *(feminine)*   *summer*
estero   *abroad*
euro *(masculine)*   *Euro*

F

fa   *ago*
Fa brutto tempo!   *The weather's awful!*
Fa caldo!   *It's hot!*
Fa freddo!   *It's cold!*
faccia   *face*
facile   *easy*
facilità   *ease, facility*
fame *(feminine)*   *hunger*
famiglia   *family*
fantascienza   *science fiction*
fare   *to do, to make*
fare delle spese   *to shop in general*
fare il biglietto   *to buy a travel ticket*
fare la spesa   *to shop for food*
fare male a   *to hurt*
febbraio   *February*
febbre *(feminine)*   *fever*
felice   *happy*
ferroviario   *railway (of the railway)*
festa   *party*
figlio / figlia   *son / daughter*
film *(masculine)*   *movie, film*
finalmente   *finally, at last*
finestra   *window (of a house or building)*
finestrino   *window (of a vehicle)*
finire (isc)   *to finish*
fino a   *up to, until*
fiorentino   *Florentine*
focaccia   *focaccia (sandwich)*
forchetta   *fork*
formaggio   *cheese*
forse   *maybe*
forte   *strong*
fotografia   *photograph*
fra   *in, between, among*
fra qualche minuto   *in a few minutes*
francese   *French*
fratello   *brother*
freddo   *cold*
fresco   *cool*
frigorifero   *refrigerator*
fronte *(feminine)*   *forehead*
frutta   *fruit*
fuoco   *fire*

G

gamba   *leg*
gara   *competition*
generalmente   *generally*
genitore / genitrice   *parent (male / female)*
gennaio   *January*
gentile   *kind*
già   *already*
giacca   *jacket*

giallo   *yellow*
giapponese   *Japanese*
ginnastica   *gymnastics*
ginocchio   *knee*
giornale *(masculine)*   *newspaper*
giornata   *day (= in the sense of all day long)*
giorno   *day*
giovane   *young person (male / female)*
giovedì   *Thursday*
girare   *to turn*
giugno   *June*
gli   *to him, to them*
gola   *throat*
gomito   *elbow*
gomma   *tire*
gonna   *skirt*
grammatica   *grammar*
grande   *big, large*
grasso   *fat*
grazie   *thank you*
greco   *Greek*
grigio   *gray*
grosso   *big, large*
guancia   *cheek*
guardare   *to watch*
guidare   *to drive*

I

ieri   *yesterday*
imparare   *to learn*
impiegato / impiegata   *employee, clerk (male / female)*
importante   *important*
in   *in*
in poi   *(from) then on*
in punto   *on the dot*
in saldo   *on sale*
incontro   *match, encounter*
indimenticabile   *unforgettable*
indirizzo   *address*
infatti   *in fact*
infine   *finally*
influenza   *flu*
informatica   *computer science*
informazione *(feminine)*   *information*
inglese   *English (language)*
inglese   *English*
insegnante *(masculine/feminine)*   *teacher (male / female)*
insegnare   *to teach*
intelligente   *intelligent*
invece   *instead*
inverno   *winter*
io   *I*
ironico   *ironic*
isolato   *street block*

Italia   *Italy*
italiano   *Italian (language)*
italiano / italiana   *Italian (male / female)*

L

la   *her, it (feminine)*
là   *over there*
labbro   *lip*
lago   *lake*
lasciare   *to leave (behind)*
lavorare   *to work*
le   *to her, them (feminine)*
leggere   *to read*
Lei   *you (polite)*
lei   *she*
lezione *(feminine)*   *lesson, class*
li   *them (masculine)*
lì   *there*
libraio / libraia   *book vendor (male / female)*
libreria   *bookstore*
libretto   *bankbook*
libro   *book*
lieto / lieta   *delighted (masculine / feminine)*
lingua   *tongue*
liquido   *liquid*
lo   *him, it (masculine)*
locale notturno   *nightclub*
lontano   *far*
loro   *they*
luglio   *July*
lui   *he*
lunedì   *Monday*
lungo   *long*

M

ma   *but*
macchina   *car*
madre *(feminine)*   *mother*
maggio   *May*
magro   *skinny*
mai   *ever*
mal di   *ache (headache, stomachache, …)*
male   *bad*
mamma   *mom*
Mamma mia!   *My heavens! (literally: My mother!)*
mancia   *tip*
mangiare   *to eat*
mano   *hand*
marito   *husband*
marrone   *brown (invariable)*
martedì   *Tuesday*
marzo   *March*
mattino   *morning*
meccanico   *mechanic*

medico   *medical doctor*
melone *(masculine)*   *cantaloupe*
meno   *less, minus*
mentre   *while*
menù *(masculine)*   *menu*
mercoledì   *Wednesday*
mese *(masculine)*   *month*
messicano   *Mexican*
mettere   *to put*
mettersi   *to put on*
mezzanotte *(feminine)*   *midnight*
mezzo   *half*
mezzogiorno   *noon*
mi   *me, to me, myself*
migliore   *best*
miliardo   *billion*
milione *(masculine)*   *million*
mille   *one thousand*
minerale   *mineral*
minestra   *soup*
minuto   *minute*
mio   *my (masculine, singular)*
misura   *measurement*
mobilia   *furniture*
moda   *fashion*
modulo   *form (to fill out), slip*
moglie   *wife*
molto   *a lot, very much, very*
molto bene   *very well*

N

naso   *nose*
ne   *of it, of them*
necessario   *necessary*
nero   *black*
nervoso   *nervous*
nessuno   *no one*
nevicare   *to snow*
niente   *nothing*
nipote   *nephew / niece, grandchild*
no   *no*
no? / vero?   *no? / right? / aren't you? / correct?*
noi   *we*
noleggiare   *to rent (a vehicle)*
nome *(masculine)*   *name*
non   *not*
Non c'è di che!   *Don't mention it! No need to thank me!*
Non c'è male!   *(I'm) not bad!*
Non importa!   *It doesn't matter!*
non...niente   *nothing*
non...più   *no longer, no more*
nonno / nonna   *grandfather / grandmother*
nono   *ninth*
norvegese   *Norwegian*

nostro   *our*
notte *(feminine)*   *night*
novanta   *ninety*
nove   *nine*
novembre   *November*
numero   *number, shoe size*
nuovo   *new*

O

o   *or*
occhio   *eye*
oggi   *today*
ogni   *every*
olandese   *Dutch*
olio   *oil*
opera   *work (literary, artistic, etc.)*
ora   *hour*
orario   *schedule, timetable*
orecchino   *earring*
orecchio   *ear*
origine *(feminine)*   *origin*
ottanta   *eighty*
ottavo   *eighth*
ottimo   *great, wonderful, excellent*
otto   *eight*
ottobre   *October*

P

padre *(masculine)*   *father*
paese *(masculine)*   *country*
pagare   *to pay*
paio   *pair*
pallacanestro *(feminine)*   *basketball*
pane *(masculine)*   *bread*
panino   *sandwich (bun style)*
pantaloni *(masculine plural)*   *pants*
parabrezza   *windshield*
parente   *relative (male / female)*
parlare   *to speak*
partire*   *to leave*
partita   *match, game*
passaporto   *passport*
passo   *pace*
pasta   *pasta*
pattinaggio   *skating*
pensarci   *to take care of*
pensare   *to think*
pensare di sì / no   *to think so / not*
per   *for, in order to, through*
per favore   *please*
perché   *because, why*
perdere   *to lose*
perfettamente   *perfectly*
persona   *person*
petto   *chest*

piacere* *to be pleasing to, to like, a pleasure*
piano *floor*
piatto *dish*
piccolo *small*
piede *foot*
pieno *full*
pigro *lazy*
piovere *to rain*
più *more, plus*
poco *little, few*
poi *then, after*
polacco *Polish*
poltrona *armchair*
popolare *popular*
porta *door*
portare *to wear, to carry*
portoghese *Portuguese*
possibile *possible*
postale *postal, mailing*
posto *place, seat*
potere *to be able to*
povero *poor*
praticare *to practice*
preciso *precise*
preferire (isc) *to prefer*
preferito *favorite*
Prego! *You're welcome!*
prelevare *to withdraw*
prendere *to take, to get, to have something to eat or drink*
prenotazione *(feminine)* *reservation*
prescrivere *to prescribe*
presentare *to introduce, to present*
presto *early*
prima *first, at first*
primavera *spring*
primo *first*
problema *problem*
professore / professoressa *Professor (male / female) / high school teacher*
programma *(masculine)* *program*
Pronto? *Hello? (on the phone)*
proprio *really*
prosciutto *ham (cured)*
prossimo *next (as in: next week)*
provarsi *to try on*
pugilato *boxing*
pulire (isc) *to clean*
puntata *episode*
punto *dot, point*
purtroppo *unfortunately*

Q

qualche *some*
qualcosa *something*

quale *which, what*
quando *when*
quanto *how much / how many*
quaranta *forty*
quarto *fourth, quarter*
quasi *almost*
quattordici *fourteen*
quattro *four*
quello *that*
questo *this*
qui *here*
quindici *fifteen*
quinto *fifth*

R

raffreddore *common cold*
ragazza *girl*
ragazzo *boy*
regista *movie director (male / female)*
ricco *rich*
ricevere *to receive*
riscuotere *to cash*
ristorante *(masculine)* *restaurant*
ristretto *strong, short (coffee)*
rivista *magazine*
romanzo *novel*
rosa *pink (invariable)*
rosso *red*
russo *Russian*

S

sabato *Saturday*
saldo *sale*
salotto *living room*
sapere *to know (in general)*
scarpa *shoe*
scelta *choice*
scherzare *to joke (around)*
scontrino *cash register tape, receipt*
scorso *last (previous)*
scrivere *to write*
scusi *excuse me (polite)*
se *if*
secondo *according to, second*
sedia *chair*
sedici *sixteen*
sei *six*
semaforo *trafficlight*
sempre *always*
sentirsi *to feel*
senza *without*
sera *evening*
serata *evening (all evening)*
servire a *to need*
sessanta *sixty*

sesto   sixth
sete (feminine)   thirst
settanta   seventy
sette   seven
settembre   September
settimana   week
settimo   seventh
si   himself, herself, themselves
sì   yes
sicuro   sure
signora   Mrs. / Ms. / madam
signore   Mr. / sir / gentleman
signorina   Ms. / Miss / young lady
simpatico   nice
sinistra   left
soldi (masculine, plural)   money
solo   only
sonno   sleep
Sono di...   I'm from...
sorella   sister
spaghetti (masculine, plural)   spaghetti
spagnolo   Spanish
spalla   shoulder
spazioso   spacious
specialmente   especially
spesa / spese (feminine, plural)   food shopping / shopping in general (plural)
spesso   often
spiccioli (masculine, plural)   coins, loose change
sport (masculine)   sport
sposato / sposata   married (male / female)
stanco   tired
stare*   to stay, to be (in some expressions)
stare* bene a   to look good on
stare* zitto   to be quiet
stasera   tonight, this evening
Stati Uniti   United States
stato civile   marital status
stazione   station
stivale   boot
stomaco   stomach
studente / studentessa   student (male / female)
studiare   to study
studio medico   doctor's office
stufo   fed up
su   on
subito   right away (after)
succedere*   to happen
svedese   Swedish
svizzero   Swiss

T

taglia   size (of clothes)
taglio   cut, size (of bill)

tanto   much, many
tardi   late
tavolo   table
tedesco   German
telecomando   remote control
telefilm   TV movie
telefonare   to phone
telefonata   phone call
telequiz   TV game show
televisione (feminine)   television
televisore (masculine)   TV set
tema   composition (written)
tempo   time (in general), weather
tennis (masculine)   tennis
terzo   third
testa   head
ti   you, to you, yourself (familiar)
Ti presento...   Let me introduce you to... (familiar, singular)
Tira vento!   It's windy!
tornare*   to return, to get back
tra   in, between, among
traslocare   to move (from one place to another)
trattoria   family restaurant
tre   three
trecento   three hundred
tredici   thirteen
tremila   three thousand
treno   train
trenta   thirty
triste   sad
troppo   too (much)
trovare   to find
tu   you (familiar)
tuo   your (familiar, singular)
turista   tourist (male / female)
tutto   everything

U

ufficio   office
ultimo   last
umile   humble
un po' di   a little bit, some
undici   eleven
unghia   fingernail
università (feminine)   university
uno   one
uomo   man
uscire*   to go out
uscita   gate, exit

V

Va bene!   OK!
vacanza   vacation

valere*   to be worth
valigia   suitcase
vecchio   old
vedere   to see
venerdì   Friday
venire*   to come
venti   twenty
vento   wind
veramente   actually, truly
verde   green
vero   true
versamento   deposit
verso   towards, around
vestito   dress, suit
vetrina   shop window
vi   you, to you, yourselves (plural)
via   street
viaggio   trip

vicino   near
viggiare   to travel
vigile / vigilessa   policeman / policewoman
   (traffic)
vino   wine
viola   purple (invariable)
visitare   to visit
voi   you (plural)
volare   to fly
volere   to want
volo   flight
volta   time (as in: first time, second time, …)

Z

zero   zero
zio / zia   uncle / aunt
zucchero   sugar

English-Italian Glossary

Adjectives (descriptive, demonstrative, possessive, etc.) and nouns are listed in their masculine singular forms.

Verbs with **isc** in parentheses are those that require this affix when they are conjugated in the present tense and in the imperative.

Verbs with an asterisk ***** are those that are conjugated with **essere** in compound tenses.

Nouns ending in **-e** will be specified as either *masculine* or *feminine.*

A

a lot   molto
abroad   estero
according to   secondo
account   conto
ache (headache, stomachache, ...)   mal di
actor (male / female)   attore / attrice
actually   veramente
address   indirizzo
African   africano
after   dopo, poi
ago   fa
air   aria
airplane   aereo
aisle   corridoio
almost   quasi
already   già
also   anche
always   sempre
American (male / female)   americano / americana
among   fra, tra
and   e
announce   annunciare
anthropologist   antropologo
antibiotic   antibiotico
appetite   appetito
appetizer   antipasto
appliance   elettrodomestico
appointment   appuntamento
April   aprile
arm   braccio
armchair   poltrona
around   verso
arrive   arrivare*
as a matter of fact   anzi
as soon as   appena
ask for   chiedere
at   a
at last   finalmente
August   agosto
aunt   zia
Australian   australiano
automobile   automobile *(feminine)*
awful   brutto

B

bad   male, cattivo
baggage   bagaglio
bank   banca
bankbook   libretto
barely   appena
bartender (male / female)   barista
basketball   pallacanestro *(feminine)*
be   essere*
be able to   potere
be afraid   avere paura
be called   chiamarsi
be here / there   esserci*
be hungry   avere fame
be pleasing to, like   piacere*
be quiet   stare* zitto
be right   avere ragione
be sleepy   avere sonno
be thirsty   avere sete
be worth   valere*
be...years old   avere...anni
beautiful, nice   bello
because   perché
become   diventare*
bedroom   camera
begin   cominciare
best   migliore
between   fra, tra
bicycle   bicicletta
big   grande, grosso
bill   biglietto, conto
billion   miliardo
biologist   biologo
birthday   compleanno
bit   un po' di
black   nero
blouse   camicetta
blue   azzurro
boarding pass   carta d'imbarco
body   corpo
book   libro
book vendor (male / female)   libraio / libraia
bookstore   libreria
boot   stivale

bottle bottiglia
boxing pugilato
boy ragazzo
bread pane *(masculine)*
brother fratello
brown marrone *(invariable)*
bus autobus *(masculine)*
but ma
buy comprare
buy a travel ticket fare il biglietto
Bye! Ciao!

C

call chiamare
calm calmo
Canadian canadese
cantaloupe melone *(masculine)*
cappuccino coffee cappuccino
car macchina
card carta
carry portare
cash riscuotere
cash (noun) contanti
cash register tape scontrino
category categoria
cellphone cellulare *(masculine)*
certainly certo
chair sedia
change cambiare
channel canale *(masculine)*
check controllare
check (noun) assegno, conto
cheek guancia
cheese formaggio
chest petto
child (male / female) bambino / bambina
Chinese cinese
choice scelta
city città *(feminine)*
class lezione *(feminine)*
clean pulire (isc)
coffee caffè *(masculine)*
coins spiccioli *(masculine, plural)*
cold freddo
color colore
come venire*
common cold raffreddore
company ditta
competition gara
composition (written) tema
computer science informatica
concert concerto
cool fresco
corner angolo
cost costare*
count contare
country paese *(masculine)*
cousin (male / female) cugino / cugina
credit card carta di credito
cure curare
customer (male / female) cliente
cut, size (of bill) taglio

D

dance ballare
Danish danese
date appuntamento, data
daughter figlia
day giorno
day (= in the sense of all day long) giornata
December dicembre
decide decidere
delighted (masculine / feminine) lieto / lieta
deposit depositare
deposit (noun) versamento
desire, want desiderare
dessert dessert *(masculine)*
different differente
difficult difficile
dish piatto
do fare
doctor, Dr. (male / female) dottore / dottoressa
doctor's office studio medico
documentary cronaca
Don't mention it! No need to thank me! Non c'è di che!
door porta
dot punto
downtown centro
dress vestito
drink bere
drive guidare
Dutch olandese
dwell abitare

E

ear orecchio
early presto
earring orecchino
ease facilità
easy facile
eat mangiare
Eat up! (literally: Have a good appetite!) Buon appetito!
economical economico
efficient efficiente
eight otto
eighteen diciotto
eighth ottavo
eighty ottanta
elbow gomito
eleven undici
employee (male / female) impiegato / impiegata
encounter incontro
energetic energico
English inglese
English (language) inglese
enjoy oneself divertirsi
enjoyment divertimento
enough abbastanza
episode puntata
especially specialmente
espresso coffee espresso

493

Euro   euro
evening   sera
evening (all evening)   serata
ever   mai
every   ogni
everything   tutto
excuse me (polite)   scusi
exit   uscita
eye   occhio

F

face   faccia
facility   facilità
fall   autunno
family   famiglia
family restaurant   trattoria
far   lontano
fashion   moda
fat   grasso
father   padre *(masculine)*
favorite   preferito
February   febbraio
fed up   stufo
feel   sentirsi
fever   febbre *(feminine)*
few   poco
fifteen   quindici
fifth   quinto
fifty   cinquanta
fill out   compilare
finally   finalmente, infine
find   trovare
finger   dito
fingernail   unghia
finish   finire (isc)
fire   fuoco
firm   ditta
first, at first   primo, prima
five   cinque
flight   volo
floor   piano
Florentine   fiorentino
flu   influenza
fly   volare
focaccia (sandwich)   focaccia
food shopping   spesa
foot   piede
for   per
forehead   fronte *(feminine)*
forget   dimenticare
fork   forchetta
form (to fill out), slip   modulo
forty   quaranta
four   quattro
fourteen   quattordici
fourth   quarto
French   francese
Friday   venerdì
friend (male / female)   amico / amica
from   da
from then on   in poi
fruit   frutta
full   pieno

fun   divertimento
furniture   mobilia

G

game   partita
gas   benzina
gas attendant   benzinaio
gate   uscita
generally   generalmente
German   tedesco
get back   tornare*
get up   alzarsi
get, to have something to eat or drink
   prendere
girl   ragazza
give   dare
glass (drinking)   bicchiere *(masculine)*
go   andare*
go out   uscire*
good   buono
Good afternoon!   Buon pomeriggio!
Good day!   Buongiorno!
Good evening!   Buonasera!
Good morning!   Buongiorno!
Good night!   Buonanotte!
Good-bye! (polite / familiar)   ArrivederLa! /
   Arrivederci!
grammar   grammatica
grandfather   nonno
grandmother   nonna
gray   grigio
great, wonderful, excellent   ottimo
Greek   greco
green   verde
gymnastics   ginnastica

H

hair (on the head)   capelli *(masculine, plural)*
half   mezzo
ham (cured)   prosciutto
hand   mano
hand in   consegnare
happen   succedere*
happy   felice
have   avere
have to   dovere
he   lui
head   testa
Hello? (on the phone)   Pronto?
help   aiutare
help (noun)   aiuto
her, it (feminine)   la
here   qui
here is / here are   ecco
Hi!   Ciao!
him, it (masculine)   lo
himself, herself, themselves   si
hole   buco
home   casa
hot   caldo
hotel   albergo
hotel room   camera
hour   ora

house   casa
how (what), like   come
How are you? (polite / familiar)   Come sta? / Come stai?
how much / many   quanto
How's it going?   Come va?
How's the weather?   Che tempo fa?
humble   umile
hundred   cento
hunger   fame *(feminine)*
hurt   fare male a
husband   marito

I

I   io
I'm from…   Sono di…
if   se
important   importante
in   in
in a few minutes   fra qualche minuto
in fact   infatti
in order to   per
information   informazione *(feminine)*
instead   invece
intelligent   intelligente
introduce   presentare
ironic   ironico
It doesn't matter!   Non importa!
It's cold!   Fa freddo!
It's hot!   Fa caldo!
It's windy!   Tira vento!
Italian (language)   italiano
Italian (male / female)   italiano / italiana
Italy   Italia

J

jacket   giacca
January   gennaio
Japanese   giapponese
joke (around)   scherzare
July   luglio
June   giugno
just   appena

K

key   chiave *(feminine)*
kind   gentile
kiosk   chiosco
kitchen   cucina
knee   ginocchio
knife   coltello
know (in general)   sapere
know (someone), meet (for the first time)   conoscere

L

lake   lago
large   grande, grosso
last   ultimo
last (previous)   scorso
late   tardi
lazy   pigro

learn   imparare
leave   partire*
leave (behind)   lasciare
lecture   conferenza
left   sinistra
leg   gamba
less   meno
lesson   lezione *(feminine)*
like   piacere*
like this   così
lip   labbro
liquid   liquido
little   poco, un po' di
live   abitare
living room   salotto
long   lungo
look after   curare
look for   cercare
look good on   stare* bene a
loose change   spiccioli *(masculine, plural)*
lose   perdere
love   amare

M

magazine   rivista
mailing   postale
make   fare
man   uomo
March   marzo
marital status   stato civile
married (male / female)   sposato / sposata
match   partita, incontro
May   maggio
maybe   forse
me, to me, myself   mi
measurement   misura
meat   carne *(feminine)*
mechanic   meccanico
medical doctor   medico
meet (for the first time)   conoscere
menu   menù
Mexican   messicano
midnight   mezzanotte *(feminine)*
million   milione *(masculine)*
mineral   minerale
minus   meno
minute   minuto
mom   mamma
Monday   lunedì
money   soldi *(masculine, plural)*
month   mese *(masculine)*
more   di più
more, plus   più
morning   mattino
mother   madre *(feminine)*
mouth   bocca
move (from one place to another)   traslocare
movie director (male / female)   regista
movie, film   film *(masculine)*
movies   cinema *(masculine)*
Mr. / sir / gentleman   signore
Mrs. / Ms. / madam   signora
Ms. / Miss / young lady   signorina

much, many   tanto
my (masculine, singular)   mio
My heavens! (literally: My mother!)   Mamma mia!

N

name   nome *(masculine)*
near   vicino
necessary   necessario
neck   collo
need   avere bisogno di, servire a
nephew / niece, grandchild   nipote
nervous   nervoso
new   nuovo
newspaper   giornale *(masculine)*
next (as in: next week)   prossimo
nice   simpatico
night   notte *(feminine)*
nightclub   locale notturno
nine   nove
nineteen   diciannove
ninety   novanta
ninth   nono
no   no
no longer   non…più
no more   non…più
no one   nessuno
no? / right? / aren't you? / correct?   no? / vero?
noon   mezzogiorno
Norwegian   norvegese
nose   naso
not   non
Not bad!   Non c'è male!
nothing   niente
novel   romanzo
November   novembre
now   adesso
number   numero

O

October   ottobre
of   di
of course   certo
of it, of them   ne
office   ufficio
often   spesso
oil   olio
OK!   Va bene!
old   vecchio
on   su
on sale   in saldo
on the dot   in punto
one   uno
one thousand   mille
only   solo
open   aprire
or   o
orange   arancione
origin   origine *(feminine)*
other   altro
otherwise   altrimenti
our   nostro
over there   là

P

pace   passo
pair   paio
pants   pantaloni *(masculine plural)*
parent (male / female)   genitore / genitrice
party   festa
passport   passaporto
pasta   pasta
pay   pagare
perfectly   perfettamente
person   persona
petrol   benzina
phone   telefonare
phone call   telefonata
photograph   fotografia
pink   rosa *(invariable)*
place   posto
please   per favore
point   punto
policeman / policewoman (traffic)   vigile / vigilessa
Polish   polacco
poor   povero
popular   popolare
Portuguese   portoghese
possible   possibile
postal   postale
practice   praticare
precise   preciso
prefer   preferire (isc)
prescribe   prescrivere
present   presentare
problem   problema
professor (male / female)   professore / professoressa
program   programma *(masculine)*
purple   viola *(invariable)*
put   mettere
put on   mettersi

Q

quarter   quarto
question   domanda
quite   abbastanza
quite   assai
Quite well!   Abbastanza bene!

R

railway (of the railway)   ferroviario
rain   piovere
read   leggere
really   proprio
receipt   scontrino
receive   ricevere
red   rosso
refrigerator   frigorifero
relative (male / female)   parente
remote control   telecomando
rent (a vehicle)   noleggiare
reservation   prenotazione *(feminine)*
restaurant   ristorante *(masculine)*
return   tornare*

rich   ricco
right   destra
right away (after)   subito
Russian   russo

S

sad   triste
sale   saldo
sandwich (bun style)   panino
Saturday   sabato
say   dire
schedule   orario
science fiction   fantascienza
search for   cercare
seat   posto
second   secondo
see   vedere
See you soon!   A presto!
See you!   Ci vediamo!
September   settembre
seven   sette
seventeen   diciassette
seventh   settimo
seventy   settanta
several   alcuni
she   lei
shirt   camicia
shoe   scarpa
shoe size   numero
shoe store   calzoleria
shop for food   fare la spesa
shop in general   fare delle spese
shop window   vetrina
shopping in general   spese (feminine, plural)
short   basso
shoulder   spalla
silkworm   baco
sister   sorella
six   sei
sixteen   sedici
sixth   sesto
sixty   sessanta
size (of clothes)   taglia
skating   pattinaggio
skinny   magro
skirt   gonna
sleep   dormire
sleep (noun)   sonno
small   piccolo
snow   nevicare
so   allora, così, dunque
soccer   calcio
sofa   divano
some   qualche, un po' di
something   qualcosa
son   figlio
so-so   così, così
soup   minestra
spacious   spazioso
spaghetti   spaghetti (masculine, plural)
Spanish   spagnolo
speak   parlare
special interest show   cronaca
spoon   cucchiaio

sport   sport (masculine)
spring   primavera
start   cominciare
station   stazione
stay, be (in some expressions)   stare*
steak   bistecca
still   ancora
stomach   stomaco
store clerk (male / female)   commesso / commessa
straight   diritto
street   via
street block   isolato
strong   forte
strong, short (coffee)   ristretto
student (male / female)   studente / studentessa
study   studiare
sugar   zucchero
suit   vestito
suitcase   valigia
summer   estate (feminine)
Sunday   domenica
sure   sicuro
Swedish   svedese
sweet pastry   dolce
Swiss   svizzero

T

table   tavolo
take   prendere
take care of   pensarci
tall   alto
teach   insegnare
teacher (male / female)   insegnante (masculine / feminine)
television   televisione (feminine)
tell   dire
ten   dieci
tennis   tennis (masculine)
tenth   decimo
thank you   grazie
that   quello
that, which   che
That's enough!   Basta!
The weather's awful!   Fa brutto tempo!
them (masculine)   li
then   poi
there   lì
therefore   allora, dunque
they   loro
think   pensare
think so / not   pensare di sì / no
third   terzo
thirst   sete (feminine)
thirteen   tredici
thirty   trenta
this   questo
three   tre
three hundred   trecento
three thousand   tremila
throat   gola
through   per
Thursday   giovedì

497

thus così
ticket biglietto
tie cravatta
time (as in: first time, second time, ...) volta
time (in general), weather tempo
timetable orario
tip mancia
tire gomma
tired stanco
to a
to her, them (feminine) le
to him gli
to the left a sinistra
to the right a destra
to them gli
today oggi
tomorrow domani
tongue lingua
tonight, this evening stasera
too anche
too (much) troppo
tourist (male / female) turista
towards verso
trafficlight semaforo
train treno
travel viggiare
trip viaggio
true vero
truly veramente
try on provarsi
Tuesday martedì
turn girare
TV game show telequiz
TV movie telefilm
TV set televisore *(masculine)*
twelve dodici
twenty venti
two due
two hundred duecento
two thousand duemila

U

ugly brutto
uncle zio
understand capire (isc)
unforgettable indimenticabile
unfortunately purtroppo
United States Stati Uniti
university università *(feminine)*
unpleasant antipatico
until fino a
up to fino a
us, to us, ourselves ci
usually di solito

V

vacation vacanza
very molto
very much molto
very well molto bene
visit visitare

W

wait for aspettare
waiter cameriere *(masculine)*
want volere
warm caldo
watch guardare
water acqua
we noi
wear portare
Wednesday mercoledì
week settimana
well bene
what che, che cosa, quale
What day is it today? Che giorno è oggi?
What's up? Che c'è?
What's your name? (polite / familiar) Come si chiama? / Come ti chiami?
when quando
where dove
Where are you from? (polite / familiar) Di dove è? / Di dove sei?
which che, quale
while mentre
white bianco
who (relative pronoun) che
who / whom chi
why perché
wife moglie
wind vento
window (of a house or building) finestra
window (of a vehicle) finestrino
windshield parabrezza
wine vino
winter inverno
with con
withdraw prelevare
without senza
woman donna
work lavorare
work (literary, artistic, etc.) opera
write scrivere

Y

year anno
year (all year) annata
yellow giallo
yes sì
yesterday ieri
yet ancora
you (familiar) tu
you (plural) voi
you (polite) Lei
you, to you, yourself (familiar) ti
you, to you, yourselves (plural) vi
You're welcome! Prego!
young person (male / female) giovane
your (familiar, singular) tuo

Z

zero zero

Answers

[Answers are given only to those exercises that have straightforward responses. Answers are not given in "open-ended" activities, such as those that require you to write free compositions. Self-study users of this book should try these as well as best they can.]

UNIT 1

A.
1. Vero
2. Vero
3. Falso
4. Falso
5. Vero
6. Falso

B.
1. Molto lieto!
2. Molto lieta!
3. Il piacere è mio!
4. Paul è un altro italiano? / È un altro italiano, Paul?
5. Dina è un'altra americana? / È un'altra americana, Dina?
6. Vi presento Dina Siracusa.
7. Le presento Mark Cardelli.
8. Signorina, Lei è americana, vero?
9. Signore, anche Lei è americano, no?

C. [Provide the information requested]
1. Mi chiamo …
2. Sì / No
3. Sono d'origine …

D.

A	M	E	R	I	C	A	N	A	I
S	A	S	I	G	N	O	R	E	T
C	D	A	S	C	D	R	S	A	A
S	I	G	N	O	R	I	N	A	L
O	D	C	B	B	N	G	S	N	I
N	A	C	A	D	B	I	A	C	A
O	S	M	L	L	D	N	A	H	N
M	A	L	T	O	D	E	M	E	O
C	L	E	R	C	C	D	A	S	L
L	C	E	O	D	A	M	M	A	S

E.
[Give it a good try.]

F.
1. *Mark:* Molto lieto!
2. *Dina:* Molto lieta!
3. *Mark:* Io sono americano.
4. *Giusti:* Io sono italiana.
5. *Paul:* Io sono un altro americano.
6. *Dina:* Anch'io sono un'altra americana.

G.
1. è
2. è
3. E
4. chiamo
5. Anche

H.
1. Professoressa Giusti, Le presento Dina Siracusa.
2. Professoressa Giusti, Le presento Paul Giannetti.
3. Professoressa Giusti, Le presento Jim Carducci.
4. Professoressa Giusti, Le presento Debbie Di Nardo.
5. Vi presento Dina Siracusa.
6. Vi presento Paul Giannetti.
7. Vi presento Jim Carducci.
8. Vi presento Debbie Di Nardo.
9. Mi chiamo Dina Siracusa. Sono americana, ma sono d'origine italiana.
10. Mi chiamo Paul Giannetti. Sono americano, ma sono d'origine italiana.
11. Mi chiamo Jim Carducci. Sono americano, ma sono d'origine italiana.
12. Mi chiamo Debbie Di Nardo. Sono americana, ma sono d'origine italiana.

I.

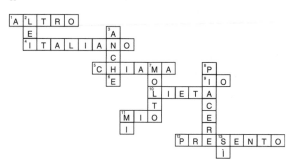

J.

1. Shake hands.
2. Greet him or her and maybe pat him or her on a shoulder.
3. Greet him or her, giving a kiss on both cheeks, barely making contact, while patting him or her on a shoulder.

UNIT 2

A.

1. a
2. a
3. b
4. b
5. a
6. a
7. b
8. a
9. a
10. b

B.

1. Dina, come stai?
2. Signora Martini, come sta?
3. (Io) sto bene.
4. (Sto) non c'è male.
5. ArriverLa, signora Martini
6. Buongiorno, signora Martini
7. Mark, ti presento Dina
8. Dina, dove vai?
9. Ciao, Paul!
10. Ciao, Paul! / Ci vediamo, Paul! / Arrivederci, Paul!

C. [Answers will vary.]

1. Ciao / Buongiorno
2. Le presento …
3. Ti presento …
4. Come si chiama?
5. Come ti chiami?
6. Mi chiamo …
7. Arrivederci
8. Come sta?
9. Come stai?
10. Di dove è (Lei)?
11. Di dove sei (tu)?
12. Dove va (Lei)?
13. Dove vai (tu)?
14. (Io) sono di Chicago.
15. (Io) sono di qui.

D.

1. Ciao
2. stai/va
3. male
4. così
5. centro
6. vediamo

E.

1. Signor Cardelli, come sta?
2. Signora Martini, come sta?
3. Signorina Siracusa, come sta?
4. Dottoressa Franchi, come sta?
5. Dottor Bruni, come sta?
6. Professoressa Gianmarchi, come sta?
7. Professor Santucci, come sta?
8. Dina, come stai?
9. Mark, come stai?
10. [This will vary]

F.

1. Buongiorno, dottor Giusti!
2. Ciao, Dina!
3. ArrivederLa, professoressa Martini!
4. Arrivederci/Ciao, Mark!
5. Come sta, signor Santucci?
6. Come stai, Paul?
7. Come ti chiami?
8. Come si chiama?
9. Signor Giusti, Le presento la signora Martini.
10. Mirella, ti presento Gino.

G. [Text will vary according to person.]

H.

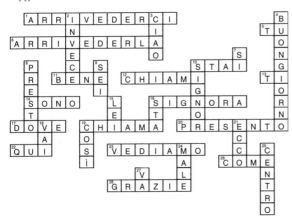

I.

1. Buongiorno, avvocato / Avvocato Martini.
2. Buongiorno, ragionier / Ragionier Nardini.
3. Buongiorno, signor Di Nardo.
4. Buongiorno, signora Rossini.
5. Buongiorno, geometra / Geometra Martelli.
6. Buongiorno, professoressa / Professoressa Giusti.
7. Buongiorno, professor / Professore Verdi.
8. Buongiorno, dottor / Dottor Brunetti.
9. Buongiorno, dottoressa / Dottoressa Carducci.

UNIT 3

A.

1. Buonasera
2. Abbastanza
3. Molto
4. Che
5. orario
6. Quando
7. qualche
8. Dove
9. Ecco

B.

1. Buonasera!
2. Abbastanza bene, grazie!
3. Il treno arriva fra /tra qualche minuto.
4. Che cosa è quello?
5. Prego!
6. È un orario in italiano.
7. Quando arriva il treno?
8. Dove va, signorina Siracusa?
9. A Firenze. È bella?

10. Sì, molto!
11. Buonasera! / Buon pomeriggio!

C.

1. che / che cosa
2. treno
3. arriva
4. minuto
5. Ciao!/Arrivederci!/A presto!/Ci vediamo!

D.

1. (Sto) abbastanza bene.
2. Che cosa è? / Che è? / Che cosa è quello?
3. Dove è l'orario? / Dov'è l'orario?
4. Quando arriva il treno?
5. Buonasera!

E. [Examples of uses are only illustrative. There are other possibilities.]

1. ArrivederLa!
2. Arrivederci! / Ciao!
3. Ciao!
4. Buongiorno!
5. Buon pomeriggio!
6. Buonasera!
7. Come si chiama?
8. Come ti chiami?
9. Come sta?
10. Come stai?
11. Di dove è? / Di dov'è?
12. Di dove sei?
13. Molto lieto!
14. Molto lieta!
15. Ti presento …
16. Le presento …
17. Vi presento …

F. [This exercise will, of course, vary.]

G.

1. a
2. b
3. a
4. a
5. a
6. a
7. c

H.

1. minuto
2. treno
3. orario
4. signorina
5. dottoressa

I.
1. il centro / un centro
2. il minuto / un minuto
3. il dottore / un dottore
4. il professore / un professore

J.

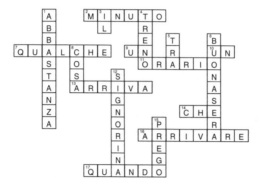

K.
1. con l'aereo / con il treno / con l'automobile
2. con la metropolitana / con l'autobus / con l'automobile
3. con l'autobus / con il treno / con l'automobile
4. con l'aereo

UNIT 4

A.
1. Dina va a dormire.
2. Perché Dina ha sonno.
3. Sì, Dina è stanca.
4. Domani Dina ha un appuntamento.
5. Con un'amica.

B.
1. No, Dina ha sonno.
2. No, Dina è stanca.
3. No, Dina ha un appuntamento con un'amica.
4. No, Dina ha un appuntamento domani.

C.
1. Lei è italiana.
2. La signora è stanca.
3. Lei ha un appuntamento con un'amica.
4. La dottoressa è italiana.
5. Lei è stanca.
6. L'amica di Mark è americana.
7. La professoressa ha sonno.

D.
1. È un orario.
2. Vado a Firenze.
3. Perché sono stanco / stanca e ho sonno.
4. Domani ho un appuntamento con un amico / un'amica.
5. Buonanotte!

E.
1. Chi è stanco? / Come è Mark? *(How is Mark?)*
2. Che cosa ha Dina? / Che ha Dina? Chi ha sonno?
3. Che cosa hai domani? / Con chi hai un appuntamento domani?
4. Come stai? / Come sta?
5. Come ti chiami? / Come si chiama?
6. Di dove sei *(familiar)*? / Di dove è *(polite)*?
7. Perché vai a dormire?

F.
1. un treno
2. un'amica
3. un'italiana
4. un italiano
5. un amico
6. un orario
7. un minuto

G.
1. Io ho sonno.
2. Dina ha sonno.
3. Dina è italiana.
4. Anche lui è italiano.
5. Io sono americano / americana.
6. Lei è stanca.
7. Lui è stanco
8. Dina, di dove sei?
9. Dina, hai sonno?
10. Dina, sei stanca?
11. Dina, sei di qui?
12. Professoressa Giusti, di dove è / dov'è?
13. Professoressa Giusti, ha sonno?
14. Professoressa Giusti, è stanca?
15. Professoressa Giusti, è di qui?

H.

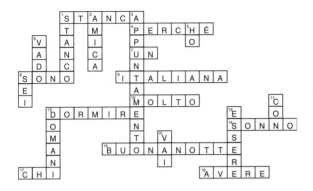

I.

1. Anywhere from age 2 to about 4 or 5.
2. Usually around age 4 or 5.
3. From around age 5 to age 9 or 10.
4. From around age 10 to 13 or 14.
5. From around age 13 or 14 to 18 or 19.
6. This varies. Usually university starts after high school.

UNIT 5

A.

1. d
2. a
3. b
4. f
5. c
6. g
7. i
8. e
9. l
10. h
11. j
12. k

B.

1. zero, uno, due, tre, quattro, cinque, sei, sette, otto, nove, dieci
2. undici, dodici, tredici, quattordici, quindici, sedici, diciassette, diciotto, diciannove
3. venti, trenta, quaranta, cinquanta, sessanta, settanta, ottanta, novanta, cento

C.

1. cento
2. dodici
3. trenta
4. trecento

5. cinquanta
6. quaranta
7. ottanta
8. novanta
9. settanta
10. sessanta

D.

1. Mamma mia!
2. Mi può insegnare a contare?
3. Chi è l'insegnante?
4. Voglio imparare i numeri da uno a dieci.
5. Come sono lunghi!
6. Ha un milione di euro.
7. No, ha un miliardo di euro!
8. Basta così!
9. Va bene!
10. Ecco altri numeri.

E.

1. ottantasei, novantacinque, sessantatré, ventidue, ottantotto, novantaquattro, novantotto, settantuno, settantadue
2. cento ventitré, duecento quarantacinque, trecento settantotto, quattrocento ventuno, cinquecento cinquantatré, seicento ventuno, settecento novantotto, ottocento ottantotto, novecento novantanove
3. duemila trecento quarantatré, cinquemila seicento settantotto, novemila ottocento settantuno, settemila cinquecento quarantanove
4. dodici mila quattrocento cinquantotto, venticinque mila settecento ottantanove
5. trecento quarantacinque mila settecento novantotto, novecento ottantanove mila quattrocento ventuno
6. un milione seicento cinquantaquattro mila ottocento novantatré, due milioni trecento quarantatré mila settecento ottantanove
7. un miliardo quattrocento cinquantasei milioni settecento novantotto mila trecento quarantacinque, cinque miliardi cinquecento cinquantacinque milioni cinquecento cinquantacinque mila cinquecento cinquantacinque

F.

1. l'amico
2. l'amica
3. l'americano
4. l'americana
5. l'appuntamento
6. il centro
7. l'insegnante
8. l'italiano

9. l'italiana
10. il milione
11. il miliardo
12. il minuto
13. il numero
14. l'orario
15. l'euro

G.

1. b
2. b
3. a
4. a
5. a
6. a
7. b

H.

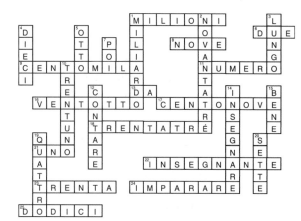

I.

1. venticinque euro [Exchange rate will vary.]
2. centocinquanta euro [Exchange rate will vary.]
3. mille cinquecento euro [Exchange rate will vary.]
4. ventunmila euro [Exchange rate will vary.]

REVIEW PART 1

A.

1. Molto lieto!
2. Molto lieta!
3. Vi presento Mark Cardelli.
4. Le presento Dina Siracusa.
5. Buonasera / Buona sera!
6. Prego!
7. Buon pomeriggio!

8. Mamma mia!
9. Voglio imparare a contare da uno a dieci.
10. Va bene!

B.

1. Dina e Marco, vi presento Paul Giannetti.
2. Jim, ti presento Debbie Di Nardo.
3. Dina, come stai?
4. Dottoressa Martini, come sta?
5. ArrivederLa, Dottoressa Martini.
6. Dina, di dove sei?
7. Dottoressa Martini di dove è / dov'è?
8. Paul, come stai?
9. Signor Franchi, come sta?
10. Mark, hai sonno?
11. Professoressa Giusti, è italiana (Lei)?
12. Professoressa Giusti, è stanca (Lei)?

C. [Answers will vary].

1. Mi chiamo …
2. Sì / No. Sì, sono americano / a. / No, non sono americano / a.
3. Sono d'origine …
4. (Io) sto bene / molto bene / non c'è male / così, così, / abbastanza bene

D. [Try your best.]

E.

M	I	N	U	T	O	E	R	T	C	B	S	Q	W	E	R	T	Y	U	I
A	S	D	F	G	H	J	K	L	H	Z	O	X	C	V	B	N	M	G	Q
W	E	R	T	Y	I	T	A	L	I	A	N	O	T	Y	U	I	O	R	P
A	S	D	F	G	H	J	K	L	A	Z	O	X	C	V	B	S	T	A	I
N	M	Q	W	E	R	T	Y	U	M	I	O	P	P	O	U	I	Y	Z	T
C	H	I	A	M	A	G	F	D	O	V	E	D	S	A	Q	W	E	I	R
E	Q	S	T	T	T	T	N	Q	Q	Z	Z	X	C	C	B	N	M	E	J
N	Z	Z	X	X	C	C	V	B	U	O	N	A	S	E	R	A	W	W	B
T	C	V	V	W	W	R	R	T	Y	U	U	Y	T	N	R	E	W	W	U
R	A	N	O	V	A	N	T	O	T	T	O	R	Q	T	Q	Q	N	N	O
O	W	W	E	R	T	Y	T	W	N	W	W	D	W	O	W	W	O	M	N
X	Z	P	E	R	C	H	É	Z	M	Z	Z	O	Z	M	Z	Z	V	K	G
Q	X	R	X	X	X	Q	G	X	B	X	X	M	X	I	X	X	E	L	I
A	C	E	C	C	C	W	X	C	B	C	C	A	C	L	C	C	M	O	O
Z	V	G	V	V	V	E	X	V	E	V	V	N	V	A	V	V	I	K	R
X	B	O	B	B	B	R	X	B	S	B	B	I	B	A	B	B	L	M	N
C	N	G	N	N	N	T	G	N	S	N	N	N	N	E	N	N	A	N	O
V	M	G	M	M	M	Y	G	M	E	M	M	M	A	M	M	K	Q	E
G	B	G	B	B	B	N	G	B	R	B	B	B	C	E	N	T	O	Q	R
B	U	O	N	A	N	O	T	T	E	B	B	A	G	G	G	G	G	Q	Q

UNIT 6

A.

1. Falso
2. Vero
3. Vero
4. Vero

5. Vero
6. Falso

B.
1. Che ora è?
2. Sono le undici in punto.
3. Veramente?
4. Quando parte l'autobus?
5. Non sono sicuro / sicura.
6. Di solito parte alle nove e un quarto ogni giorno.
7. Non capisco.
8. C'è un orario differente domani.
9. L'informazione non è precisa.

C.
1. È l'una e dodici.
2. Sono le due e venti.
3. Sono le tre e quindici. / Sono le tre e un quarto.
4. Sono le quattro e trenta. / Sono le quattro e mezzo.
5. Sono le cinque e quarantacinque. / Sono le sei meno un quarto.
6. Sono le sei e cinque.
7. Sono le sette e cinquantanove. / Sono le otto meno uno (un minuto).
8. Sono le otto precise. / Sono le otto in punto.
9. È l'una precisa. / È l'una in punto.
10. Sono le nove e trenta. / Sono le nove e mezzo.
11. Sono le dieci e venti.
12. Sono le undici e quindici. / Sono le undici e un quarto.
13. Sono le dodici e quaranta. / È l'una meno venti.

D.
1. Di solito l'autobus parte alle nove e cinquanta / alle dieci meno dieci.
2. Di solito l'autobus parte all'una e trenta / all'una e mezzo.
3. Di solito l'autobus parte alle dodici e quindici / alle dodici e un quarto.
4. Di solito l'autobus parte alle cinque precise / alle cinque in punto.
5. Di solito l'autobus parte alle sei e quarantacinque / alle sette meno un quarto.

E. [Answers will vary].

F. [The answers given are illustrative. There are, in some cases, other possibilities.]
1. È l'una precisa del mattino. / È l'una in punto del mattino.

2. È l'una e quindici (un quarto) del pomeriggio. / Sono le tredici e quindici (un quarto).
3. Sono le due e quarantacinque del mattino. / Sono le tre meno un quarto del mattino.
4. Sono le tre e quarantacinque del pomeriggio. / Sono le quattro meno un quarto del pomeriggio. / Sono le quindici e quarantacinque.
5. Sono le quattro e dieci del mattino.
6. Sono le sei meno cinque del pomeriggio. / Sono le diciassette e cinquantacinque.
7. Sono le sei e trenta (mezzo) del mattino.
8. Sono le sette e trenta (mezzo) di sera. / Sono le diciannove e trenta.
9. Sono le otto precise del mattino. / Sono le otto in punto del mattino.
10. Sono le nove precise (in punto) della sera. / Sono le ventuno precise (in punto).
11. Sono le dieci e dodici del mattino.
12. Sono le undici e uno della sera. / Sono le ventitré e uno.
13. Sono le dodici della sera. / È mezzanotte.
14. Sono le dodici del pomeriggio. / È mezzogiorno.

G.
1. L'autobus parte alle otto del mattino.
2. È l'una precisa del pomeriggio.
3. Sono le nove e trenta della sera.
4. Il treno parte all'una e dieci del pomeriggio.
5. Sono le venti in punto.

H.

I.

1. le tredici (people are probably having lunch)
2. le diciannove (people are probably starting to have dinner)
3. le ventitré (people are going to bed, unless it is the summer)
4. le diciotto (people are engaged in various late afternoon activities)
5. le ventuno (except for the summer, people are probably watching TV, reading, or doing other typical evening things)

UNIT 7

A.

1. a
2. b
3. a
4. b
5. a
6. b

B.

1. È proprio una bella giornata.
2. Di solito fa brutto tempo.
3. Fra freddo oggi.
4. Tira vento.
5. Nevica oggi.
6. Di primavera / In primavera piove troppo e fa fresco.
7. Tira vento in autunno / d'autunno.
8. Fa freddo d'inverno / in inverno.
9. Fa sempre caldo d'estate / in estate.
10. Che tempo fa generalmente d'inverno / in inverno?
11. Che tempo fa di solito di primavera / in primavera?
12. Che tempo fa generalmente d'estate / in estate?
13. Che tempo fa generalmente d'autunno / in autunno?
14. Alessandro, scherzi, vero?

C.

1. Fa freddo. / Nevica. / È inverno.
2. Fa bel tempo. / Fa caldo. / È estate.
3. Fa brutto tempo. / Piove. / Fa fresco. / È primavera. / È autunno.
4. È estate. / Fa caldo. / Fa bel tempo.
5. È autunno. / Fa fresco.
6. È inverno.

D. [Answers will vary.]

E.

1. Oggi nevica, ma domani fa bel tempo.
2. Di solito tira vento in autunno / d'autunno.
3. D'inverno / In inverno fa (è) sempre freddo, ma oggi non fa (è) freddo.
4. D'estate / In estate fa (è) sempre troppo caldo.
5. Oggi è proprio una bella giornata, ma tira molto vento.
6. D'autunno / In autunno fa (è) sempre molto fresco.
7. Anche di primavera / in primavera fa (è) sempre molto fresco e tira molto vento.

F.

1. bella
2. bel
3. bello
4. bell'
5. bell'
6. bel
7. bel

G. [Paragraphs will vary.]

H.

I.

The regions (in alphabetical order) are:
1. gli Abruzzi
2. la Valle d'Aosta
3. la Basilicata
4. la Calabria
5. la Campania
6. l'Emilia Romagna
7. il Friuli Venezia Giulia
8. il Lazio
9. la Liguria
10. la Lombardia
11. la Lucania
12. il Molise
13. il Piemonte
14. la Puglia, le Puglie
15. la Sardegna
16. la Sicilia
17. la Toscana
18. il Trentino Alto Adige
19. l'Umbria
20. il Veneto

UNIT 8

A.
1. Dina
2. giorno
3. lunedì, martedì, mercoledì, giovedì, venerdì, sabato, domenica
4. testa
5. centro
6. domenica
7. vuoi
8. mese
9. gennaio, febbraio, marzo, aprile, maggio, giugno, luglio, agosto, settembre, ottobre, novembre, dicembre
10. freddo
11. paese
12. il cinque novembre.

B.
1. Pronto?
2. Certo.
3. Se vuoi tu.
4. Non sempre.
5. Sara, hai ragione.
6. Sono io.
7. Oggi vado in centro come ogni sabato.
8. Fa sempre molto freddo in questo paese.
9. Fa già assai freddo.
10. È il dieci ottobre.
11. Che c'è?
12. Che giorno della settimana è?
13. Hai perso la testa?
14. Che dici?
15. Alessandro, anche tu vieni alla festa?
16. Che mese dell'anno è?
17. Che giorno è?
18. Dov'è il cellulare?
19. Sara, hai un cellulare?

C.
1. Il giorno dopo è mercoledì.
2. Il giorno dopo è venerdì.
3. Il giorno dopo è domenica.
4. Il mese dopo è febbraio.
5. Il mese dopo è aprile.
6. Il mese dopo è giugno.
7. Il mese dopo è agosto.
8. Il mese dopo è ottobre.
9. Il mese dopo è dicembre.

D. [Answers will vary.]

E. [Dialogues will vary.]

F. [Note: numbers ending in uno, such as ventuno, change in form before a noun. They are to be treated as indefinite article forms. Thus, ventuno settembre is changed to ventun settembre.]

1. È il ventun settembre, mille novecento novantotto
2. È il tre maggio, mille novecento settanta-due.
3. È il quattro dicembre, mille novecento settantuno.
4. È il quindici settembre, mille novecento novantaquattro.
5. È il primo ottobre, duemila e quattro.
6. È il primo gennaio, duemila e sei.
7. È il diciannove febbraio, duemila e sette.

G. [Answer will vary.]

H.
1. Alessandro viene alla festa domenica. Lui va con Dina. E lei dice che è vero.
2. Io dico che Sara e Dina vanno alla festa. Tu che dici?
3. Che (cosa) dicono? Vengono? Se no, venite voi?
4. Dove andate (voi)? Andiamo alla festa.
5. Veniamo anche noi, se voi dite dov'è.
6. Vado anch'io alla festa. Vengo con Dina.

I.

1. Dina, vai in centro?
2. Dina, che (cosa) dici?
3. Dina, con chi vieni alla festa?
4. Professoressa Giusti, va in centro?
5. Professoressa Giusti, che (cosa) dice?
6. Professoressa Giusti, con chi viene alla festa?
7. Dina e Alessandro, andate in centro?
8. Dina e Alessandro, che (cosa) dite?
9. Dina e Alessandro, con chi venite alla festa?

J.

K.

1. il Natale
2. il Capo d'Anno
3. la Pasqua
4. il Ferragosto
5. il presepio
6. il Bambino
7. il panettone
8. il Carnevale
9. la Befana

A.

1. Dina vuole conoscere la famiglia di Alessandro.
2. Il padre di Alessandro si chiama Paolo.
3. Il padre di Alessandro è molto alto.
4. La madre di Alessandro si chiama Maria.
5. Anche la madre di Alessandro è molto alta.
6. Nella famiglia di Alessandro c'è anche un fratello (che si chiama Mario) e una sorella (che si chiama Claudia).
7. La famiglia di Dina è grande.
8. La casa di Dina è molto grande.
9. Il nonno, la nonna, lo zio e la zia vivono *(live)* con loro.

B.

1. Vorrei conoscere la famiglia di Alessandro.
2. Va bene!
3. Mio padre è molto alto.
4. Anche mia madre è molto alta.
5. Ho anche un fratello e una sorella.
6. Ho una famiglia grande.
7. Abbiamo il nonno e la nonna in casa.
8. Abbiamo anche lo zio e la zia in casa.
9. La nostra casa è molto grande.

C.

1. madre
2. nonno
3. sorella
4. zio

D. [Answers will vary.]

1. Mia madre si chiama…
2. Mio padre si chiama…
3. Mio fratello si chiama…
4. Mia sorella si chiama…
5. Mio nonno si chiama…
6. Mia nonna si chiama…
7. Mia zia si chiama…
8. Mio zio si chiama…

E. [Compositions will vary.]

F.

1. Alessandro, tua sorella è bella? / Sì, mia sorella è bella.
2. Alessandro, tuo zio è stanco? / Sì, mio zio è stanco.
3. Alessandro, tua zia è alta? / Sì, mia zia è alta.

4. Alessandro, tuo fratello è bello? / Sì, mio fratello è bello.

5. Alessandro, tua madre è stanca? / Sì, mia madre è stanca.

6. Alessandro, tuo padre è preciso? / Sì, mio padre è preciso.

7. Alessandro, tua nonna è bella? / Sì, ma nonna è bella.

8. Alessandro, tuo nonno è preciso? / Sì, mio nonno è preciso.

G.

1. la genitrice / una genitrice
2. il parente / un parente
3. la parente / una parente
4. la famiglia / una famiglia
5. lo zio / uno zio
6. la zia / una zia
7. l'amica / un'amica
8. l'orario / un orario
9. il cellulare / un cellulare
10. il giorno / un giorno
11. la giornata / una giornata
12. il mese / un mese
13. l'origine / un'origine
14. l'amico / un amico
15. lo zero / uno zero

H.

1. (Io) ho una famiglia grande.
2. (Io) sono stanco / stanca.
3. Dina è stanca.
4. Alessandro non è stanco.
5. (Noi) abbiamo una famiglia grande.
6. (Noi) non siamo d'origine italiana.
7. Alessandro e Dina hanno una famiglia grande.
8. (Loro) sono in centro oggi.

I.

1. Dina, hai sonno?
2. Dina, sei stanca?
3. Professoressa Giusti, ha sonno?
4. Professoressa Giusti, è stanca?
5. Mark e Paul, avete sonno?
6. Mark e Paul, siete stanchi?

J.

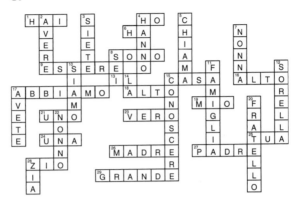

K. [Answers will vary.]

UNIT 10

A.

1. d
2. f
3. e
4. g
5. c
6. b
7. a

B.

Ask Sara…

1. Sara, vuoi vedere queste fotografie?
2. Sara, vedi quei due ragazzi?
3. Sara, chi è quella donna?
4. Sara, chi è quell'uomo?
5. Sara, chi sono quelle due ragazze?
6. Sara, vedi quei due bambini?
7. Sara, chi sono quei bambini?
8. Quell'uomo è il migliore amico di mio padre.
9. Quella donna è un'amica di mia madre.
10. Quel ragazzo piccolo è mio nipote.
11. Quell'altro ragazzo più grande è mio cugino.
12. (Loro) sono due amiche di mia sorella.
13. (Loro) sono i bambini di mia cugina.
14. Che belle fotografie!

C.

1. quella donna
2. quel bambino
3. piccolo
4. più

5. quel cugino
6. quel genitore
7. quel nipote

D. [Dialogues will vary.]

E.
1. le americane
2. gli uomini
3. i bambini
4. le donne
5. gli zeri
6. le fotografie
7. i ragazzi
8. le ragazze
9. le nipoti
10. i nipoti
11. i parenti
12. i genitori
13. gli italiani
14. gli anni
15. i cellulari
16. gli zii
17. gli studenti
18. le italiane

F.
1. questo cugino / questi cugini
2. questa ragazza / queste ragazze
3. quest'amico / questi amici
4. quest'amica / queste amiche
5. questo studente / questi studenti
6. questo cellulare / questi cellulari
7. questo zio / questi zii
8. questa donna / queste donne
9. quest'uomo / questi uomini

G.
1. quel cugino / quei cugini
2. quella ragazza / quelle ragazze
3. quell'amico / quegli amici
4. quell'amica / quelle amiche
5. quello studente / quegli studenti
6. quel cellulare / quei cellulari
7. quello zio / quegli zii
8. quella donna / quelle donne
9. quell'uomo / quegli uomini

H.
1. La figlia di mia zia è mia cugina.
2. La sorella di mia madre è mia zia.
3. Il fratello di mio padre è mio zio.
4. Il padre di mia madre è mio nonno.
5. La madre di mia madre è mia nonna.
6. Il figlio di mio fratello è mio nipote.
7. La figlia di mia sorella è mia nipote.

I. [Answers will vary.]

J.

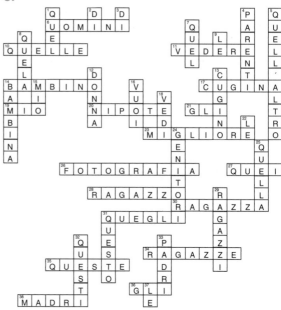

K. [Descriptions will vary.]
1. la damigella d'onore
2. il compare d'anello
3. le damigelle
4. i cavalieri
5. lo sposalizio
6. il matrimonio
7. la sposa
8. lo sposo
9. la luna di miele

REVIEW PART 2

A.
1. Che ora è? / Che ore sono?
2. È mezzanotte.
3. Sono le cinque e mezzo del pomeriggio. / Sono le diciassette e trenta.
4. Sono le nove e cinquanta di sera. / Sono le ventuno e cinquanta. / Sono le dieci meno dieci di sera.
5. Di solito, l'autobus parte all'una in punto.
6. Pronto?
7. Vengo alla festa sabato se vuoi tu.
8. (Loro) hanno una famiglia grande.
9. (Loro) sono d'origine italiana.

B.

1. Oggi fa brutto tempo.
2. Di solito fa bel tempo.
3. Fa (È) sempre freddo d'inverno / in inverno.
4. Nevica generalmente d'inverno /in inverno.
5. Piove troppo d'estate / in estate.
6. Sono io!
7. Domani vado in centro come ogni venerdì.
8. È il quindici settembre.
9. Vorrei conoscere la famiglia e i parenti di Sara.
10. Ho una famiglia grande.
11. La mia / nostra casa è molto grande.
12. Che c'è?
13. Che dici *(familiar)*? / Che dice *(polite)*?
14. Sara, vieni anche tu alla festa?
15. Sara, domani vai in centro?
16. Signora Martini, che (cosa) dice?
17. Mark e Paul, con chi venite alla festa?
18. Dina, vuoi vedere quelle fotografie?
19. Dina, chi sono queste due ragazze?
20. Dina, chi sono quei bambini?

C. [Answers will vary.]

D. [Compositions will vary.]

E.

A	Z	Q	E	D	C	V	G	M	T	Y	U	I	O	P	A	S	D	S	D
H	K	J	L	G	I	O	Z	I	X	C	V	T	E	M	P	O	M	A	L
L	G	I	O	R	N	A	T	A	D	J	K	L	K	J	H	G	B	B	M
P	S	D	F	A	B	B	B	A	A	A	Q	R	T	Y	P	S	N	A	M
A	S	A	S	N	D	P	R	O	N	T	O	R	R	R	L	S	M	T	M
D	D	D	D	D	D	G	G	G	G	C	C	C	R	B	U	R	O	N
R	C	D	A	E	G	C	D	A	G	C	B	R	U	T	T	O	T	U	N
E	S	Z	C	X	Z	C	X	Z	C	X	Z	D	A	R	B	M	T	R	N
X	T	R	O	P	P	O	S	D	F	G	C	A	A	R	N	O	T	D	S
X	X	X	Q	Q	Q	S	S	S	R	B	X	G	A	F	N	A	F	Q	E
X	X	X	R	Q	Q	Q	P	R	E	C	I	S	E	F	B	C	R	Z	T
C	F	S	A	Q	Z	X	V	X	R	B	Z	C	A	F	E	M	A	X	T
C	A	S	G	D	D	D	X	T	R	C	C	D	A	T	L	M	T	C	E
A	M	M	A	Q	G	I	O	R	N	O	X	A	A	T	L	M	E	V	M
D	I	M	Z	E	Q	Y	X	S	T	S	Z	G	A	T	A	N	L	B	B
A	G	M	Z	D	E	Y	X	Q	T	R	C	C	A	T	Q	Y	L	N	R
A	L	D	I	Y	D	Y	X	I	N	F	O	R	M	A	Z	I	O	N	E
Q	I	D	R	Y	Y	V	Z	Q	T	Q	X	D	A	B	Q	T	T	T	O
Q	A	U	T	O	B	U	S	Z	V	S	E	T	T	I	M	A	N	A	M
D	Z	Z	X	X	Q	R	Z	V	Q	V	A	A	B	Q	G	T	B	N

A.

1. Vero
2. Falso
3. Vero
4. Falso
5. Vero
6. Vero
7. Vero

B.

1. Purtroppo, (io) non parlo italiano.
2. Io e mio marito non parliamo italiano molto bene.
3. Voi parlate italiano molto bene.
4. Per via Garibaldi, voi dovete andare a sinistra fino al semaforo.
5. A destra, c'è la via.
6. Lei parla inglese?
7. Ci può aiutare a trovare via Garibaldi?

C.

1. Scusi!
2. Lei è molto gentile.
3. Tu sei molto gentile.
4. Voi siete molto gentili.
5. Lei parla molto bene.
6. Tu parli molto bene.
7. Voi parlate molto bene.
8. Mia moglie parla molto bene.
9. Nostro figlio e nostra figlia non parlano italiano.
10. Lei è molto umile.
11. Tu sei molto umile.
12. Voi siete molto umili.
13. Dunque!

D.

1. Dov'è via Boccaccio? / Via Boccaccio è a sinistra.
2. Ci può aiutare trovare il semaforo? / Il semaforo è a destra.
3. Lei parla inglese? / Sì, lo parlo.
4. Cosa desidera? / Purtroppo, (io) non parlo italiano.

E. [Instructions will vary.]

F.

1. C'è il mio amico?
2. C'è la mia amica?
3. C'è mio cugino?
4. C'è mia cugina?
5. C'è la mia bella madre?
6. Ci sono i miei genitori?
7. C'è il mio fratello alto?
8. Ci sono i miei nonni?
9. Ci sono le mie cugine?
10. Ci sono le mie amiche?
11. C'è il tuo amico?
12. C'è la tua amica?
13. C'è tuo cugino?
14. C'è tua cugina?
15. C'è la tua bella madre?
16. Ci sono i tuoi genitori?
17. C'è il tuo fratello alto?
18. Ci sono i tuoi nonni?
19. Ci sono le tue cugine?
20. Ci sono le tue amiche?
21. C'è il nostro amico?
22. C'è la nostra amica?
23. C'è nostro cugino?
24. C'è nostra cugina?
25. C'è la nostra bella madre?
26. Ci sono i nostri genitori?
27. C'è il nostro fratello alto?
28. Ci sono i nostri nonni?
29. Ci sono le nostre cugine?
30. Ci sono le nostre amiche?

G.

1. Io parlo italiano.
2. Io aiuto sempre i miei amici.
3. Di solito io arrivo presto.
4. Io insegno inglese.
5. Io non scherzo sempre.
6. Tu parli italiano.
7. Tu aiuti sempre i tuoi amici.
8. Di solito tu arrivi presto.
9. Tu insegni inglese.
10. Tu non scherzi sempre.
11. Lei parla italiano.
12. Lei aiuta sempre i Suoi amici.
13. Di solito Lei arriva presto.
14. Lei insegna inglese.
15. Lei non scherza sempre.
16. Lui / Lei parla italiano.
17. Lui / Lei aiuta sempre i suoi amici.
18. Di solito lui / lei arriva presto.
19. Lui / Lei insegna inglese.
20. Lui / Lei non scherza sempre.
21. Noi parliamo italiano.
22. Noi aiutiamo sempre i nostri amici.
23. Di solito noi arriviamo presto.
24. Noi insegniamo inglese.
25. Noi non scherziamo sempre.
26. Voi parlate italiano.
27. Voi aiutate sempre i vostri amici.
28. Di solito voi arrivate presto.
29. Voi insegnate inglese.
30. Voi non scherzate sempre.
31. Loro parlano italiano.
32. Loro aiutano sempre i loro amici.
33. Di solito loro arrivano presto.
34. Loro insegnano inglese.
35. Loro non scherzano sempre.

H. [Answers will vary.]

I.

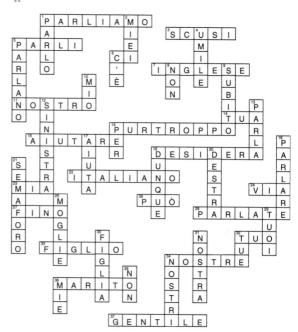

J.

1. il balcone
2. il carnevale
3. il costume
4. la malaria
5. l'opera
6. il piano(forte)
7. il pilota
8. lo stucco
9. lo studio
10. l'ombrello
11. il vulcano

UNIT 12

A.
1. a
2. a
3. a
4. a
5. a
6. b
7. a

B.
1. (Io) capisco l'italiano e lo scrivo bene.
2. Sono molti anni che studio (l') italiano.
3. Io e il mio amico / la mia amica capiamo quasi tutto.
4. Debbie e Sharon, dovete scrivere i vostri nomi, altrimenti non vi posso aiutare.
5. Debbie, parli italiano?
6. Chi parla italiano molto bene?
7. Debbie e Sharon, avete un indirizzo postale qui in Italia?

C.
1. (Io) studio l'italiano ogni sera.
2. (Io) scrivo l'italiano molto bene.
3. Altro?
4. (Noi) capiamo tutto.
5. Sono quasi le nove.
6. L'impiegata dice che (lei) capisce l'inglese.
7. Le mie amiche, Debbie e Sharon, dicono che anche loro vengono alla festa.

D. [Answers will vary.]

E. [Compositions will vary.]

F.
1. C'è il vostro amico? / Sì, ecco il nostro amico.
2. C'è la vostra amica? / Sì, ecco la nostra amica.
3. C'è vostro fratello? / Sì, ecco nostro fratello.
4. C'è vostra sorella? / Sì, ecco nostra sorella.
5. C'è la vostra bella madre? / Sì, ecco la nostra bella madre.
6. Ci sono i vostri genitori? / Sì, ecco i nostri genitori.
7. C'è il vostro cugino alto? / Sì, ecco il nostro cugino alto.
8. Ci sono i vostri nonni? / Sì, ecco i nostri nonni.
9. Ci sono le vostre cugine? / Sì, ecco le nostre cugine.
10. Ci sono le vostre amiche? / Sì, ecco le nostre amiche.
11. C'è il loro amico? / Sì, ecco il loro amico.
12. C'è la loro amica? / Sì, ecco la loro amica.
13. C'è il loro fratello? / Sì, ecco il loro fratello.
14. C'è la loro sorella? / Sì, ecco la loro sorella.
15. C'è la loro bella madre? / Sì, ecco la loro bella madre.
16. Ci sono i loro genitori? / Sì, ecco i loro genitori.
17. C'è il loro cugino? / Sì, ecco il loro cugino.
18. Ci sono i loro nonni? / Sì, ecco i loro nonni.
19. Ci sono le loro cugine? / Sì, ecco le loro cugine.
20. Ci sono le loro amiche? / Sì, ecco le loro amiche.

G.
1. Io scrivo l'italiano molto bene.
2. Io capisco l'italiano e l'inglese.
3. Io conosco i loro cugini.
4. Tu scrivi l'italiano molto bene.
5. Tu capisci l'italiano e l'inglese.
6. Tu conosci i loro cugini.
7. Lei scrive l'italiano molto bene.
8. Lei capisce l'italiano e l'inglese.
9. Lei conosce i loro cugini.
10. Lui / lei scrive l'italiano molto bene.
11. Lui / lei capisce l'italiano e l'inglese.
12. Lui / lei conosce i loro cugini.
13. Noi scriviamo l'italiano molto bene.
14. Noi capiamo l'italiano e l'inglese.
15. Noi conosciamo i loro cugini.
16. Voi scrivete l'italiano molto bene.
17. Voi capite l'italiano e l'inglese.
18. Voi conoscete i loro cugini.
19. Loro scrivono l'italiano molto bene.
20. Loro capiscono l'italiano e l'inglese.
21. Loro conoscono i nostri cugini.

H.

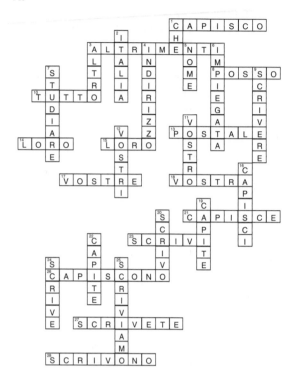

I. [Answers will vary.]

UNIT 13

A.
1. sa
2. parte
3. vicino
4. Vada
5. giri
6. passi

B.
1. Il mio treno parte tra qualche minuto.
2. La stazione ferroviaria è qui vicino.
3. La stazione è a due passi dopo il semaforo.
4. Vada diritto per due isolati.
5. Giri a sinistra al semaforo.
6. Mi sa dire dov'è la stazione ferroviaria?

C.
1. Mi sa dire dov'è la stazione ferroviaria? / La stazione ferroviaria è a due passi.
2. Mi sa dire dov'è l'isolato? / L'isolato è qui diritto.
3. Mi sa dire dov'è il vigile? / Il vigile è qui vicino.
4. Mi sa dire dov'è la vigilessa? / La vigilessa è a due isolati qui diritto.
5. Mi sa dire dov'è il turista / la turista? / Il turista / La turista è a destra.

D. [Instructions will vary.]

E.
1. Io parto domani per l'Italia.
2. Io finisco alle tre e mezzo.
3. Io dormo sempre fino a tardi.
4. Io do tutto a mio fratello.
5. Io faccio tutto in casa.
6. Io voglio andare in centro.
7. Tu parti domani per l'Italia.
8. Tu finisci alle tre e mezzo.
9. Tu dormi sempre fino a tardi.
10. Tu dai tutto a tuo fratello.
11. Tu fai tutto in casa.
12. Tu vuoi andare in centro.
13. Lei parte domani per l'Italia.
14. Lei finisce alle tre e mezzo.
15. Lei dorme sempre fino a tardi.
16. Lei dà tutto a Suo fratello.
17. Lei fa tutto in casa.
18. Lei vuole andare in centro.
19. Lui / Lei parte domani per l'Italia.
20. Lui / Lei finisce alle tre e mezzo.
21. Lui / Lei dorme sempre fino a tardi.
22. Lui / Lei dà tutto a suo fratello.
23. Lui / Lei fa tutto in casa.
24. Lui / Lei vuole andare in centro.
25. Noi partiamo domani per l'Italia.
26. Noi finiamo alle tre e mezzo.
27. Noi dormiamo sempre fino a tardi.
28. Noi diamo tutto a nostro fratello.
29. Noi facciamo tutto in casa.
30. Noi vogliamo andare in centro.
31. Voi partite domani per l'Italia.
32. Voi finite alle tre e mezzo.
33. Voi dormite sempre fino a tardi.
34. Voi date tutto a vostro fratello.
35. Voi fate tutto in casa.
36. Voi volete andare in centro.
37. Loro partono domani per l'Italia.
38. Loro finiscono alle tre e mezzo.
39. Loro dormono sempre fino a tardi.
40. Loro danno tutto al loro fratello.
41. Loro fanno tutto in casa.
42. Loro vogliono andare in centro.

F.

1. Dina, parla italiano!
2. Dina, scrivi alla professoressa Giusti!
3. Dina, dormi fino a mezzogiorno!
4. Dina, finisci il caffè!
5. Dina, va' (vai) in centro!
6. Dina, abbi pazienza!
7. Dina, da' (dai) tutto a tuo fratello!
8. Dina, di' (dici) sempre la verità!
9. Dina, sii sempre gentile!
10. Dina, fa' (fai) tutto in casa!
11. Dina, vieni alla festa!
12. Signora Martini, parli italiano!
13. Signora Martini, scriva alla professoressa Giusti!
14. Signora Martini, dorma fino a mezzogiorno!
15. Signora Martini, finisca il caffè!
16. Signora Martini, vada in centro!
17. Signora Martini, abbia pazienza!
18. Signora Martini, dia tutto al signor Martini!
19. Signora Martini, dica sempre la verità!
20. Signora Martini, sia sempre gentile!
21. Signora Martini, faccia tutto in casa!
22. Signora Martini, venga alla festa!
23. Alessandro e Sara, parlate italiano!
24. Alessandro e Sara, scrivete alla professoressa Giusti!
25. Alessandro e Sara, dormite fino a mezzogiorno!
26. Alessandro e Sara, finite il caffè!
27. Alessandro e Sara, andate in centro!
28. Alessandro e Sara, abbiate pazienza!
29. Alessandro e Sara, date tutto a vostra madre!
30. Alessandro e Sara, dite sempre la verità!
31. Alessandro e Sara, siate sempre gentili!
32. Alessandro e Sara, fate tutto in casa!
33. Alessandro e Sara, venite alla festa!
34. Signor e signora Martini, parlino italiano!
35. Signor e signora Martini, scrivano alla professoressa Giusti!
36. Signor e signora Martini, dormano fino a mezzogiorno!
37. Signor e signora Martini, finiscano il caffè!
38. Signor e signora Martini, vadano in centro!
39. Signor e signora Martini, abbiano pazienza!
40. Signor e signora Martini, diano tutto ai vostri (ai Loro) parenti!
41. Signor e signora Martini, dicano sempre la verità!
42. Signor e signora Martini, siano sempre gentili!
43. Signor e signora Martini, facciano tutto in casa!
44. Signor e signora Martini, vengano alla festa!
45. Parliamo italiano!
46. Scriviamo alla professoressa Giusti!
47. Dormiamo fino a mezzogiorno!
48. Finiamo il caffè!
49. Andiamo in centro!
50. Abbiamo pazienza!
51. Diamo tutto ai nostri amici!
52. Diciamo sempre la verità!
53. Siamo sempre gentili!
54. Facciamo tutto in casa!
55. Veniamo alla festa!

G.

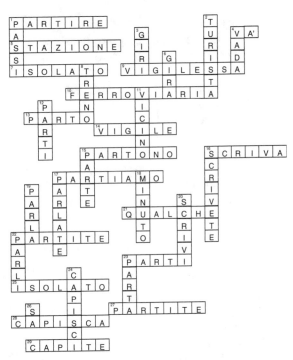

H. [Answers will vary.]

UNIT 14

A.

1. Claudio chiama Carla.
2. Carla è in centro.
3. Carla fa delle spese.
4. Torna a casa fra un'ora.
5. Claudio ha bisogno del pane, dell'olio, dello zucchero, degli spaghetti e della carne.
6. Perché stasera Claudio fa da mangiare.
7. Fra una settimana c'è il compleanno della mamma.

8. Secondo Claudio è più facile comprare gli orecchini.

B.

1. Sono io!
2. Faccio delle spese in centro.
3. Torno tra / fra un'ora.
4. Ho bisogno del pane.
5. Claudio ha bisogno dell'olio.
6. Carla e Claudio hanno bisogno dello zucchero.
7. Ho bisogno degli spaghetti.
8. I miei genitori hanno bisogno della carne.
9. Stasera faccio io da mangiare.
10. Tra /fra una settimana è il mio compleanno.
11. Voglio comprare dei pantaloni.
12. Mio fratello vuole comprare delle scarpe.
13. Mia sorella vuole comprare degli orecchini.
14. Non importa!
15. Forse è più facile comprare gli orecchini.
16. Chi parla?
17. Carla, dove sei?
18. Claudio, che fai?
19. Sara, quando torni a casa?
20. Carla, puoi comprare qualcosa per me?
21. Claudio, che (cosa) vuoi?
22. Claudio, che (cosa) devo comprare?
23. Carla, compra qualcosa per la mamma.
24. Carla, fa' da mangiare stasera.

C.

1. Voglio dell'olio.
2. Voglio degli orecchini.
3. Voglio del pane.
4. Voglio dei pantaloni.
5. Voglio delle scarpe.
6. Voglio degli spaghetti.
7. Voglio dello zucchero.

D.

1. Il mio compleanno è tra un mese.
2. L'italiano è facile.
3. Faccio sempre io la spesa nella mia famiglia.
4. Faccio sempre delle spese in centro.
5. Ho bisogno di qualcosa stasera.
6. Torno a casa tra / fra qualche minuto.

E. [Answers will vary.]

F. [List will vary.]

G.

1. Dov'è sua sorella?
2. Dov'è suo fratello?
3. Dov'è il suo amico?
4. Dov'è la sua amica?
5. Dov'è il suo amico?
6. Dov'è la sua amica?
7. Dov'è il suo zio alto?
8. Dov'è il suo zio alto?
9. Dov'è la sua scarpa?
10. Dov'è la sua scarpa
11. Dov'è il suo numero?
12. Dov'è il suo numero?
13. Dov'è il Suo amico?
14. Dov'è la Sua amica?
15. Dov'è Suo cugino?
16. Dove sono le sue sorelle?
17. Dove sono i suoi fratelli?
18. Dove sono i suoi amici?
19. Dove sono le sue amiche?
20. Dove sono i suoi amici?
21. Dove sono le sue amiche?
22. Dove sono i suoi zii?
23. Dove sono i suoi zii?
24. Dove sono le sue scarpe?
25. Dove sono le sue scarpe
26. Dove sono i suoi numeri?
27. Dove sono i suoi numeri?
28. Dove sono i Suoi amici?
29. Dove sono le Sue amiche?
30. Dove sono i Suoi cugini?

H.

1. Dina, vuoi dell'olio?
2. Dina, vuoi del pane?
3. Dina, vuoi degli spaghetti?
4. Dina, vuoi dei cellulari?
5. Dina, vuoi delle scarpe?
6. Dina, vuoi dei pantaloni?
7. Dina, vuoi della carne?
8. Dina, vuoi degli euro?
9. Dina, vuoi degli orecchini?

I.

1. Voglio andare in Italia, ma non posso quest'anno.
2. Tu vuoi andare a fare delle spese, ma non puoi.
3. Lui vuole mangiare la carne, ma non può.
4. Lei vuole mangiare gli spaghetti, ma non può.
5. Noi possiamo mangiare solo la carne.
6. Voi potete mangiare la carne, vero?
7. I miei genitori non possono mangiare la carne.

J.

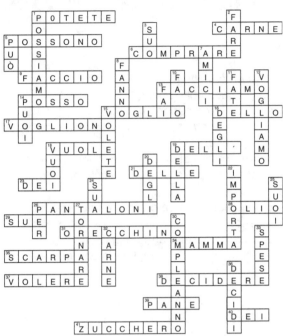

K.
1. president of the republic
2. prime minister
3. minister of foreign affairs
4. minister of education

UNIT 15

A.
1. e
2. a
3. b
4. g
5. f
6. c
7. d

B.
1. Mi piace la casa nuova di Carla.
2. La casa ha un salotto grande.
3. La cucina è bella.
4. La casa ha delle belle finestre e delle belle porte.
5. La nostra (La mia) casa nuova ha delle camere molto spaziose.
6. Abbiamo (Ho) bisogno di mobilia e di elettrodomestici.
7. Abbiamo (Ho) bisogno specialmente di un tavolo per adesso.
8. Vogliamo (Voglio) comprare un divano nuovo e un televisore nuovo.
9. Abbiamo (Ho) bisogno delle sedie e di un frigorifero nuovo.
10. Alessandro, ti piace la mia casa nuova?
11. Alessandro, sai dove andare per comprare tutto?
12. Alessandro, vuoi comprare una casa nuova?

C.
1. Allora, ti piacciono quelle camere? / Sì, mi piacciono.
2. Allora, ti piace la cucina nuova? / Sì, mi piace.
3. Allora, ti piacciono le porte nuove? / Sì, mi piacciono.
4. Allora, ti piace questo tavolo? / Sì, mi piace.
5. Allora, ti piacciono quelle sedie? / Sì, mi piacciono.
6. Allora, ti piace quel salotto spazioso? / Sì, mi piace.
7. Allora, ti piace la mobilia nuova? / Sì, mi piace.
8. Allora, ti piace quel divano? / Sì, mi piace.
9. Allora, ti piace il nostro frigorifero nuovo? / Sì, mi piace.
10. Allora, ti piacciono le poltrone? Sì, mi piacciono.

D. [Answers will vary.]

E. [Commercial will vary.]

F.
1. Ti piace la nostra bella casa? / Certo che mi piace.
2. Ti piacciono le nostre belle poltrone? / Certo che mi piacciono.
3. Ti piace il nostro bell'elettrodomestico? / Certo che mi piace.
4. Ti piace la nostra bell'amica? /Certo che mi piace.
5. Ti piacciono i nostri begli elettrodomestici / Certo che mi piacciono.
6. Ti piacciono le nostre belle amiche? / Certo che mi piacciono.
7. Ti piace il nostro bello zio? / Certo che mi piace.
8. Ti piacciono i nostri begli zii? / Certo che mi piacciono.
9. Ti piace il nostro bel televisore? / Certo che mi piace.

10. Ti piacciono i nostri bei tavoli? / Certo che mi piacciono.

G.
1. Mi piacciono quelle case spaziose.
2. Mi piace il suo tavolo nuovo / nuovo tavolo.
3. Mi piacciono le sue sedie nuove / nuove sedie.
4. Mi piace la tua poltrona nuova / nuova poltrona.
5. Mi piacciono i loro elettrodomestici nuovi / nuovi elettrodomestici.
6. Mi piace quella camera spaziosa.
7. Mi piace quell'uomo umile.
8. Mi piacciono quegli uomini umili.
9. Mi piace quella donna gentile.
10. Mi piacciono quelle donne gentili.
11. Mi piacciono le sue scarpe grandi.
12. Mi piacciono i suoi pantaloni grandi.

H.

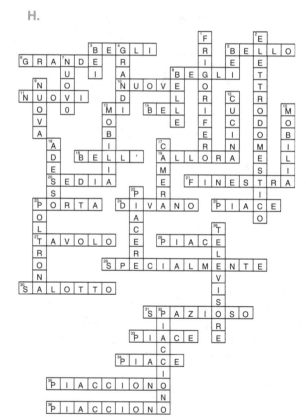

I. [Answers will vary.]

A.
1. Scusi!
2. (Lei) è molto gentile.
3. (Tu) sei molto umile.
4. (Loro) non parlano italiano.
5. L'impiegata dice che (lei) capisce e scrive l'inglese.
6. I tuoi amici dicono che vengono alla festa.
7. Vostro fratello conosce i vostri amici molto bene.
8. Alessandro dorme sempre fino a tardi il sabato.
9. (Loro) vogliono andare in Italia.
10. (Noi) vogliamo mangiare la carne, ma non possiamo.

B.
1. Purtroppo io e il mio amico / la mia amica non parliamo italiano.
2. Per via Garibaldi, Lei deve andare a destra e poi a sinistra.
3. I miei amici sono al semaforo.
4. (Io) capisco, parlo e scrivo l'italiano molto bene.
5. Sono cinque anni che studio l'italiano.
6. (Io) ho bisogno del pane, dell'olio, dello zucchero, degli spaghetti e della carne.
7. (Io) voglio comprare dei pantaloni, delle scarpe e degli orecchini.
8. Domani (io) vado in centro a fare delle spese.
9. (Io) voglio dello zucchero.
10. Mi piace la loro casa nuova / nuova casa.
11. La casa ha un salotto grande e una bella cucina.
12. Ho / Abbiamo un frigorifero nuovo / un nuovo frigorifero e un bel televisore / un televisore bello.
13. Sara, va' diritto per un isolato!
14. Sara, gira a destra al semaforo!
15. Sara, studia l'italiano!
16. Sara, finisci alle cinque e un quarto!
17. Sara, compra gli orecchini!
18. Signora Martini, vada diritto per un isolato!
19. Signora Martini, giri a destra al semaforo!
20. Signora Martini, studi l'inglese!
21. Signora Martini, finisca alle cinque e un quarto!
22. Mi sa dire dov'è la stazione ferroviaria?
23. Signor Martini, (Lei) parla italiano?
24. Chi parla italiano molto bene?

25. Mark e Paul, avete un indirizzo postale qui in Italia?
26. Professoressa Giusti, mi può aiutare a trovare via Nazionale?
27. Alessandro, che (cosa) vuoi?
28. Sara, che (cosa) devo comprare?
29. Dina, ti piacciono le sedie nuove / nuove sedie?
30. Carla, ti piace il salotto spazioso?

C. [Answers will vary.]

D. [Lists will vary.]

E.

V	E	R	A	M	E	N	T	E	X	X	X	D	I	R	E	C	A	D	S
C	A	D	D	A	C	A	A	C	A	D	D	A	C	A	A	X	X	X	A
S	T	U	D	I	O	D	S	E	M	A	F	O	R	O	C	D	X	A	D
C	A	D	D	A	C	A	A	C	A	D	D	A	C	A	A	X	X	X	E
S	T	A	Z	I	O	N	E	S	D	I	R	I	T	T	O	S	S	S	S
V	V	B	N	M	J	K	L	L	C	V	C	A	D	D	A	C	A	A	S
X	M	B	N	M	J	K	L	L	C	P	C	A	D	D	A	C	A	A	A
C	P	B	N	M	J	K	L	L	C	I	C	A	D	D	A	C	A	A	A
S	I	B	N	M	J	K	L	L	C	A	C	A	D	D	A	C	A	A	G
N	A	B	N	M	J	K	L	L	C	C	C	D	F	G	H	J	K	J	R
B	C	P	P	P	X	X	X	S	S	C	B	N	M	K	L	K	L	Y	A
V	E	A	S	D	F	C	A	D	D	I	A	C	C	B	B	B	C	C	N
X	X	X	C	C	C	A	D	D	D	O	A	A	A	A	I	X	X	X	D
L	K	J	H	G	F	P	D	S	A	N	Q	E	R	T	S	Y	U	I	E
Q	W	E	R	T	Y	I	U	I	O	O	P	L	K	J	O	H	G	F	V
P	A	R	L	A	N	S	M	L	C	A	D	C	S	L	G	M	C	D	S
A	V	B	N	Q	C	C	D	D	E	A	A	A	P	B	N	E	A	R	O
G	E	N	T	I	L	E	S	D	R	Q	T	R	E	P	O	J	S	K	N
Q	E	R	T	Y	U	I	U	Y	T	Z	C	V	S	C	A	D	A	A	O
D	E	S	T	R	A	A	A	M	O	G	L	I	E	A	S	D	F	G	H

UNIT 16

A.
1. Vero
2. Vero
3. Vero
4. Vero
5. Vero
6. Falso
7. Vero

B.
1. (Io) lavoro qui da due anni. / Sono due anni che lavoro qui.
2. (Io) ho cominciato il mese scorso.
3. Mi piace molto lavorare qui.
4. È la prima volta che lavoro per una ditta d'informatica.
5. (Io) ho conosciuto alcune persone al sesto piano la settimana scorsa.
6. (Io) non conosco ancora nessuno lì.

7. D'accordo! / Sono d'accordo!
8. Dina, quanto tempo è che lavori qui?
9. Claudio, ti piace lavorare qui?
10. Signor Marchi, (Lei) conosce la signora Di Nardo che lavora al decimo piano?
11. Dina, sei mai andata all'ottavo piano?
12. Alessandro e Claudio, andiamo a prendere un caffè a mezzogiorno? / volete venire a prendere un caffè con me a mezzogiorno?

C.
1. Ho lavorato al primo piano per due anni.
2. Ho lavorato al secondo piano per alcuni anni.
3. Ho lavorato al terzo piano per molti anni.
4. Ho lavorato al quarto piano per sei anni.
5. Ho lavorato al quinto piano per un anno.
6. Ho lavorato al sesto piano per otto anni.
7. Ho lavorato al settimo piano per troppi anni.
8. Ho lavorato all'ottavo piano per sette anni.
9. Ho lavorato al nono piano per tanti anni.
10. Ho lavorato al decimo piano per nove anni.
11. Ho conosciuto Marco Pisani la settimana scorsa.
12. Ho conosciuto Dina ieri.
13. Ho conosciuto suo fratello il mese scorso.
14. Ho conosciuto sua sorella l'anno scorso.
15. Ho conosciuto quella persona ieri.

D. [Answers will vary.]

E. [Descriptions will vary.]

F.
1. Sono tre mesi che Mark lavora al diciannovesimo piano.
2. Sono sei settimane che il signor Martini lavora al diciottesimo piano.
3. È un anno che la signora Di Nardo lavora al dodicesimo piano.
4. È molto tempo che Alessandro lavora al quindicesimo piano.
5. Sono alcuni anni che Sara lavora al ventunesimo piano.
6. l'undicesimo caffè
7. la tredicesima donna
8. il quattordicesimo uomo
9. il diciassettesimo giorno / la diciassettesima giornata
10. la trentaseiesima volta
11. il quarantottesimo minuto
12. il cinquantatreesimo numero

13. il sessantanovesimo giorno / la sessan-tanovesima giornata
14. la settantasettesima volta
15. l'ottantatreesimo piano
16. il novantaseiesimo compleanno
17. Tu mangi sempre gli spaghetti.
18. Tu cominci alle sette a lavorare.
19. Tu cerchi la sua casa.
20. Tu paghi domani.
21. Lei mangia sempre gli spaghetti.
22. Lei comincia alle sette a lavorare.
23. Lei cerca la sua casa.
24. Lei paga domani.
25. Noi mangiamo sempre gli spaghetti.
26. Noi cominciamo alle sette a lavorare.
27. Noi cerchiamo la sua casa.
28. Noi paghiamo domani.
29. Voi mangiate sempre gli spaghetti.
30. Voi cominciate alle sette a lavorare.
31. Voi cercate la sua casa.
32. Voi pagate domani.
33. Lui / Lei mangia sempre gli spaghetti.
34. Lui / Lei comincia alle sette a lavorare.
35. Lui / Lei cerca la sua casa.
36. Lui / Lei paga domani.
37. Loro mangiano sempre gli spaghetti.
38. Loro cominciano alle sette a lavorare.
39. Loro cercano la sua casa.
40. Loro pagano domani.

G.

1. Io ho già parlato al professore.
2. Io ho già mangiato gli spaghetti.
3. Io sono già andato / andata in Italia.
4. Io sono già tornato / tornata a casa.
5. Io sono arrivato / arrivata alle sei e mezzo.
6. Io ho già pagato tutto.
7. Io non ho trovato la sua casa.
8. Tu hai parlato al professore la settimana scorsa.
9. Tu hai mangiato gli spaghetti ieri.
10. Tu sei andato / andata in Italia l'anno scorso.
11. Tu sei tornato / tornata a casa alcuni minuti fa.
12. Tu sei arrivato / arrivata due minuti fa.
13. Tu hai pagato ieri.
14. Tu non hai trovato la sua casa.
15. Lui / Lei ha parlato al professore ieri.
16. Lui / Lei ha mangiato gli spaghetti ieri.
17. Lui / Lei è andato / andata in Italia tre anni fa.
18. Lui / Lei è tornato / tornata a casa alcuni minuti fa.

19. Lui / Lei è già arrivato / arrivata.
20. Lui / Lei ha pagato ieri tutto.
21. Lui / Lei non ha trovato la sua casa.
22. Noi abbiamo già parlato alla profes-soressa.
23. Noi abbiamo già mangiato gli spaghetti.
24. Noi siamo andati / andate in Italia l'anno scorso.
25. Noi siamo tornati / tornate a casa un'ora fa.
26. Noi siamo arrivati / arrivate ieri.
27. Noi abbiamo già pagato tutto.
28. Noi non abbiamo trovato la sua casa.
29. Voi avete parlato alla professoressa ieri.
30. Voi avete già mangiato gli spaghetti.
31. Voi siete già andati / andate in Italia.
32. Voi siete tornati / tornate a casa due minuti fa.
33. Voi siete arrivati / arrivate alcuni giorni fa.
34. Voi avete già pagato tutto.
35. Voi non avete trovato la sua casa.
36. Loro hanno già parlato alla signora Martini.
37. Loro hanno già mangiato la carne.
38. Loro sono andati / andate in Italia ieri.
39. Loro sono già tornati / tornate a casa.
40. Loro sono arrivati / arrivate alcuni minuti fa.
41. Loro hanno già pagato tutto.
42. Loro non hanno trovato la sua casa.

H.

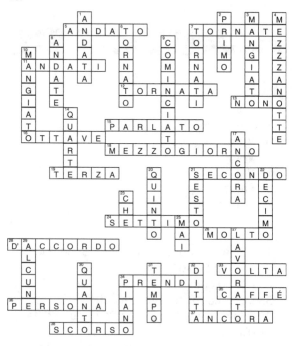

I.

1. Ho comprato software per il mio computer la settimana scorsa.
2. Ho comprato uno schermo e una tastiera per il mio computer il mese scorso.
3. Ho comprato una stampante per il mio computer l'anno scorso.
4. Ho comprato un CD-ROM e un DVD la settimana scorsa.

UNIT 17

A.

1. b
2. b
3. b
4. b
5. a
6. a
7. b
8. b

B.

1. Vorrei lavorare per questa ditta.
2. (Io) ho lavorato per una banca due anni fa.
3. La banca era troppo lontana da casa mia.
4. (io) ero un impiegato / un'impiegata di quella banca.
5. (Io) abito in via Boccaccio, numero settantadue.
6. Ho ventidue anni.
7. Claudio è sposato con tre figli.
8. Per adesso, ho finito.
9. Signora Di Nardo, La chiamo tra / fra qualche settimana / tra alcune settimane.
10. Dina, hai mai lavorato in un altro ufficio?
11. Signor Marchi, che (cosa) faceva nella banca?
12. Qual è il Suo indirizzo, signora Di Nardo?
13. Signorina Nardini, quanti anni ha?
14. Signor Marchi, qual è il Suo stato civile?

C.

1. Dove abita?
2. Qual è il Suo indirizzo?
3. Ha mai lavorato per un'altra ditta?
4. Che (cosa) faceva nella banca?
5. Qual è il Suo stato civile?

D. [Answers will vary.]

E. [Descriptions will vary.]

F.

1. Io ho voluto mangiare tutti gli spaghetti.
2. Io ho dormito tutta la giornata ieri.
3. Io ho conosciuto la professoressa alcune settimane fa.
4. Io ho già finito di studiare.
5. Io sono partito / partita per l'Italia ieri.
6. Tu hai voluto mangiare tutti gli spaghetti.
7. Tu hai dormito tutta la giornata ieri.
8. Tu hai conosciuto la professoressa alcune settimane fa.
9. Tu hai già finito di studiare.
10. Tu sei partito / partita per l'Italia ieri.
11. Lui / Lei ha voluto mangiare tutti gli spaghetti.
12. Lui / Lei ha dormito tutta la giornata ieri.
13. Lui / Lei ha conosciuto la professoressa alcune settimane fa.
14. Lui / Lei ha già finito di studiare.
15. Lui / Lei è partito / partita per l'Italia ieri.
16. Noi abbiamo voluto mangiare tutti gli spaghetti.
17. Noi abbiamo dormito tutta la giornata ieri.
18. Noi abbiamo conosciuto la professoressa alcune settimane fa.
19. Noi abbiamo già finito di studiare.
20. Noi siamo partiti / partite per l'Italia ieri.
21. Voi avete voluto mangiare tutti gli spaghetti.
22. Voi avete dormito tutta la giornata ieri.
23. Voi avete conosciuto la professoressa alcune settimane fa.
24. Voi avete già finito di studiare.
25. Voi siete partiti / partite per l'Italia ieri.
26. Loro hanno voluto mangiare tutti gli spaghetti.
27. Loro hanno dormito tutta la giornata ieri.
28. Loro hanno conosciuto la professoressa alcune settimane fa.
29. Loro hanno già finito di studiare.
30. Loro sono partiti / partite per l'Italia ieri.

G.

1. Che cosa ha dato alla professoressa?
2. Che cosa ha deciso di fare ieri?
3. Che cosa ha detto ieri?
4. Dove è stata ieri?
5. Che cosa ha fatto la settimana scorsa?
6. Che cosa ha perso ieri?
7. Che cosa ha preso?
8. A chi ha scritto ieri?
9. Chi ha visto ieri?
10. A che ora è venuto ieri?
11. Che cosa hanno dato alla professoressa?
12. Che cosa hanno deciso di fare ieri?
13. Che cosa hanno detto ieri?

14. Dove sono state ieri?
15. Che cosa hanno fatto la settimana scorsa?
16. Che cosa hanno perso ieri?
17. Che cosa hanno preso?
18. A chi hanno scritto ieri?
19. Chi hanno visto ieri?
20. A che ora sono venuti ieri?

H.

1. Io ero stanco / stanca ieri perché facevo troppo.
2. Tu eri stanco / stanca ieri perché facevi troppo.
3. Alessandro era stanco ieri perché faceva troppo.
4. Sara era stanca ieri perché faceva troppo.
5. Noi eravamo stanchi / stanche ieri perché facevamo troppo.
6. Voi eravate stanchi / stanche ieri perché facevate troppo.
7. I bambini erano stanchi ieri perché facevano troppo.

I.

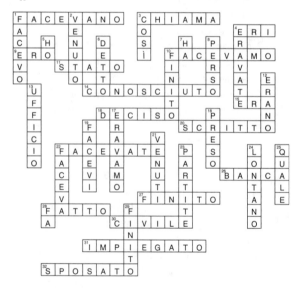

J. [Answers will vary.]

UNIT 18

A.

1. ho capito
2. Legga
3. deve
4. abbiamo studiato
5. consegni
6. era
7. devo
8. Sono

B.

1. Professore / Professoressa, non ho capito la lezione.
2. Signor Marchi, legga anche questo libro!
3. Signora Di Nardo, scriva le domande che ha sulla grammatica che ha studiato oggi!
4. Signora Di Nardo, le consegni domani dopo la lezione!
5. La lezione di oggi era difficile.
6. La lezione di oggi era molto importante.
7. Sono d'accordo!
8. Professore / Professoressa, che (cosa) devo fare?
9. Professore / Professoressa, che (cosa) devo leggere?

C.

1. Ieri ho consegnato i miei temi.
2. Ieri ho letto un libro.
3. Ieri ho mangiato della carne.
4. Ieri ho studiato la lezione.
5. Ieri ho letto un libro di grammatica.

D. [Answers will vary.]

E. [Descriptions will vary.]

F.

1. La professoressa Mirri è andata in centro ieri. / Professoressa Mirri, è vero che Lei è andata in centro ieri?
2. Il dottor Nardini è andato in centro ieri. / Dottor Nardini, è vero che Lei è andato in centro ieri?
3. Il signor Gardini è andato in centro ieri. / Signor Gardini, è vero che Lei è andato in centro ieri?
4. La signora Gardini è andata in centro ieri. / Signora Gardini, è vero che Lei è andata in centro ieri?
5. La dottoressa Giusti è andata in centro ieri. / Dottoressa Giusti, è vero che Lei è andata in centro ieri?

G.

1. la madre del ragazzo
2. la madre della ragazza
3. le scarpe dello zio
4. le scarpe dell'amica
5. la madre dei ragazzi
6. la madre delle ragazze
7. dal centro
8. dai tavoli
9. dallo zio
10. dagli zii
11. dalla ragazza

12. dalle amiche
13. al semaforo
14. agli insegnanti
15. allo zio
16. agli zii
17. ai ragazzi
18. alla ragazza
19. alle ragazze
20. nell'autobus
21. nella banca
22. nelle banche
23. nel treno
24. negli spaghetti
25. sugli spaghetti
26. sulla carne
27. sul pane
28. sui tavoli

H.

1. Io abitavo in centro da bambino / da bambina.
2. Io arrivavo spesso in ritardo mentre il professore faceva lezione.
3. Io mangiavo spesso gli spaghetti da giovane.
4. Io pagavo tutto da giovane.
5. Tu abitavi in centro da bambino / da bambina.
6. Tu arrivavi spesso in ritardo mentre il professore faceva lezione.
7. Tu mangiavi spesso gli spaghetti da giovane.
8. Tu pagavi tutto da giovane.
9. Lui / Lei abitava in centro da bambino / da bambina.
10. Lui / Lei arrivava spesso in ritardo mentre il professore faceva lezione.
11. Lui / Lei mangiava spesso gli spaghetti da giovane.
12. Lui / Lei pagava tutto da giovane.
13. Noi abitavamo in centro da bambini / da bambine.
14. Noi arrivavamo spesso in ritardo mentre il professore faceva lezione.
15. Noi mangiavamo spesso gli spaghetti da giovani.
16. Noi pagavamo tutto da giovani.
17. Voi abitavate in centro da bambini / da bambine.
18. Voi arrivavate spesso in ritardo mentre il professore faceva lezione.
19. Voi mangiavate spesso gli spaghetti da giovani.
20. Voi pagavate tutto da giovani.
21. Loro abitavano in centro da bambini / da bambine.
22. Loro arrivavano spesso in ritardo mentre il professore faceva lezione.
23. Loro mangiavano spesso gli spaghetti da giovani.
24. Loro pagavano tutto da giovani.

I.

1.
Io devo partire (*I have to leave*)
Io posso partire (*I can leave*)
Io voglio partire (*I want to leave*)

2.
Tu devi mangiare (*You have to eat*)
Tu puoi mangiare (*You can eat*)
Tu vuoi mangiare (*You want to eat*)

3.
Dina deve parlare italiano (*Dina has to speak Italian*)
Dina può parlare italiano (*Dina can speak Italian*)
Dina vuole parlare italiano (*Dina wants to speak Italian*)

4.
Noi dobbiamo comprare gli orecchini (*We have to buy the earrings*)
Noi possiamo comprare gli orecchini (*We can buy the earrings*)
Noi vogliamo comprare gli orecchini (*We want to buy the earrings*)

5.
Voi dovete lavorare (*You have to work*)
Voi potete lavorare (*You can work*)
Voi volete lavorare (*You want to work*)

6.
I ragazzi devono venire alla festa (*The boys have to come to the party*)
I ragazzi possono venire alla festa (*The boys can come to the party*)
I ragazzi vogliono venire alla festa (*The boys want to come to the party*)

7.
Io sono dovuto / dovuta partire (*I had to leave*)
Io sono potuto / potuta partire (*I was able to leave*)
Io sono voluto / voluta partire (*I wanted to leave*)

8.
Tu hai dovuto mangiare (*You had to eat*)
Tu hai potuto mangiare (*You were able to eat*)
Tu hai voluto mangiare (*You wanted to eat*)

9.

Dina ha dovuto parlare italiano *(Dina had to speak Italian)*

Dina ha potuto parlare italiano *(Dina was able to speak Italian)*

Dina ha voluto parlare italiano *(Dina wanted to speak Italian)*

10.

Noi abbiamo dovuto comprare gli orecchini *(We had to buy the earrings)*

Noi abbiamo potuto comprare gli orecchini *(We were able to buy the earrings)*

Noi abbiamo voluto comprare gli orecchini *(We wanted to buy the earrings)*

11.

Voi avete dovuto lavorare *(You had to work)*

Voi avete potuto lavorare *(You were able to work)*

Voi avete voluto lavorare *(You wanted to work)*

12.

I ragazzi sono dovuti venire alla festa *(The boys had to come to the party)*

I ragazzi sono potuti venire alla festa *(The boys were able to come to the party)*

I ragazzi sono voluti venire alla festa *(The boys wanted to come to the party)*

J.

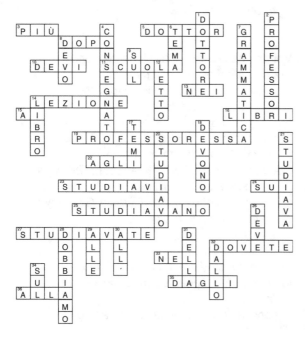

K.

1. un articolo
2. una preposizione
3. un avverbio
4. un verbo
5. un nome
6. un aggettivo

UNIT 19

A.

1. Il primo cliente vuole comprare una giacca, una camicia, una cravatta e forse anche un paio di pantaloni.
2. La seconda cliente vuole comprare una gonna, una camicetta e un vestito da sera.
3. Il primo cliente preferisce l'azzurro, il rosso, il verde, il nero e anche il bianco.
4. La seconda cliente preferisce l'arancione, il marrone, il giallo, il grigio, il rosa e il viola.
5. Il primo commesso scherza.
6. La seconda commessa prende le misure della cliente.

B.

1. Vorrei comprare una giacca nera.
2. Il mio amico / La mia amica ha bisogno di una camicia bianca.
3. Mio fratello ha bisogno di una cravatta e forse anche di un paio di pantaloni neri.
4. Non sono sicuro / sicura (di) che taglia porto.
5. Vorrei i pantaloni verdi e una cravatta rossa.
6. Mia sorella vuole un paio di pantaloni bianchi.
7. Mio fratello vuole una camicia azzurra.
8. Ci devo pensare!
9. Oggi tutto è in saldo.
10. Mia madre ha comprato una camicetta gialla la settimana scorsa.
11. Mia sorella ha comprato una camicetta marrone la settimana scorsa.
12. Mia madre ha comprato anche un vestito da sera rosa.
13. Mia sorella ha comprato anche una gonna viola e una camicetta grigia.
14. Non c'è problema.
15. Desidera?
16. Che taglia porta?
17. Che / Quale colore preferisce?
18. Lei scherza, vero?

19. Prendo le Sue misure, va bene?
20. Quali colori preferisce di solito?

C.

1. Sì, mi piacciono quelle camicie bianche.
2. Sì, mi piace quella camicetta arancione.
3. Sì, mi piacciono quelle cravatte marrone.
4. Sì, mi piace quella giacca gialla.
5. Sì, mi piace quel paio di pantaloni neri.
6. Sì, mi piacciono quelle paia di pantaloni rossi.
7. Sì, mi piace il vestito da sera verde.
8. Sì, mi piacciono le camicette rosa.
9. Sì, mi piacciono le scarpe viola.

D. [Answers will vary.]

E. [Descriptions will vary.]

F.

1. Quale giacca preferisce?
2. Quali pantaloni vuole?
3. Quali scarpe preferisce?
4. Quanta carne vuole?
5. Quanti spaghetti vuole?
6. Quante giacche vuole?
7. Che cosa è quello?
8. Chi è quella persona?
9. Come si chiama?
10. Quando ha comprato quel vestito?
11. Perché ha comprato quel vestito?
12. Dove ha comprato quel vestito?

G.

1. Io conoscevo Franco da bambino.
2. Io leggevo tanti libri da giovane.
3. Io avevo molti amici da giovane.
4. Tu conoscevi Franco da bambino.
5. Tu leggevi tanti libri da giovane.
6. Tu avevi molti amici da giovane.
7. Dina conosceva Franco da bambina.
8. Dina leggeva tanti libri da giovane.
9. Dina aveva molti amici da giovane.
10. Noi conoscevamo Franco da bambini.
11. Noi leggevamo tanti libri da giovani.
12. Noi avevamo molti amici da giovani.
13. Voi conoscevate Franco da bambini.
14. Voi leggevate tanti libri da giovani.
15. Voi avevate molti amici da giovani.
16. Le tue amiche conoscevano Franco da bambine.
17. Le tue amiche leggevano tanti libri da giovani.
18. Le tue amiche avevano molti amici da giovani.

H.

1. Mi piace quella camicia.
2. Ti piace quella camicia.
3. Gli piace quella camicia.
4. Le piace quella camicia.
5. Ci piace quella camicia.
6. Le piace quella camicia.
7. Vi piace quella camicia.
8. Gli piace quella camicia.
9. Quella camicia piace alla donna.
10. Quella camicia piace agli uomini.
11. Mi piacciono quei pantaloni.
12. Ti piacciono quei pantaloni.
13. Gli piacciono quei pantaloni.
14. Le piacciono quei pantaloni.
15. Ci piacciono quei pantaloni.
16. Le piacciono quei pantaloni.
17. Vi piacciono quei pantaloni.
18. Gli piacciono quei pantaloni.
19. Quei pantaloni piacciono alla donna.
20. Quei pantaloni piacciono agli uomini.

I.

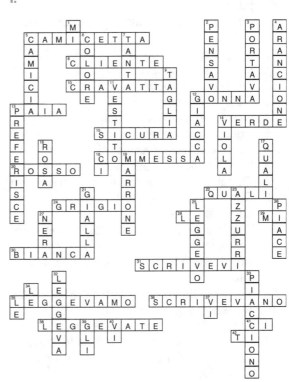

J.

1. il quarantotto / il quarantadue
2. il cinquantadue / il quarantotto
3. il trentasette
4. il trentotto
5. il quarantuno

UNIT 20

A.

1. e
2. a
3. b
4. c
5. d

B.

1. Vorrei un caffè lungo, per favore.
2. Vorrei un caffè ristretto, per favore.
3. Io amo il caffè molto.
4. Mi è sempre piaciuto.
5. Prendo una focaccia.
6. Dopo prendo anche un dolce.
7. Forse prendo un panino.
8. Oggi pago io.
9. Dina sei sempre così gentile.
10. Signorina, cosa desidera?
11. Dina, non hai appena finito di bere un cappuccino?
12. Dina, prendiamo qualcosa da mangiare?

C.

1. Io bevo il cappuccino.
2. Tu bevi il cappuccino.
3. Quel barista beve il cappuccino.
4. Quelle bariste bevono il cappuccino.
5. Noi beviamo il cappuccino.
6. Voi bevete il cappuccino.
7. Io ho bevuto il cappuccino anche ieri.
8. Tu hai bevuto il cappuccino anche ieri.
9. Quel barista ha bevuto il cappuccino anche ieri.
10. Quelle bariste hanno bevuto il cappuccino anche ieri.
11. Noi abbiamo bevuto il cappuccino anche ieri.
12. Voi avete bevuto il cappuccino anche ieri.
13. Alessandro bevi il caffè lungo!
14. Signora Martini, beva il caffè lungo!
15. Dina e Alessandro, bevete il caffè lungo!
16. Signora Martini e signor Giusti, bevano il caffè lungo!
17. Beviamo il caffè lungo!

D. [Answers will vary.]

E. [Descriptions will vary.]

F.

1. Io dormivo molto da bambino.
2. Io preferivo l'inverno da giovane.
3. Io davo spesso i miei euro alla famiglia.
4. Io dicevo sempre tutto alla mamma.
5. Io non bevevo mai il caffè.
6. Tu dormivi molto da bambino.
7. Tu preferivi l'inverno da giovane.
8. Tu davi spesso i tuoi euro alla famiglia.
9. Tu dicevi sempre tutto alla mamma.
10. Tu non bevevi mai il caffè.
11. Dina dormiva molto da bambina.
12. Dina preferiva l'inverno da giovane.
13. Dina dava spesso i suoi euro alla famiglia.
14. Dina diceva sempre tutto alla mamma.
15. Dina non beveva mai il caffè.
16. Noi dormivamo molto da bambini.
17. Noi preferivamo l'inverno da giovani.
18. Noi davamo spesso i nostri euro alla famiglia.
19. Noi dicevamo sempre tutto alla mamma.
20. Noi non bevevamo mai il caffè.
21. Voi dormivate molto da bambini.
22. Voi preferivate l'inverno da giovani.
23. Voi davate spesso i vostri euro alla famiglia.
24. Voi dicevate sempre tutto alla mamma.
25. Voi non bevevate mai il caffè.
26. Gli amici di Alessandro dormivano molto da bambini.
27. Gli amici di Alessandro preferivano l'inverno da giovani.
28. Gli amici di Alessandro davano spesso i loro euro alla famiglia.
29. Gli amici di Alessandro dicevano sempre tutto alla mamma.
30. Gli amici di Alessandro non bevevano mai il caffè.

G.

1. Mi è piaciuto il cappuccino. / Ma da giovane non mi piaceva.
2. Ti è piaciuto il cappuccino. / Ma da giovane non ti piaceva.
3. Le è piaciuto il cappuccino. / Ma da giovane non Le piaceva.
4. Gli è piaciuto il cappuccino. / Ma da giovane non gli piaceva.
5. Le è piaciuto il cappuccino. / Ma da giovane non le piaceva.
6. Ci è piaciuto il cappuccino. / Ma da giovani non ci piaceva.
7. Vi è piaciuto il cappuccino. / Ma da giovani non vi piaceva.
8. Gli è piaciuto il cappuccino. / Ma da giovani non gli piaceva.

9. Mi sono piaciute quelle città. / Ma da giovane non mi piacevano.
10. Ti sono piaciute quelle città. / Ma da giovane non ti piacevano.
11. Le sono piaciute quelle città. / Ma da giovane non Le piacevano.
12. Gli sono piaciute quelle città. / Ma da giovane non gli piacevano.
13. Le sono piaciute quelle città. / Ma da giovane non le piacevano.
14. Ci sono piaciute quelle città. / Ma da giovani non ci piacevano.
15. Vi sono piaciute quelle città. / Ma da giovani non vi piacevano.
16. Gli sono piaciute quelle città. / Ma da giovani non gli piacevano.

H.

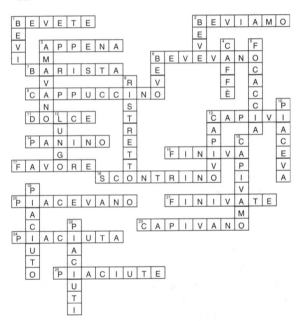

I.

1. Vorrei un caffellatte, per favore.
2. Vorrei un cappuccino, per favore.
3. Vorrei un caffè corretto, per favore.
4. Vorrei un caffè decaffeinato, per favore.
5. Vorrei un espresso doppio, per favore.
6. Vorrei un caffè lungo, per favore.
7. Vorrei un espresso macchiato, per favore.
8. Vorrei un caffè ristretto, per favore.

REVIEW PART 4

A.

1. Lavoro per una ditta d'informatica da alcuni anni. / Sono alcuni anni che lavoro per una ditta d'informatica.
2. Ho cominciato a lavorare l'anno scorso.
3. Non è la prima volta che lavoro per una ditta d'informatica.
4. Ho conosciuto alcune persone che lavorano lì alcune settimane fa.
5. Ho lavorato per quella banca alcuni anni fa.
6. Il mio amico/La mia amica abita in via Verdi, numero centoventitré.
7. Mio fratello è sposato con quattro bambini.
8. La lezione di oggi era difficile, ma era molto importante.
9. Vorrei comprare una nuova giacca e una camicia bianca.
10. Mio fratello ha comprato una bella cravatta nuova due settimane fa.
11. Oggi tutto è in saldo, ma non so che cosa comprare.
12. Mi piace il caffè ristretto/forte.
13. Mi piacciono solo le facacce.
14. Desidera? Che taglia porta?
15. Quali colori preferisce per il vestito da sera?
16. Professore/Professoressa, non ho capito le lezioni della settimana scorsa.
17. Signor Marchi, legga questo libro e scriva le domande che ha!
18. Signora Di Nardo, scriva le domande che ha sulla grammatica che ha studiato oggi!
19. Sara, quanto tempo è che lavori per quell ditta?/Sara, da quanto tempo lavori per quella ditta?
20. Signora Marchi, ha conosciuto il Signor Pasquali che lavora al sesto piano?
21. DIna, hai mai lavorato per un'altra ditta?
22. Sara, qual è il tuo indirizzo?
23. Alessandro, quanti anni hai?
24. Professore/Professoressa, che (cosa) devo fare per imparare la grammatica?
25. Che taglia porti?
26. Che colore preferisci?
27. Dina, vuoi/prendi un cappuccino?

B.

1. (Io) ho lavorato al decimo piano per sei anni.
2. Mio fratello ha conosciuto Dina due anni fa.
3. (Loro) hanno letto un libro sulla grammatica italiana ieri.
4. (Noi) non abbiamo consegnato il (nostro) tema al professore / alla professoressa.

C. [Answers will vary.]

D. [Lists will vary.]

E.

A	A	N	D	A	T	A	A	P	A	D	P	P	D	S	T	A	T	O	X
T	X	X	X	C	C	C	B	I	B	A	R	P	D	E	R	T	P	X	X
A	X	X	X	C	C	C	N	A	N	D	O	O	S	R	T	Y	L	X	X
G	X	X	X	C	C	F	M	C	M	A	F	I	A	T	Y	V	K	X	M
L	X	X	X	C	C	I	K	C	K	D	E	U	D	Y	U	O	J	L	A
I	Q	E	D	R	T	N	L	I	L	C	S	Y	E	Q	I	R	K	E	R
A	Q	E	D	R	T	I	M	O	G	C	S	T	S	Q	P	R	L	G	C
Q	W	E	R	T	Y	T	V	N	H	C	O	R	I	A	L	E	G	G	A
N	E	S	S	U	N	O	B	O	S	A	R	A	D	D	Q	I	M	E	M
S	D	F	G	H	J	K	K	M	G	N	B	V	E	C	P	G	N	V	N
S	D	F	G	H	J	K	L	M	E	N	B	V	R	Q	I	L	P	O	I
C	A	P	I	T	O	M	N	J	N	J	K	L	A	V	A	Q	E	D	S
Q	E	D	X	X	X	A	A	C	T	C	B	V	N	T	C	Q	E	D	P
Q	E	D	X	X	X	A	A	C	I	C	B	V	N	T	E	Q	E	D	I
Q	E	D	X	X	X	A	A	C	L	C	B	V	N	T	V	R	E	D	A
Q	E	D	X	X	X	A	A	C	E	C	B	V	N	T	A	R	E	D	C
A	N	N	I	A	D	C	B	N	L	C	B	V	N	T	N	R	E	D	I
Q	E	D	X	X	X	A	A	B	I	T	O	X	X	X	O	R	E	D	U
Q	E	D	X	X	X	A	A	C	D	C	B	V	N	T	D	Q	E	D	T
P	I	A	C	E	Q	L	A	V	O	R	A	T	O	Q	P	I	A	N	O

UNIT 21

A.

1. Vero
2. Falso
3. Vero
4. Vero
5. Vero
6. Vero
7. Vero
8. Falso

B.

1. b
2. b
3. b
4. b
5. a
6. b
7. b
8. a
9. a
10. a
11. b
12. a
13. a
14. b

C. [Answers will vary.]

D.

1. Cerco un romanzo, un giornale o anche una rivista.
2. Ne abbiamo molti.
3. Mi piace quello di fantascienza in vetrina.
4. Desidera altro?
5. Abbiamo solo questi due / queste due.
6. Va bene, li / le prendo.
7. Penso di sì.
8. Ecco il giornale!
9. Mi serve un paio di stivali neri.
10. Questi Le / ti stanno bene.

E. [Lists will vary.]

F.

1. parlando
2. mangiando
3. prendendo
4. scrivendo
5. capendo
6. preferendo
7. dando
8. stando
9. venendo
10. essendo
11. Quella camicia ti sta bene.
12. Quella camicia ti stava bene, ma non più.
13. Dina, sta' (stai) zitta!
14. Signora Martini, stia zitta!
15. Carla e Claudio state zitti!
16. Signore e signori, stiano zitti!
17. Siamo stati in Italia!
18. Anche loro sono stati in Italia!
19. Stiamo zitti!
20. Bill, sei stato mai in Italia?

G.

1. (Io) sto leggendo.
2. (Noi) stiamo bevendo un caffè.
3. (Loro) stanno dormendo.
4. Alessandro sta dormendo.
5. Sara sta andando in centro con un'amica.
6. I miei genitori stanno bevendo il caffè.
7. (Noi) stiamo parlando.
8. Mark sta dicendo tutto al professore.
9. Carla sta dicendo qualcosa a sua cugina.
10. (Io) sto leggendo un bel libro.

H.

1. La camicia sta bene a Marco.
2. La camicia sta bene a quell'uomo là.
3. La camicia ti sta bene.
4. La camicia / camicetta sta bene al tuo amico / alla tua amica.
5. La camicia sta bene a quei ragazzi.
6. La camicia gli sta bene.
7. La camicia / camicetta Le sta bene.
8. La camicia /camicetta mi sta bene.
9. Gli stivali vi stanno bene.
10. Gli stivali stanno bene a quella donna là.
11. Gli stivali ci stanno bene.
12. Gli stivali le stanno bene.

I.

1. Ti servono dei libri / Ti servono alcuni libri / Ti serve qualche libro.
2. Gli servono degli stivali / Gli servono alcuni stivali / Gli serve qualche stivale.
3. Le servono delle scarpe / Le servono alcune scarpe / Le serve qualche scarpa.
4. Ci servono delle camicie / Ci servono alcune camicie / Ci serve qualche camicia.
5. Vi servono delle fotografie / Vi servono alcune fotografie / Vi serve qualche fotografia.
6. Mi servono dei tavoli / Mi servono alcuni tavoli / Mi serve qualche tavolo.
7. Ti servono degli orecchini / Ti servono alcuni orecchini / Ti serve qualche orecchino.
8. Gli servono delle sedie / Gli servono alcune sedie / Gli serve qualche sedia.
9. Gli servono delle poltrone / Gli servono alcune poltrone / Gli serve qualche poltrona.

J.

1. No, ne ho mangiata troppa.
2. No, ne ho mangiati troppi
3. No, ne ho mangiato troppo.
4. No, ne ho mangiate troppe.
5. No, ne ho mangiati troppi

K.

1. Telefono a quella stasera.
2. Ieri ho parlato a quelli.
3. Anche la settimana scorsa hai mangiato queste.
4. Hai visto quello ieri.
5. Hai visto quella la settimana scorsa.
6. Non ho mai mangiati quelli.
7. Tutti hanno letto questi.
8. Domani vado a quella.

L.

M.

1. Dante è considerato il padre della lingua italiana.
2. La *Divina Commedia* è considerata l'opera che stabilisce la lingua toscana come la lingua letteraria di tutti gli italiani.
3. A Dante va il merito di aver dato al volgare italiano la dignità di lingua d'arte.
4. È stata completata nel 1321.
5. L'Inferno significa *Hell*, il Purgatorio significa *Purgatory* e il Paradiso significa *Paradise*.
6. Virgilio accompagna Dante nell'Inferno.
7. Beatrice accompagna Dante in Paradiso.

UNIT 22

A.

1. a
2. a
3. b
4. b
5. a
6. b

B.
1. Vorrei depositare un assegno nel mio conto.
2. Mia madre aprì un conto molti anni fa.
3. Vorrei riscuotere un altro assegno.
4. Vorrei (dei) biglietti di taglio grosso, non piccolo.
5. Non ho degli spiccioli.
6. Vorrei prelevare un po' di soldi da un altro conto.
7. Ecco tutto fatto!
8. Mi deve dare il Suo libretto.
9. Lei deve compilare questo modulo.
10. Lei ha un conto in questa banca?

C. [Answers of partner will vary.]
1. Signora Martini, quando ha aperto un conto?
2. Signor Nardini, quando ha riscosso quell'assegno?
3. Dottor Marchi, quando ha compilato quel modulo?
4. Dottoressa Di Nardo, quando ha riscosso i soldi in contanti?
5. Dina, quando hai depositato i soldi?
6. Dina, quando hai perso il tuo libretto?
7. Alessandro, quando hai prelevato i soldi?
8. Signora Martini, quando ha compilato il modulo di versamento?

D. [Answers will vary.]

E. [Lists will vary.]

F.
1. Buon viaggio!
2. Buona notte!
3. Buona serata!
4. Buone vacanze!
5. Buon divertimento!
6. Buona scelta!
7. Buon anno!
8. Buon'annata!

G.
1. Dina mi chiama ogni giorno.
2. Dina ti chiama ogni giorno.
3. Dina La chiama ogni giorno.
4. Dina ci chiama ogni giorno.
5. Dina vi chiama ogni giorno.
6. Dina le chiama ogni giorno.
7. Dina li chiama ogni giorno.

H.
1. Vuoi la camicia? / No, non la voglio perché l'ho comprata già.
2. Vuoi il cellulare? / No, non lo voglio perché l'ho comprato già.
3. Vuoi le cravatte? / No, non le voglio perché le ho comprate già.
4. Vuoi i dolci? / No, non li voglio perché li ho comprati già.
5. Vuoi gli elettrodomestici? / No, non li voglio perché li ho comprati già.
6. Vuoi quella giacca? / No, non la voglio perché l'ho comprata già.
7. Vuoi quelle gonne? / No, non le voglio perché le ho comprate già.
8. Vuoi quei libri? / No, non li voglio perché li ho comprati già.
9. Vuoi quegli orecchini? / No, non li voglio perché li ho comprati già.
10. Vuoi quelle scarpe? / No, non le voglio perché le ho comprate già.

I.
1. Io andai in Italia molto tempo fa.
2. Io dovei / dovetti lavorare molti anni fa.
3. Io partii per gli Stati Uniti nel 1996.
4. Io conobbi Dina nel 1995.
5. Io ebbi una casa in quella città molto tempo fa.
6. Io decisi di traslocare a un'altra città molto tempo fa.
7. Io presi una vacanza nel 1990.
8. Io venni negli Stati Uniti nel 1999.
9. Tu andasti in Italia molto tempo fa.
10. Tu dovesti lavorare molti anni fa.
11. Tu partisti per gli Stati Uniti nel 1996.
12. Tu conoscesti Dina nel 1995.
13. Tu avesti una casa in quella città molto tempo fa.
14. Tu decidesti di traslocare a un'altra città molto tempo fa.
15. Tu prendesti una vacanza nel 1990.
16. Tu venisti negli Stati Uniti nel 1999.
17. Lui / Lei andò in Italia molto tempo fa.
18. Lui / Lei dové / dovette lavorare molti anni fa.
19. Lui / Lei partì per gli Stati Uniti nel 1996.
20. Lui / Lei conobbe Dina nel 1995.

21. Lui / Lei ebbe una casa in quella città molto tempo fa.
22. Lui / Lei decise di traslocare a un'altra città molto tempo fa.
23. Lui / Lei prese una vacanza nel 1990.
24. Lui / Lei venne negli Stati Uniti nel 1999.
25. Noi andammo in Italia molto tempo fa.
26. Noi dovemmo lavorare molti anni fa.
27. Noi partimmo per gli Stati Uniti nel 1996.
28. Noi conoscemmo Dina nel 1995.
29. Noi avemmo una casa in quella città molto tempo fa.
30. Noi decidemmo di traslocare a un'altra città molto tempo fa.
31. Noi prendemmo una vacanza nel 1990.
32. Noi venimmo negli Stati Uniti nel 1999.
33. Voi andaste in Italia molto tempo fa.
34. Voi doveste lavorare molti anni fa.
35. Voi partiste per gli Stati Uniti nel 1996.
36. Voi conosceste Dina nel 1995.
37. Voi aveste una casa in quella città molto tempo fa.
38. Voi decideste di traslocare a un'altra città molto tempo fa.
39. Voi prendeste una vacanza nel 1990.
40. Voi veniste negli Stati Uniti nel 1999.
41. Loro andarono in Italia molto tempo fa.
42. Loro doverono / dovettero lavorare molti anni fa.
43. Loro partirono per gli Stati Uniti nel 1996.
44. Loro conobbero Dina nel 1995.
45. Loro ebbero una casa in quella città molto tempo fa.
46. Loro decisero di traslocare a un'altra città molto tempo fa.
47. Loro presero una vacanza nel 1990.
48. Loro vennero negli Stati Uniti nel 1999.

J.
1. scrisse
2. vollero
3. riscossi
4. bevemmo
5. deste
6. disse
7. fu / stette
8. fece
9. fummo / stemmo

K.

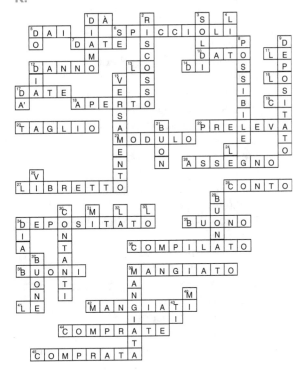

L.
1. Gioacchino Rossini / 1829
2. Giacomo Puccini / 1904
3. Giacomo Puccini / 1896
4. Giuseppe Verdi / 1871
5. Giuseppe Verdi / 1853
6. Vincenzo Bellini / 1831
7. Vincenzo Bellini / 1831
8. Gioacchino Rossini / 1816
9. Gaetano Donizetti / 1832
10. Gaetano Donizetti / 1835

UNIT 23

A.
1. bel
2. mancia
3. un po' di frutta e di caffè
4. un po' di formaggio
5. il conto
6. fame e sete
7. il melone e prosciutto
8. alla fiorentina
9. una bottiglia di acqua minerale

B.

1. (Io) ho fame e sete.
2. Per me / Vorrei l'antipasto di melone e prosciutto.
3. Per il primo piatto, vorrei / per me un piatto di pasta.
4. Generalmente mi piacciono gli spaghetti per secondo (piatto).
5. Oggi prendo una bistecca alla fiorentina per secondo (piatto).
6. I miei genitori prendono una bottiglia di vino.
7. Noi (Io e il mio amico / la mia amica) siamo troppo giovani.
8. Prendo / Per me una bottiglia di acqua minerale.
9. Noi (Io e il mio amico / la mia amica) prendiamo un po' di frutta.
10. Vorrei / Per me anche un po' di formaggio.
11. Chiederò il conto.
12. Non è sempre necessario lasciare una mancia in Italia.
13. Mio padre chiese a mia madre di venire negli Stati Uniti molti / tanti anni fa.
14. (Io) chiesi a mia madre perché venimmo / siamo venuti negli Stati Uniti molto / tanto tempo fa.
15. Alessandro, non dimenticare di lasciare una bella mancia!
16. Cameriere, il menù per favore!
17. Dina, hai fame e sete anche tu?
18. Alessandro, vuoi un po' di minestra per primo (per il primo piatto)?
19. Dina, vuoi qualcosa da bere?
20. Signora Martini, Le piace il formaggio?

C.

1. Che bel ristorante!
2. Che bella bistecca!
3. Che bel vestito!
4. Che bei pantaloni!
5. Che bei libri!
6. Che bella città!
7. Che bel tempo!
8. Buon appetito!
9. Che bei menù!
10. Voglio / Per me una bistecca alla fiorentina.

D.

1. Vorrei una bottiglia di acqua minerale.
2. Vorrei una bistecca.
3. Vorrei un l'antipasto di prosciutto e melone.
4. Vorrei un espresso.
5. Vorrei del formaggio / un po' di formaggio.
6. Vorrei della frutta / un po' di frutta.
7. Vorrei un piatto di minestra.
8. Vorrei un piatto di pasta.

E. [Answers will vary.]

F. [Compositions will vary.]

G.

1. Dina, vieni con me!
2. Dina, non mangiare la pasta senza (di) lui!
3. Dina, parla a noi, non a loro!
4. Dina, va' con loro al ristorante!
5. Dina, non dire che io non vengo mai con te!
6. Signora Marchi, mangi molta minestra!
7. Signora Marchi, non mangi troppi dolci!
8. Signora Marchi, beva tanta acqua minerale!
9. Signora Marchi, non parli a lui e non chiami lei!
10. Mark e Paul, mangiate quel panino al prosciutto!
11. Mark e Paul, non mangiate quel dolce al formaggio!
12. Mark e Paul, mangiate quella bistecca alla fiorentina!

H.

1. Non andiamo in centro!
2. Non andare in centro!
3. Non beva l'acqua!
4. Non bere l'acqua!
5. Non dire tutto a loro!
6. Non dica tutto a loro!

I.

1. Dina ha molta sete. / Alessandro, invece, ha poca sete.
2. Dina ha molti amici. / Alessandro, invece, ha pochi amici.
3. Dina ha molto sonno. / Alessandro, invece, ha poco sonno.
4. Dina ha molti soldi. / Alessandro, invece, ha pochi soldi.

J.

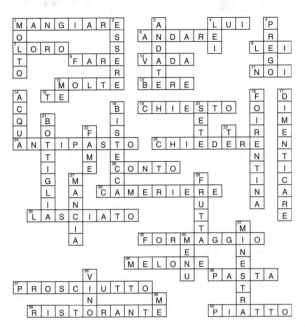

K. [Answers will vary.]

UNIT 24

A.

1. Alessandro chiede a Dina di uscire.
2. Alessandro pagherà tutto.
3. Secondo Dina, Alessandro è sempre ironico.
4. Prima Alessandro vuole andare a una conferenza all'università.
5. Dopo Alessandro vuole andare a ballare o al cinema.
6. Dina preferirebbe andare a un concerto o a un locale notturno.
7. Alessandro telefonerà a Dina verso le venti.

B.

1. Sono io.
2. Pago tutto io!
3. C'è una conferenza all'università.
4. Dopo possiamo andare a ballare.
5. (Io) preferirei andare al cinema.
6. O preferirei andare a un concerto o a un locale notturno.
7. Ti telefono più tardi.

8. Ti telefono verso le diciassette.
9. Aspetto la tua telefonata.
10. Dina, vuoi uscire?
11. Alessandro, perché sei sempre così ironico?
12. Alessandro, dove andiamo?
13. Dina, che (che cosa) ne pensi?
14. Dina, a che ora vuoi uscire?

C.

1. Io esco con loro stasera. / Io sono uscito / uscita con loro anche ieri sera.
2. Tu esci con lei stasera. / Tu sei uscito / uscita con lei anche ieri sera.
3. Lui esce con noi stasera. / Lui è uscito con noi anche ieri sera.
4. Noi usciamo con loro stasera. / Noi siamo usciti / uscite con loro anche ieri sera.
5. Voi uscite con lui stasera. / Voi siete usciti / uscite con lui anche ieri sera.
6. Loro escono con noi stasera. / Loro sono usciti / uscite con noi anche ieri sera.

D.

1. Alessandro, esci con me al cinema!
2. Signor Martini, esca con me al cinema!
3. Mark e Paul, uscite con me al cinema!
4. Signor e signora Martini, escano con me al cinema!

E. [Answers will vary.]

F. [Compositions will vary.]

G.

1. Dina mi telefona spesso. / Dina mi ha telefonato anche ieri.
2. Dina ti telefona spesso. / Dina ti ha telefonato anche ieri.
3. Dina Le telefona spesso. / Dina Le ha telefonato anche ieri.
4. Dina ci telefona spesso. / Dina ci ha telefonato anche ieri.
5. Dina vi telefona spesso. / Dina vi ha telefonato anche ieri.
6. Dina gli telefona spesso. / Dina gli ha telefonato anche ieri.
7. Dina gli telefona spesso. / Dina gli ha telefonato anche ieri.
8. Dina mi aspetta spesso. / Dina mi ha aspettato anche ieri.
9. Dina ti aspetta spesso. / Dina ti ha aspettato anche ieri.

10. Dina Le aspetta spesso. / Dina Le ha aspettato (aspettata) anche ieri.
11. Dina ci aspetta spesso. / Dina ci ha aspettato anche ieri.
12. Dina vi aspetta spesso. / Dina vi ha aspettato anche ieri.
13. Dina li aspetta spesso. / Dina li ha aspettati anche ieri.
14. Dina le aspetta spesso. / Dina le ha aspettate anche ieri.

H.
1. Chi ha pagato quei conti? Li ha pagati Alessandro.
2. Chi ha cercato Dina? Loro l'hanno cercata.
3. Loro hanno detto tutto a me, non a lei.
4. A chi hai / ha dato il menù? Lo hai / ha dato a lui o a lei?
5. Ho visto quei due film. Li ho visti / veduti ieri.

I.

J.
1. La letteratura italiana traccia le sue radici all'inizio del Duecento.
2. Promuove molti movimenti che hanno avuto grande impatto sulle altre letterature nazionali.
3. L'italiano diventò una lingua ufficiale nel 1870.
4. Dante scrisse la *Divina Commedia*.
5. Petrarca scrisse il *Canzoniere*, una collezione di 366 poesie che trattano dell'amore di Petrarca per una donna chiamata Laura.
6. Boccaccio scrisse il *Decamerone*, una collezione di cento novelle che trattano della vita quotidiana medievale dal punto di vista psicologico.

A.
1. j
2. i
3. h
4. g
5. f
6. e
7. d
8. c
9. b
10. a

B.
1. Dottore / Dottoressa, mi fa male la gola.
2. Dottore / Dottoressa, ho la febbre.
3. Dottore / Dottoressa, ho un forte mal di testa.
4. Dottore / Dottoressa, ho anche mal di stomaco.
5. Dottore / Dottoressa, mi sento / sto veramente male.
6. Dottore / Dottoressa, ho un forte raffreddore.
7. Dottore / Dottoressa, ho l'influenza?
8. Dottore / Dottoressa, che (cosa) devo fare per curare il raffreddore?
9. Dottore / Dottoressa, devo stare a casa?
10. Dottore / Dottoressa, devo bere liquidi?
11. Dottore / Dottoressa, che (cosa) devo fare se peggiora?
12. Dottore / Dottoressa, devo tornare da Lei?
13. Dottore / Dottoressa, mi prescrive antiobiotici?

C.
1. Mio fratello ha la febbre.
2. Mio fratello ha mal di gola. / A mio fratello fa male la gola.
3. Mio fratello ha un forte mal di testa.
4. Mio fratello ha mal di stomaco.
5. Mio fratello potrebbe avere l'influenza.
6. Mio fratello deve prendere gli antibiotici.
7. Mio fratello deve bere tanti liquidi.
8. Mio fratello deve stare a casa.

D. [Answers will vary.]

E. [Compositions will vary.]

F.

1. Le fa male il braccio? / Mi fanno male le braccia!
2. Le fa male il dito? / Mi fanno male le dita!
3. Le fa male la gamba? / Mi fanno male le gambe!
4. Le fa male il ginocchio? / Mi fanno male le ginocchia!
5. Le fa male il gomito? / Mi fanno male i gomiti!
6. Le fa male la guancia? / Mi fanno male le guance!
7. Le fa male il labbro? / Mi fanno male le labbra!
8. Le fa male la mano? / Mi fanno male le mani!
9. Le fa male l'occhio? / Mi fanno male gli occhi!
10. Le fa male il piede? / Mi fanno male i piedi!
11. Le fa male la spalla? / Mi fanno male le spalle!
12. Le fa male l'unghia? / Mi fanno male le unghie!

G.

1. Le fa male il collo.
2. I suoi capelli sono molto lunghi.
3. Ti fa male il corpo.
4. Tu hai una faccia lunga!
5. Lei ha una fronte grossa.
6. Mi fa male la lingua.
7. Tu hai un naso piccolo.
8. Ci fa male il petto.
9. Mi fa male la testa.

H.

1. le amiche
2. gli amici
3. gli antibiotici
4. le bocche
5. i chioschi
6. gli antropologi
7. gli elettrodomestici
8. le grammatiche
9. i medici
10. i fuochi
11. i bachi
12. i buchi
13. i laghi
14. gli alberghi
15. i biologi

I.

1. Me lo ha dato.
2. Me li ha dati.
3. Me l'ha data.
4. Me le ha date.
5. Te lo ha dato.
6. Te li ha dati.
7. Te l'ha data.
8. Te le ha date.
9. Glielo ha dato.
10. Glieli ha dati.
11. Gliel'ha data.
12. Gliele ha date.
13. Glielo ha dato.
14. Glieli ha dati.
15. Gliel'ha data.
16. Gliele ha date.
17. Ce lo ha dato.
18. Ce li ha dati.
19. Ce l'ha data.
20. Ce le ha date.
21. Ve lo ha dato.
22. Ve li ha dati.
23. Ve l'ha data.
24. Ve le ha date.
25. Glielo ha dato.
26. Glieli ha dati.
27. Gliel'ha data.
28. Gliele ha date.

J.

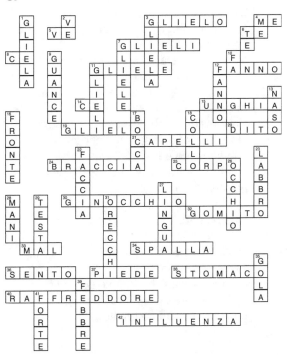

K.

1. Federico Fellini è considerato uno dei più grandi registi del cinema italiano.
2. Fellini combina elementi satirici con elementi di fantasia in film come *La Dolce Vita* e *Amarcord*.
3. Il suo primo film fu *Città Aperta*.
4. Lo fece con Roberto Rossellini, un altro grande regista del cinema italiano.
5. Il film *I Vitelloni* stabilì la sua fama internazionale.
6. I suoi film che hanno vinto premi internazionali sono *La Strada*, *Le Notti di Cabiria*, *8 1/2* e *Amarcord*.

REVIEW PART 5

A.

1. Gli stivali mi stanno veramente bene.
2. Li prendo.
3. È una scelta ottima! / È un'ottima scelta!
4. (Io) sto leggendo, mentre mia sorella sta mangiando.
5. Quegli stivali mi stavano bene.
6. Ho mangiato un po' di carne ieri.
7. Ho depositato un assegno in banca (nella mia banca) ieri.
8. Mio padre aprì un conto molti anni fa.
9. Prendo l'antipasto di melone e prosciutto e poi la pasta e una bistecca.
10. Vorrei anche un po' di formaggio, perché ho ancora molta fame.
11. Vorrei andare a un conferenza all'università.
12. Vorrei andare a ballare a un locale notturno stasera (questa sera).
13. Preferisco andare al cinema il venerdì.
14. Dottore, Dottoressa, mi fanno male la gola e lo stomaco e ho la febbre.
15. Dottore, Dottoressa, che (cosa) devo fare per curare l'influenza?
16. Signorina, (che cosa) desidera?
17. Che numero (di scarpa) porta?
18. Che taglia di giacca porta?
19. Quanto costano gli stivali?
20. Ha aperto un conto in questa banca?
21. Signora Martini, ha fame e sete?
22. Professoressa Giusti, vuole un po' di minestra per primo (piatto)?
23. Dina, vuoi andare al cinema?
24. Alessandro che (cosa) ne pensi?
25. Dottore / Dottoressa, devo prendere gli antibiotici?

B.

1. Lei può / Tu puoi comprare il giornale al chiosco all'angolo.
2. Ho comprato una rivista ieri. L'ho comprata perché mi piace leggere.
3. Lascia una bella mancia, Alessandro!
4. Che bella giornata!
5. Loro vennero negli Stati Uniti (in America) nel 1956.
6. La nostra famiglia comprò quella casa nel 1990.
7. Loro venivano sempre al cinema con me quando eravamo giovani.
8. Ieri (lui) aveva molta fame.
9. Lui gli ha dato i libri, vero? Sì, glieli ha dati.

C. [Answers will vary.]

D. [Stories will vary.]

E.

R	O	M	A	N	Z	O	B	V	B	V	F	V	S	G	L	G	F	G
A	D	F	G	H	J	K	I	B	O	B	O	B	P	H	I	H	A	H	I
R	I	V	I	S	T	A	L	M	T	M	R	M	I	N	B	N	N	N	O
A	D	F	G	H	J	K	P	N	T	N	M	N	C	X	R	X	T	X	R
A	S	S	E	G	N	O	N	L	I	L	A	L	C	R	E	R	A	R	N
A	D	F	G	H	J	K	D	O	G	O	G	O	I	C	T	C	S	C	A
C	O	N	T	O	D	D	F	P	L	P	G	P	O	D	T	D	C	D	L
A	D	F	G	H	J	K	G	L	I	L	I	L	L	B	O	B	I	B	E
M	A	N	C	I	A	D	H	J	A	J	O	J	I	A	D	X	E	V	B
A	D	F	G	H	J	K	J	Y	B	Y	S	Y	A	T	V	B	N	X	I
B	I	S	T	E	C	C	A	L	G	H	J	K	L	E	K	J	Z	L	N
A	D	F	G	H	J	K	T	K	B	N	B	S	D	L	C	V	A	B	F
C	I	N	E	M	A	K	T	K	B	N	A	D	E	E	C	V	B	N	L
K	T	K	B	N	Q	K	T	K	B	N	L	A	D	F	X	X	X	V	U
U	S	C	I	R	E	N	M	J	K	I	L	A	D	O	M	M	M	M	E
N	M	J	K	I	O	N	M	J	K	I	A	A	D	N	L	A	L	L	N
P	I	E	D	E	X	X	X	A	A	A	R	A	S	A	T	N	T	T	Z
N	M	J	K	I	O	N	M	J	K	I	E	B	N	T	O	O	O	O	A
N	M	J	K	I	O	N	M	J	K	I	P	H	D	A	I	V	I	I	D
R	A	F	F	R	E	D	D	O	R	E	M	E	D	A	U	M	U	U	D

UNIT 26

A.
1. Vero
2. Vero
3. Vero
4. Vero
5. Vero
6. Vero
7. Vero
8. Falso
9. Vero

B.
1. Le mie gomme hanno bisogno di un po' d'aria.
2. La mia macchina è economica e efficiente.
3. La mia macchina si guida con grande facilità.
4. Dovrei cambiare l'olio.
5. Tornerò la prossima settimana.
6. Il pieno, per favore!
7. Ci metta un po' d'aria. / Ci metta l'aria.
8. Può controllare l'olio e l'acqua?
9. Può anche pulire il parabrezza?
10. Le piace guidare una macchina giapponese?

C.
1. d
2. g
3. a
4. b
5. c
6. h
7. e
8. f

D.
1. Io ho messo la benzina nella macchina ieri, ma lui, invece, la mise nella macchina la settimana scorsa.
2. Noi abbiamo messo la benzina nella macchina ieri, ma tu, invece, la mettesti nella macchina la settimana scorsa.
3. Voi avete messo la benzina nella macchina ieri, ma io, invece, la misi nella macchina la settimana scorsa.
4. Loro hanno messo la benzina nella macchina ieri, ma noi, invece, la mettemmo nella macchina la settimana scorsa.
5. Io ho messo la benzina nella macchina ieri, ma voi, invece, la metteste nella macchina la settimana scorsa.
6. Lei ha messo la benzina nella macchina ieri, ma loro, invece, la misero nella macchina la settimana scorsa.

E. [Answers will vary.]

F. [Compositions will vary.]

G.
1. Quando vai in centro? / Ci vado domani.
2. Quando vai dal medico? / Ci vado tra un'ora.
3. Quando vai a Firenze? / Ci vado tra alcuni giorni / tra qualche giorno.
4. Quando vai a Roma? / Ci vado tra poco.
5. Quando vai in Calabria? / Ci vado tra un mese.
6. Quando sei andato / andata in Toscana? / Ci sono andato / andata ieri.
7. Quando sei andato / andata dal medico? / Ci sono andato / andata un'ora fa.
8. Quando sei andato / andata a Pisa? / Ci sono andato / andata alcuni giorni fa / qualche giorno fa.
9. Quando sei andato / andata a Milano? / Ci sono andato / andata poco tempo fa.
10. Quando sei andato / andata in Sicilia? / Ci sono andato / andata un mese fa.

H.
1. Dove si guidano le macchine giapponesi?
2. Dove si studia l'italiano?
3. Dove si mangiano gli spaghetti alla bolognese?
4. Dove si beve un buon espresso?
5. Dove si sta veramente bene?

I.
1. Io arriverò domani. / Io arriverei domani, ma…
2. Io prenderò un espresso. / Io prenderei un espresso, ma…
3. Io uscirò stasera. / Io uscirei stasera, ma…
4. Io traslocherò tra una settimana. / Io traslocherei tra una settimana, ma…
5. Io pagherò tutto. / Io pagherei tutto, ma…
6. Io comincerò a lavorare la settimana prossima. / Io comincerei a lavorare la settimana prossima, ma…
7. Io mangerò gli spaghetti. / Io mangerei gli spaghetti, ma…

8. Tu arriverai domani. / Tu arriveresti domani, ma…
9. Tu prenderai un espresso. / Tu prenderesti un espresso, ma…
10. Tu uscirai stasera. / Tu usciresti stasera, ma…
11. Tu traslocherai tra una settimana. / Tu traslocheresti tra una settimana, ma…
12. Tu pagherai tutto. / Tu pagheresti tutto, ma…
13. Tu comincerai a lavorare la settimana prossima. / Tu cominceresti a lavorare la settimana prossima, ma…
14. Tu mangerai gli spaghetti. / Tu mangeresti gli spaghetti, ma…
15. Lui / Lei arriverà domani. / Lui / Lei arriverebbe domani, ma…
16. Lui / Lei prenderà un espresso. / Lui / Lei prenderebbe un espresso, ma…
17. Lui / Lei uscirà stasera. / Lui / Lei uscirebbe stasera, ma…
18. Lui / Lei traslocherà tra una settimana. / Lui / Lei traslocherebbe tra una settimana, ma…
19. Lui / Lei pagherà tutto. / Lui / Lei pagherebbe tutto, ma…
20. Lui / Lei comincerà a lavorare la settimana prossima. / Lui / Lei comincerebbe a lavorare la settimana prossima, ma…
21. Lui / Lei mangerà gli spaghetti. / Lui / Lei mangerebbe gli spaghetti, ma…
22. Noi arriveremo domani. / Noi arriveremmo domani, ma…
23. Noi prenderemo un espresso. / Noi prenderemmo un espresso, ma…
24. Noi usciremo stasera. / Noi usciremmo stasera, ma…
25. Noi traslocheremo tra una settimana. / Noi traslocheremmo tra una settimana, ma…
26. Noi pagheremo tutto. / Noi pagheremmo tutto, ma…
27. Noi cominceremo a lavorare la settimana prossima. / Noi cominceremmo a lavorare la settimana prossima, ma…
28. Noi mangeremo gli spaghetti. / Noi mangeremmo gli spaghetti, ma…
29. Voi arriverete domani. / Voi arrivereste domani, ma…
30. Voi prenderete un espresso. / Voi prendereste un espresso, ma…
31. Voi uscirete stasera. / Voi uscireste stasera, ma…
32. Voi traslocherete tra una settimana. / Voi traslochereste tra una settimana, ma…
33. Voi pagherete tutto. / Voi paghereste tutto, ma…
34. Voi comincerete a lavorare la settimana prossima. / Voi comincereste a lavorare la settimana prossima, ma…
35. Voi mangerete gli spaghetti. / Voi mangereste gli spaghetti, ma…
36. Loro arriveranno domani. / Loro arriverebbero domani, ma…
37. Loro prenderanno un espresso. / Loro prenderebbero un espresso, ma…
38. Loro usciranno stasera. / Loro uscirebbero stasera, ma…
39. Loro traslocheranno tra una settimana. / Loro traslocherebbero tra una settimana, ma…
40. Loro pagheranno tutto. / Loro pagherebbero tutto, ma…
41. Loro cominceranno a lavorare la settimana prossima. / Loro comincerebbero a lavorare la settimana prossima, ma…
42. Loro mangeranno gli spaghetti. / Loro mangerebbero gli spaghetti, ma…

J.

K.
1. La FIAT fu fondata nel 1899.
2. Alcuni industriali, tra cui Giovanni Agnelli, hanno fondato la FIAT.
3. Acquistò la Lancia nel 1969.
4. Acquistò l'Alfa Romeo nel 1986.
5. Compleò una joint venture con la Chrysler nel 1995.
6. Con la francese Lohr firmò un accordo per lo sviluppo delle loro attività nel settore dei trasporti urbani.

UNIT 27

A.
1. a
2. a
3. a
4. a
5. a
6. b
7. a

B.
1. Sto cercando il mio biglietto e passaporto.
2. Vorrei un posto al corridoio.
3. Non preferirei un posto al finestrino.
4. Il mio aereo partirà dall'uscita numero S21.
5. Sara, è tanto tempo che non ci vediamo.
6. Sara, purtroppo devo andare perché hanno annunciato il mio volo.
7. Prego, il Suo biglietto, per favore?
8. Hai la mia carta d'imbarco?
9. Mark, buon viaggio!

C.
1. Il mio aereo partirà tra un'ora.
2. Annunceranno il tuo volo tra poco.
3. Ecco la Sua carta d'imbarco.
4. Lui preferirebbe un posto al corridoio, perché non gli piacciono i posti al finestrino.
5. Dov'è l'uscita?

D. [Answers will vary.]

E. [Compositions will vary.]

F.
1. a
2. a
3. b
4. b
5. b
6. a
7. a
8. a

G.
1. Tu andrai in centro domani.
2. Tu andresti in centro domani, ma non hai tempo.
3. Lui avrà / avrebbe tempo domani.
4. Lei berrebbe il cappuccino, ma non le piace.
5. Noi daremmo quel libro a Carla, ma lo abbiamo perso.
6. Voi direte tutto alla professoressa domani.
7. Loro dovrebbero andare in Italia, ma non hanno soldi.
8. Lei sarà molto stanca, dopo che ha lavorato.
9. Io farò il biglietto domani.
10. Loro non potranno venire al cinema perché lavorano.

H.
1. vi piacerebbero
2. ci piacerà
3. vi piacerebbe
4. gli piacerà
5. le piacerebbe
6. ti piacerà
7. mi piacerebbe
8. loro vorrebbero
9. io verrò
10. noi vedremo
11. tu staresti
12. io saprò

I.

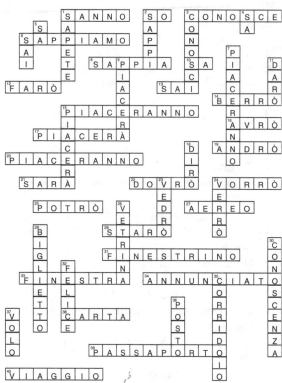

J. [Compositions will vary.]

UNIT 28

A.
1. all'estero
2. indimenticabile
3. divertimento
4. da vedere
5. la chiave
6. gli alberghi
7. noleggiare
8. carta di credito
9. due valige

B.
1. Voglio andare all'estero.
2. Mi divertirò di più in Italia.
3. Voglio fare una vacanza indimenticabile.
4. Voglio visitare molti bei paesi e molte belle città.
5. Mi piacciono solo gli alberghi di prima categoria.
6. Vorrei noleggiare la macchina.
7. Ci penso io!

8. Non ho tanto bagaglio.
9. Ho solo due valige.
10. Non ho bisogno di aiuto.
11. Mi dia la Sua carta di credito, per favore.
12. Ha ricevuto la mia prenotazione?
13. Mi potrebbe dare / Potrei avere due chiavi per la mia camera?

C.
1. a
2. b
3. a
4. b
5. a
6. b
7. a
8. b

D. [Answers will vary.]

E. [Dialogues will vary.]

F.
1. Loro andranno al cinema, appena che io avrò finito di lavorare.
2. Loro andranno al cinema, appena che tu sarai arrivato / arrivata.
3. Loro andranno al cinema, appena che lui sarà venuto.
4. Loro andranno al cinema, appena che avremo mangiato.
5. Loro andranno al cinema, appena che voi vi sarete alzati / alzate.
6. Loro andranno al cinema, appena che i miei amici si saranno alzati / le mie amiche si saranno alzate.

G.
1. Io avrei finito di lavorare prima, ma…
2. Tu saresti arrivato / arrivata prima, ma…
3. Lui sarebbe venuto prima, ma…
4. Noi avremmo mangiato prima, ma…
5. Voi vi sareste alzati / alzate prima, ma…
6. I miei amici si sarebbero alzati prima, ma… / Le mie amiche si sarebbero alzate prima, ma…

H.
1. Io mi alzo sempre presto. Anche da giovane mi alzavo sempre presto. E mi alzerò sempre presto.
2. Tu ti alzi sempre presto. Anche da giovane ti alzavi sempre presto. E ti alzerai sempre presto.

3. Lui / Lei si alza sempre presto. Anche da giovane si alzava sempre presto. E si alzerà sempre presto.

4. Noi ci alziamo sempre presto. Anche da giovani ci alzavamo sempre presto. E ci alzeremo sempre presto.

5. Voi vi alzate sempre presto. Anche da giovani vi alzavate sempre presto. E vi alzerete sempre presto.

6. Loro si alzano sempre presto. Anche da giovani si alzavano sempre presto. E si alzeranno sempre presto.

7. Io mi metto sempre la giacca. Anche da giovane me la mettevo sempre. E me la metterò sempre.

8. Tu ti metti sempre la giacca. Anche da giovane te la mettevi sempre. E te la metterai sempre.

9. Lui / Lei si mette sempre la giacca. Anche da giovane se la metteva sempre. E se la metterà sempre.

10. Noi ci mettiamo sempre la giacca. Anche da giovani ce la mettevamo sempre. E ce la metteremo sempre.

11. Voi vi mettete sempre la giacca. Anche da giovani ve la mettevate sempre. E ve la metterete sempre.

12. Loro si mettono sempre la giacca. Anche da giovani se la mettevano sempre. E se la metteranno sempre.

13. Io mi diverto sempre. Anche da giovane mi divertivo sempre. E mi divertirò sempre.

14. Tu ti diverti sempre. Anche da giovane ti divertivi sempre. E ti divertirai sempre.

15. Lui / Lei si diverte sempre. Anche da giovane si divertiva sempre. E si divertirà sempre.

16. Noi ci divertiamo sempre. Anche da giovani ci divertivamo sempre. E ci divertiremo sempre.

17. Voi vi divertite sempre. Anche da giovani vi divertivate sempre. E vi divertirete sempre.

18. Loro si divertono sempre. Anche da giovani si divertivano sempre. E si divertiranno sempre.

I.

1. Dina, alzati presto!
2. Dina, mettiti un nuovo paio di pantaloni!
3. Dina, divertiti!
4. Signora Martini, si alzi presto!
5. Signora Martini, si metta un nuovo paio di pantaloni!

6. Signora Martini, si diverta!
7. Dina e Alessandro, alzatevi presto!
8. Dina e Alessandro, mettetevi un nuovo paio di pantaloni!
9. Dina e Alessandro, divertitevi!
10. Signor e signora Martini, si alzino presto!
11. Signor e signora Martini, si mettano un nuovo paio di pantaloni!
12. Signor e signora Martini, si divertano!

J.

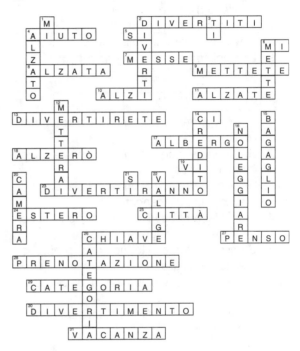

K. [Compositions will vary.]

UNIT 29

A.

1. Stasera Dina vuole guardare il programma di pattinaggio.
2. Alessandro invece vuole guardare la partita di calcio e poi la partita di pallacanestro.
3. Domani Dina vuole guardare l'incontro di tennis.
4. La sera dopo Alessandro vuole guardare il pugilato e la gara di bicicletta.
5. Dina va a fare un po' di ginnastica.
6. Secondo Dina, Alessandro dovrebbe praticare di più lo sport.
7. Domani Alessandro comincerà a fare il footing.

B.
1. Stasera c'è un bel programma di pattinaggio in televisione.
2. Più tardi c'è una partita importante di calcio in televisione.
3. Domani ci sarà una partita di pallacanestro in televisione.
4. Domani voglio guardare l'incontro di tennis.
5. La sera dopo c'è il pugilato in televisione.
6. Ogni martedì / Il martedì c'è una gara di bicicletta d'estate in televisione.
7. Esco per fare un po' di ginnastica.
8. Dovrei praticare di più lo sport.
9. Domani comincerò a fare il footing.
10. Dina, divertiti!

C.
1. Sì mi piacerebbe / No, non mi piacerebbe praticare il calcio.
2. Sì mi piacerebbe / No, non mi piacerebbe fare ginnastica.
3. Sì mi piacerebbe / No, non mi piacerebbe praticare la pallacanestro.
4. Sì mi piacerebbe / No, non mi piacerebbe praticare il pattinaggio.
5. Sì mi piacerebbe / No, non mi piacerebbe praticare il pugilato.
6. Sì mi piacerebbe / No, non mi piacerebbe praticare il tennis.
7. Sì mi piacerebbe / No, non mi piacerebbe fare il footing.

D. [Answers will vary.]

E. [Lists will vary.]

F.
1. il film / i film
2. il programma / i programmi
3. il problema / i problemi
4. il tema / i temi

G.
1. Mia sorella è calma, ma mio fratello è nervoso.
   Infatti, tutte le mie amiche sono calme, ma i miei amici sono nervosi.
   Ci telefoniamo spesso.

2. Mia sorella è energica, ma mio fratello è pigro.
   Infatti, tutte le mie amiche sono energiche, ma i miei amici sono pigri.
   Ci telefoniamo spesso.

3. Mia sorella è giovane, ma mio fratello è vecchio.
   Infatti, tutte le mie amiche sono giovani, ma i miei amici sono vecchi.
   Ci telefoniamo spesso.

4. Mia sorella è piccola, ma mio fratello è grande.
   Infatti, tutte le mie amiche sono piccole, ma i miei amici sono grandi.
   Ci telefoniamo spesso.

5. Mia sorella è intelligente, ma mio fratello è stupido.
   Infatti, tutte le mie amiche sono intelligenti, ma i miei amici sono stupidi.
   Ci telefoniamo spesso.

6. Mia sorella è magra, ma mio fratello è grasso.
   Infatti, tutte le mie amiche sono magre, ma i miei amici sono grassi.
   Ci telefoniamo spesso.

7. Mia sorella è ricca, ma mio fratello è povero.
   Infatti, tutte le mie amiche sono ricche, ma i miei amici sono poveri.
   Ci telefoniamo spesso.

8. Mia sorella è simpatica, ma mio fratello è antipatico.
   Infatti, tutte le mie amiche sono simpatiche, ma i miei amici sono antipatici.
   Ci telefoniamo spesso.

H.
1. Dina, parlagli!
2. Dina, mangiali!
3. Dina, chiamaci!
4. Dina, bevilo!
5. Dina, parlale!
6. Signora Martini, gli parli!
7. Signora Martini, li mangi!
8. Signora Martini, ci chiami!
9. Signora Martini, lo beva!
10. Signora Martini, le parli!
11. Dina e Alessandro, parlategli!
12. Dina e Alessandro, mangiateli!
13. Dina e Alessandro, chiamateci!
14. Dina e Alessandro, bevetelo!
15. Dina e Alessandro, parlatele!
16. Signor e signora Martini, gli parlino!

17. Signor e signora Martini, li mangino!
18. Signor e signora Martini, ci chiamino!
19. Signor e signora Martini, lo bevano!
20. Signor e signora Martini, le parlino!

I.

1. Io gli avevo già parlato.
2. Io mi ero alzato / alzata presto ieri.
3. Io ero venuto / venuta tardi.
4. Tu gli avevi già parlato.
5. Tu ti eri alzato / alzata presto ieri.
6. Tu eri venuto / venuta tardi.
7. Lui gli aveva già parlato.
8. Lui si era alzato presto ieri.
9. Lui era venuto tardi.
10. Lei gli aveva già parlato.
11. Lei si era alzata presto ieri.
12. Lei era venuta tardi.
13. Noi gli avevamo già parlato.
14. Noi ci eravamo alzati / alzate presto ieri.
15. Noi eravamo venuti / venute tardi.
16. Voi gli avevate già parlato.
17. Voi vi eravate alzati / alzate presto ieri.
18. Voi eravate venuti / venute tardi.
19. Loro gli avevano già parlato.
20. Loro si erano alzati / alzate presto ieri.
21. Loro erano venuti / venute tardi.

J.

K. [Compositions will vary.]

UNIT 30

A.
1. d
2. c
3. a
4. b
5. g
6. e
7. f

B.
1. Stasera vorrei guardare l'ultima puntata del telefilm.
2. Dopo voglio guardare il telequiz su RAI Uno.
3. A me piace più la cronaca che i programmi popolari.
4. Io ho il telecomando. / Il telecomando l'ho io.
5. Sono stufo / stufa dei programmi popolari.
6. Non li voglio guardare più.
7. La cronaca in italiano è un po' troppo difficile per me.
8. I programmi in italiano sono, anzi, facili per me.
9. Il telefilm non vale niente.
10. Alessandro, non essere cattivo!
11. Alessandro, cambia canale!
12. Alessandro, finalmente capisci qualcosa!

C.
1. a
2. a
3. a
4. a
5. a
6. a
7. b

D.
1. Quel film non vale niente.
2. Quel film non valeva niente.
3. Quel film varrà qualcosa.
4. Varrebbe vedere quel film, ma non ho tempo.

E. [Answers will vary.]

F. [Lists will vary.]

G.

1. Mio fratello è stanco, ma mia sorella è più stanca.
   Io sono meno stanco / stanca di lui, ma più stanco / stanca di lei.

2. Mio fratello è simpatico, ma mia sorella è più simpatica.
   Io sono meno simpatico / simpatica di lui, ma più simpatico / simpatica di lei.

3. Mio fratello è intelligente, ma mia sorella è più intelligente.
   Io sono meno intelligente di lui, ma più intelligente di lei.

4. Mio fratello è grande, ma mia sorella è più grande.
   Io sono meno grande di lui, ma più grande di lei.

5. Mio fratello è ironico, ma mia sorella è più ironica.
   Io sono meno ironico / ironica di lui, ma più ironico / ironica di lei.

6. Mio fratello è umile, ma mia sorella è più umile.
   Io sono meno umile di lui, ma più umile di lei.

7. Mio fratello è felice, ma mia sorella è più felice.
   Io sono meno felice di lui, ma più felice di lei.

8. Mio fratello è triste, ma mia sorella è più triste.
   Io sono meno triste di lui, ma più triste di lei.

H.

1. Mio fratello è più grande che piccolo, ma mia sorella è meno grande che piccola.
   Io sono così grande come lui.
   Ma nostra madre è la più grande della famiglia.

2. Mio fratello è più simpatico che gentile, ma mia sorella è meno simpatica che gentile.
   Io sono così simpatico /simpatica come lui.
   Ma nostra madre è la più simpatica della famiglia.

3. Mio fratello è più energico che umile, ma mia sorella è meno energica che umile.
   Io sono così energico / energica come lui.
   Ma nostra madre è la più energica della famiglia.

4. Mio fratello è più forte che energico, ma mia sorella è meno forte che energica.
   Io sono così forte come lui.
   Ma nostra madre è la più forte della famiglia.

I.

1. facilmente
2. calmamente
3. certamente
4. efficientemente
5. economicamente
6. difficilmente
7. differentemente
8. felicemente
9. fortemente
10. gentilmente
11. umilmente
12. sicuramente

J.

1. Quell'uomo è svizzero e quella donna è svedese.
2. Quell'uomo è spagnolo e quella donna è russa.
3. Quell'uomo è portoghese e quella donna è olandese.
4. Quell'uomo è polacco e quella donna è norvegese.
5. Quell'uomo è messicano e quella donna è italiana.
6. Quell'uomo è inglese e quella donna è greca.
7. Quell'uomo è giapponese e quella donna è svedese.
8. Quell'uomo è danese e quella donna è cinese.
9. Quell'uomo è africano e quella donna è australiana.
10. Quell'uomo è americano e quella donna è tedesca.

K.

1. Lei mi piace, ma io non piaccio a lei (ma io non le piaccio).
2. Noi le piacevamo, ma adesso solo voi le piacete.
3. Lui gli piacerà molto (Lui piacerà molto a loro).

4. Mi piacerebbe andare in Italia, ma non ho abbastanza soldi.
5. Non ci sono piaciuti gli spaghetti (A noi non sono piaciuti gli spaghetti), ma sono piaciuti molto a lei.
6. Vi piaccio?
7. Lei piace a lui e anche lui piace a lei.
8. Dina piace a Alessandro e lui piace a lei.
9. Ti è piaciuta la carne?
10. No, non mi è piaciuta.

L.

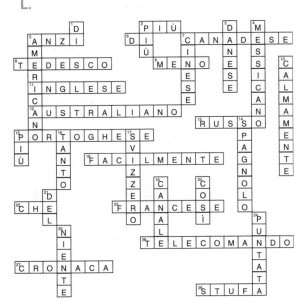

M. [Compositions will vary.]

REVIEW PART 6

A.
1. Le mie gomme hanno bisogno di / un po' d'aria e dovrei cambiare l'olio.
2. La mia macchina si guida con grande facilità, perché è economica e efficient.
3. Ho dimenticato il mio biglietto e il mio passaporto nella macchina.
4. Preferirei un posto al corridoio.
5. Vorrei andare all'estero per una vacanza indimenticabile.
6. Vorrei noleggiare la macchina per visitare molti bei paesi.
7. Ho sempre molto bagaglio e, allora, ho sempre bisogno di aiuto.
8. Stasera c'è una partita di calcio in televisione e più tardi un incontro di tennis.

9. Faccio un po' di ginnastica due giorni alla settimana / ogni settimana.
10. Tutti dovrebbero praticare di più lo sport.
11. Stasera vorrei gurdare l'ultimo episodio del telefilm, non il telequiz.
12. A me piace più la cronaca italiana che i programmi popolari, perché li capisco di più.
13. Dina, non essere cattiva, cambia il canale!
14. Il pieno, per favore e metta un po' d'aria nelle gomme.
15. Può controllare l'olio e l'acqua e poi pulire il parabrezza?
16. Sara, hai visto la mia carta d'imbarco?
17. Perché non ha ancora ricevuto la mia prenotazione?

B.
1. Le amiche di Dina andranno in Italia tra un mese.
2. Alessandro mangerebbe la carne, ma non ha molta / tanta fame.
3. L'aereo partirà tra un'ora dall'uscita numero A1521.
4. Preferirei un posto al corridoio, ma se non c'è, prenderò un posto al finestrino.
5. Conosci Mark? Sai se verrà al cinema con noi?
6. Lui si divertirà in Italia, perché gli piace il bel tempo.
7. Signorina, si provi queste scarpe!
8. Dopo che erano arrivati /arrivateri, abbiamo deciso di andare al cinema.
9. Non ho mangiato la carne, perchè veramente non mi piaceva / mi è piaciuta.

C. [Answers will vary.]

D. [Accounts will vary.]

E.

A	C	O	N	T	R	O	L	L	A	R	E	X	X	X	B	U	O	N	C
Z	A	S	D	F	G	H	J	K	L	M	N	M	K	L	O	P	P	H	D
P	A	R	A	B	R	E	Z	Z	A	A	M	A	C	C	H	I	N	A	A
K	A	S	D	F	G	H	J	K	L	M	P	H	D	P	H	D	A	D	P
T	O	R	N	E	R	Ò	A	U	S	C	I	T	A	X	P	Q	P	N	A
J	A	S	D	F	G	H	J	K	L	M	D	F	L	X	I	W	R	M	E
C	O	N	O	S	C	E	N	Z	A	L	H	J	T	X	G	E	I	L	S
G	A	S	D	F	G	H	J	K	L	M	N	M	O	X	R	R	M	S	I
V	O	L	O	A	E	S	T	E	R	O	O	F	T	X	A	T	A	D	I
S	A	S	D	F	G	H	J	K	L	M	Q	A	G	C	B	Y	S	P	O
N	O	L	E	G	G	I	A	R	E	S	P	I	B	A	N	D	D	D	H
A	S	D	F	G	H	J	K	L	M	P	S	O	F	L	M	E	T	I	K
A	S	D	F	G	H	J	K	L	M	I	U	C	G	C	O	L	F	H	L
A	S	D	F	G	H	J	K	L	M	U	T	H	J	I	P	L	V	N	M
A	D	F	G	H	J	K	L	B	M	H	H	E	H	O	H	A	H	H	H
A	S	D	E	G	D	X	X	X	A	D	C	Q	E	D	A	C	X	X	X
A	S	D	E	G	D	X	X	X	A	D	C	Q	E	D	A	C	X	X	X
A	S	D	E	G	D	X	X	X	A	D	C	Q	E	D	A	C	X	X	X
A	S	D	E	G	D	X	X	X	A	D	C	Q	E	D	A	C	X	X	X
A	S	D	E	G	D	X	X	X	A	D	C	Q	E	D	A	C	X	X	X